Julius Caesar

Julius Caesar
The Life and Times of the People's Dictator

Luciano Canfora

Translated by Marian Hill and Kevin Windle

University of California Press
Berkeley   Los Angeles

University of California Press, one of the most distinguished university presses in the United States, enriches lives around the world by advancing scholarship in the humanities, social sciences, and natural sciences. Its activities are supported by the UC Press Foundation and by philanthropic contributions from individuals and institutions. For more information, visit www.ucpress.edu.

University of California Press
Berkeley and Los Angeles, California

English language edition published by arrangement with Eulama Literary Agency, Rome.
First published in Italy as *Giulio Cesare: Il Dittatore Democratico*.
First published in the UK by Edinburgh University Press Ltd, 22 George Square, Edinburgh.

Library of Congress Cataloging-in-Publication Data

Canfora, Luciano.
　　[Giulio Cesare. English]
　　Julius Caesar : the life and times of the people's dictator / Luciano Canfora ; translated by Marian Hill and Kevin Windle.
　　　　p.　　cm.
　　With minor corrections to the text by the author.
　　Includes bibliographical references and index.
　　ISBN-13: 978-0-520-23502-1 (cloth : alk. paper)
　　1. Caesar, Julius.　2. Heads of state—Rome—Biography.　3. Generals—Rome—
Biography.　4. Rome—History—Republic, 265–30 B.C.　I. Title.

DG261.C34313　2007
937'.05092—dc22　　　　　　　　　　　　　　　　　　　　　　　　　　　2006051434

Manufactured in Great Britain

16　15　14　13　12　11　10　09　08　07
10　9　8　7　6　5　4　3　2　1

The paper used in this publication meets the minimum requirements of ANSI/NISO z39.48-1992 (R1997) (Permanence of Paper).

The translation of this work has been funded by SEPS
SEGRETARIATO EUROPEO PER LE PUBBLICAZIONI SCIENTIFICHE

Contents

Translators' Note   vii
Acknowledgements   viii
Foreword   ix

PART I   FROM SULLA TO CATILINE   1

1   In Flight from Sulla: First Experiences of
    an Aristocratic Youth   3
2   Prisoner of the Pirates (75–74 BC)   9
3   The Rise of a Party Leader   14
4   *Pontifex Maximus*   23
5   The 'Affairs' of Mr Julius Caesar and Others   26
6   The Political Market   33
7   Inside and Outside the Conspiracy   39
8   Caesar's Senate Speech Rewritten by Sallust   54

**PART II   FROM THE TRIUMVIRATE TO THE
             CONQUEST OF GAUL**   61

9   The 'Three-Headed Monster'   63
10   The Consequences of the Triumvirate:
     The View of Asinius Pollio   72
11   The First Consulship (59 BC)   78
12   An Inconvenient Ally: Clodius   83
13   Semiramis in Gaul   88
14   The Conquest of Gaul (58–51 BC)   98
15   The Black Book of the Gallic Campaign   118

PART III   THE LONG CIVIL WAR   125

16   Towards the Crisis   127
17   Striving after Tyranny?   137

18   Attacking the World with Five Cohorts   141
19   Caesar's 'Programme': In Search of Consensus   150
20   'Amicitia'   159
21   From the Rubicon to Pharsalus   165
22   Against Subversion   184
23   Alexandria   188
24   Caesar Saved by the Jews   209
25   From Syria to Zela   218
26   The Long Civil War   229
27   The Shoot of a Palm Tree: The Young Octavius
     Emerges   245
28   'Anticato'   256

PART IV   FROM THE CONSPIRACY TO THE
          TRIUMPH OF CAESARISM   261

29   Inklings of Conspiracy   263
30   'Iure caesus'   269
31   The Lupercalia Drama   281
32   The Dictatorship   287
33   Epicureans in Revolt?   296
34   The *Hetairia* of Cassius and the Recruitment of
     Brutus   306
35   A Conspirator's Realism: Cassius Settles for the
     Second Rank   311
36   Some Unexpected Refusals   314
37   Cicero – an Organiser of the Conspiracy?   317
38   The Serious Mistake of Dismissing the Escort   322
39   The Dynamics of the 'Tyrannicide'   325
40   'Where's Antony?'   334
41   Caesar's Body: How to Turn Victory into Defeat   337
42   The Wind   344

Chronology   349
Bibliography   370
Index   377

Translators' Note

This English translation is based on the Laterza edition of *Giulio Cesare: il dittatore democratico*, published in 1999. It departs from that edition at occasional points where the author has made minor corrections to the text.

Where the author cites classical sources such as Plutarch, Suetonius, Cicero or Caesar himself, we have generally used the Loeb dual-language series, except in cases where the Loeb Greek or Latin text differs from that used by the author. For English translations we have mostly followed the Loeb versions but adapted these where necessary to suit the author's purposes.

The translators are deeply grateful for the generous assistance and support of their friends and colleagues at a time when serious illness in the Hill family threatened to derail the project, in particular: Rosh Ireland, who checked many chapters and filled large gaps; Margaret Travers, who traced and double-checked quotations and read draft chapters; Robert Barnes, who read the whole work in draft from the viewpoint of a classical historian.

Roberta Bonalume, Piera Carroli and Francesca Foppoli were always willing to clarify ambiguities in the Italian; Morrell Aston was a source of valuable comments on a late draft, and the author gave prompt guidance at many points where only he could help.

To all, our thanks.

Kevin Windle
Marian Hill

Australian National University, Canberra
November 2005

Acknowledgements

My thanks to all who have helped and advised me, in particular Giorgio Fabre and Marina Silvestrini.

Luciano Canfora

Foreword

'While writing my *Caesar*, I have realised that I must never for a moment let myself believe that things necessarily had to turn out the way they did', wrote Brecht in his *Arbeitsjournal*.[1] After this his lines take a wandering course, detracting somewhat from the force of that initial thought. Brecht becomes entangled in unprofitable reflections on the non-inevitability of the ancient slave-owning social order. But a little later he returns to his initial idea and takes issue with the optimistic and ultimately arbitrary notion of 'seeking the causes of everything that happened'. Hence the pungent criticism of those impersonal expressions so commonly found in historical writing ('this or that was done because . . .'), which should lead any historian to ask, 'done *by whom*'?

The events which provide the material for this book lend themselves as much as any to such anti-deterministic reservations. We are dealing with political and military facts which might at any juncture have yielded results quite opposite to those which actually transpired. To take only the last phase, this is clear from the extraordinary strength and endurance of Caesar's opponents in the civil war: it took years of fierce, pitiless and bloody fighting to wear them down, without any truly decisive battle taking place.

1 WAS HIS SHADOW THE WHOLE WORLD?

A poem by Jorge Luis Borges, plainly inspired by Shakespeare's *Julius Caesar*, sums up in a few lines the 'providential' view of Caesar's life and its importance. 'Here lies that thing the daggers left behind, / that poor wretched thing, a dead man / who was known as Caesar' ('Aquí lo que dejaron los puñales. / Aquí esa pobre cosa, un hombre muerto / que se llamaba César'); these words echo Mark Antony's first words on seeing the body in Shakespeare's play: 'O mighty Caesar! Dost thou lie so low? / Are all thy conquests, glories, triumphs, spoils, / Shrunk to this little measure?' But Borges' short poem concludes with the emergence of 'the other Caesar': 'the future Caesar, / whose great shadow will be the whole world' ('el otro, el venidero / cuya sombra será el orbe entero').

The underlying idea is clear: Caesar is seen here as one of those men whose works leave 'deep traces'. Epoch-making changes result from their actions: in the case of Caesar, the Romanisation of Celtic Europe and the birth of an enduring universal monarchy. Men of his stamp are seen as 'instruments' of history. And by virtue of giving form to *necessary* changes, transformations which somehow *had to* come about because 'their time had come', the results of their actions and their successes are perceived to be almost inscribed in some immanent 'logic' of history.

Brecht's self-admonition in his *Arbeitsjournal* poses a fundamental challenge to this kind of certainty, this 'faith' in the 'providential' coincidence between 'that poor wretched thing' stabbed by his enemies' daggers, and that 'other Caesar, whose shadow will be the whole world', as if the long-term historical result could already be perceived in embryo in the works of that bold and unfortunate faction leader.

At all times, and especially at decisive moments, the end result of Caesar's political and military actions was wide open. He played for high stakes, risking all, especially during the protracted conflict that ended with his violent death. His undoing came in a spectacular operation, which should not, however, have come as a complete surprise: a conspiracy among his own men. And yet he retained an abiding posthumous prestige, and his power to fascinate has made him and his very name an archetype. Was this due solely to able management on the part of Octavian, his 'son' and heir, who became the emperor Augustus? Octavian in effect 'restyled' Caesar's image in order to present himself for a great part of his career as 'the heir', but later let that image recede into the background and gave preference to a formula which reflected favourably upon himself, 'the son': *Divi filius*.[2] This complicates the work of the historian, who must distinguish between the 'real' Caesar and the Caesar of the tradition filtered through Octavian. This tradition has not only influenced contemporary historiography; it has also determined the dominant interpretative approach which – rightly or wrongly – took Caesar as its point of departure.

We should consider ourselves fortunate that this man left us his own account of his political and military actions during the decisive decade of his public life (58–48 BC), and that this is the most authentic self-perception that 'the dead man known as Caesar' could have wished to leave. And we know how perilous it is – and how tempt-ing – to declare what a historical figure *was*, besides what he *wished to be*, and above all what he *claimed to have been*.

The solution, then, lies in the telling, in the depiction of a career dedicated to overturning the *res publica*, the traditional order of the Roman state. But such an account cannot be complete because the tradition has been subject to manipulation from the very beginning. It was Caesar himself, with his *Commentaries*, who initiated the manipulation. The search for a connection between the ambitions and the career of a faction leader and the 'historical role' played by him in terminating the ancient *res publica* comes up against his repeated claim to have acted as a staunch defender of the rules and laws of the traditional order. But to mistrust that self-representation systematically is to risk continually falling into a kind of teleological vision, a sort of historical metaphysics.

2 THE CAESAR OF THE RULERS

One cannot, however, leave out of account the long historiographical tradition and the Caesar created by it. If, for example, the notion of 'Caesarism', still alive and still ambiguous today, recurs throughout the centuries as a term in a typology of power, this means that the Caesar who is the product of that tradition is accepted as fact. But which tradition? On the one hand the tradition of the rulers, ever ready to identify with this model, and on the other a highly critical interpretative tradition which may be described by the formula dear to Ronald Syme as 'republican pessimism'.

A glimpse of the rulers' interest in the archetypal Caesar is offered by one of the rulers, Napoleon III, in the introduction he prepared for the second volume of his very scholarly but never completed *Histoire de Jules César* (1866). 'In publishing this second volume of the *Histoire de César*, written by the Emperor,' writes the publisher, clearly prompted by the imperial author, 'it is not without interest to recall the names of the sovereigns and rulers who have taken an inter-est in this subject.' He then lists some names which are salient enough to deserve mention: Charles VIII, 'who was particularly fond of Caesar's *Commentaries*', to the extent that he persuaded the monk Robert Gaguin to prepare a translation of the commentaries on Caesar's *Gallic War* (1480); and Charles V, who left a copy of the *Commentaries* with marginal notes in his own hand. Charles V was so interested in the strategic aspects of Caesar's account that he dispatched a scientific mission to France to study the topography of the Gallic campaigns. The result was Giacomo Strada's high-quality publication (1575) of some forty maps, one of which features the siege of Alesia. A contemporary and emulator of Charles V, the Turkish sultan Suleiman the Magnificent, ordered searches throughout all Europe for editions of Caesar's *Commentaries*. He had them collected and classified, and initiated their translation into Turkish, and they became part of the sultan's daily reading. Henri IV and Louis XIII translated, respectively, the first two *Commentaries* and the last two. (An edition containing both translations was published in 1630 'au Louvre', that is, by the royal publishing house.) Louis XIV (who did not exert himself unduly) retranslated the first *Commentary*, already translated by Henri IV, and produced a sumptuous illustrated edition in 1651, when he was still under the tutelage of Mazarin. The publisher of *Histoire de Jules César* then goes on to mention the Grand Condé, who had made a serious study of Caesar's campaigns. He had Perrot d'Ablancourt translate all the *Commentaries*, and this translation became the best known and the most widely used in the eighteenth century. After a note on the biographical work on Caesar by Queen Christina of Sweden and the map of the Gallic campaigns commissioned by Philippe of Orléans, the real precursor of Napoleon III's impressive work is listed: *Le Précis des guerres de César*, dictated by Napoleon I to Count Marchand on St Helena and published by Marchand in Paris in 1836.

3 BONAPARTE'S CAESAR

Napoleon Bonaparte really did identify himself with Caesar. In his *Mémorial de Sainte-Hélène*, the faithful Las Cases recorded some comparative musings which certainly originated with the emperor: 'Napoleon fought sixty battles; Caesar no more than fifty.'[3] And the emperor confided a prediction to Count Marchand: 'his death would be marked in the way that Caesar's was' (a reference to the appearance of a comet at the moment of Caesar's death).[4] In conversation with Las Cases the emperor claimed to have planned to drain the Pontine Marshes, like Caesar before him.[5] Overturning these analogies, the Baron de Pommereul declared in his *Campagnes du général Bonaparte en Italie* (1797) that, compared to Bonaparte, Caesar was merely a candidate for military glory.

But unlike some of his predecessors who embraced the 'cult of Caesar', Napoleon did more than adopt a model of leadership. He was also extremely conscious of Caesar's special relationship with 'the people': *le peuple* was a term much in vogue in the years of the French revolution (Marat's newspaper had the title *L'Ami du peuple*); the word denoted the politically active part of the lowest social strata that actually shaped political life and influenced the holders of power. We have only to mention a few typical observations which help us understand what Napoleon meant by 'le peuple': in January 49 BC Pompey could have taken up position to confront Caesar in Rome, but '*the people* were against him' (p. 209); '*the people* were overwhelmingly in favour of Caesar' (p. 125); 'when Caesar, still a very young man, delivered a eulogy for Julia, his father's sister and the wife of Gaius Marius, *the people* enthusiastically welcomed the return of the images of Marius in a public ceremony' (p. 26). He uses 'le peuple' in the same sense as Suetonius in some parts of his *Life of Caesar* uses 'plebs': it is the mass of the working people but also the social pressure group which had played a crucial role in the civil war. Napoleon seized on one core element: he identified an initial strategy which allowed Caesar to use all possible tactics to get the better of his adversaries, a strategy from which he never deviated. Napoleon was right to locate the cause of 'discontent in the *parti populaire* and the army' in certain concessions to the aristocracy after Caesar's victory in the civil war. Napoleon focuses his attention on one point which lay very close to his own heart: the 'legitimacy' of the personal power of Caesar,[6] who remained the leader of 'the people' even in his new role of sole ruler ('perpetual dictator'). Having in mind the decline of the Senate, the perversion of its operations, and the presence in Italy of a great number of veterans, 'attendant tout de la grandeur de quelques hommes et rien de la République', Napoleon proposed the theory of the '*person* of Caesar as the guarantee of Roman supremacy' and the guarantee of 'the security of the citizens of all parties'.

The emphatic way in which Napoleon dismisses as libellous inventions all reports that Caesar aspired to the title of king is further evidence of his self-identification with Caesar: with Caesar not as king, but as 'perpetual dictator', and thus the guarantee of Roman supremacy and the security of all.

This self-identification should come as no surprise (Napoleon's Italian campaign was to him what the Gallic campaign was to Caesar: a preparation for more decisive and critical battles). In France's military academies Caesar's *Commentaries* were required reading:[7] a page such as that in the *Précis* where Napoleon discusses – seriously and with expert knowledge of the logistical difficulties – which kind of attack would work best against the Parthians, and by which routes, is also a textbook exercise in military studies.[8]

4 THE CAESAR OF THE 'REPUBLICANS'

Napoleon Bonaparte seems to suggest (*pro bono suo*) that the only way to maintain a popular policy is to anchor it to a strong personal power which embraces all social classes.[9] At the opposite extreme is an interpretation which may be broadly described as 'republican pessimism', which had numerous representatives, including some distinguished ones, in the twentieth century. The pages of Syme's *Roman Revolution* and Gelzer's *Caesar* (and also many of his less well-known works) provide clear evidence of this. The core of this view lies in the perception of all late republican party leaders as equal and in the reduction of their statements and their 'programmes' to the level of pure propaganda. Paradoxically, this position recalls, in one essential point at least, (in its consequences, not its premises) a view which may be termed 'Marxist-Leninist'. (Its main exponents are Soviet historians, but echoes may be heard in some lines of Brecht in the pages cited above.) This reading too, though for other reasons, has tended to reduce the differences between the party leaders contending for supremacy. Even when fighting among themselves, these leaders are still seen as sharing responsibility for maintaining a common policy directed towards preserving slavery. With regard to this fundamental issue, they are all on the same side of the barricade. In Brecht's work there is just one fleeting phrase that refers to a question which seems to open a breach in this schematic pattern: when he says that 'slavery makes democratic policy impossible'. It is the merest hint, but one which might have led to a more sharply differentiated picture.

The vision imbued with 'republican pessimism' is certainly schematic. Arnaldo Momigliano, shortly after reaching his place of exile in England, was right to reject an empty but supposedly crowded 'prosopographical' universe: he pointed out that all those men whose careers in the civil war period are well known to us were not simply figures predestined to be listed in the Pauly-Wissowa *Realencyclopädie*; they were also members of diverse social strata and conflicting groupings, such as the urban proletariat, the *nobilitas*, the old aristocracy, etc.[10]

'Republican pessimism',[11] not surprisingly, is dominated by a moralising tone. The principate itself, the form of governance introduced by Augustus, is seen by Gibbon as a form of 'slavery'. In his view, as in Syme's, Cremutius, Thrasea and their ilk are martyrs to freedom under this regime, and 'the last true Romans'.

> The education of Helvidius and Thrasea, of Tacitus and Pliny, was the same as that of Cato and Cicero. From Grecian philosophy, they had imbibed the justest and most liberal notions of the dignity of human nature, and the origin of civil society. The history of their own country had taught them to revere a free, a virtuous, and a victorious commonwealth; to abhor the successful crimes of Caesar and Augustus; and inwardly to despise those tyrants whom they adored with the most abject flattery.[12]

This tone, understandable in Gibbon, becomes anachronistic in Syme.

Shifting practices in the exercise of power in the ancient republic proceeded, for two centuries at least, mostly – though with striking exceptions – in the direction of a principate which continued the ancient city-state, with its forms of political life, rather than towards a Hellenistic military monarchy, for which the Greek world had long held out an attractive ideological model in the form of Alexandria. Half-way between the two models stands Caesar. We would be doing him an injustice if we were to reduce all his endeavours to a determination, documented in the *Commentaries*, above all on the civil war, to settle scores with friends and personal enemies. Fortunately, thanks to Suetonius, fragments of information originating in Caesar's entourage have been preserved, with others that come indirectly from Caesar himself, captured, one might say, outside the self-representation of his *Commentaries* and illuminated anew by original documents that perhaps nobody since Suetonius has attempted to use for historical purposes.

The present account will attempt to negotiate the hazards of this tradition. Caesar has excited the interest of historians for millennia. Brilliant minds of great experience have described him as incomparable. 'But in this very circumstance lies the difficulty, we may perhaps say the impossibility, of depicting Caesar to the life', wrote Theodor Mommsen. 'As the artist can paint everything save only consummate beauty, so the historian, when once in a thousand years he encounters the perfect, can only be silent regarding it.'[13]

Admiration taken to this extreme does not serve the historian well. But it is noteworthy that one of the greatest historians of the nineteenth century should have surrendered so completely to the fascination exerted by his subject. This makes the task all the more difficult for those of us who come to it later.

Notes

1 *Journal Dänemark 1938/39* (Frankfurt 1994), (*Journal I, 1913–1941*, in *Werke, Grosse kommentierte Berliner und Frankfurter Ausgabe*, vol. 26), p. 312. The note of 23 July 1938 records the early idea of the (unfinished) novel *Die Geschäfte des Herrn Julius Caesar*.

2 The manner in which Caesar is treated in book 6 of the *Aeneid* (line 789) is significant: a brief note, compared to the space devoted to Augustus.

3 Emmanuel comte de Las Cases, *Mémorial de Sainte-Hélène* (Paris 1961), vol. 2, p. 610.

4 Marchand, *Mémoires* (Paris 1955), vol. 2, p. 294.

5 *Mémorial*, vol. 2, p. 107.

6 *Précis des guerres de César* par Napoléon, écrit par M. Marchand sous la dictée de l'Empereur [1819] (Paris 1836), pp. 212–13.

7 In the same way, book 6 of Polybius was studied by Macchiavelli, Justus Lipsius and Frederick II of Prussia with a view to developing a modern 'art of war'.

8 *Précis*, p. 211.

9 See the pages in his *Précis* in which he explains why it was inevitable that Caesar should seek to win back the old aristocracy.

10 Arnaldo Momigliano, review of R. Syme, *The Roman Revolution*, *JRS*, 30 (1940), p. 78.

11 The expression is derived from Ronald Syme, *The Roman Revolution* (Oxford 1939), p. 6.

12 Edward Gibbon, The *History of the Decline and Fall of the Roman Empire* [1774] (London 1994), ed. D. Womersley, vol. 1, pp. 105–6.

13 Theodor Mommsen, *Römische Geschichte* [1856], III, 4th edn (Munich 1986), vol. 5, p. 134. In English, *The History of Rome*, trans. William Purdie Dickson (London 1908), vol. 5, p. 314.

Part I

From Sulla to Catiline

In Flight from Sulla: First Experiences of an Aristocratic Youth

The early life of Caesar may be seen as the story of a young man being hunted, but possessed of an indomitable spirit and a fierce determination to defend the honour of the defeated party of the *populares*. He incurs the enmity of the dictator Sulla, who seeks to eliminate the nephew of Gaius Marius. But Caesar is also the scion of one of the most venerable patrician families, the *gens Julia*, which boasted a mythical descent from Julus, the son of Aeneas. Any overt action against the young son of Gaius Julius Caesar the Elder (who had died in 85 BC, when the future dictator was only sixteen) would have been fraught with difficulty. Instead Sulla preferred to attempt to humiliate him, trying among other things to make him leave his wife Cornelia, the daughter of Cinna, the other leader of the *populares*, whom Sulla had defeated when he marched on Rome.

For Caesar the defining experience was perhaps his first few years of 'conscious' life, under the dictatorship of Sulla. That was when he learned what it meant to stake all while facing the overwhelming power of political adversaries. He learned what the unlimited control of the *factio paucorum* could mean.

After blocking Caesar's appointment as *flamen Dialis*,[1] Sulla had planned to remove him and have him put to death. Plutarch states this clearly,[2] and Suetonius lets it be understood when he recounts that Caesar is obliged to change his hiding place every night and even bribe 'Sulla's detectives'. He is saved (*veniam impetravit*) thanks to the intercession of the Vestal Virgins and Aurelius Cotta.[3]

Sulla had encountered resistance in his own entourage to the plan to liquidate Caesar. Hence the fury he directed at those of his followers who could not grasp how dangerous Caesar was:

> Have your way and take him; only bear in mind that the man you are so eager to save will one day deal the death blow to the cause of the aristocracy (*optimates*), which you have joined with me in upholding; for in this Caesar there is more than one Marius.[4]

Although there was no shortage of anonymous and reliable assassins,[5] his quarry eluded him. The experience of 'wandering about in
the country of the Sabines, . . . changing his abode by night', as
Plutarch tells us, set Caesar firmly on a definite course.[6]

Caesar elected to disappear from Rome for some time. Here begins his
attachment as legate to Marcus Minutius Thermus. In 81 BC, as soon
as his praetorship was over, or perhaps even before the end of his term
as magistrate,[7] Thermus was sent to the province of Asia, and Caesar
accompanied him. This, it seems, was a way of getting him away from
Rome. In Asia Thermus tasked Caesar with a mission to Nicomedes,
the king of Bithynia and a good friend of the Roman republic. This
was the start of the close friendship between Caesar and Nicomedes,
on which his adversaries based persistent and unsubtle hints at the
sexual nature of the relationship. Thirty-five years later this was still
the object of mirth in the ditties Caesar's troops sang during their conquest of Gaul:[8] 'All the Gauls did Caesar vanquish, Nicomedes vanquished him',[9] and going on ironically, 'Lo! now Caesar rides in
triumph, victor over all the Gauls; Nicomedes does not triumph, who
subdued the conqueror.' Caesar ignored taunts of this kind. In any case
the mission to Asia was characterised by warlike events. Caesar distinguished himself in the siege of Mytilene, the last centre of resistance
to Rome after the defeat of Mithridates, and 'Thermus awarded him
the civic crown' *ob cives servatos* (for saving the lives of Roman
citizens).[10]

In 78 BC we find Caesar in Cilicia in the service of Servilius
Isauricus,[11] who, his consulship behind him, had been entrusted with
the delicate task of dealing with the pirates who had made Cilicia
their stronghold, their centre of operations and their refuge. Precise
information is lacking, but it seems clear that Caesar continued to
operate in Asia and did not return to Rome while Sulla was alive.
Increasingly he was entrusted with special duties and served beside
Roman commanders who were posted to Asia Minor. This was made
possible by the fact of his belonging to the patrician class. It should
also be said that magistrates in good standing with Sulla were apparently opening doors for Caesar, and this did much to ensure that he
survived and prospered.

It was only when news came of the death of Sulla and the insurrection of Marcus Emilius Lepidus (consul in 78 BC) against the
Sullan order that Caesar returned to Rome.[12] The whole story of his
return is noteworthy. This man of twenty-two, hunted, then forced to

flee for his life from Rome, utterly undaunted by the persecution, sets out promptly as soon as news comes of the passing of the dictator. He behaves like a leader who is confident of being seen as one: he weighs up Lepidus' proposals and his chances, and turns them down. Lepidus, who is his senior in years and authority, and had assumed the consulate in that year, invites him cordially and 'with highly favourable terms'[13] to share the adventure of revolution. He has recognised the popular leader in Caesar, but Caesar already possesses the mature politician's 'clinical eye', which enables him to distinguish an adventurer from a leader with prospects of success. Suetonius, who supplies these precious details, makes clear that Caesar refused to align himself with Lepidus for two reasons: he had no faith in Lepidus' character,[14] and he suddenly realised, viewing the situation at close quarters, that it was far less favourable than he had thought.[15] This speedy appraisal and reaction already show us the politician endowed with the greatest of all gifts, according to classical political science: the ability to foresee developments by intuition, to identify 'among the various possibilities the one which may most rationally be expected to eventuate',[16] an art in which the ability to assess the balance of forces is paramount.

Lepidus' revolt, premature and badly organised, ended badly. After fomenting disorder in Transalpine Gaul, the then (77 BC) proconsul marched on Rome but was defeated by Catulus and then fled in haste to Sardinia. Some of his men sought refuge with Sertorius in Spain. Lepidus had behind him a wretched career. He had been on Cinna's side and had married a woman who was related to Saturninus, the unfortunate leader of the *populares*. But when Sulla's victory seemed imminent, he rejected his wife and joined Sulla, profiting from the proscriptions and thus acquiring an indelible stain. Having become consul (within the structure devised by Sulla), he began conspiring with Pompey – who had become the creature and protégé of Sulla but who was shrewder by far – to change the Sullan constitution, the anti-libertarian provisions of which emphasised the oligarchic nature of the Roman republic. It may easily be seen that Caesar's behaviour had been quite the opposite; he had refused to divorce Cinna's daughter and had risked all by defying the dictator. This may be what Suetonius is referring to when he speaks of Caesar's mistrust of Lepidus' *ingenium*. However, in Rome politics is nothing if not a hereditary occupation, and Caesar, who was cynical enough to make use even of discredited men, in 49–48 BC, at the start of the civil war, would seek out Lepidus' son, exploit him to formalise his assumption of the dictatorship, and make him his *magister equitum*, using him as a 'rival' to the too independent and troublesome Mark Antony.[17]

Against the backers of the Sullan regime Caesar chose a more diverse and cautious strategy (and one which would also prove more productive): he would take some of them to court for their crimes. Thus he levelled accusations against Gnaeus Cornelius Dolabella (consul in 81 BC and commander of Sulla's fleet the year before), who had not preserved his innocence during the proscriptions. Caesar alleged extortion while Dolabella was proconsul in Macedonia. Since it is quite probable that Dolabella's command in Macedonia continued until Appius Claudius Pulcher (consul in 79 BC) arrived in 77 BC, this means that the trial took place in 77–76. Tacitus, however, in his *Dialogue of the Orators*, dates this memorable trial, in which Dolabella was defended and cleared by advocates of the first rank such as Quintus Hortensius, in 'the twenty-first year' of Caesar's life,[18] that is, in 79 BC or even 80. This is impossible since the trial would then have taken place during the reign of Sulla. Caesar's speech for the prosecution against the extortionist consul was still read during the time of Gellius,[19] in the second century AD. Velleius Paterculus, who lived in the time of the emperor Tiberius, described the speech for the prosecution enthusiastically as *accusatio nobilissima*. He also makes clear that public opinion was favourable to Caesar. But the extortionist was cleared thanks to the excellent and influential advocates who assisted him.[20] Caesar, who never had any illusions about the outcome of the trial, said in his speech against the accused that 'the best of causes could be defeated by the pleading of Lucius Cotta'.[21] The defeat was not without consequences. It should be borne in mind that, as may happen in such cases, the failure of Lepidus had reinforced the regime which Lepidus had tried to overthrow. Dolabella's triumph in court was a sign of the vitality and arrogance of Sulla's faction,[22] which remained firmly in power.

The Greeks, who had hoped to obtain justice against Dolabella, were disappointed. Caesar appeared for them in one last court action, this time against another figure from the Sullan coterie, Gaius Antonius Hybrida. This latter, who had a chequered career but owes his fame principally to being the uncle of the tribune Mark Antony,[23] launched into the collection of vast tributes at the expense of the Greeks while Sulla was there,[24] and on returning to Italy distinguished himself by speculating with the property of the outcasts. But his Greek victims – this was in 76 BC – denounced him to the *praetor peregrinus* of that year, Marcus Terentius Varro Lucullus. According to Plutarch,[25] Caesar, who prosecuted the Sullan extortionist on behalf of the provincials, was so efficient that Gaius Antonius finally appealed to the tribunes, on the pretext that he had not been accorded fair treatment in court. Neither Plutarch (who commits a number of chronological errors) nor the grammarian Asconius tells us how the trial concluded, but all the indications are that Gaius Antonius avoided punishment.

What is certain is that in the wake of these political and judicial events Caesar again decided to 'withdraw', 'to escape from the ill-will which he had incurred', as Suetonius puts it.[26] What better opportunity than an educational visit to Rhodes, the meeting place and site of pilgrimage of young Romans of the upper classes who aspired to a good 'Greek' education?

Notes

1 Cinna and Marius had intended Caesar to take this appointment.
2 Plutarch, *Caesar* 1.4.
3 Suetonius, *Caesar* 1.3. Aurelius Cotta was the brother of Aurelia, Caesar's mother, but during the Marian conflict he had returned to Rome in Sulla's retinue (Cicero, *Brutus* 311). On intercession of this kind, based on the right of asylum in the temples, see Cicero, *In Defence of Fonteius* 46; Suetonius, *Tiberius* 2.4; Tacitus, *Annals* 11.32.
4 Suetonius, *Caesar* 1.
5 Suetonius, *Caesar* 1.2 ('inquisitores').
6 Plutarch, *Caesar* 1.6. Experiences such as this did not always dictate a consistent pattern of behaviour. In 49 BC Marcus Junius Brutus, the future assassin of Caesar, chose to follow Pompey, the murderer of his father.
7 This may be deduced from Suetonius, *Caesar* 2.1. Cf. Broughton, *MRR*, vol. II, p. 76.
8 Celebrated in 46 BC, after the return from Africa (Suetonius, *Caesar* 37).
9 Suetonius, *Caesar* 49.
10 Suetonius, *Caesar* 2. The conquest of Mytilene is recorded by Livy, *Periochae* 89.
11 Suetonius, *Caesar* 3.
12 In L. Labruna's happy phrase from the book of the same name, 'the subversive consul'. L. Labruna, *Il console sovversivo* (Naples 1975).
13 'Magnis condicionibus', says Suetonius, *Caesar* 3.
14 'Ingenio eius diffisus.'
15 'Cum ingenio eius diffisus tum occasione, quam minorem opinione offenderat.'

16 Thucydides 1.22.4: τὸ γενησόμενον τῶν μελλόντων.
17 Of course the nature of Lepidus, father and son, as 'professional' traitors was universally known, and Cicero speaks contemptuously of it in private letters to Brutus and Cassius (*Letters to his friends* 12.8.1).
18 Tacitus, *Dialogue of the Orators* 34.7.
19 Gellius 4.16.8.
20 This Dolabella is no relation of Cicero's son-in-law Dolabella, the follower of Caesar in the civil war.
21 The fragment is cited by Valerius Maximus (8.9.3). Lucius Aurelius Cotta, with Hortensius, defended Dolabella ably and successfully.
22 Only a few years later, in the consulship of Crassus and Pompey (70 BC), the cornerstones of the revised constitution would be dismantled.
23 In 63 BC he would be a consul with Cicero and tasked with the military repression of the Catilinarian conspirators.
24 Asconius, p. 75 Kiessling-Schoell (= p. 84 Clark).
25 Plutarch, *Caesar* 4.1–3. Suetonius makes no mention of this trial.
26 Suetonius, *Caesar* 4.1 'ad declinandam invidiam'.

CHAPTER 2

Prisoner of the Pirates (75–74 BC)

An unforeseen event marred the journey. Off the island of
Pharmacussa – one of the Sporades to the south of Miletos – Caesar's
ship was seized by pirates, the ferocious pirates of Cilicia. The most
colourful account of this episode, which is also found in the historical
writing of Velleius,[1] is by Plutarch, and Suetonius too provides details
which concur with the vivid account by his Greek contemporary. It is
difficult to imagine that anybody but Caesar himself could be the
source of the story. The sardonic self-confidence with which the whole
episode is related must come from him. 'The pirates demanded twenty
talents for his ransom,' says Plutarch, 'and he laughed at them for not
knowing who their captive was, and of his own accord agreed to give
them fifty.'[2] He dispatched messengers from his entourage to collect
the money, keeping only his personal doctor and two slaves at his
side.[3] Although a hostage for thirty-eight days while waiting for the
messengers to return with the money, he quickly assumed a leading
position. When it was time to sleep, he would send one of the two
slaves to command silence. When his captors were practising their
sports and exercises, he gave directions, as if he had assumed
command with their consent. They even provided him with an audience. To make profitable use of the enforced idleness of captivity, he
composed poetry and speeches, which he recited in the presence of his
captors, expecting their admiration. If this was not sufficiently forthcoming, he belaboured them with insults, calling them 'illiterate
Barbarians', and sometimes uttering more serious threats, but all in
jesting tone, saying that he would have them all hanged, for example.
The pirates were greatly amused, 'attributing his boldness of speech to
a certain simplicity and boyish mirth'.[4] At last the ransom was raised,
the fifty talents paid and Caesar was put ashore. How had he raised
the large ransom amount? Velleius is very precise on this point: 'His
ransom was paid by the cities of Asia',[5] but on condition that the
hostages should be released before payment of the ransom. This can
be more clearly understood if we bear in mind that Caesar was able to

exploit the fact that he had been captured because the 'coastguard' mounted by the community (*civitates*) of the region had been insufficiently vigilant.[6] This was in the year 74 BC, when Marcus Juncus was *propraetor* of the province of Asia – an unfavourable moment for Roman maritime power.[7] Servilius Isauricus' campaign had not in fact struck at the root of the endemic scourge of piracy. The economic and military power of the Roman state was concentrated on the hard-fought war against Sertorius in Spain, a war which was then at its height. Piracy in Cilicia in particular was therefore now flourishing and dominated the eastern Mediterranean above all. The coastal towns of Asia were thrown onto the defensive. Faced with a peremptory request from Caesar, a Roman nobleman seized by pirates just off their shores thanks to their ineffective control, they could only comply, and raise the very considerable sum in a relatively short period.

No sooner had he been freed than Caesar set about punishing his captors. At Miletos he fitted out some ships and moved to entrap the pirates while they still lay at anchor off Pharmacussa. Velleius correctly points out that Caesar carried out this whole operation as a *privatus*,[8] a private individual: in the absence of any firm 'public' power of control over the seas, he proceeded, we may suppose, much as he had done when he raised the ransom from *pecunia publica*, availing himself of the assistance of *privati* to prepare the ships and take personal and direct command of them, without assuming any public office which might authorise him to do so. A naval engagement took place: some of the pirate vessels took flight, some were sunk, others were captured and many prisoners taken.

At this time Juncus, the *propraetor* of the province of Asia with proconsular *imperium* (authority), was in Bithynia as executor of the will of Nicomedes III, who had bequeathed the kingdom of Bithynia 'to the people of Rome'. Caesar therefore made his way to Bithynia with his 'human booty' of captive pirates, expecting the *propraetor* to impose exemplary punishment upon them. This did not in fact happen.

Juncus had no intention of imposing capital punishment. According to Plutarch, 'he had eyes above all for the booty', since Caesar had recovered 'no small sum' when he had captured the pirates.[9] But the information provided by Velleius must be taken to be more accurate: Juncus hoped to profit greatly by selling the pirates,[10] and indeed he issued orders to this effect, but Caesar put back to sea at once, before the *propraetor*'s orders were received and on his own initiative set about crucifying the prisoners. History is, as usual, kind to Caesar. In a separate part of his biography – as an indication of Caesar's mercy even in revenge! – Suetonius notes that before having them hung on their crosses, a torture leading to a very slow and agonising death, he 'ordered that their throats be cut first'.[11] Plutarch is careful to point out that Caesar was merely keeping the promise he had made when he was their prisoner, 'when they thought he was joking'.[12]

The fact that as a young man the future 'master of the world' had fallen into the hands of pirates was something that lent itself naturally to embroidery and elaboration in legend. In the account of Polyaenus, who was writing his manual of *Stratagems* at the time of Marcus Aurelius, much later than Plutarch and Suetonius, Caesar's liberation was achieved by means of a ruse worthy of Odysseus. Having collected the ransom, laden with money far beyond their expectations, the pirates were enticed to a banquet and plied with drugged wine. Caesar then had them put to death while they slept and returned the ransom money to the people of Miletos.[13] Fenestella, an antiquarian of the time of Augustus, reported in the second book of his *Epitome*, now lost, that the pirates were 'beheaded' (*decollati*) and not crucified.[14]

A speech by Caesar *To the Bithynians*, of which Gellius has preserved a few sentences,[15] must be seen in the context of his sojourn in Asia and his unhappy encounter with the governor Marcus Juncus. Judging by the little that remains, and from Gellius' scant commentary, it seems clear that Caesar was speaking in front of Juncus, since he addresses him in person (he could not avoid addressing him if Juncus was the magistrate before whom the speech was to be delivered),[16] and explaining that his long-standing friendship with Nicomedes obliged him to support the cause of the Bithynians. He also formulated a maxim which would remain a central principle of the conduct of the good Roman politician: 'one cannot abandon one's clients without earning the greatest infamy'.[17]

We have no further details of this episode, but it seems to confirm that relations with Juncus were not all they might have been (the incident of the punishment of the pirates was no trifle). And above all it adds one more piece to the picture formed by the other judicial episodes in which the very young Caesar became involved, in defence of citizens of the provinces.[18] Here he can best be understood from his own words, and against the background of a network of political relations helpful to his subsequent political ascent.

Besides the adventure with the pirates, with its sequel in Bithynia, the journey first undertaken towards Rhodes held other surprises in store. In the province of Asia Caesar took part in operations against one of Mithridates' generals, whose name is not supplied by Suetonius – the sole source.[19] The story may be briefly told: the province was afflicted by this general's raids; Caesar recruited auxiliary militia forces, drove out the invader and succeeded in restoring the friendship for Rome of those towns whose loyalty was wavering, owing to the evident weakness of Roman control not only in this region. Just as he had earlier fitted out ships to pursue the pirates as a *privatus*, he now recruited auxiliaries and gained some experience, if only marginal experience, of a very serious conflict. So if the 'Gaius Julius' named with Publius Autronius as a legate of Antonius Creticus in a Greek inscription from 71 BC is Caesar,[20] another fragment of his travels and activities in Greece before his return to Rome can be recovered.

Meanwhile Caesar was elected in his absence to the college of *pontifices* in place of Gaius Aurelius Cotta, who had died.[21] To Velleius this was compensation for the loss of the *flamen Dialis*, which had come about as a result of Sulla's persecution. From the very beginning Caesar had understood very clearly the importance of sacred duties, although for him, as for any member of the Roman ruling class, personal religious views had no effect on political decisions. He did not become a leader by chance. He built up his own power base, tenaciously, little by little, and the pontificate rightly formed part of it.

Notes

 1 Velleius 2.42.
 2 Plutarch, *Caesar* 2.1.
 3 Suetonius, *Caesar* 4.1.
 4 Plutarch, *Caesar* 2.4.
 5 Velleius 2.42.2: 'publica civitatium pecunia redemptus est'. Polyaenus (8.23.1) states categorically that the ransom sought was paid by Miletos.
 6 Matthias Gelzer, *Caesar, Politician and Statesman* (Oxford 1968), trans. Peter Needham, p. 24.
 7 Velleius 2.42.3; Plutarch, *Caesar* 2.6.
 8 Velleius 2.42.2.
 9 Plutarch, *Caesar* 2.7.
10 Velleius 2.42.3.
11 Suetonius, *Caesar* 74.1.
12 Plutarch, *Caesar* 2.7.

13 Polyaenus 8.23.1.

14 Fragment 30 of the collection by Peter, *HRR*, vol. II, p. 87.

15 Gellius 5.13.6.

16 Although Gellius describes Caesar at this point as *pontifex maximus*, this does not mean that Caesar held the office at the moment when he delivered this speech. On this matter see A. M. Ward, 'Caesar and the Pirates', *American Journal of Ancient History*, 2 (1977), pp. 26–36.

17 Gellius has a whole chapter (5.13) devoted to the question of the amount of attention one should pay to clients.

18 See Chapter 1.

19 Suetonius, *Caesar* 4.2.

20 *Syll.*[3], no. 748, r. 23. Broughton, *MRR*, vol. II, p. 113, tends towards this view and develops it with further arguments in his Supplement (p. 105). Dittenberger (*Syll.*[3], no. 748, n. 12) may have had in mind Caesar's first sojourn in Asia Minor (81–68 BC).

21 Velleius 2.43.1: 'absens pontifex factus erat in Cottae consularis locum'.

CHAPTER 3

The Rise of a Party Leader

On returning to Rome from a journey during which, according to Velleius, he was again harassed by pirates, the 'masters of the seas',[1] Caesar achieved an early electoral success: he was elected a military tribune in 72 BC for the following year.[2] He was the first to be elected,[3] no doubt because he was well aware of the way to win an electoral campaign. He deployed his energies in the battles characteristic of the tradition and the politics of the *populares*, all the more significant while the war against Spartacus was raging in Italy. He strove to support, says Suetonius somewhat vaguely, those who tried 'to re-establish the authority of the tribunes of the plebs, the extent of which Sulla had curtailed'. His other initiative – which is better documented – was to support the *Lex Plotia*, designed to secure the return of the followers of Lepidus, who in the meantime had taken refuge with Sertorius in Spain, among them Caesar's brother-in-law Lucius Cinna.[4]

The fact that the most delicate problem left behind by Sulla was the restoration of the rights of the tribunes of the plebs was well known to all the contending forces. It had already figured in Lepidus' programme, in the petitions of Gaius Aurelius Cotta in 75 BC, of Lucius Quintius in 74, of Licinius Macer in 73, and it would be one of the achievements of the consulate of Crassus and Pompey in 70. So to which specific initiatives of Caesar, the soldiers' tribune, could Sulla's vague statement ('he ardently supported the leaders in the attempt to re-establish the authority of the tribunes of the plebs') refer? Perhaps to his contribution to the election of Crassus. The consular elections for the year 70 BC took place in 71: it is more than likely that Caesar and his supporters backed a candidate who, to be sure, did not lack the means to gain a majority, but who could certainly benefit from the support of a recognised and energetic leader of the *populares*.

In his *Life of Crassus* Plutarch mentions – without naming his source – that when Caesar was captured by the pirates he exclaimed, 'How you will rejoice, Crassus, when you learn that I have been captured!'[5] If this is not the purest invention, it implies a certain friction, even rivalry, between Caesar, still an apprentice in politics, and Crassus, a wealthy and authoritative claimant to the consulate, despite a great disparity in power and resources. 'But later they became friends', Plutarch goes on. And indeed, as we shall see, Crassus came to be linked with Caesar, a central figure in the decade 70–60 BC, in various ways, including the widespread belief that both were behind a series of dark conspiracies.[6] It is therefore probable that it was precisely the election campaign of 71 BC, when Crassus sought the consulate (and secured it by means of an agreement with Pompey) and Caesar was the soldiers' tribune, that provided the occasion for an alliance of convenience between the two.

The year 70 BC proved a defining one for the constitution and for Roman politics. The two consuls, who were also the two dominant political figures, were at one not only during the election campaign but also later, when in power, in wanting to demolish the Sullan constitutional framework, and in particular in wanting to restore the rights of the tribunes. The climate, however, had changed. This may readily be seen when Caesar, having assumed office as *quaestor* on 5 December 70 BC,[7] began a series of gestures with obvious symbolic significance, officially restoring 'political honour' to the Marian faction.[8] Speaking from the rostra in the Forum, 'according to the custom',[9] he delivered the eulogies for his paternal aunt Julia, the widow of Gaius Marius, and his own wife Cornelia, the daughter of Cinna, both of whom died in 69 BC. During the funeral procession, he had portraits of Gaius Marius and his son Marius the Younger displayed in public for the first time since Sulla's victory, and in the first rank.[10] He countered protests from some quarters by citing public enthusiasm for this initiative: 'the people answered with loud shouts, received Caesar with applause, and admired him for bringing back after so long a time, as it were from Hades, the honours of Marius into the city'.[11] Conscious of the power of symbols and buoyed by his success, as *aedile* four years later he would also restore Marius' trophies.[12]

Caesar's eulogy for Julia is better known than his other public speeches because Suetonius preserved a substantial excerpt.[13] The passage cited by the biographer appears to have been selected with some malice. In it Caesar dwells on Julia's ancestry *on her mother's side*, stressing that she was descended from Ancus Marcius (while the *gens Julia* was descended from Venus). In laying claim to this royal lineage Caesar is also extolling the charisma of royalty. Among other things, he says: 'Our stock therefore has at once *the sanctity of kings,* whose power is supreme among mortal men, and the claim to reverence which attaches to the Gods, *who hold sway over kings themselves.*' The choice may be deliberate. Suetonius wished to point out this forceful claim to *royalty,* and Caesar's manner of locating himself complacently in the regal tradition. Suetonius was certainly mindful of the traditional image of Caesar with his aspirations to the *regnum* in perpetuity (something to which Suetonius himself makes a substantial contribution with his biography), and this excerpt from Caesar's speech suited his purpose well. The image of a 'monarchic' Caesar emerges from it reinforced.

The eulogy for Cornelia seems unusual: it was not the custom to deliver funeral orations for young women.[14] Caesar was an innovator in this. According to Plutarch it was precisely this unusual and innovative gesture that won him even more public favour. The people, he writes, were moved to admire him 'as a man who was gentle and full of feeling'.[15] The support secured among the public by this official innovation,[16] an expression of greater consideration for a young female figure, rather than a powerful matron, deserves attention.

Caesar's most significant political experience as *quaestor* was the period of months spent in Further Spain – the far south of Spain, opposite Morocco – under Gaius Antistius Vetus, *praetor* in 70 BC and governor the following year in precisely this region. Years later, and in a completely different context, when in 45 BC he had to confront Pompey's sons in Further Spain, he recalled that he had chosen this region with particular enthusiasm 'at the beginning of his quaestorship', that he had preferred it 'to all other provinces', and that at that time he had done his best to bestow his bounty upon it. The quotations are known to us from the anonymous author of *Bellum Hispaniense* (*Spanish War*).[17] In the speech, which the author paraphrases, Caesar also recalls his own good works for the benefit of the province when *praetor* (he had lifted the burden of Metellus' taxes) and later during his first consulship. All of this indicates – and we have it in Caesar's very own words – that he tried from the beginning to build up connections in the province: the development of a network of clients in the various regions of the empire was clearly important to him as a principal means to advance his political career. We may recall the brief lesson he inflicted upon the *praetor* Juncus in Bithynia on the importance of the clientship and how to protect it.

The prime example is clearly provided by Pompey, who in those years was busy constructing his network of clients in grand style – a web which enveloped the most distant provinces and constituted the true foundation of Pompey's power and the guarantee of its stability. Thus, when on becoming a *praetor* (in 62 BC) he had to choose a province to administer, his choice fell on Further Spain, where in 61 he launched into an extensive campaign of gubernatorial activities.

Of his energetic activity as *quaestor* in Spain we gain an impression from Suetonius, who shows him engaged in frenetic judicial work in various towns across the country, including Cadiz (Gades).[18] Velleius writes, with his usual emphasis, of a quaestorship 'in which he showed wonderful energy and valour'.[19] The particular mandate entrusted to Caesar by Antistius was *iure dicundo* (the administration of justice). This was a formative experience which allowed him to learn the mechanisms of provincial administration.[20] The connections which he established at this time were to be developed later. Plutarch asserts that, having become *praetor*, Caesar in his turn wished to have the son of Antistius Vetus as his *quaestor*.[21]

Caesar left the province before his term was completed, having 'straightway asked for his discharge, to grasp the first opportunity for greater enterprises at Rome', to quote Suetonius, whose account is very detailed.[22] Suetonius gives swift confirmation that Caesar departed the province early, before the expiry of his term of office. The motivation accepted by the biographer for this premature departure is somewhat doubtful, if not mythological: the episode – variously dated – of the sudden comparison which occurred to Caesar between himself and Alexander the Great. This episode, like the dream attributed to him ('he dreamed that he had a sexual relationship with his own mother'), has become part of the tradition.[23] Plutarch, for example, places Caesar's anguished realisation that he was lagging behind Alexander in the pace of his career in the time when he was *praetor* (62 BC),[24] and the dream on the night before he crossed the Rubicon.[25] It is precisely the chronological uncertainty that makes these episodes untenable. In the case of Caesar's self-comparison with Alexander, the context also varies. In Suetonius' account it came to Caesar as he stood before a statue of Alexander by the temple of Hercules at Cadiz.[26] In Plutarch's version, Caesar burst into tears while reading: 'Do you not think it is a matter for sorrow that while Alexander, at my age, was already king of so many peoples, I have as yet achieved no brilliant success?'[27] Thus began the tradition –

inaugurated by Caesar himself – of *synkrisis*, the Caesar-Alexander comparison, which subsequently developed into a kind of literary genre. It no longer figures at the conclusion of Plutarch's *Lives* (of Alexander and Caesar), but Appian gives us a sample of it at the end of the second book of his *Civil Wars* and informs us that this comparison was commonly drawn.[28] The connection between Caesar's nightmare of Alexander's superiority and the decision to return to Rome early is obvious: the thought of Alexander's brilliant career is, according to Suetonius, the spur which drove Caesar to grasp with both hands the chance to do great things at the centre of power, that is, in Rome.

An episode related only by Suetonius is connected to Caesar's return journey to Rome, but in this instance Suetonius' account is extremely vague. Before returning to Rome, Caesar is said to have visited 'the Latin colonists who were in a state of unrest and meditating a demand for citizenship'. This clearly refers to the colonies of Gallia Transpadana, which did not enjoy full citizenship, only the 'Latin law', until the end of the 'Social War' (88 BC).[29] What follows is not so much a statement as a conjecture: 'and he might have spurred them on to some rash act, had not the consuls, in anticipation of that very danger, detained there for a time the legions which had been enrolled for service in Cilicia'.[30] The consul in question can only be Quintus Marcius Rex, consul in 68 BC, who in that year was fighting in Cilicia.[31] This therefore provides the chronological framework for the reconstruction adopted here.

That Marcius Rex would really have postponed his departure in order to frustrate with his legions the vague but fell designs of the young *quaestor* on his way home from Spain is difficult to believe. It is probably correct to suppose[32] that this story derives from the same hostile sources of which Suetonius avails himself in the pages that follow.[33] This section is rich in indiscretions and insinuations concerning the agreements of Caesar and Crassus in the 'conspiracies' which characterised this decade. Of these the best known was that of Catiline, and the most successful might be considered the 'triumvirate'.

It was with the aedileship, which he assumed with Marcus Bibulus in 65 BC, that Caesar, having ended his quaestorship and become a senator in 68 BC, finally asserted himself as a leader. From this point he formulated his own policies and commanded attention in 'high' politics. Throughout this 'march' – in which he and Crassus were often side by side – he never lost sight of Pompey, the real master of Roman politics in those years. In 67 BC he supported the *Lex Gabinia*, by which Pompey was granted command in the struggle against the pirates.[34] In 66 BC, with Cicero, he supported the *Lex Manilia*, which gave Pompey command in the war against Mithridates.[35] These were two astute and far-sighted decisions which would assume some importance when Caesar, having upset many people and disrupted traditional power-balances, made the most decisive move of his career and in the history of the republic by reaching a rapprochement and a political understanding with Pompey.

Now, as *aedile*, he enjoyed plenty of room to manoeuvre and achieve personal advancement through the accepted methods of securing and consolidating a consensus. He adopted first of all a comprehensive policy of public works, or rather, of bestowing gifts. 'Caesar decorated not only the Comitium and the Forum with its adjacent basilicas, but the Capitol as well, building temporary colonnades for the display of a part of his material.'[36] He also staged wild-beast hunts and other spectacles. For these he took the credit himself, even though Bibulus was the one who footed the bill. Bibulus was not a colourful individual, but on this occasion he was able to sum up the situation with an apt joke, saying that he felt like Pollux confronted with the temple built in the Forum to honour the twin deities, which was known colloquially as 'the temple of Castor'.[37] A further opportunity for the public displays of generosity, and at the same time for political and familial self-celebration, came with the gladiatorial games which he organised to honour the memory of his own father.[38] He hired 320 pairs of gladiators and would have liked to hire many more.[39] However, his opponents took fright at the great number of gladiator teams which he had called in from every hand and enacted a law by which it was illegal to own and train more than a limited number of gladiators in the city of Rome.

Managing gladiators is always an extremely delicate matter in a slave-owning society as highly militarised as that of Rome, especially at a time following a fierce war such as that fought a few years earlier – in 73–71 BC – against the gladiator army of Spartacus and Crixus. We need look no further for an example than the decisive role played by Decimus Brutus in March 44 BC: he was responsible for managing the numerous teams of gladiators in the city, a fact which was important at the time of the plot against Caesar and in the days immediately following it. But on this occasion there was another consideration: the use of gladiatorial spectacles for electoral purposes.

Two years later, in 63 BC, Cicero as consul would introduce the *Lex Tullia de ambitu*, a law forbidding candidates to office to hold gladiatorial games in the two-year period preceding their candidacy unless the date had been set in the will of a deceased official.[40] In the case of Caesar's games of 65 BC, Suetonius unfortunately does not state exactly who was responsible for passing the ruling *de numero gladiatorum*, or what might have been the motive.

To the recruitment and care of his gladiators Caesar devoted almost obsessive attention. He well understood how central these tragic slave-warriors were in the violent imagination of all classes. He possessed his own 'intelligence service', charged with identifying the best and most aggressive gladiators, those who 'fought without winning the favour of the people', says Suetonius,[41] in a pitiless turn of phrase (those who 'never died', or survived innumerable duels).[42] He did not entrust his gladiators to those schools where paid professionals gave instruction, but had them trained 'in private houses by Roman knights and even senators who were skilled in arms, earnestly beseeching them, *as is shown by his own letters*, to give the recruits individual attention and personally direct their exercises'.[43] Years later, when his daughter died, he promised the people a gladiatorial spectacle – something unheard of previously.

All of this was naturally very expensive: the most detailed information on the effects of the aedileship on Caesar's finances, on the colossal debt he incurred as *aedile* and then as *praetor*, is to be found in Appian, from a source very close to Caesar (as is clear from the whole of Appian's second book).[44] This is the starting point of the acute need for money which determined a series of political steps taken during his career, some of which resonated long afterwards.[45] His abortive plan to have an 'extraordinary mission' to Egypt entrusted to him by plebiscite probably bears some relation to his great need for money. But in the end he had to renounce it on account of 'the opposition of *the aristocratic party* [*optimates*]'.[46]

This was the start of open warfare against those whom the *populares* termed 'the party of the *optimates*'. He responded with a move which was the purest propaganda, but highly effective. He ordered the restoration of the monuments to Marius' great military victories over the Cimbri and the Teutoni, which Sulla had earlier torn down. In addition, as *aedile* it was his duty to preside at murder trials, and he extended the category to those suspected of the murder of outlaws during the proscriptions, cases which under Sulla's laws had been exempt and declared immune from any judicial retribution.[47]

Thus the war of symbols became increasingly bitter, and the position of the new leader emerged from it strengthened, thanks to the stubborn resistance of his opponents.

Notes

1 Velleius 2.43.1–2.
2 If the epigraph *Syll.*³, no. 748, refers to Caesar, he could only have taken part in the elections of 72 BC, not those of 73.
3 Plutarch, *Caesar* 5.1.
4 Suetonius, *Caesar* 5; Dio Cassius 44.47.4. This may be why, in his speech in support of the *Lex Plotia* (*rogatio Plotia*), Caesar had written, '*as our kinship demanded*, I have failed neither in labour, in pains, nor in industry', that is, Gellius explains, 'for the bond of relationship' (Gellius, *Attic Nights* 13.3.5).
5 Plutarch, *Crassus* 7.5.
6 See below, Chapter 7.
7 I follow the chronology of Caesar's quaestorship proposed and argued by Broughton, *MRR*, vol. II, p. 136, note 7; vol. III (Suppl.), pp. 105–6.
8 Caesar began his service as *quaestor* in Spain under Antistius Vetus only in spring 69, so these political moves date from his first months in office.
9 Suetonius, *Caesar* 6.1.
10 Plutarch, *Caesar* 5.2.
11 Plutarch, *Caesar* 5.3.
12 Velleius 2.43.4: 'et restituta in aedilitate adversante quidem nobilitate monumenta C. Marii'.
13 Suetonius, *Caesar* 6.
14 Plutarch, *Caesar* 5.4.
15 Plutarch, *Caesar* 5.5.
16 There was nothing more official than a *laudatio funebris*.
17 *Spanish War* 42.1, the last part of the *corpus Caesarianum*.
18 Suetonius, *Caesar* 7.1.
19 Velleius 2.43.4. He uses the opportunity to pay homage to the Antistius Vetus of his day, a descendant of the praetor of 70 BC.
20 Suetonius, *Caesar* 7.1.
21 See also A. Garzetti (ed.), *Plutarchi Vita Caesaris* (Florence 1954), pp. 17–18. But D. R. Shackleton-Bailey, *Two Studies in Roman Nomenclature*, 2nd edn (Atlanta, GA, 1991), pp. 8–9, claims that this son of Antistius Vetus never existed. On this point Broughton agrees with him: *MRR*, vol. III, p. 18.
22 Suetonius, *Caesar* 7.1.
23 A dream laden with meaning, suggesting a need to return to one's homeland (Artemidorus 1.79; Dio Cassius 37.52.2; see Hippia's similar dream: Herodotus 6.107).

24 Plutarch, *Caesar* 11.5–6.

25 Plutarch, *Caesar* 32.9.

26 Suetonius, *Caesar* 7.1. The circumstances are the same in Dio Cassius 37.52.2, but the year is that of his praetorship.

27 Plutarch, *Caesar* 11.6.

28 Appian, *Civil Wars* 2.149, 2.620.

29 Cf. A. N. Sherwin-White, *The Roman Citizenship*, 2nd edn (Oxford 1973), pp. 157–9; E. Badian, 'Caesar', *Oxford Classical Dictionary* (Oxford 1996), p. 780.

30 Suetonius, *Caesar* 8.

31 The conduct of the difficult conflict in the East had first been entrusted to Lucullus. Lucius Caecilius Metellus, co-consul of Marcius Rex, died at the beginning of the year, and the consul *suffectus*, Servilius Vatia, who should have succeeded him, died before he could take office. This is why Marcius Rex was already departing for Cilicia in spring 68 BC.

32 H. E. Butler and M. Cary (eds), *Suetoni Tranquilli Divus Iulius* (New York and Oxford 1927), p. 51.

33 Suetonius, *Caesar* 9.

34 Plutarch, *Pompey* 25.8.

35 Dio Cassius, 36.43.2–4.

36 Suetonius, *Caesar* 10.1.

37 Ibid. 10.1.

38 Pliny (*Natural History* 33.53) and Dio Cassius (37.8.1) claim that this was the purpose of the games. The biographical sources mostly emphasise the fact that they were magnificent. It should be borne in mind that during his quaestorship Caesar had celebrated Julia and his maternal ancestors.

39 The exact figure is given in Plutarch, *Caesar* 5.9.

40 See G. Rotondi, *Leges publicae populi Romani* (Milan 1912), p. 379; also M. H. Crawford (ed.), *Roman Statutes*, vol. II (London 1996), pp. 761–2.

41 Suetonius, *Caesar* 26.

42 The crowd and also the leisured classes sought strong emotions: they wanted to see the gladiators killed rather than emerging victorious.

43 Suetonius, *Caesar* 26. There were, therefore, first-hand documents attesting to this.

44 Appian, *Civil Wars* 2.1.3.

45 His 'affairs', to use Brecht's term, really were of crucial importance.

46 Suetonius, *Caesar* 11: 'adversante optimatium factione'. This expression points to a source close to Caesar rather than his opponents, who would not have referred to themselves in this way.

47 Suetonius, *Caesar* 11.2.

CHAPTER 4

Pontifex Maximus

sed pietate ac religione [. . .] omnes gentes nationesque superavimus.
Cicero

The *démarche* which led to the surprise capture of the office of *pontifex maximus* (high priest) in 63 BC was one of Caesar's most successful. Thanks to his efforts, the pontificate had again become an elected office – another blow against Sulla's constitutional reforms.[1] This sacred office carried with it immense importance in Roman politics. Caesar, a sceptic ever close to the Epicureans in his beliefs,[2] clearly did not hesitate for an instant to compete for the role of supreme guardian of the religion of the state, a post which by its nature stood above everyday political squabbles. Being an Epicurean in his intellectual sympathies, Caesar understood the power of this *instrumentum regni*. He realised full well that false notions concerning the gods had generated fear, and that this fear had produced a false religion, a cult which rested on an almost commercial relationship with the gods. Caesar had much respect for the Epicureans – both militant and moderate – who propagated the 'dangerous' doctrine, as Benjamin Farrington aptly put it, 'that God does not dwell in a temple made with hands – *even if the authority responsible for its erection be the State*'.[3] He also knew that Greek political writers were deeply involved in Roman reality, to the point of being champions of 'realpolitik'. The historian from Megalopolis, Polybius, for example, setting forth his policy in book 6, says that superstition, 'which among other peoples is an object of reproach, . . . maintains the cohesion of the Roman state', and he adds that 'these matters . . . are introduced to such an extent into public and private life that nothing could exceed it'.[4]

Here Polybius sets out his entire creed, which is also the creed of the 'enlightened' ruling classes of the ancient city: the Romans

adopted this course for the sake of the common people. It is a course which *perhaps* [this *perhaps* is significant!] would not have been necessary had it been possible to form a state composed of wise men,

> but as every multitude is fickle, full of lawless desires, unreasoned
> passion, and violent anger, the multitude must be held in *by invisible
> terrors* and suchlike pageantry.

Polybius writes in Greek, but all of his work is aimed at an essentially
Roman audience. With words like this he praises and at the same time
instructs the Roman ruling class, using a language which only the
ruling class and educated slaves (those brought up indoors but
deprived of political rights) could understand. Such reflections were
read by Romans of the most diverse opinions. Even Brutus, the Stoic,
composed an epitome of Polybius in his spare time. And when these
same Romans wished to limit their conversations strictly to the elite,
they spoke Greek.

Caesar was familiar with this kind of secular and practical view of
religion, and he was not alone. It must have amused him to find
himself *pontifex maximus* of this gigantic and deceptive religious, cultural and political machine. But for him the conquest of political
power was such a serious and compelling aim that in his view there
was little point in seeking to reconcile his inner religious beliefs and
his public behaviour. He knew that he had to do everything that this
key office demanded of him, and do it with full seriousness.

To achieve this end, however, to emerge victorious in the hard-fought
electoral contest, he had to pay a very high price: he had to borrow
enormous sums – *profusissima largitione*, in Suetonius' words.[5]
While contemplating the vast debts caused by the campaign, he made
a telling remark. On the day of the election, as he took his leave of his
mother, he said, 'I shall never return except as *pontifex*.'[6] He brilliantly defeated his two rivals, Quintus Lutatius Catulus and Servilius
Isauricus, who were his superiors in age and rank (the pontificate was
viewed as the culmination of a glorious career). 'He polled more votes
in their tribes than were cast for both of them in all the tribes.'[7]

This stunning and costly triumph came at the end of a series of initiatives of greater or lesser success: from Caesar's 'support' for Crassus
in 64 BC, in the campaign to elect Cicero, to the trial of Rabirius
(accused of high treason for having taken part in the murder of
Saturninus forty years earlier),[8] and the trial of Gaius Piso, also
defended and 'saved' by Cicero.[9] But the greatest coup against his
adversaries was his election as *pontifex maximus*. Plutarch, in his
account of this triumph, observes that the *optimates* were gripped by
panic, 'afraid that he would lead the people on to every form of

recklessness'. To mark the event publicly, Caesar decided upon a solemn and symbolic gesture: having been elected *pontifex maximus* he moved into a public building on the Via Sacra, leaving his old home in Subura.[10] Buoyed by this great success he then achieved another, which served to confirm his heightened popularity, above all in the eyes of his opponents: for the next year, 62 BC, he was elected *praetor*. When in November and December 63 the Senate was faced with the Catilinarian affair, Caesar, who since 68 had sat in the Senate, could speak with the authority of *pontifex maximus* as well as *praetor* elect. Meanwhile his connection with Pompey remained unbroken. Titus Labienus, who the previous year had secured the restoration of elections for the pontificate, for Caesar's benefit, now availed himself of Caesar's backing to promote an initiative favourable to Pompey: with the tribune Titus Ampius,[11] he passed a plebiscite conferring upon Pompey the right to wear the *toga praetexta* and golden crown at the theatre and triumphal robes at the circus.[12]

Notes

1 Dio Cassius 37.37.1.

2 C. Castner, *Prosopography of Roman Epicureans* (Frankfurt 1988), pp. 83–6.

3 Benjamin Farrington, 'The Gods of Epicurus and the Roman State', in *Head and Hand in Ancient Greece* (London 1947), p. 97.

4 Polybius 6.56.7. In speaking of 'religious superstition' Polybius uses the precise term, well established in literature and used by Theophrastus, for example, τὴν δεισιδαιμονίαν, which means 'fear of superior beings'.

5 Suetonius, *Caesar* 13.1.

6 Plutarch, *Caesar* 7.4 offers a variant: 'Mother, today thou shalt see thy son either *pontifex maximus* or an exile.'

7 Suetonius, *Caesar* 13.1.

8 Suetonius, *Caesar* 12: in an ancient practice revived for the occasion, Caesar, as *duovir perduellionis*, played a major role in the condemnation of Rabirius. Rabirius appealed against his sentence and was defended by Cicero. Cf. Dio Cassius 37.26.

9 Sallust, *The Catilinarian Conspiracy* 49.2; Cicero, *In Defence of Flaccus* 98.

10 Suetonius, *Caesar* 46.

11 This man, who was loyal to Pompey to the very end, later became a bitter foe of Caesar.

12 Velleius 2.40.4. Cf. G. Rotondi, *Leges publicae populi Romani* (Milan 1912), p. 380.

CHAPTER 5

The 'Affairs' of Mr Julius Caesar and Others

The costs of these two hugely expensive election campaigns had exhausted Caesar's finances, and his debts were a continuing concern. He knew very well that the last resort of those beset by debts was civil war. When young men of his class utterly ruined by debt sought his assistance, if there was no other way to help them out of their difficulties, he replied with pitiless realism that 'what they needed was civil war'.[1] At first sight this seemed a paradoxical witticism, but it well illustrates an immediate connection in Caesar's mind: war as a response to debt and economic ruin for groups of the ruling classes who found themselves in serious difficulties. This line of thinking is not so remote from the idea which Asinius Pollio reports Caesar expressing to those close to him when he saw the vanquished at Pharsalus: 'They would have it so. Even I, Gaius Caesar, after so many great deeds, should have been found guilty, if I had not turned to my army for help.'[2] Asinius places much emphasis on this statement, which was another indication of the true motives that brought Caesar to the rift and subsequent civil war: Asinius plainly understood it to mean that Caesar was one of those young men for whom recourse to civil war was the last resort in extricating oneself from extreme personal difficulties. Asinius himself, a friend and companion of Catullus, must also have had some knowledge of those young men.[3] It is significant for us, as we seek among partisan and one-sided analyses of events which have manifold causes, that Asinius attributes this explanation to Caesar himself – if only in general terms.

Caesar's debts, swollen by the election campaigns for the pontificate and the praetorship, had further contributing causes. The day-to-day political activities of a 'potentate' presented a constant need for money. Suetonius tells us that, 'He had put all Pompey's friends under obligation, as well as the great part of the Senate, through loans made without interest or at a low rate.' In addition, he 'lavished gifts on men of all other classes, . . . including even freedmen slaves who were special favourites of their masters or patrons'.[4] From this it is clear that behind this apparent munificence lay a certain logic and that in this giddying whirl of money (at whose source not infrequently lay the virtually inexhaustible reserves of Marcus Licinius Crassus) a tell-tale thread again provided a firm link to Pompey. Without the consent of Pompey no political activity was possible other than small-scale agitation à la Publius Clodius.

Interest-free or cheap loans were an unsurpassed means to secure support. Great reserves were naturally required to maintain this scale of largesse. The day-to-day management of these vast amounts of money – most of it not his own – did not always run smoothly. The scene imagined by Bertolt Brecht in his novel on the life of Caesar, showing a night-time assault on Caesar's house in Subura, illustrates well the kind of everyday distress that this caused him. The attackers were 'a motley crowd from the city fringes, mostly youths and *déclassé* elements', demanding money that Caesar had promised but had no access to. ('Where are the campaign funds, you cheating windbag?') Caesar tries in vain to hide behind an enormous amphora but is discovered and has to wipe away his assailants' spittle with the tatters of his dressing gown. Clodius comes to him the next day to 'present formal apologies'.[5] In daily close-quarter combat Caesar had to suffer many severe setbacks without ever losing sight of his aims and ambitions. This is part of his tenacity, but it is also an essential part of his experience of life. The awareness of the fact that one could lose everything had never left him since the time when he had been hunted by Sulla. It had accompanied him to Munda, and in the famous siege of Alexandria, when, with a rain of Egyptian arrows falling around him, he swam in the sea with one hand raised above the water, holding the documents he would not be parted from. The ever-present danger of financial ruin was one of those extreme experiences.

In the election campaign for the consulate, in a situation very different from that in which he was the sole candidate, it was necessary to have recourse to new financiers. He sensed that the third and weakest candidate offered an opportunity: Lucius Lucceius, a rival to Bibulus and himself, was extremely wealthy. Caesar suggested the idea of an electoral alliance: Lucceius would buy votes in the legions in the name of both candidates, paying for them by himself. Caesar thus stood a chance not only of winning, but also of having a pliant colleague beside him in office. The *optimates*, in high dudgeon, decided to reply in kind. Their candidate, Bibulus, offered the voters the same amount as Lucceius and more. The upright Cato, a sworn enemy of Caesar and supreme moral arbiter of all right-thinking people, when asked for his opinion replied that 'bribery in such circumstances was for the good of the commonwealth'.[6] Even donations of grain appeared legitimate to the austere Cato, if these were designed to undermine the popularity of an opponent. To return to the year of the elections to the pontificate and the appointment to the praetorship, the *optimates* were again in a state of panic (this was also the year of Catiline's conspiracy). Plutarch, in an aside to his account of the conspiracy, places in this year a record donation of grain, proposed by Cato and intended to 'strike a blow' at Caesar.[7]

Fearing more than anything – he writes – a revolt of the poor, who had pinned their hopes on Caesar and could ignite the entire people, Cato persuaded the Senate to distribute a monthly ration of grain. By this means 7.5 million *denarii* (1,250 talents) were added to the annual expenditure of the state. This measure clearly did much to dispel the pervasive fear, sap the power of Caesar, and weaken his influence at just the right moment, when he was ready to assume the praetorship, and thus presented an even greater danger.[8]

As may readily be imagined, many legends circulated regarding Cato's electoral probity. He won praise for his proposal that magistrates could be called personally to account even without charges being laid or legal proceedings set in train. His election campaigns were remembered because he had lost them only by forbidding his supporters to buy influence, which was then considered normal practice.[9] Some may perhaps have neglected to point out that these were campaigns in which the politically untalented Cato was in any case condemned to failure.

His nephew Brutus, the stern Marcus Junius Brutus, on the other hand, known after the Ides of March as a 'liberator', practised usury, but this was not entirely obvious even to his contemporaries. When Cicero was governor of Cilicia in 51–50 BC, Arnold Toynbee writes with graceful irony, 'he discovered, to his astonishment and indignation, that Brutus, who presented such an austere and impeccable image of himself in Rome, was investing his capital in usury, on extortionate terms, in Rome's Levantine possessions and dependencies'.[10] Cicero, who saw himself as no less expert in human nature than Odysseus, was more than a little put out when he realised that Brutus expected him to continue supporting his financial speculation at the expense of his debtors, just as the previous governor had done.[11]

Cicero writes of this disagreeable matter in confidential letters such as those he sends to Atticus, but even here his tone is extremely restrained in view of Atticus' friendship for Brutus, of which Cicero was well aware. It is instructive to read how he presents matters:[12]

> Now let me tell you about Brutus.[13] Among his intimates your friend Brutus [a most eloquent opening!] has some creditors among the people of Salamis in Cyprus, M. Scaptius and P. Matinius, whom he recommended to me warmly.[14] Matinius I have not met: Scaptius came to see me in camp. For the sake of Brutus I promised that the people of Salamis should settle their debts to him.

But this was not enough for Scaptius. He had urged Cicero to nominate him as prefect, but the proconsul had flatly refused, even suggesting that if Scaptius wished only to get his hands on the money he had lent, he, Cicero, would see to it that debt-recovery took place regularly. Cicero's predecessor Appius Claudius Pulcher had permitted this and more to Scaptius:[15] he had made him prefect of the cavalry purely in order to enable him to recover his money from his debtors in Cyprus without too much ceremony and with military force, for the benefit of Brutus, of course.[16] Cicero was courteous but adamant. He comments:

> Our friend Appius had given him some squadrons to put pressure on the people of Salamis, and had also given him the office of prefect. He was causing trouble to the people of Salamis. I gave orders that his cavalry should leave the island. That annoyed him.[17]

There is no need to go into greater detail. Suffice it to say that Cicero had the delicate task of mediating in the conflict between Scaptius and the Salaminians, who were grateful to him at least for having revealed an awkward fact: some years earlier, in 56 BC, Brutus' friends had passed a law in the Senate raising the tax *ad hoc* for the inhabitants of Salamis (Brutus' debtors) from 1 per cent to 4 per cent a month, or 48 per cent per annum.[18] 'At first I was horror stricken', comments Cicero, who in the end yielded to Scaptius' urging and left this dispute unresolved: the next governor would certainly be more brazen. And Cicero ends ironically: 'if Brutus does not approve, there is no reason why I should be friendly with him'.[19] And he observes with obvious irony: 'Certainly his uncle [that is, the unbending Cato] will approve.'

Though deep in debt and harried for years by his creditors, a faction leader who acquires a flourishing province, or succeeds immediately in imposing his dominance in the republic, may secure great riches if he shares the not unreasonable belief that this is the foundation of the political system. Edward Gibbon recorded with some insistence that the real motive for Caesar's landing in Britain was 'the pleasing, though doubtful intelligence, of a pearl fishery',[20] and cited Suetonius' pungent words about Caesar greedily weighing British pearls in the palm of his hands.[21] Suetonius provides a fairly comprehensive picture of the procedures by which Caesar was able to recover from the results of his disastrous extravagance:[22]

> When he was proconsul in Spain [that is, after his praetorship, in 61 BC] he not only begged money from the allies, to help pay his debts, but also attacked and sacked some towns of the Lusitanians although they did not refuse his terms and opened their gates to him on his arrival. In Gaul he pillaged shrines and temples of the gods filled with offerings, and oftener sacked towns rather for the sake of plunder than for any fault.

By this means he acquired large quantities of gold and sold it in the market in Italy and in the provinces at 3,000 sesterces a pound. Moreover, if Suetonius is to be believed, he committed a theft during his first consulship (59 BC): 'He stole 3,000 pounds of gold from the Capitol, replacing it with the same weight of gilded bronze.' Here the biographer's tone becomes even sharper: 'He made alliances and thrones a matter of barter, for he extorted from Ptolemy alone in his own name and that of Pompey nearly 6,000 talents.' At this point the tone becomes almost defiant: Caesar engaged in 'bare-faced pillage and sacrilege' to finance his civil wars. Reports of this nature, for which Suetonius is often the only source, cannot be verified. What is certain is that in the propaganda of Caesar's adversaries this delicate aspect becomes the focal point at issue.

Again it is Suetonius who records the taunts of the soldiery, who, many years later, when victory in Gaul was celebrated at last, sang: 'Gold in Gaul you spent in dalliance, which you borrowed here in Rome.'[23] This razor-sharp and accurate formulation combines two central points in the one verse: a catastrophic level of debt at the stage when Caesar became a magistrate, and the large-scale economic 'revenge' during the subsequent period of his provincial administration. For Caesar this period was one of a great war of conquest, the most challenging and bloody that Rome had ever fought, followed by a devastating civil war.

This war began for Caesar with an act of violence of indisputable significance: the plunder of the state treasury. In April 49 BC Caesar, now at open war with the republican authorities (who had fled Rome in ignominy), forced the doors of the *aerarium sanctum*, entered and took possession of 45,000 gold and silver ingots and 30,000,000 sesterces.[24] It is noteworthy that Caesar himself, in his own *Commentaries* on the civil war, glosses over this moment in the conflict. He reports in some detail that the consul Lentulus indeed made haste 'to open the treasury for the purpose of providing a sum of money for Pompey, in accordance with a decree of the Senate,' but that fearing Caesar's imminent arrival Lentulus fled the city leaving the *aerarium* doors open.[25] That is all. Caesar does not state explicitly that on his arrival he helped himself. Instead he says that *his enemies* intended to do exactly that, but did not.

Notes

1 Suetonius, *Caesar* 27.2.
2 Suetonius, *Caesar* 30.4; Plutarch, *Caesar* 46.1. On the question of the 'true' cause of the civil war see Chapter 16 below.
3 Catullus 12.1–6 (*Pollioni fratri*).
4 Suetonius, *Caesar* 27.1.
5 Bertolt Brecht, *Die Geschäfte des Herrn Julius Caesar*, in *Werke* (Frankfurt 1989), vol. 17, p. 248.
6 'Eam largitionem e re publica fieri' (Suetonius, *Caesar* 19.1).
7 Plutarch, *Cato the Younger* 26.1; *Caesar* 8.6–7; cf. *Moralia* 818d (*Political precepts*).
8 Plutarch, *Caesar* 8.1.
9 Plutarch, *Cato the Younger* 44 and 49.
10 Arnold Toynbee, *Hannibal's Legacy* (London 1965), vol. 2, p. 630.
11 In the case of illegal loans the annual rate of interest was 48 per cent! Cicero's administration had become very strict (see his *Letters to Atticus* 5.21.5).
12 Cicero, *Letters to Atticus* 5.21.10–13 (written from Laodicea on 15 February 50 BC).
13 Atticus had apparently spoken to Cicero about Brutus.
14 Scaptius was looking after Brutus' economic interests in Cappadocia.
15 Appius had been consul in 54 BC.
16 See Broughton, *MRR*, vol. II, p. 239, and the profile of Scaptius in R. Y. Tyrell and L. C. Purser, *The Correspondence of M. T. Cicero*, vol. III, 2nd edn. (Dublin and London 1914), pp. 337–44. The reconstruction of the whole episode owes much to an essay by T. Mommsen, 'Der Zinswucher des M. Brutus', *Hermes*, 34 (1899), pp. 145–50. Mommsen started *ab ovo*, i.e. from Brutus' loans to the people of Salamis in 56 BC.
17 Cicero, *Letters to Atticus* 5.21.10.

18 Cicero, *Letters to Atticus* 5.21.11–12.
19 Cicero, *Letters to Atticus* 5.21.13: 'nescio cur illum amemus'!
20 Edward Gibbon, *The Decline and Fall of the Roman Empire* (New York 1932), vol. 1, p. 3.
21 Suetonius, *Caesar* 47.
22 Suetonius, *Caesar* 54: '*monumentis suis* [in memoirs?] testati sunt'.
23 Suetonius, *Caesar* 51: 'aurum in Gallia effutuisti, hic sumpsisti mutuum'.
24 Pliny, in *Natural History* 33.56, gives the fullest account. Lucan (3.156ff.) tells of it in dramatic terms. Petronius in his *Satyricon* (ch. 124, line 291) places much emphasis on the 'burglary' by which Caesar was able to seize the treasure.
25 Caesar, *Civil War* 1.14.1.

CHAPTER 6

The Political Market

The trade in votes, which celebrated its greatest triumphs in Roman election campaigns, is eloquent testimony to the well-known fact that only members of the wealthiest families could contemplate and pursue a career in politics. The Roman republic was, as we know, an oligarchic republic in the sense that all its leading political figures were drawn from a patrician-plebeian *nobilitas* characterised by being able to boast that its forebears had reached the rank of consul (the highest political and military office). It was an oligarchy which sought and directed the 'popular' vote in order to perpetuate itself, but it did not systematically exclude all contributions from other family groups (some of whom came from the Italic ruling strata after the 'Social War'). The *homines novi* were able, with commitment and determination, to forge a career, but to do so they had not only to come from rich families (to afford to enter politics), but also to have the ability to form connections, at least in the preliminary stages, with the great and powerful families of the day. We need look no further than Marcus Tullius Cicero, perhaps the most famous of the *homines novi* in the late Roman republic, and his entry into politics (and his subsequent career). A *homo novus*, especially if he had money and training in oratory and the law, might be co-opted.

The history of electoral corruption in Rome is a long one. To a great moralist like Sallust the problem of political corruption was a fundamental feature of Roman political life and took pride of place in his historical writing (as far as this is known to us). We might even say that the picture of Roman politics which he presents is, from this point of view, a hopeless one. Sallust seemed to wish to explain that in his judgement the traditional republic (which Caesar had swept away) would not have been able to survive its own inexorable decline. The scene in which he depicts Jugurtha bitterly taking his leave of Rome as a city where everything is venal, a city which would sell itself if a buyer could be found,[1] acquires to Sallust a symbolic meaning which goes beyond the specific circumstances of the conflict between the republic and a client king who was particularly able and unscrupulous. The catastrophic level of debt of important families of the ruling class, and the consequent political immorality, which did not stop at crime, are seen by Sallust as central elements, helpful in explaining the causes of the episode which he takes as the theme of his first historical monograph: the Catilinarian conspiracy. But he is so firmly focused on the mechanics of the conspiracy that in his account the electoral excesses of Catiline's enemies remain in the background. Nevertheless it is clear that the means by which Catiline's path to the consulship was repeatedly barred were illegal or on the fringes of legality. Manoeuvres ensured that in any case the election result went against him. In this salient and important illustration of the political and electoral struggle in the late republic, the manipulation of the vote was the instrument by which a politician who was himself the catalyst of troublesome dissent could be marginalised (and provoked into taking desperate measures).

We know much about the Catilinarian conspiracy thanks to the great number of extant sources, some of which can be traced back to participants in the events (Cicero's orations) – to those on the winning side, it is true. But the fact that, for reasons which cannot be elaborated here, Cicero's correspondence (in which he was less circumspect than in his orations) has survived makes it possible to glean some less than complimentary details. One of his first letters to Atticus begins with the statement, 'I am thinking about defending my fellow-candidate Catiline.'[2] Catiline was in the throes of an embarrassing trial over extortion, following the theft which had occurred while he held the office of *propraetor* in Africa (67–66 BC). Cicero was considering offering a helping hand so as to have him as an ally in the election campaign. He knew full well, however, that this was a lost cause: 'Catiline will be sure to be standing', he writes at another point, 'if the verdict is, No sun at midday.'[3]

Electoral pacts between candidates were not a novelty in Roman elections. Of course, when they were exposed in scandalous fashion they could spell political disaster, or at least temporary eclipse, for the scions of the great Roman families, who were tireless electoral contenders.

The case of Gaius Memmius is well known, particularly because of his connection with the Epicurean poet Lucretius. As is known, *De rerum natura* was dedicated to Memmius, but his name disappears at a certain point from the poem. It has been supposed, with good grounds, that this disappearance has to do with his political ruin. Memmius, who was a *praetor* in 58 BC, became *propraetor* in Bithynia and Pontus the next year. From Catullus (poems 10 and 28) we know something (and nothing edifying) of his governorship of these provinces: briefly, Catullus, who nurtured hopes of making some money in Memmius' retinue, complained indignantly that the only one to get rich in the province was the *propraetor* himself. And yet it was normal practice to go to the provinces the year after holding a magistracy, in order to recoup the vast electoral expenses incurred to attain the office.

On his return in 56 BC, Memmius could not claim the consulate at once because the triumvirs had decided to reserve the position for themselves. That decision had immediate effect, given the high degree of manipulation in Roman elections: in 56 BC Pompey and Crassus were elected for the year 55. For 54 the triumvirs succeeded in installing one of their own as consul, Appius Claudius Pulcher, while their opponents brought Domitius Ahenobarbus, a sworn enemy of Caesar, to the consulship. This meant that Memmius was able to secure the consulship for himself only in 54 for the year 53. To achieve this end he severed at one resounding stroke the political and family alliance with Pompey (even rejecting his own wife, the scandal-prone daughter of Sulla, to mark a final breach with that political faction) and secured the backing, including financial backing, of Caesar for the election campaign. The 'team' comprised Memmius and Gnaeus Domitius Calvinus (with Caesar in support). To be assured of success they promised a colossal sum, ten million sesterces, to the centuries who cast their ballots first (the importance of the vote of the first centuries in Roman elections is well known), and offered the consuls then in office four million to bribe the augurs. As early as July the scandal was becoming known: in a letter to his brother Cicero tells him that 'the biggest case of electoral corruption in the history of the republic' is about to burst out.[4] Very soon financial circles were also gripped by unease: the interest rate on credit, mentioned by Cicero in the same letter, rose rapidly from 4 to 8 per cent. In September, with the election fast approaching, Memmius decided on an almost desperate move: he would confess all in the Senate, in the hope of saving his skin at the last moment (a move that we today would call 'the Craxi option'). Cicero, not sparing his barbs, writes to his brother that it was generally expected either that the candidates would commit suicide in shame or that a violent coup would result, leading to something resembling dictatorship ('aut hominum aut legum interitus').

Caesar promptly abandoned Memmius to his fate, which meant a fatal trial *de ambitu,* on charges of corruption. Thus it was that at the beginning of 53 BC there were no consuls, and an 'interregnum' resulted because it had not been possible to hold elections. Memmius escaped his trial and moved to Athens, where he devoted himself unhindered to construction speculation, and probably bribing the local authorities, as may be inferred from a letter to him from Cicero written in July 51 BC.[5] This episode would have passed unnoticed if Memmius had not had the bizarre idea of building on the ground where the (presumed) remains of the house of Epicurus lay.

Political corruption in Rome has many other facets to it. While briefly setting out the most obvious one, electoral corruption (*ambitus*), we indicated others, which are often linked to it: shameless exploitation of the provinces, and extortion (an important aspect of the exploitation). Extortion became such a widespread phenomenon that a special tribunal was needed to deal with it, this being the first case in Roman law of a tribunal dedicated to combating a single crime. Control of these tribunals was the cause of conflict between the *equites* and the senators for half a century, from the reforms of Gaius Gracchus (*Lex Sempronia iudicaria* in 123 BC) to the Sullan restoration (81 BC), which returned control to the senators. With regard to the crisis in the republic, a crisis aggravated rather than alleviated by the dire and bloody Sullan restoration, this was a decisive half-century. It is not difficult to argue that the conflict over control of these tribunals contributed to the 'revolution' and the intractable crisis of the republic. What was at stake was the opportunity to reserve for either the senators alone or the *equites* the exploitation of the provinces. The tribunal charged with combating the crime of extortion was, it is clear, a vital cog in the mechanism.

In a recent edition of Cicero's *Verrine Orations* the very competent scholar Marinone has clearly set out the further implications: extortion was often coupled with embezzlement of state funds. 'In the same charge, evidence of both crimes was sometimes adduced, as shown in the trial of Verres.'[6] And when the theft included cult objects it became sacrilege, while on the other hand extortion

> in its most serious forms could verge on the crime of *lèse majesté*, since the behaviour of a magistrate publicly diminished the dignity of the state, and when this was linked with embezzlement with disastrous consequences for the state it was regarded as treason.[7]

It is no accident that the *Lex Cornelia de maiestate* (81 BC) included under the crime of *lèse majesté* (*laesa maiestas*) 'generally speaking, acts by magistrates injurious to the dignity of the state'.[8]

In a passage of his speech *In Defence of Murena*, Cicero recalls that,

> a decree of the Senate decision was passed declaring that the Calpurnian law was contravened, if men were paid to meet the candidates, if hirelings followed in their train, if at the gladiatorial fights places were given for the crowd, tribe by tribe, and if likewise indiscriminate feasts were given.[9]

Although based on the sale of votes, or, as is often said, on trading favours, the Roman electoral system did have inbuilt auto-correction, which, however, often did little more than describe the reality of the 'elections' by enumerating 'offences'. The degree to which the problem was recognised is clear also from the amount of consideration surrounding the phenomenon of 'elections'. This has come down to us in an essay in epistolary form written by Quintus Tullius Cicero to his more famous brother on the occasion of the memorable election campaign for the consulship in 63 BC (fought in 64 against opponents of Catiline's calibre and lack of scruple). This is his so-called *Commentariolum petitionis*, whose authenticity was long disputed but probably without good grounds.[10]

Some years ago, in connection with a new edition of the works of Gaetano Mosca, Norberto Bobbio wrote a workmanlike commentary on Mosca's critique of the mechanisms of parliamentary elections. Bobbio summarised the criticisms which the twenty-five-year-old Mosca had levelled at an electoral system reduced to a 'market', and added, 'What the young Mosca did not realise was that the defect he laments is inherent in the democratic system as such, and more specifically in the system of representative democracy.' And he concludes,

> The idea – not, incidentally, a new one – that democracy may be compared to a large free market in which the principal commodity is the vote is not elevating. But it is one that we must bear constantly in mind if we wish to understand the behaviour of politicians faced with elections. Like the economic market, the political market defies all control that one might wish to impose from above, so the analogy holds good even in this respect.[11]

Notes

1 Sallust, *Jugurthine War* 35.10.
2 Cicero, *Letters to Atticus* 1.2.
3 Cicero, *Letters to Atticus* 1.1.
4 Cicero, *Letters to brother Quintus* 2.15b.4.
5 Cicero, *Letters to his friends* 13.1.
6 See Cicerone, *Il processo di Verre*, intro. N. Marinone (Milan 1992), p. 11.
7 Ibid.
8 G. Rotondi, *Leges publicae populi Romani* (Milan 1912), p. 360.
9 Cicero, *In Defence of Murena* 67.
10 On the *Commentariolum* see P. Fedeli (ed.), *Manualetto di campagna elettorale* (Rome 1987).
11 Norberto Bobbio, 'Mercato politico', *La Stampa* (Turin), 3 January 1983.

CHAPTER 7

Inside and Outside the Conspiracy

Caesar's career was marked by two conspiracies: in one of them, which failed, he was a participant 'from a distance', or was at least aware of it; of the other, which succeeded, he was the target. He was on the fringes of the Catilinarian conspiracy, but he stood to be swept away by it. It was Cicero who came to his rescue. Somebody had produced documents, possibly not genuine, which seemed to implicate Caesar in the plot. Lucius Vettius, a Roman knight who in his youth had known Cicero at the time of the social war (89 BC: both had fought at Ascoli), later a friend of Catiline and a participant in the conspiracy,[1] went over to the other side and denounced the plotters.[2] He declared before the investigation carried out by Novius Niger that he was in possession of compromising letters to Catiline signed by Caesar. Caesar had in the meantime taken up the praetorship, and the accusation could have cost him his life: in January Catiline and his followers had fought with astonishing bravery against the army of the consuls at the battle of Pistoia in Tuscany. Caesar 'appealed', as Suetonius puts it, to Cicero for help.[3] But that help, according to Suetonius, could not consist in proving that the documents were forged. The best that Cicero could do in response to Caesar's plea was to testify that Caesar had actually on his own initiative confided to the consul those details that he knew of the conspiracy months earlier, when the conspiracy was in train.[4] This was a somewhat lame defence, raising the question: how did Caesar happen to know such precise details of the conspiracy? At that point Cicero showed the good-will that Caesar himself had shown earlier, and his assistance was valuable. Partly because of Caesar's great popular prestige, the action against him turned out to be damaging not only for his denouncer Lucius Vettius, who was subjected to violent attacks and spent some time in prison, but also for Novius himself, who was imprisoned 'for allowing an official of superior rank to be arraigned before his tribunal'.[5]

Cicero's stance also freed Caesar from the dangerous accusation made by Quintus Curius before the Senate. Curius, in Sallust's account a grotesque figure,[6] had an important role in betraying the plot: not only did he save Cicero's life,[7] but he also named all the conspirators in the plot, which was defused thanks to him. But his list of names included that of Caesar.[8] And it would have been strange if his was the only name falsely included. Curius was interested primarily in the reward promised to him for denunciation, so he had little motive to spoil his own denunciation by a false accusation and see the reward slip from his grasp. It is a fact that Cicero's statement in Caesar's favour (made under pressure from the latter) was also used against Curius, who was denied the reward because it turned out that he had inserted a name, that of Caesar, by mistake. We may wonder about the reasons which induced Cicero to abandon with such alacrity a man who had done him good service. The explanation can only be in the form of cautious conjecture. It may have been dangerous to confront Caesar. There may also have been some calculation in Cicero's choice: an 'investment in the future', since Caesar's star was steadily rising and gaining prestige, and he was very close to Crassus, who remained 'untouchable' in spite of a long-standing and well-known friendship with Catiline. From a later perspective, Cicero may have miscalculated. In this episode he chose a course of action which brought him little benefit. While rescuing Caesar he destroyed Curius by disqualifying his evidence. Later, when forced into exile by Caesar's power play as consul, he began to set down his 'truth' about the conspiracy, implicating Caesar and Crassus.[9] But he chose to keep this document secret, stipulating that it should be made public only after his death.[10] On Caesar's sudden end, however, when he seemed to be at the height of his power, Cicero did begin to release some of that 'truth' (for example, in a meaningful but not entirely explicit outline of his *On duties* [*De officiis*]).[11] Even before this he had begun circulating his explosive *anecdota* within a restricted circle of trusted friends.[12]

The suggestion that Sallust's extraordinary book *The Catilinarian Conspiracy* was intended as a response to Cicero's document, then already in circulation, has much to recommend it.[13] Since we do not know the exact date of Sallust's composition, we cannot give a fully accurate appraisal of the rich series of allusions contained in it. (We can be sure, however, that Sallust assumes a knowledge of the tragedy of the proscriptions.)[14] In general terms this work reaches its culmination in a kind of 'apotheosis' of both Caesar and Cato, that is, of the two men who had fought with no holds barred and whose struggle went on after the death of Cato, thanks to the campaign initiated by his supporters in 46 BC. Caesar had not taken kindly to the posthumous beatification of his most implacable adversary, and in the heat of the moment had even dispensed harsh treatment to a tame and harmless intellectual such as Cicero, whom he usually treated with great consideration and respect. Sallust's decision in this short book of political history to idealise both parties in the never-ending debate pro and contra Cato was therefore politically unwise. His book also abounds in barbs aimed at the 'liberators' (whose *coniuratio* he compares to the crime of the Catilinarians from the very first lines) and the triumvirs. Caesar addresses the latter in a long speech which Sallust has him make, clearly post mortem.[15] In it Caesar foresees the possibility of further proscriptions along the lines of Sulla's, and his words appear to be aimed at Octavian. Caesar, contrasted with Cato, appears remote from the conspiracy, yet able in the situation to choose the path of clemency. The apologetic tendency is apparent. From Sallust's account the reader gains the impression from the beginning of a Caesar not even remotely involved in the plot,[16] but well able to handle the delicate problem of overcoming it, without, however, going to brutal lengths.

Of course Caesar was a very different character from the person so idealised by Sallust. In one of the last chapters of his biography of Caesar, dealing with his behaviour towards his friends, Suetonius paints a realistic picture of a man with no qualms about using others for his own purposes: 'If he had been helped in defending his honour by brigands and cut-throats,' he is said to have replied to those who rebuked him for bestowing honours on people of *infimi generis* (humble origins), 'he would have requited even such men in the same way.'[17]

There is no doubt that a man like Caesar had nothing against exploiting people such as the Catilinarians, but he had realised in good time *that they were of no use to him*. However, the fact of having had dealings with them was bound to have consequences, like the denunciations, perhaps with some truth in them, but the 'best consul' himself was there to fend them off, to his subsequent regret.

What he needed to do vis-à-vis the Catilinarians was demonstrate that he had no connection with the repressive machinery set in motion by the Senate. He knew that those men enjoyed the sympathy of the public, and he did not intend to forfeit that sympathy, although he realised that if he had placed himself at the head of a movement of popular discontent he would not have got far. But at the same time he could not have got far *against* that traditional 'social basis' of the *partes populares*. Hence his choice.[18]

Plutarch (or the source he used in the first fourteen chapters of his *Life of Caesar*) sums up Caesar's problem well: it is the delicate essence of Caesarism as an attempt to overcome the old, traditional politics of the *populares*, knowing that that social basis will not get one far, yet unable to do without it. Plutarch depicts a confrontation with the *optimates* (which probably did not take place), which he places at the beginning of Caesar's first term as consul (59 BC), when the *optimates* were represented at the very highest level by the other consul, Caesar's colleague Marcus Calpurnius Bibulus. Plutarch imagines Caesar, faced with the protests of the *optimates* against his proposed agrarian laws, erupting with rage in the Senate – in a reaction which in a way demonstrates how far he has become detached from the tradition of the *populares*:

> In the Senate the opposition of the *optimates* gave him the pretext which he had long desired. He cried with loud adjurations that he was driven forth into the popular assembly against his wishes, and was compelled to court its favour by the insolence and obstinacy of the Senate.[19]

This is an imagined Caesar,[20] but the story conveys well the nature of the crisis of identity and of values afflicting the faction of the *populares*, a crisis to which he had sought an end and a new solution,[21] always taking care to maintain intact his traditional good relations with the urban plebs, with whom he had joined his political fortunes from the very start, and to consider their demands. This does not mean that in this 'idyll' there were no moments of drama. There were, after all, the risings of Caelius Rufus and Dolabella in 48 and 47 BC (see Chapter 22), but Caesar always remained the nephew of Marius. Yet when he was killed there was no immediate popular upheaval. This came later and with some orchestration, at least, which is symptomatic of a somewhat strained relationship. The rantings of various liberators, who made themselves heard here and there, were greeted by a puzzled silence: 'The people listened to what [Brutus] said without either expressing resentment at what had been done or appearing to approve of it', writes Plutarch. 'They showed, however, by their deep silence, that while they pitied Caesar, they respected Brutus.'[22]

But this was still far in the future. Caesar the *praetor* nominated for the year 63 BC, who spoke out against the death penalty for the Catilinarians, was not yet the consul of 59 BC, having the security of the triumviral pact behind him, let alone the dictator for life (*dictator perpetuus*) with ill-defined plans for institutional change. He was an influential representative of the *populares* caught in a disagreeable moment of eclipse. Such moments sometimes occur in the lives of great political figures – times which they would rather not recall, in which they have accepted dubious compromises or played their part in questionable manoeuvrings; episodes which might have spelt their ruin if a pitiless light had fallen upon them before they had come to be what they were later. If this light comes too late it is ineffective. It is possible, for example, that the real nature of Caesar's involvement with the Catilinarian plotters was as confided by Cicero, in a tortuous denunciation, to his *De consiliis suis*. But by this time the complex public profile of his personality, the balances of pro and contra, had taken firm shape, and paradoxically it was the 'revelation' itself that was in danger of losing clarity.

Thus it is more than likely that Caesar, like Crassus, who then enjoyed greater power than Caesar (due to his impressive wealth), should have been implicated in the Catilinarian affair. And it is the more admirable that he managed to pull out in time. Fifteen years earlier, when much younger, he had been able to discern with a clinical eye the flimsiness of Lepidus' putsch, in which his involvement had seemed natural. This time he pulled back, but he could hardly fail to intervene on behalf of the arrested conspirators. It is also reasonable to suppose that the repression was so prompt and pitiless precisely because the names of the great and famous were not among them. It is touching to see Cicero in his *Fourth Catilinarian* – clearly rewritten after the event – expatiating on the distinction between the thoughtlessness of the agitators (*levitas contionatorum*) and the 'genuinely popular' policies of Caesar, who truly had the common good at heart!

'Caesar's influence in Senate circles was so strong and his popularity among the plebs so great that his name was not even mentioned in the Catilinarian affair, even though everybody knew of his involvement in the conspiracy', wrote Mashkin.[23] Rumours of Caesar and Crassus being implicated in the so-called 'first' conspiracy (66–65 BC) are even more insistent: after being removed as consul by Caesar, his partner in office in 59 BC, Bibulus, in enforced inactivity, spoke clearly – but to no avail – in 'edicts' issued from his home on the transgressions of his fellow-consul.

On this matter the most extensive evidence is again supplied by Suetonius.[24] Suetonius knew the 'edicts' of Bibulus and the historical writings of Tanusius Geminus,[25] who deals at length with this matter, as well as the collection of letters by Cicero entitled *Ad Axium* (which has not survived). In this collection Cicero set down a statement very like one that appeared in *On duties* about the subversive streak which, in his view, stood out clearly throughout the entire career of Julius Caesar. In a letter to Axius, probably written in the year when Caesar was consul, Cicero observed that Caesar 'during his consul-ship had secured that monarchic power [*regnum*] to which he had aspired when *aedile*'.[26] To this streak in Caesar's make-up Cicero returns twice in *On duties* (written only after Caesar's assassination): once when he recalls Caesar's constant references to that eloquent line of *The Phoenicians* ('si violandum est ius, regnandi gratia violandum est'),[27] and above all when he refers openly to Caesar's involvement in the Catilinarian affair in 63 BC and again links the victor of the long civil war with the then indigent and indebted revolutionary in defeat, whose direct and personal interests might be served by the imple-mentation of the Catilinarian programme.[28] Thus, according to Cicero, there is a thread which connects Caesar the conspirator in 66–65 BC and Caesar the consul, abusing his office and ruling as a true 'monarch' (once he had displaced Bibulus), in 59 BC; just as there is a thread connecting the defeated Catilinarian of 63 BC with the dic-tator of 48–44 BC, who implemented a Catilinarian programme (*sic!*).

But the details of this first conspiracy of 66–65 BC, in which pro-vision was made for Crassus to assume the dictatorship with Caesar as his *magister equitum*, were taken by Suetonius from a contempor-ary historian who was implacably hostile to Caesar, Tanusius Geminus. Tanusius may have had a seat in the Senate and thus been in a position to have direct knowledge of Cato's propaganda call to have Caesar handed over to the Tencteri for violations of human rights during his term as proconsul. He also knew a great deal about the first failed scheme, in which Catiline had planned the dictatorship of Crassus with the support of Caesar.

The plan was this: to storm the Senate in early 65 BC, when the new consuls took office, and kill not only the consuls but also their main opponents. In the chaos that followed, Crassus was to have the dic-tatorship placed in his hands (since the consuls would be dead, this would obviously have to be proclaimed by other magistrates, as was the case with Sulla), and Crassus would nominate Caesar as his *magister equitum*. Following the Sullan model, the result would be a *rei publicae constituendae*, permitting them both to proceed to a radical reform of the constitution, and – among other things – the two candidates defeated in the elections of 66 BC would be nominated as consuls (Publius Sulla and Lucius Autronius). But Tanusius also knew (although Bibulus in his *Edicts* is silent on this score) that Crassus had changed his mind at the last moment, 'on the day appointed for the massacre', and 'therefore Caesar did not give the signal which it had been agreed that he should give'.[29] According to Curio the Elder (the father of the Curio who was Caesar's man in the conflict with the Senate in 49 BC), the signal which Caesar would give was an inconspicuous gesture: he would let his toga slip from his shoulders. Curio also knew of something else that Caesar was involved in. For this episode Suetonius found confirmation in other memoirs from the period, in the writings of Marcus Actorius Naso, who purported to be very well informed about Caesar, including his love affair with the African queen Eunoë, wife of King Bogudes.[30] Curio and Actorius Naso speak of a conspiracy raised by Caesar with Gnaeus Calpurnius Piso. The terms in which Suetonius reports this are vague: 'they agreed to rise in revolt at the same time, Piso abroad and Caesar at Rome, aided by the Ambrani and the peoples beyond the Po; but Piso's death brought both their designs to naught'. The difficulties of modern historians faced with this information spring from the fact that Sallust, a vitally important source, says something very different. Right in the middle of his *Catilinaria* (chapters 18–19), describing the conspiracy of 63 BC and having listed the ring-leaders, Sallust feels the need to insert a digression on the conspiracy of 66 BC: a fairly ample account which he himself describes as 'most truthful', and which does not in any way square with that which Suetonius builds from his contemporary sources. To Sallust the bloody coup planned for 1 January 65 BC and the Piso plot are one and the same thing. His account, however, is far from clear at precisely the point where he should explain the connection between what was planned in Rome and what it was proposed to do in Spain. This is not all: he writes – barely credibly – that the conspiracy, once discovered, is merely 'put back by one month'. On the Nones of February the conspirators are in place and ready for action, but the plan falls through because Catiline 'gives the signal too soon' (but Sallust then explains that it fell through because the number of conspirators who had assembled was too small). This is followed by the observation that Piso was sent to Hither Spain

(Hispania Citerior) as *propraetor* 'through the efforts of Crassus, who knew him to be a deadly enemy of Pompey',[31] and a detailed survey of the theories surrounding Piso's mysterious murder. We shall never know exactly what the real dynamics of this episode were. What stands out in Sallust's confused account is the obscure link between the plot set to be enacted in Rome and the fate of Piso in Spain, but above all the careful removal of Caesar from the events. What Caesar was said to have done, according to Tanusius Geminus, here is done by Catiline himself. Sallust knew very well, as did all his contemporaries, just how close Caesar and Crassus were in those years, but manages to cast a shadow only upon Crassus (for both the first conspiracy and the second), meticulously expunging the name of Caesar from the story. This runs counter to any semblance of verisimilitude, given that at the time Crassus had Caesar as his 'political brain', the weapon with which to oppose Pompey wherever possible and to attract popular sympathy. Crassus would have been unable to achieve anything – and least of all in this field – had he been unable to count on Caesar's support. Thus the account proclaimed as the 'most truthful' is certainly the worst we have, being intended purely and simply to keep Caesar well clear of the dark shadow of the Catilinarian conspiracy.[32] In Sallust's reconstruction Caesar first appears in the Senate debate as one of the two 'great men' of politics, Caesar and Cato. Polar opposites they might be, but both are depicted as supreme masters.

The Catilinarian conspiracy is one of those episodes in which the abundance of sources adds to the confusion, as the voices we hear are almost exclusively those of the contending parties: Cicero as a protagonist who tried to make of his consulship a monument (not merely to his own career, but to his age), and Sallust, who opted for the role of vindicator of Caesar's memory, while opting out of any effective or rigorous search for truths however painful. By the merest chance a corrective has come from a private letter from Cicero to Atticus, dated 17 March 45 BC, dealing in angry tones with a third person, Marcus Junius Brutus (who twelve months later would be the ringleader of the plotters who assassinated Caesar).[33] At that moment Caesar was fighting the battle of Munda (the most difficult in his long career as general), while in Rome a kind of verbal battle was being waged to honour Cato, who had committed suicide at Utica after Caesar's victory in Africa. Cicero and Brutus should have been on the same side. A little earlier Cicero had written his *Laudes Catonis* at the request of Brutus (who was Cato's nephew and perhaps dreamed in moments of high optimism of one day being his equal). It seems, however, that Brutus was dissatisfied with the result and set about the same task himself. But his text irked and offended Cicero on a matter that he felt to be of primary importance: Brutus attributed to Cato – to his speech in the Senate so elegantly set down by Sallust – the repression of the Catilinarian conspiracy.[34] One could do anything at all to the 'best consul' of 63 BC, save that! But the letter in which Cicero is severely critical of his friend's account offers useful information by which to balance the reconstruction of the events. The fact that Brutus ascribes to Cato a role which Cicero claimed as his own is instructive. In a sense this tallies with the rhetorical and edifying account provided by Sallust. Moved by a need to contradict Brutus, Cicero reconstructs precisely (as far as he is able to recollect) the sequence of speeches in the Senate in the session of 5 December – information which is completely absent in Sallust. Here Cicero seeks to diminish as much as possible the merits of Cato, and provides a most valuable piece of information: 'Cato was not the first to speak of the punishment to be imposed. All who had spoken before him had done this.' Nor, he adds, did Cato say anything particularly new: 'He expressed the same view as all the others, but used language more showy and prolix.'[35] Suetonius gives a different report: Caesar, the only one to oppose the death penalty, 'would have prevailed' (*obtinuisset*), since he had even won over Cicero's brother to his side.[36] Cato's words carried weight: he turned the mood of the assembly back in the opposite direction. From this angle, Sallust did well to focus all that day's debates on two main speakers, Caesar and Cato. But, wishing to keep any bad light from his hero, Sallust is silent about what happened to Caesar after Cato had, in Suetonius' words, 'kept the wavering Senate in line'.[37] As a true *popularis*, Caesar refused to concede defeat. He did his best to prevent the now inevitable conclusion, following Cato's hard-line speech. He tried to achieve two separate votes on the death penalty and the confiscation of property, and, in spite of furious opposition, secured the floor for a speech by the tribunes.

But at this point something happened which the pro-Caesar Sallust in his hagiography manipulates, confining himself to an evasive summary: 'Cato was hailed as great and noble, and a decree of the Senate was passed in accordance with his recommendation.'[38] What actually happened was that Caesar, clinging on desperately ('immoderatius', says Suetonius) to his position, risked his life in the Senate.

A group of knights, Suetonius relates, placed round the Curia for security purposes, burst into the Senate with weapons drawn and threatened Caesar. The senators seated beside him withdrew, leaving him on his own (as had happened to Catiline when Cicero had attacked him without warning in the Senate on 7 November), and Caesar was saved only thanks to a small number of loyalists who stepped in to shield him and carry him out of the Senate.[39] Tiberius and Gaius Gracchus in their day were murdered by hotheads like those of the bodyguard of the 'best consul'. Plutarch, who tells of the attack on Caesar by those whom he calls 'Cicero's bodyguard', adds a detail and sheds further light on the sources. He says that Caesar really would have been put to death by these armed men if Cicero had not given the signal to stop.[40] He adds that Cicero stopped them at the last moment 'either through fear of the people, or because he thought the murder would be wholly contrary to law and justice'.[41] Twenty years before his assassination, Caesar had come very close to being killed in the Senate.

This is not an unimportant incident. It signifies two things, both of which shed light on the real nature of the conspiracy: (a) that Caesar knew he could not abandon those men because he was conscious of having been, until very recently, closely bound to them; (b) that although Cicero and his henchmen had tolerated the oratorical duel (in which Cato had tipped the balance back in their favour), when they were in danger of losing the battle, they decided to act against Caesar *as against a conspirator*.[42] They continued to regard him in large measure as an accomplice in the conspiracy, a sort of 'external conspirator'.

We cannot turn away from this topic without asking what place the whole 'Catilinarian' experience came to occupy in the last crisis of the republic. It is not necessary to review the whole of the lengthy history of the 'reception' of Catiline. That is a matter not only of historiography but also of literature.[43] On the one hand we have the Catiline of Mommsen and of Eduard Meyer: the leader of the 'social revolution' (to quote Arthur Rosenberg, the pupil and in a sense continuer of Meyer), and on the other the Catiline of Gelzer, a link in the chain that runs from Cinna through Sulla to Caesar, all of them men who pursued a common political aim: to replace the ailing republic with a monarchy.[44]

Gelzer places much emphasis on the homogeneity of the phenomenon: the momentum of the leaders' drive towards the installation of a dictatorial regime, which is, he adds, the 'governance model of the future'.[45] This tendency had been apparent already in the designs and authoritarian ambitions of Gnaeus Pompeius Strabo, the father of Pompeius Magnus (Pompey). Cinna and Carbo would bring it out more clearly, as would the one who defeated them, Sulla. In 78 BC Marcus Emilius Lepidus repeated the attempt, rebelling against Sulla's rule. In 65 BC Crassus and Caesar would attempt something similar (the aim of the plotters in the 'first conspiracy' was also dictatorship), and the same may be said of Catiline and his followers in 63 BC. This was the route that led to Caesar, and then to Augustus.[46] In support of his theory, Gelzer turns to Sallust, who asserts at one point in his account that if Catiline had achieved his goal, or at least had not given up the fight, the victors would have been unable to enjoy the fruits of their victory for long, and in the end 'a more powerful adversary would have wrested from them *imperium atque libertatem*'.[47] Again it is Sallust who supports the theory of the monarchic ambitions of the leaders with the following points: Publius Cornelius Lentulus Sura, one of the most prominent nobles who stood with Catiline at the head of the conspiracy, was fond of repeating that it was written in the Sybilline oracles that three Cornelii would hold monarchic power in Rome, and he implied that he would be the third, following Cinna and Sulla, both of them Cornelii though each other's bitterest foes.[48] Other leaders, such as Gaius Cornelius Cethegus and Lucius Cassius Longinus, pursued similar aims. At the time when he was recruiting followers, Catiline had not hesitated to promise them 'magistracies and priesthoods'.[49] And in his *Second Catilinarian* Cicero lends much emphasis to the expectations of the conspirators: 'They could already see themselves as consuls, dictators, or even kings' (§19). The scene sarcastically outlined by Caesar in his *Commentaries* on the civil war has similarities: the ugly brawl which breaks out in Pompey's camp only hours before the battle of Pharsalus[50] between Domitius Ahenobarbus, Scipio the father-in-law of Pompey and Lentulus Spinther for the prize of the office of *pontifex maximus*, held by Caesar.[51] In spite of the apparent objectivity of his account, it is clear that Caesar enjoys this moment; glad to be able to place this scene at this precise point, before he tells of the disaster that all these people met with a little later at Pharsalus: 'Already they openly contended for rewards and priesthoods and apportioned the consulship for successive years.'[52] The scene is similar to the one with which the *Commentaries* open: when all Caesar's proposals have been rejected out of hand, even the most conciliatory, 'everything is done in hurry and confusion',[53] 'the provinces are decreed to private persons',[54] and even then the distribution is conducted in the most brazenly egoistic manner.

The behavioural similarities are plain to see. Caesar himself in fact did something similar after his victory, deciding the succession of consulships and distributing provinces, but he did this with a broader perspective in view, not with the factious small-mindedness of the grasping, clamorous clique which surrounded Pompey, nor with the orotund revolutionary promises of Catiline (remission of debts, curtailment of wealth, etc.). To Gelzer Catiline's programme is nothing more than a linguistic exercise: the crisis which he provoked was merely a stage in the struggle between oligarchy and military monarchy as forms of governance, of which the latter seemed to him the midwife of a new and increasingly distinctive order.[55] Certainly it is very likely that Catiline's demagogy would have been short-lived, and, if he had won, would have led to a fierce personal contest for real pre-eminence between the leaders, and thus in a sense to a repetition of the Sullan episode. Had Catiline himself in 66–65 BC not foreseen the possibility of resorting to a renewed Sullan solution, with Crassus as dictator and Caesar as *magister equitum*? Amidst all the uncertainty of dubious, partisan or misinformed sources, one certain fact deserves attention: Caesar, who grew up with the programmes of the *populares*, did not adopt any of their demands – not at the moment when he chose the risky path of civil war, not when the flight of his opponents delivered Rome to him, and not after his victory. In fact he had even crushed some Catilines writ small such as Caelius Rufus and Dolabella. He had understood the change of course: once installed in power he would not promulgate any 'agrarian laws' or 'cancellations' of debt, but instead extend the rights of citizens and seek to involve to the utmost the ruling strata, including the old ruling strata, in his far-reaching realignment. If his career spans a period between two conspiracies, filled with an endless civil war, this bloody and violent path accurately shows how hard it proved for the aristocratic and imperial republic to give way to personal power, and how fiercely it fought to survive.

Notes

1 Dio Cassius 37.41.2.
2 Ibid. Sallust's statement (*Catilinarian Conspiracy* 36.5), in which he says that 'nobody betrayed the conspiracy for hope of gain' (*praemio*

inductus), is an exaggeration. In the case of Vettius, however, the denunciation was not prompted by any *praemium*.

3 Suetonius, *Caesar* 17.
4 Ibid. 'quaedam se de coniuratione *ultro* ad eum detulisse'.
5 Ibid.
6 Sallust, *Catilinarian Conspiracy* 23: a sort of politicised *miles gloriosus*.
7 Sallust, *Catilinarian Conspiracy* 28.2.
8 Suetonius, *Caesar* 17.
9 Plutarch, *Crassus* 13.
10 Dio Cassius 39.10.
11 Cicero, *On duties* 2.84.
12 See *Letters to Atticus* 2.6.2: ''Ανέκδοτα quae tibi uni legamus' (April 59 BC). Here, however, we are dealing only with a plan ('*pangentur*', says Cicero). According to Schwartz, Cicero was referring to *De consiliis suis*.
13 E. Schwartz, 'Die Berichte über die catilinarische Verschwörung', *Hermes*, 32 (1897), pp. 554–608; also in *Gesammelte Schriften*, vol. II (Berlin 1956), pp. 275–336.
14 See L. Canfora, 'Sallustio e i triumviri', *Studi di storia della storiografia romana* (Bari 1993), pp. 121–6.
15 Sallust, *Catilinarian Conspiracy* 51.
16 Note the patently apologetic lines in Sallust 49, where he delivers himself of a veritable speech for the defence addressed to anybody who might dare to suggest that Caesar was complicit in the conspiracy.
17 Suetonius, *Caesar* 72.
18 This was a decision in keeping, in a way, with some of his actions in a more personal sphere, for example his famous decision not to testify against Clodius, who by seeking to commit adultery with Caesar's wife in Caesar's own house had profaned the mysteries of Bona Dea. Clodius was a favourite with the plebeians of the city, and Caesar would have been foolish to make an enemy of him.
19 Plutarch, *Caesar* 14.
20 Garzetti, in the commentary accompanying his Italian translation of Plutarch, makes no mention of any parallels.
21 The granting of citizenship rather than the agrarian laws.
22 Plutarch, *Caesar* 67.7.
23 N. A. Mashkin, *Printsipat Avgusta: proiskhozhdenie i sotsial'naia sushchnost'* (Moscow and Leningrad 1949), p. 14.
24 Suetonius, *Caesar* 9.
25 On this figure see the excellent article 'Tanusius' by F. Münzer, *RE*, cols 2231–2.
26 Fr. 5 Watt (*ex libro incerto*).
27 Cicero, *On duties* 3.21.81 (= Euripides, *The Phoenicians* 524–5).
28 Cicero, *On duties* 2.24.84.
29 Suetonius, *Caesar* 9.

30 Suetonius, *Caesar* 52.1.
31 Sallust, *Catilinarian Conspiracy* 19.1.
32 Concealment of the 'revolutionary' past of politicians who later rise to high office is a familiar phenomenon.
33 Cicero, *Letters to Atticus* 12.21.
34 Sallust, *Catilinarian Conspiracy* 52.
35 'Verbis luculentioribus et pluribus'.
36 Suetonius, *Caesar* 14: 'transductis ad se iam pluribus et in his Cicerone consulis fratre'.
37 Ibid. 'nisi labantem ordinem confirmasset M. Catonis oratio'.
38 Sallust, *Catilinarian Conspiracy* 53.1. Sallust deliberately brings forward the knights' attack on Caesar in the Senate (*Catilinarian Conspiracy* 49). This distortion was the only way to preserve the saintly aura with which he surrounds the name of Caesar and his speech.
39 Suetonius, *Caesar* 14.
40 Plutarch, *Caesar* 8.3.
41 Plutarch comments: 'I do not see why Cicero did not mention it in the treatise *De consulatu suo*' (*Caesar* 8.4). He may mean that in other writings by Cicero on the same theme this detail does appear, for example in the commentary in Greek (which Plutarch used in his *Life of Cicero* 10–23) or in *De consiliis suis* (of which Cicero delayed distribution until after Caesar's death, and which contained the most damaging revelations).
42 It is no accident that Plutarch says that Cato in his speech 'helped to raise suspicion against Caesar'. Plutarch, *Caesar* 8.2.
43 Some entertainment may be derived from edifying dramas such as Voltaire's *Rome sauvée*.
44 For the traditional view see Theodor Mommsen, *Römische Geschichte* [1856], vol. III, pp. 174–92; in English, *The History of Rome*, trans. William Purdie Dickson (London 1908), vol. IV, book V, ch. V, pp. 465–85. E. Meyer, *Cäsars Monarchie und das Principat des Pompeius* (Stuttgart and Berlin 1918), p. 25; A. Rosenberg, *Geschichte der Römischen Republik* (Leipzig 1921), pp. 91–2 (but the volume was written by Rosenberg in 1917–18, when he was still politically close to his master Eduard Meyer); Mashkin, *Printsipat*, p. 14. Among the admirers of Catiline as a social agitator and luckless revolutionary was Concetto Marchesi, whose many pertinent writings include his commentary on Sallust's monograph and a chapter dedicated to Cicero in his *Storia della letteratura latina* [1925–7], (Milan and Messina 1958). A judgement of Catiline the revolutionary may clearly be in terms of rejection (as in Mommsen and Meyer, for whom 'anarchist' and 'communist' were synonymous), or admiration, as in the case of Rosenberg and Marchesi. Gelzer's view is contained in his well-documented article on Catiline ('Sergius', *RE*, no. 23 [1923], cols 1702–3 and 1711).

45 M. Gelzer, 'Staatsform der Zukunft' ('future' from the perspective of the moribund republic). In 'Sergius', *RE*, no. 23 [1923].
46 Paraphrase of Gelzer, ibid. col. 1702, 68–1703, 11.
47 Sallust, *Catilinarian Conspiracy* 39.4.
48 Sallust, *Catilinarian Conspiracy* 47.2.
49 Sallust, *Catilinarian Conspiracy* 21.2.
50 Which will spell disaster for Pompey's side from its very beginning.
51 Caesar, *Civil War* 3.83.1: 'ad gravissimas verborum contumelias descenderunt'.
52 Caesar, *Civil War* 3.82.3.
53 Caesar, *Civil War* 1.5.1.
54 Caesar, *Civil War* 1.6.5.
55 Gelzer, 'Staatsform der Zukunft', col. 1711, 35–51.

CHAPTER 8

Caesar's Senate Speech Rewritten by Sallust

Sallust maintains that the plan for a coup arose long before Catiline's defeat in the consular elections of 63 BC. This date is one of the most controversial points in Sallust's reconstruction. The initial exposure was due, according to Sallust, to the mistress of the conspirator Curius, a certain Fulvia, who learned it from pillow-talk. It was the alarm consequently raised that led to Catiline's electoral defeat in 63 BC (for the consulship of 62). Catiline, undeterred by this defeat, persevered with his preparations for the coup. The Senate responded by granting the consuls Cicero and Antony full power to defend the city and the peninsula. His bravura performance in facing the Senate having achieved nothing, Catiline fled the city (8 November 63 BC), leaving Lentulus to win over more supporters. Lentulus, through the agency of Umbrenus, made contact with the delegates of the Allobroges, who were then in Rome to present their complaints about the maladministration of the province. But the fearful delegates exposed the stratagem, agreeing to play along in order to entrap the conspirators: they accepted explicit and compromising letters signed by the conspirators, and by agreement with Cicero allowed themselves to be arrested on the Milvius bridge on the night of 2 December. With this evidence in hand, the consul was able to indict Lentulus, Cethegus and their accomplices before the Senate and arrest them. In the Senate debate that followed, the first to speak was the consul-elect, Decimus Julius Silanus, who demanded the death penalty and won general support. When it was the turn of Caesar, then *pontifex maximus* and *praetor*-elect for the year 62 BC, the situation seemed to change: his speech, to which Sallust attaches great significance,[1] argued a case completely opposite to that of Silanus and, as Sallust emphasises, won the agreement even of Silanus himself. All of Cato's eloquence and persuasive powers would be needed to reverse the trend and bring a majority of the senators round to the proposal to execute the Catilinarians immediately, without trial.[2]

Cato's speech, also recorded by Sallust, is memorably harsh and uncompromising. Velleius writes that Cato was among the last to speak in the session, and that he spoke with such passion (*vis animi*), such conviction (*vis ingenii*) and such oratorical power (*ardor oris*) that 'he caused those who in their speeches had urged leniency to be suspected of complicity in the plot'.[3] Thus Velleius indicates that Cato spoke in such a way as to cast Caesar in the worst possible light. Cato's wish to present Caesar to the Senate as an accomplice in the conspiracy was so obvious that he placed himself in a ridiculous situation, which is described for us by Plutarch:

> It is said that when the great conspiracy of Catiline, which came near overthrowing the city, had come to the ears of the Senate, Cato and Caesar, who were of different opinions about the matter, were standing side by side, and just then a little note was handed to Caesar from outside, which he read quietly. But Cato cried out that Caesar was outrageously receiving letters of instruction from the enemy. At this, a great tumult arose, and Caesar gave the missive, just as it was, to Cato. Cato found, when he read it, that it was a wanton bit of writing from his sister Servilia,[4] and throwing it to Caesar with the words 'Take it, thou sot,' turned again to the business under discussion.[5]

Cato, raising the alarm because Caesar had received a message, was angry and bent on finding 'objective proof' against the man whose complicity in the plot was for him a certainty. In fact Caesar was in Cato's eyes the most dangerous element in the plot because he was a fellow-traveller with a clean slate, and therefore in a position to influence the decisions of a constitutional body such as the Senate. It is virtually certain that the speech with which Cato turned around the mood in the Senate after Caesar's speech was much harsher than it appears in Sallust's version. Cato's speech against clemency for the plotters and in favour of their immediate condemnation to death is the only one of his speeches to have been preserved. Cato was one of those orators who did not write, but whose rhetorical gifts were remembered long after him. As luck would have it, we know from Plutarch that the only one of Cato's speeches to survive in written form was this one, and it survived because Cato had placed in the Senate hall a number of outstanding note-takers, skilled in a particularly fast and efficient form of shorthand: his intention was to preserve a complete and faithful record of that crucial debate in every detail.[6] This means that the speech Cato delivered must have circulated, and therefore Sallust was obliged to provide a version that was not totally fanciful. It is possible, however, that Sallust's rendering of

Caesar's words is closer to the reality. Sallust was close to Caesar, at least during certain periods of the civil war – witness the so-called *Epistulae ad Caesarem senem,* an exercise in rhetoric which arose at precisely the time when the two are known to have been in contact – and had come to occupy a privileged position rather like that held by Thucydides in relation to the great Athenian politicians of his day.

In Sallust's account, Caesar begins his speech with an extended overture, in which he stresses the need for a balanced decision rather than one made in anger, and above all the risk of creating a damaging precedent by condemning the plotters, a precedent which might one day be exploited by others to enforce political repression. He then sets forth his proposal: in his view the captured conspirators should be held in those towns in which they can best be guarded; their property should be distrained and there should be no further discussion of their fate, whether in the Senate or among the people; anyone who failed to comply would be declared a public enemy.[7]

This last and decisive passage must have been based on the record of the debate in the Senate *(acta Senatus).* A difficulty arises, however, from the fact that the other records at our disposal mention Caesar's proposal in ways which differ in some degree, especially the most important contemporary source. This is Cicero's *Fourth Catilinarian,* a speech delivered after the event – like the other *Catilinaria* – but no less important for this as first-hand evidence at the highest level. Cicero relates Caesar's proposal from a noticeably different conceptual viewpoint, while reporting some details which Sallust does not mention. Then we have the accounts of Plutarch[8] and Appian,[9] which should probably be seen less as alternative versions of Caesar's argument than as interpretations of it.

For Sallust the Thucydidean model is decisive. For him, as for many other scholars of antiquity, the work of Thucydides is the archetypal 'historiographic monograph'. It is therefore Thucydides who provides the direct inspiration for him, even in the design of his Catilinarian monograph. This applies especially to his treatment of speeches, and the place they occupy in his narrative. Just as Thucydides has speeches or groups of speeches providing the rhetorical or dramatic climax of the narrative, so the conceptual and dramatic core of Sallust's Catilinarian monograph is without any doubt the pair of counterpoised speeches by Caesar and Cato, for and against capital punishment for the conspirators. Like Thucydides, Sallust 'chooses' the characters whose speeches he will report, reformulating them as he does so: he begins with a context in which many others have spoken, and in which his chosen ones are the only ones – in his opinion – to stand out as important figures in weighty debates. That Sallust modelled the situation on a Thucydidean pattern is clear if one compares his account with that of Plutarch in his *Life of Cicero*,[10] which is probably based on the autobiographical account of Cicero himself. In Plutarch the debate develops in a much more clearly articulated form. After Silanus, who receives much support for his plea for the 'severest penalty', Caesar speaks. His proposal is so effective that not only Cicero begins to agree (on the advice of his closest friends), but even Silanus himself is swayed and attempts to modify his interpretation of the phrase 'severest penalty' (for a Roman senator the 'severest penalty' would be imprisonment!); at this point Lutatius Catulus takes the floor and is the first to speak out sharply against Caesar's well-received speech. Cato then speaks and casts upon Caesar the shadow of suspicion that he might be implicated in the plot. The Caesar-Cato opposition is thus the creation of Sallust.

Like Thucydides, Sallust had been a political activist and a pugnacious orator before turning to the writing of history. In his commentary on Cicero's *Miloniana*, Asconius describes Quintus Pompeius, Sallust and Munatius Plancus as the tribunes of the plebs most antagonistic to Milo in 52 BC, and the ones who, in those troubled times, 'inimicissimas contiones de Milone habebant, invidiosas etiam de Cicerone quod Milonem tanto studio defenderet'.[11] Whether the *Invectiva in Ciceronem* is really Sallust's we cannot say; but it is certain that Ventidius turned to him as an orator of renown in 38 BC to ask him to write a good speech 'ad victoriam suam praedicandam' (as we learn from a letter from Frontos to Lucius Verus). It is this that persuades us of the fundamental credibility of the speeches which he places in the mouths of his central characters. When he 'invents' Caesar's speech in the Senate in December 63 BC, we may be sure that he is reproducing oratory 'adapted' to Senate debates. Sallust's own personal experience enables him to move with ease between exhortations to the troops, speeches by tribunes of the plebs, and Senate debates. All these are situations which he knows at first-hand. Naturally it is part of his craft (and part of the tradition) to insert thoughts actually expressed by Caesar in a largely reconstituted speech. An example is Caesar's criticism of the death penalty from an Epicurean point of view (death is not a punishment but 'requies aerumnarum' – a respite from tribulations). Sallust knew from Cicero's *Fourth Catilinarian* that Caesar had said this.[12] In the same way Thucydides had placed in the mouth of Pericles words which the great statesman had actually spoken (describing Athens as an 'imperfect island' in the first speech; the idea of the great value of 'unwritten laws' in the epitaph, etc.), but Thucydides had embedded these thoughts in the context of his own.

In the works of Thucydides Sallust also found documents quoted verbatim (the treaties), and from this drew justification for his own citing of documents, such as Catiline's letter to Quintus Catulus (Chapter 35), which Sallust claimed to be 'copying exactly'.[13]

What Sallust scrupulously avoids is a free rendering of speeches that were already circulating in written form, such as Cicero's *First Catilinarian*. Sallust recalls the dramatic session of 7 November 63 BC, when Catiline addressed the Senate 'in order to conceal his designs or to clear himself', and Cicero had 'delivered a brilliant speech of great service to the State', which – Sallust hastens to add – 'he later wrote out and published', that is, he distributed it in written form.[14] Sallust, as may be seen, is familiar with the collection of consular speeches that Cicero had planned as early as 60 BC,[15] and therefore discounts any possibility of 'rewriting' another *First Catilinarian* (let alone of inserting such a speech into his narrative). The principle of not repeating verbatim rhetorical texts available from other sources was set down by Livy[16] and Tacitus,[17] and was to become a firm 'stylistic rule' in classical historiography.[18]

The context into which the two speeches by Caesar and Cato are inserted forms a *topos*: the decision on the fate of a group of 'the vanquished'. Sallust has a great many models in mind. In particular, Caesar's own speech[19] refers to a primary text which is also a model, if not the *locus classicus*: Cato's *In defence of the Rhodeans*, the speech with which Cato had persuaded the Senate not to discuss in any vengeful spirit the behaviour of the Rhodeans (who had proved disloyal allies during the Third Macedonian War, against Perseus). It is significant that his *In Defence of the Rhodeans* also opens with an exordium on the frame of mind in which those called upon to make decisions generally deliberate (and implicitly on how they ought to deliberate) – precisely the subject with which Caesar begins his speech, paraphrasing a famous overture by Demosthenes. Sallust's other great model is the oratorical duel between Cleon and Diodotos in the third book of Thucydides, in which the former advocates and the latter attacks the ferocious 'exemplary' punishment to be inflicted upon some rebellious allies, the citizens of Mytilene.[20] In this case too, Sallust alludes clearly to his model, in particular the thoughts with which Diodotos begins his speech.[21] For Caesar's speech another model is a long speech by Euryptolemos in Xenophon's *Hellenika*, a skilfully constructed address by which Alcibiades' powerful relative seeks to save the generals from a death sentence imposed upon them in haste.[22] These generals had won the battle of the Arginusae but were hauled before the court for failing to assist the shipwrecked sailors. The two situations have a great deal in common: Caesar, like Euryptolemos before him, has to turn back the tide and win over a hostile audience; in the case of the trial of the generals, again a handful of men of high social standing have to answer for a most serious omission, and their trial takes place before a political body endowed with judicial functions. We may also note how Caesar, like Euryptolemos, in the closing part of his speech appeals to the laws on the treatment of accused persons.[23] And the last model is the debate, or rather the oratorical duel, over the fate to be meted out to the Athenian prisoners, between the gentle and humane Nikolaos and the crude and vengeful Spartan general Gylippus, a debate which Ephorus dramatised after the Athenian siege of Syracuse.[24]

But the conceptual core of Caesar's speech is not his call for clemency, or for a reasoned debate without animosity or over-hasty intransigence. Clearly this is what Caesar is seeking, as is known from other sources, above all Cicero's *Fourth Catilinarian*. The central point, however, around which Sallust appears to construct Caesar's speech,[25] relates to the repression of the Catilinarians as a possibly dangerous precedent for future proscriptions. Ronald Syme has written convincingly that, by attributing to Caesar these alarming and prophetic words, Sallust is using Caesar against the heirs of Caesar, condemning the triumviral proscriptions in Caesar's own words. In a cluster of paragraphs placed at the mid-point of the speech, the reference to the present becomes very much clearer.[26] This is a striking example of the deliberate interweaving of past and present in historical writing. And when Sallust speaks clearly his tone becomes increasingly sarcastic, as when Caesar says, 'For my own part, I fear nothing of that kind for Marcus Tullius or for our times' ('Atque haec non in Marco Tullio neque his temporibus vereor'). In order to grasp the relevance of the allusion, we have to realise that in reality it is not Caesar but Sallust speaking here. And as if this were not enough, he goes on: 'at another time, when someone else is consul and is likewise in command of an army' ('alio tempore, alio consule, cui item exercitus in manu sit' – a reference to Octavian, who imposed himself as consul at nineteen and relied on illegally recruited armies), 'some falsehood may be believed to be true' ('falsum aliquid pro vero credi').

If this reading is correct, the meaning of the entire work is enriched by further topical allusions: not only was the conspiracy a precursor of the equally criminal *coniuratio* against Caesar, but the emergency powers employed to put its leaders to death sowed the seed for further illegal acts, to which Cicero himself fell victim.

Notes

1   Sallust, *Catilinarian Conspiracy* 51.
2   Sallust, *Catilinarian Conspiracy* 52.
3   Velleius 2.35.3.
4   A sister of Cato, mother of Brutus, mistress of Caesar.
5   Plutarch, *Brutus* 5.
6   Plutarch, *Cato the Younger* 23.3.
7   Sallust, *Catilinarian Conspiracy* 51.43.
8   Plutarch, *Cicero* 21.1.
9   Appian, *Civil Wars* 2.6.20.
10 Plutarch, *Cicero* 20–1.
11 Asconius, p. 37, 18–21 Clark.
12 Cicero, *Fourth Catilinarian* 7.
13 Sallust, *Catilinarian Conspiracy* 34.3; 'earum [*scil.* litterarum] exemplum infra scriptum est'.
14 Sallust, *Catilinarian Conspiracy* 31.6.
15 Cicero, *Letters to Atticus* 2.1.30.
16 Livy 45.25.3.
17 Tacitus, *Annals* 15.63.7.
18 E. Norden, *Die antike Kunstprosa* (Leipzig 1915), p. 88.
19 Sallust, *Catilinarian Conspiracy* 51.5.
20 Thucydides, 3.37–48.
21 Thucydides, 3.42.1.
22 Xenophon 1.7.16–33.
23 Further evidence of use of Xenophon's *Hellenika* occurs in the body of Caesar's speech, in Sallust, *Catilinarian Conspiracy* 51.28–31, where some phrases from the *Hellenika* concerning the installation of the 'Thirty Tyrants' are transcribed almost verbatim.
24 This oratorical duel is reproduced with the usual fidelity to Ephorus by Diodorus Siculus, *Historical Library* 13.20–32. The credit for recognising the coincidences between the speeches of Caesar and Nikolaos, on the one hand, and those of Cato and Gylippus, on the other, belongs to Willy Theiler.
25 Sallust, *Catilinarian Conspiracy* 51.25–36.
26 Especially *Catilinarian Conspiracy* 51.35–36. See R. Syme, *Sallust* (Berkeley 1964).

Part II

From the Triumvirate to the Conquest of Gaul

CHAPTER 9

The 'Three-Headed Monster'

In politics nothing is contemptible.

Disraeli

Had the *optimates* not been utterly obsessed with the idea that some-body – and that somebody could only be Pompey – was striving after a new form of personal power, they would probably not have offered Pompey to Caesar as a valuable ally. To the republic, Pompey was an extremely burdensome legacy of Sulla, the more so because his power and military prestige had grown, resting on a fine web of clientship relations which reached from one end of the empire to the other. He had followed in the footsteps of Sulla, the victor in the civil war against Marius.[1] After Sulla's death, he had lent decisive support to the victory over Sertorius when the latter, at the head of the revolt in Spain, threatened to detach a part of the empire, one of the most important parts for the domination of the West. And already on that occasion he had made it quite plain to the Senate that he too – like Sulla before him – would march on Rome if the Senate did not supply everything he needed for his campaigns.[2] And all things considered, Pompey's decision to align himself with Crassus, when both were consuls in 70 BC, to demolish jointly the foundations of the Sullan constitution, was from the *optimates*' point of view a sort of de facto bloodless *coup d'état*. He owed his subsequent career to an unbroken series of military and diplomatic successes, as well as some astute manoeuvring, but by the time he at last returned to Italy in 62 BC, having claimed the East for Rome, 'from Thrace to the Caucasus and down to Egypt the eastern lands acknowledged his predominance'.[3] He had built an empire and with it established his personal hegemony. The people of Miletopolis greeted him with their customary title of honour, 'lord of the heavens and the earth'.[4] He was beyond doubt a *princeps*, but not in Rome.[5] There it was precisely the *nobiles*, with whom he had stood since the very beginning of his career, who received him coolly and subtly boycotted him. His two main requests

– that the Senate should confirm the new order which he had imposed on his eastern conquests, and reward his veterans with plots of land – were blocked by cavilling objections. Lucius Lucullus, for example, demanded that the changes in the East be discussed one by one, rather than en bloc.[6] Pompey had also attempted to establish links by marriage with the faction that dominated the Senate. He divorced his own wife, the half-sister of Metellus Celer, and sought the hand of Cato's niece, but the stern answer came back: no.[7]

There was much fear of the new Sulla, while Cicero, who had 'saved' the republic from the Catilinarians without any recourse to Pompey's armies,[8] dreamed of the coming of a *princeps*.[9] He had become convinced that the republic now needed a constitutionally enshrined leader, but to the very end he remained uncertain who might be suited for the role in the given situation. Then events took their own course, civil war broke out, and in his private correspondence Cicero gave harsh judgements of the 'Sullan' ambitions of both parties. Since it seems unimaginable that he really had in mind the rise of a new Scipio in the role of *princeps in re publica*, the suspicion remains that as he mused on the 'great' Catilinarian episode he must have been toying with the idea of himself taking the reins of the republic that he longed to see. Had he not saved the republic at the hour of its greatest peril? His tireless efforts to keep alive the memory of that event can only feed this suspicion.

Be that as it may, it is significant that Caesar, when he returned from provincial government in Spain in time for the electoral campaign of 60 BC for the consulship, had at a certain point, when the election was already won, considered drawing Cicero into a secret compact which would guarantee the parties against the excessive power of the *factio*. In a letter to Atticus, dated late December 60 BC, Cicero relates with some irritation Caesar's proposals and the rebuff with which Cicero has finally decided to respond.[10] The text is illuminating because it tells us plainly that the 'pact' was to come into force on 1 January, the day when Caesar took office:

> It really is a point that requires much consideration. For either I have got to resist the agrarian measure strongly, which would mean something of a fight, though I should gain prestige by it; or I must hold my peace, which is equivalent to retiring to Solonium or Antium; or else I must assist the measure, and that is what they say Caesar expects me to do beyond a doubt. For Cornelius paid me a visit – I mean Balbus, Caesar's great friend. He assured me that Caesar will take my

own and Pompey's opinion on everything, and that he will make an effort to reconcile Pompey and Crassus.

These were Caesar's proposals, which in essence may be summarised as a tempting offer of participation in a four-cornered alliance, *in return for Cicero's support for Caesar's agrarian legislation* (designed primarily to reward Pompey's veterans).

Cicero comments: 'On this side of the sheet may be placed an intimate connection with Pompey and, if I like, with Caesar too, reconciliation with my enemies, and ease in my old age.' The irony is palpable, although it may arise from an error of judgement, but perhaps above all from a moment of humour, which takes the somewhat narcissistic form of self-quotation: 'But my blood is still stirred by the *finale* I laid down for myself in the third book of my poem.' He then quotes:

> Meantime the course you chose in youth's first spring
> And held to, heart and soul, 'mid civic strife
> Keep still, with growing fame and report.'[11]

Here he drops these reflections for the moment, in somewhat embarrassed fashion, and jokes about the respect which these injunctions demand of him, given that in his poem it was Calliope who guided his hand. But this is not the end of the correspondence with Atticus: he takes it up again on 1 January of the next year. Then there is a pause in the exchange of letters, the next one being dated April 59 BC,[12] when the moment of decision is overtaken by events.

This letter also contains information on the careful manner in which Caesar, still as consul-elect, went about constructing his 'plot'. Balbus, who was intensely loyal to Caesar and his right hand in the complicated network of personal relations, while being a former beneficiary of Pompey's protection, let Cicero know that Caesar's accord with the other two potentates (Crassus and Pompey) was in the wind but not yet signed and sealed. ('We are doing our best to draw Crassus and Pompey together.') In reality things looked different. The three-cornered pact was taking shape even in the electoral campaign of 60 BC for the year 59. Asinius Pollio was sure of his ground when he pointed to the triple alliance, the 'triumvirate', as the true starting point of the civil war and spoke of the 'civil strife begun during the consulship of Metellus' (that is, in 60).[13] This places the birth of the triumvirate firmly in the year 60, or more precisely, in the election campaign of that year for the consulship in 59. This is why Plutarch, relying on the decidedly anti-Caesar source on which he based the first part of his biography of Caesar, writes that Caesar, 'encompassed and protected by the friendship of Crassus and Pompey, entered the canvass for the consulship and was triumphantly elected'.[14] Velleius, on the other hand, maintains that the pact, the 'partnership in political power', as he calls it, was concluded when Caesar was already consul.[15] This chronology accords with what Cicero writes in his letter to Atticus at the end of December 60 BC. Suetonius dates the pact at a precise moment before Caesar and Bibulus took office: at the moment of the allocation of provinces for the next year (which took place *before the election results were known*),[16] the Senate, sure that Caesar would emerge victorious, provocatively took care to allot to the future consuls 'the forests and pastures', in other words an utterly derisory portion. It is claimed that it was this slight that moved Caesar to take the serious step of concluding a secret pact with Crassus and Pompey, cutting through the long-standing and undying hostility between the two.[17] This reconstruction of the facts may have a documentary basis, since Suetonius had Caesar's letters (including those in code)[18] to hand while he wrote, and the phrase 'incensed by this slight' may reflect judgements or opinions expressed by Caesar in his letters of those months.[19] But it must also be said that Caesar probably felt the need for such an alliance, which would enable him to avoid wearisome and protracted static warfare, even before being provocatively awarded a comic-opera province. The electoral strategy which he deployed on his return from Spain suggests the possibility of a secret accord. Finally, we should not delude ourselves that even the confidential letters to which Suetonius had access contained any explicit reference to a secret accord.[20] The most important exchanges are not committed to writing.[21]

For all its succinctness, which we trust does not distort the substance of the original, the version which we read in Livy's book 103 seems the most convincing account: on his return from Spain, Caesar decides to stand for the consulship and 'attack the constitution', and to this end 'a conspiracy [*conspiratio*] was made by him, Pompey and Crassus'.[22] The crux of the agreement – a private agreement, but with clearly stated mutual responsibilities, and in this sense a true conspiracy – is described by Suetonius, who plainly had a reliable source: 'that no step should be taken in public affairs which did not suit any one of the three'.[23] The uncertainty in the dating has to do with the need for secrecy.

There is no historical source which does not comment critically on this pact. Pollio, who saw in it the origin of the civil war, is broadly in agreement with Velleius, who warmly welcomed the rise of Augustus and was also an admirer of Caesar. Velleius is quick to point out that the 'partnership in political power' (*potentiae societas*) was disastrous for the city and the whole world, and, at various times, for all three participants.[24] Florus (who may owe much more to Seneca the Elder than to Livy) follows the same line of argument: the triumvirate is a pact designed 'to seize control of the State',[25] and the first act of the civil war. Livy also speaks of 'control of the State',[26] and Suetonius waxes eloquent in his description of the brazen illegality of the triumvirate's plan to control every political decision. Marcus Terentius Varro even wrote a satire about the triumvirate, with the title *The Three-Headed Monster*, Τρικάρανος.[27] As for Cicero, once he had decided to stand aside and turn down Caesar's offer, he suffered great personal disadvantage from the triumvirate (exile, temporary loss of vitally important property), and it is obvious that his views of the pact were entirely negative. In the judgement of the historians, in what concerns this fundamental turnabout by Caesar, the opinion of the Cato school – one of total rejection and condemnation – has held sway. They had feared the rise of another *princeps* like Sulla, and all of a sudden they had three. There are several reasons why this losing faction proved so strong and durable in the historiography: one is the strength of the senatorial tradition in Roman historiography;[28] another is the partial repudiation of Caesar's career in the Augustan reinterpretation of the long civil war. Augustus, the devoted 'son' determined to avenge his father's murder, gradually replaced the cult of Caesar with the cult of himself, and to this end it was necessary to diminish somewhat the figure of Caesar.[29] This is why Velleius found cause for some irritation in the 'Augustan' condemnation of the triumviral pact of 60 BC, given the criminal triumvirate of 43 BC, in which Octavian was a prime mover, participant and accomplice who shared the responsibility for the crimes committed.

Technically it had been a masterstroke to break the deadlock and bring Crassus and Pompey together. This move had robbed the Cato faction of the opportunity to paralyse the main actors by playing one off against another, as had happened all too obviously after the return of Pompey. On the other hand, it had allowed Caesar to free himself from a position of financial dependence on Crassus,[30] a dependence which, as long as the rivalry endured between Crassus and Pompey, inevitably forced Caesar to align himself with one or the other (and it was quite clear to him that the future figure of importance was not Crassus but Pompey). Finally it had allowed Caesar to claim the rank of third potentate, on equal footing with the other two, if not directly, as Plutarch maintains, 'by concentrating their united strength upon himself'.[31] His status as third potentate was ratified by his triumphant election for the consulship. The other two had been consuls together ten years earlier. With Caesar's election the consulship returned after an interval of many years to a member of the *gens Julia*.[32]

With the 'triumviral' accord, Caesar began to shake off the image which had clung to him up to that time, as a less impetuous Lepidus, or a less gifted Catiline. From Lepidus to Catiline, in fifteen years of political struggle, Caesar had been through many compromising episodes, often courting disaster, yet coming through unscathed. His intuitive sense of the need for the triumvirate had been formed by these experiences. His intuition told him that the traditional politics of the *populares* had by now run into a blind alley: it was necessary to identify other forces and other partners, but without losing any of the hinterland already consolidated, which was an important factor at critical moments. When Caesar joined the triumvirate, he no longer had any rivals in his own camp, so could permit himself, in certain circumstances, from political necessity or opportunity, to deceive his followers.

He was very much aware of the conspiratorial nature (to use Livy's term) of the secret pact: this was a 'plot' involving people quite different from Catiline and his desperate adventurers in their financial and military significance. This point is the watershed in Caesar's biography. It is his masterstroke: the available sources unanimously agree that the initiative was his. Cicero's letter to Atticus, which tells of Caesar's attempt to include Cicero in the alliance, confirms that Caesar is the political brain of the operation.

The other two parties appear, in the accounts we have, to play walk-on parts. But this impression may depend also on the polemical stance of the sources. Pompey is reduced to the role of supporter of Caesar ('he had now wholly given himself up to do Caesar's bidding'),[33] despite the fact that he brought support, in an unpolished and threatening manner perhaps, for legislation which would be of great benefit to him.[34] His involvement in the policies of the triumvirate was total, and was a source of irritation to his old partners in politics. This is reflected in Plutarch:

> Never up to that day had Pompey said or done anything more vulgar and arrogant [than threaten to use his men to support Caesar's agrarian legislation], as it was thought, so that even his friends apologised for him and said the words must have escaped him on the spur of the moment. However, by his subsequent acts he made it clear that he had now wholly given himself up to do Caesar's bidding.[35]

Confirmation of this may be seen in the surprising political marriage of Caesar's daughter Julia to Pompey. A political alliance by marriage, of a kind quite usual in the history of the Roman ruling class, is depicted in the accounts influenced by the anti-triumviral tendency as an act of the deepest cynicism: it is stressed that Julia is virtually torn from the arms of her intended, Servilius Caepio,[36] and consigned instead to Pompey, who appeases Caepio's wrath by offering him his own daughter,[37] who had been promised to Faustus Sulla, son of the late dictator. The emphasis placed on the exploitation of family ties, which were thus subordinated to politics, derives from polemical polarisation and pushes another fact into the background: that Pompey breaks a matrimonial alliance of great importance with Faustus Sulla in order to bind himself to the driving force of the triumvirate. Meanwhile Caesar married Calpurnia, the daughter of Lucius Calpurnius Piso Caesoninus,[38] who would become consul the next year, 58 BC, in accordance with agreements concluded by the triumvirs. Cato pointedly commented on this, saying that 'the supreme power'[39] was being 'prostituted by marriage alliances', and that women were being used to share out provinces, positions and armies.[40]

Triumviral politics were for Caesar a long-term strategy. The alliances by marriage demonstrate this clearly. It is no accident that, years later, after Julia's death, at a time when deeper and deeper cracks were beginning to appear in the alliance, Caesar suggested to Pompey the prospect of establishing another matrimonial alliance: in about 54 BC or a little later, he would offer him the hand of Octavia, the granddaughter of his sister Julia the Younger.[41] But Pompey refused.[42] This view of the triumvirate as part of a long-term strategy, symbolised by marriage alliances, fits squarely into a clear framework – a plan to share power with Pompey. Speaking of the outbreak of the civil war, Syme wrote that to the last, even after the crossing of the Rubicon, Caesar's tactics had consisted in attempting to restore his *amicitia* with his one-time son-in-law. But, Syme goes on,

> With the nominal primacy of Pompeius recognized, Caesar and his adherents would capture the government – and perhaps reform the State. Caesar's enemies were afraid of that – and so was Pompeius. After long wavering Pompeius chose at last to save the oligarchy.[43]

The armed struggle for supremacy, then, came as a surprise, as an event which did not conform to Caesar's original strategy and sprang from the tension which arose on the political stage after the death of Clodius (52 BC). And even then, when the *factio* offered Pompey a new form of dictatorship (a consulship *sine collega*), Caesar would defend this choice against his own allies, who urged him to oppose it. The exclamation attributed to him by Asinius, as he viewed the battlefield of Pharsalus strewn with the bodies of the slain – 'They would have it so!' – was therefore fully justified.

Notes

1 *African War* 22.2; Velleius 2.29; Plutarch, *Pompey* 6. Pompey had privately raised three legions from farmers, clients and veterans of the campaigns of his father (who had shown his brutality and disloyalty in the war against the Italic peoples).
2 Sallust, *Histories* 2, fr. 98 (Pompey's threatening letter to the Senate).
3 R. Syme, *The Roman Revolution* (Oxford 1939), p. 30.
4 *ILS* 9459.
5 Syme, *Roman Revolution*, p. 30.
6 Dio Cassius 37.49.4.
7 Plutarch, *Pompey* 44; *Cato the Younger* 30.
8 For which Pompey would never forgive him.
9 On Cicero's understanding of *princeps*, see E. Lepore, *Il 'princeps' ciceroniano e gli ideali politici della tarda repubblica* (Naples 1954).
10 Cicero, *Letters to Atticus* 2.3.3–4.
11 From Cicero's own *On his consulship* 8.
12 Cicero, *Letters to Atticus* 2.4.
13 Horace, *Odes* 2.1.1.
14 Plutarch, *Caesar* 14.1.
15 Velleius 2.44.1: 'potentiae societas'.
16 In accordance with Gaius Gracchus' *Lex Sempronia* from the year 123 BC.
17 Suetonius, *Caesar* 19.2.
18 See Suetonius, *Caesar* 56.6, and, for a specific case of the use of these letters, 26.3.
19 Suetonius, *Caesar* 19.2.
20 Dio Cassius 37.58.1 stresses the secrecy.
21 Henry Kissinger, *White House Years* (Boston 1979), p. xxii.

22 Livy, *Periochae* 103, p. 101 Rossbach: 'eoque consulatus candidato et captante rem publicam invadere, conspiratio inter tres civitatis principes facta est'.

23 Suetonius, *Caesar* 19.2.

24 Velleius, *Caesar* 2.44.1.

25 Florus 2.13.11: 'de invadenda re publica'.

26 'Captante rem publicam invadere'.

27 Appian, *Civil Wars* 2.9.33.

28 See A. La Penna, 'Storiografia di senatori e storiografia di letterati' (1967), in *Aspetti del pensiero storico latino* (Turin 1978), pp. 43–104 (esp. pp. 101–4, where he argues persuasively against the idiosyncrasies of Ronald Syme).

29 It is sufficient to consider the amount of space allotted to the two protagonists in book 6 of the *Aeneid* (in which the descendants of the *gens Julia* are reviewed), and the space devoted to Caesar by Ovid in his *Metamorphoses*, a somewhat incongruous book, given the political and cultural directives of Augustus.

30 Plutarch, *Caesar* 11.1–2: having stepped down from the praetorship, besieged by creditors, he obtained a guarantee from Crassus for the sum of 830 talents, and thus was able to set out for Spain.

31 Plutarch, *Caesar* 13.4.

32 Sextus Caesar, a cousin of his father, had been consul in 91 BC.

33 Plutarch, *Pompey* 47.9.

34 Pompey 'would come up against swords, with sword and buckler too' (Plutarch, *Caesar* 14.3; *Pompey* 47.6).

35 Plutarch, *Pompey* 47.9.

36 Of Caepio nothing is known except that he had backed Caesar in the struggle with Bibulus (Suetonius, *Caesar* 21.1).

37 Plutarch, *Pompey* 47.10.

38 It is generally believed that the 'papyrus villa' of Herculanium belonged to him.

39 Plutarch translates τὴν ἡγεμονίαν (*Caesar* 14.7), but it is possible that Cato was referring to the consulship.

40 Plutarch, *Caesar* 14.8.

41 Octavia the Younger, sister of Octavian, later given in marriage by Octavian to Antony.

42 Suetonius, *Caesar* 27.1. See also M. Hammond, *RE*, 'Octavius', no. 96. This Octavia was already married to Gaius Claudius Marcellus (consul in 50 BC).

43 Syme, *Roman Revolution*, p. 47.

CHAPTER 10

The Consequences of the Triumvirate: The View of Asinius Pollio

> Thou art treating of the civil strife that with Metellus' consulship began, the causes of the war, its blunders, and its phases, and Fortune's game, friendship of leaders that boded ill, and weapons stained with blood as yet unexpiated – a task full of dangerous hazard – and art walking, as it were, over fires hidden beneath treacherous ashes.
>
> Horace, *Odes* 2.1, 'To Pollio'

The causal connection between the triumvirate and the civil war is stated in the opening lines of this ode to Asinius Pollio, in which the sometime republican Horace, still a sympathiser, but from a distance, salutes the birth and development of Asinius' work on the civil war.[1] To Horace, many years after the event, the battle of Philippi remained the moment at which 'Valour's self was beaten down' (*cum fracta virtus*).[2] This view, not unlike that of Cremutius, but clearly set in a poem which views everything with disenchantment, appears in a book which opens with a somewhat nervous announcement of Pollio's forthcoming historical work. It is the ode of 'a shield ingloriously abandoned', a nostalgic ode looking back on a politically critical moment.[3]

The fact that Pollio's historical writings were lost along with other Roman historical literature is a matter of particular regret. It was not exactly what might be called 'conformist' writing. The most extensive direct evidence we possess is this ode, in which Horace seems concerned above all about the risks facing the author of a work of this kind: 'thou art walking, as it were, over fires hidden beneath treacherous ashes'. But the poet does not restrict himself to this alone. He gives quite precise information on the content of the text and above all on one especially pertinent fact: the point of departure of Pollio's account.

We know that to divide an event into periods is itself an act of interpretation. Asinius makes the *motus civicus*, the civil conflict, begin not with the tension between Caesar and the Senate in 50–49 BC, but ten years earlier, with the birth of the triumvirate in 60 BC. Horace consciously places this basic fact in the opening line of his ode, using a highly deliberate form of words: 'Motum ex Metello consule civicum' ('the civil strife that with Metellus' consulship began'). This means that it began in 60 BC, the year in which Caesar, the real author of the 'three-headed monster', brought Pompey and Crassus into a power-sharing agreement. *Ex Metello consule* here becomes an epithet for *motus civicus*. That is why it is placed between the two terms, *motus* and *civicus*, and as a whole it succeeds elegantly in occupying the whole of the first line, always the most important position in an ode.

The components that follow, marking out the theme and directions of the work, appear in an apparently loose paratactic series, but are nevertheless part of the very first verse: *belli causas* (and, in a subordinate clause, *et vitia et modos*), *ludum Fortunae, gravis principum amicitias*, and finally *arma*, as the last word of the verse. The latter are described dramatically as being 'stained with blood as yet unexpiated', which does not express a reassuring view of the eventual end of the civil war. This leads into the second verse, which is entirely taken up – to the point of seeming deliberately tautologous – with phrases stressing the extreme danger confronting Asinius.[4] It is here that he describes the historian's exacting task as one 'full of dangerous *alea*', a phrase which has caused readers of the modern age much reflection, some of it quite erroneous.[5] There is no doubt that Horace chose the expression deliberately, as he is very clearly emphasising the idea of *periculum* (danger), which is much more than the proverbial 'incedis per ignis'.[6] This should provide food for thought, since in a matter like this Horace took care to weigh his words.

When we speak of 'censorship' and control, or merely of pressure on historians during the time of Augustus and Tiberius, other examples come to mind. This early case of politically motivated concern over a historical work therefore merits closer attention. Under Tiberius the *periculum* to which Cremutius Cordus was exposed was extreme, owing to the particular favour shown by this historian and senator to Brutus and even more to Cassius. An abnormally broad interpretation of the crime of *lèse majesté* made it possible to prosecute Cremutius, who committed suicide. But even under Augustus there were cases of great intolerance, especially towards 'slanderous defamations', a category of writing not easily defined.[7] Pollio himself later became the target of some menacing sarcasm from Augustus, when it was learned that he had welcomed into his home the Greek historian Timagenes of Alexandria, whom Augustus had driven out of his own house. 'You are nurturing a wild beast in your house', said the emperor in Greek, a language sometimes used by educated Romans when they felt it could express more than could or should otherwise be said.[8] Asinius replied, 'Caesar, if you order me I will at once banish him from my home.' Octavian commented, with furious irony, 'It would be a pity, now that I've just made peace between you', referring to the earlier friction between Asinius and Timagenes, which had been set aside by Asinius – says Seneca, to whom we owe the account of this conversation – only because Octavian had taken a violent dislike to Timagenes.[9] Horace's concern over the fate of Pollio's historical initiative is therefore understandable.

Moreover, we may appreciate the skill with which he arranges the cornerstones of Asinius' historical work, from the very start: *belli causas, ludum Fortunae* and *principum amicitias*.

There is, however, one source which helps us towards an understanding of the logical connection between the triumvirate and the civil war more than Horace, who refers to the work of his friend by a cautious juxtaposition of elements. It is Plutarch, writing in his *Life of Caesar* of the birth of the triumvirate:

> These men [Pompey and Crassus] Caesar brought together in friendship after their quarrel, and by concentrating their united strength upon himself, succeeded, before men were aware of it, and by an act which could be called one of kindness, in changing the form of government. *For it was not, as most men supposed, the quarrel between Caesar and Pompey that brought on the civil wars, but rather their friendship.*[10]

It is more than likely that here, as elsewhere, Plutarch draws inspiration from Pollio: the fact that his evidence coincides with that of Horace seems to confirm it. It is surely no accident that Horace's 'summary' of Pollio's work ends with a statement that all the world is subjugated (*cuncta terrarum subacta*) to Caesar, 'except stern Cato's soul', or that Plutarch also sets Cato apart in the passage in which he reaffirms Asinius' view that the pact between the three (rather than the friction between them) was the cause of war. Cato is presented as the only one to foresee the end results of Caesar's policy, and the one who therefore became Caesar's determined opponent. This might be a matter of chance, but it is also possible that Plutarch adhered very closely to the analysis offered by his source, the analysis we find in Horace, filtered through the process of poetic 'distancing'.

Be this as it may the analysis set forth by Asinius – which in essentials followed the thinking of Cato and even Cicero, until both chose to ally themselves with Pompey – became almost the accepted wisdom in later historical writing. It is the subject of a consensus of views among personalities of differing, even contrasting, orientation. Livy spoke of a 'conspiracy' (*conspiratio*) linking the three potentates,[11] that is, he gave emphasis to the illegal and subversive aspect of their private agreement. Naturally, he also thought that the civil *war* began in January 49 BC, but there is an important distinction between *bellum civile* and *motus civicus*. The latter began long before anybody took up arms. Velleius, who is in general a faithful interpreter of historical orientations, or rather of Augustan propaganda, has an almost mystical devotion to Caesar, yet still says dryly that 'in Caesar's consulship'[12] a 'partnership in political power (*potentiae societas*) was established between Caesar, Crassus and Pompey, which was fatal not only for the city and the whole world, but also for each of the three parties, though at different moments'.[13] This appraisal by the ever loyal Velleius indicates that perhaps the danger discerned by Horace in Pollio's enterprise was less acute. Annaeus Florus is another who sees the 'true cause' of the civil war in the triumvirate.[14] But Florus shows that he has a much broader notion of the whole *motus civicus*, derived, it appears from the historical writings of his distant relative Annaeus Seneca the Elder, whose *Ab initio bellorum civilium* began with the 'sedition' of Tiberius Gracchus. Florus takes a broader view, and perhaps a deeper one, than that of Asinius: its influence may be seen in the only monograph still extant on the Roman civil war – the one by Appian of Alexandria, written in Greek at the time of Marcus Cornelius Fronto and Antoninus Pius.

Asinius Pollio has enjoyed particularly favourable treatment since Ronald Syme painted a sympathetic portrait of him, making free with the facts in order to do so, in the introduction to his *Roman Revolution* (1939). This portrait is excessively audacious when it ventures to assert that 'the fragments of the preface of Sallust's *Histories*, combined with Tacitus, *Hist*. 1.1–3, will give some idea of the introduction to Pollio's work on the Civil Wars'.[15] It is not generally advisable to attempt fanciful reconstructions based on one's own intellectual or even literary tastes. Here we are dealing with the theory that Pollio's work, for which the only evidence we have is Horace and a body of biographical anecdotes, stands in the tradition of condescending pessimism which is found in the work of Sallust and Tacitus. This is possible, but in the absence of documents one risks indulging in speculation. Syme has a great fondness for Asinius, attributing to him a 'Roman and republican spirit' and declaring him 'always of the opposition'. As to why Pollio chose Caesar at the precise moment when Caesar was trampling republican laws underfoot by crossing the Rubicon under arms, Syme of course finds Pollio's justification persuasive: 'Pollio had powerful enemies on either side [. . .] he chose Caesar, his personal friend.' This less than 'republican' choice becomes in Syme's account nothing short of glorious: 'Loyal to Caesar, and proud of his loyalty, Pollio at the same time professed his attachment to free institutions.' And the proof of this is to be found in Pollio's letter to Cicero (*Letters to his friends* 10.31) at the height of the Mutina war, and for that very reason highly unreliable, or of dubious value. Soon after this, however, the reader of *The Roman Revolution* is apprised of the fact that 'Caesar the Dictator bears the heavier blame for civil war' (p. 9). But how one is to reconcile loyalty to Caesar (and later to Antony) with the 'The Roman and the senator [who] could never surrender the prerogative of liberty' (p. 5) is not at all clear, especially as the civil war, for which Caesar bore 'the heavier blame' (p. 9), was the cause of unprecedented devastation, not only for the country and the empire, but above all for the equestrian order (its 'best men', according to Syme, p. 9). And at this point the reader is suddenly confronted by a quite different diagnosis of the civil war: 'the ambitions of the dynasts provoked war between class and class' (p. 9). How the ambitions of a few could bring about 'war between class and class' is unclear. (The reverse mechanism might be easier to imagine.) Be this as it may, Syme's appraisal of these events fluctuates from one chapter to the next: on p. 9 Pompey is judged to be 'occultior non melior', in the words of Tacitus, yet on p. 47 we read that he 'chose to save the oligarchy' from the threat of Caesar. Caesar is described on p. 9 as bearing 'the heavier blame for civil war', while on p. 47 we learn that he 'strove to avert any resort to open war', 'both before and after the outbreak of hostilities'. In the end Syme seems to assume the role of Pollio (just as he later identifies himself with Sallust and Tacitus), passing on to the reader (this in June 1939!) the following message:

> Yet, in the end, the Principate has to be accepted, for the Principate, while abolishing political freedom, averts civil war and preserves the non-political classes.[16] Liberty or stable government: that was the question confronting the Romans themselves, and I have tried to answer it precisely in their fashion. (pp. vii–viii)

Asinius Pollio, who declares himself neutral on the eve of Actium but is prepared to be 'the prize of the victor',[17] comes to resemble this Syme, so severely marked by the 'spirit of Munich'.

Notes

1 Horace, *Odes* 2.1.
2 Horace, *Odes* 2.7.11.
3 The whole of book 2 of the *Odes* bears the mark of this feeling. It is symptomatic from this standpoint that in Ode 2.6.7–8 Horace confesses to being weary 'lasso maris et viarum militiaeque' 'weary with sea, with roaming, and with war'.
4 Eduard Fraenkel has aptly pointed out, 'Not content with the abstract expression *periculosae plenum opus aleae*, he adds a proverbial image and adorns it with vivid details: *et incedis per ignis suppositos cineri doloso*.' *Orazio*, Italian translation (Rome 1993), p. 323.
5 One of the greatest, Otto Seeck, felt uneasy about the idea that writing history might be a 'hazard' for a responsible member of the establishment like Pollio and thought that the reference might be to the Caesarian motto to which Pollio claimed to be living witness: 'The die is cast!' ('Iacta alea est!'), said before the crossing of the Rubicon. Otto Seeck, *Wiener Studien*, 24 (1902), p. 499.
6 It is surely no accident that this book of the *Odes* opens with anxious warnings to the figure of Pollio, who had refused to take part in the war whose victorious conclusion is hailed at the end of the preceding book (1.37: *nunc est bibendum . . .*)
7 Pierre Bayle, who was clearly highly sensitive to the matter of censorship, gives a lengthy excursus on precisely this aspect of censorship under Augustus in his *Dictionnaire historique*.
8 θηριοτροφεῖς.
9 Seneca, *On anger* 3.23. Seneca would have learned this from his father, who was extremely well informed about relations between Octavian and Timagenes.
10 Plutarch, *Caesar* 13.
11 Assuming that his *Periocha* 103 is faithful to the model.
12 As we know, this is inexact. It leaves aside the most secret and confidential part of the pact, which was actually sealed the year before. Suetonius (*Caesar* 19) offers a more accurate chronology for the birth of the triumvirate. See Chapter 9.
13 Velleius 2.44.1. See Chapter 9.
14 Annaeus Florus, *Epitoma* 2.13.8–9. Lucan in his *Pharsalia* (1.84–6) also adopts this viewpoint.
15 Ronald Syme, *The Roman Revolution* (Oxford 1963), p. 5.
16 A curious phrase which is not without interest.
17 Velleius 2.86.3.

CHAPTER 11

The First Consulship (59 BC)

Caesar's first act as consul was to enact a law requiring publication of a written record of the Senate's proceedings, as well as the minutes of proceedings in the popular assemblies (the *comitia*).[1] The aim was clearly to step up the external pressure on the Senate. Years later, Augustus repealed Caesar's law on the publication of Senate proceedings.[2] Here Caesar was clearly influenced by the Greek democratic tradition, which was firmly wedded to the public use of writing. Alert to symbolism, Caesar required the lictors to walk behind him even in the months in which his fellow-consul took precedence. It was usual for the lictors, bearing the *fasces* and axes as tokens of office, to walk in front of the consul when he appeared in public, and in alternate months each of the consuls would assume this potent symbol of power. An ancient custom, revived by Caesar, permitted each consul, in the month in which his colleague held the tokens of office, to be followed by the lictors rather than preceded by them. In the course of the year, however, this alternation soon lost its significance. The break with Bibulus, the other consul elected by the *factio*, was irreparable and so dramatic that Bibulus locked himself away in his house, issuing edicts as harsh as they were impotent against his colleague, while Caesar effectively acted as sole consul, without him.

The crisis came with the agrarian legislation:[3] when the first of Caesar's two agrarian laws was debated in the Senate, the opposition was such that he left the session and placed the laws before the assembly (the *comitia*) and won the approval of the people.[4] In order to block the passage of this decision, Bibulus decided to rule it out of order on religious grounds: he proclaimed a 'sacred period',[5] during which no meetings of the *comitia* were permitted. But Caesar had at his disposal another weapon, having for some time held the office of *pontifex maximus* (as well as consul). This enabled him to challenge his colleague's obstructive moves. Disregarding Bibulus' orders, he convened the *comitia* to get the law passed. Bibulus, however, chose to force the issue by appearing before the people himself and attempting to speak and declare the assembly (from his point of view) illegal. He was violently ejected, but his intervention could only ignite passions and lead to uncontrollable reactions. Clearly the political responsibility for this very serious act – the expulsion of a colleague from the *comitia* – could only be attributed to Caesar: for this reason many sources critical of Caesar state that Caesar 'resorted to arms and drove him from the Forum'.[6] This naturally had its sequel in the Senate, but, as Suetonius says, 'no one could be found who ventured to make a motion, or even to express an opinion about so high-handed a proceeding (although decrees had often been passed touching less serious breaches of the peace)'. It was the clearest indication of the paralysis of the *factio* when confronted with the coalition of the three potentates: in the circumstances, the *factio* could not be sure of carrying a majority of senators with them.[7] At this point Bibulus, who was obviously not acting alone but in concert with Cato and his supporters, chose a complete break, hoping by this means to provoke an institutional crisis, but this did not eventuate. As we have seen, he withdrew from his office and restricted himself to rejecting stubbornly all Caesar's legislative measures as invalid on account of the continuing 'sacred period',[8] in which he alone believed. 'Caesar managed all the affairs of state alone and after his own pleasure.'[9] Some wags began to sign and seal documents not 'done in the consulship of Caesar and Bibulus', but 'done in the consulship of Julius and Caesar'.[10] In a letter to Atticus, dated 28 April 59 BC, Cicero wrote with great political acuity, 'As to Bibulus' firmness in impeding the *comitia*, it amounts to nothing but an expression of his opinion and does not improve the position of affairs at all.'[11] And in July he wrote ironically, 'Bibulus is exalted to the sky, though I don't know why. However, he is as much praised *as though "His wise delay alone did save the State"* ' (i.e. like Fabius Maximus, *Fabius Cunctator*, in the famous description given by Ennius).[12] In the same letter, Cicero explains to Atticus the cause of his dilemma: his friendship with Pompey prevents him from taking sides against the consul and the triumvirs, but at the same time he cannot condone their actions 'without denying all of my past', he writes. Therefore, he concludes, 'I am following a middle path' – a self-deluding and precarious position, which aroused the hatred of the *factio* and did nothing to bring him under the protection of the opposing side.[13]

Having become effectively a 'consul without a colleague', but with a Senate hardly disposed to be magnanimous, Caesar pursued an overtly 'popularist' line: sharing out the *ager Campanus* (the Campanian Territory) and the *campus Stella* (the 'plain called Stellas') among 20,000 citizens who had three children or more;[14] reducing by one third the tax debt of tax-farmers. He needed to give his traditional power base tangible and positive signs that he was in control. But signs of unrest were also apparent among the people. At the games in honour of Apollo on 13 July, the actor Diphilus had recited in public a line which was in his text, so could not be avoided, 'By our misfortunes thou art great!' 'nostra miseria tu es magnus', and all his listeners understood at once how well this line applied to Pompey, who had assumed the cognomen Magnus. In a state of high excitement the audience kept calling for encores, and Diphilus had to repeat the line many times over.[15] Pompey, who was not present, was none the less deeply hurt; and Caesar wrote a very warm letter of solidarity to the great conqueror injured by the impatience of the crowd.

This is a very well known example, and a highly instructive one, of the almost pathological unpredictability of the urban masses. These constituted a hypersensitive and capricious barometer, willing to be exploited by those who traditionally despised them. Caesar, who had long been familiar with these mechanisms, could not possibly allow the *factio* to take advantage of some fleeting mood of discontent and play this card against him. He responded by inserting into his agrarian legislation provisions of guarantees favouring owners: the redistribution was aimed only at the public domain. The executive organ entrusted with the implementation of the reform was the land commission of *XX viri* elected by the tribes and sworn by oath not to oppose the law.[16] A clause obliged the senators to swear to observe the *Lex Julia* on the redistribution of land, on pain of severe punishment.[17] Even candidates for election who declared that they thought it possible to establish ownership of land in a manner different from that in the legislation faced punishment.[18] While Bibulus continued to issue edicts, in which he vented his feelings about Caesar in cheap jibes,[19] and in vain declared all the *dies comitiales* impractical (thus emphasising that Caesar was incapable of conducting legislation), Cato kept up his opposition in the Senate. He demanded that Caesar explain his actions vis-à-vis Bibulus, his colleague. Caesar's response was harsh: he ordered a lictor to remove Cato from the chamber and escort him to prison.[20]

Among Caesar's legislative measures in the year 59 BC the law on extortion stands out in particular. This was the most comprehensive legislation on the subject enacted up to that point, and in its essentials it remained in force for a very long time. The text of this law, extremely detailed (in over a hundred paragraphs) and based on a thorough knowledge of the reality of Roman provincial administration, was intended primarily to restrict as far as possible the 'normal extortion' indulged in by the pro-magistrates and their retinues in the provinces. The law prohibited the acceptance of gifts relating to the administration of justice, restricted the so-called *legationes liberae* (special commissions, which greatly increased the staff of a pro-magistrate, and hence the expenditure), fixed indemnity for the governors and protected their subjects against the exorbitant tributes imposed by the pro-magistrates. Above all it guaranteed that these rules should be obeyed by obliging every pro-magistrate to lodge two copies of the financial accounting statements for his area in two different cities of the province, and a third in the *aerarium*. By this means control was greatly enhanced. In the case of a trial, the procedures were simplified and it even became possible to take legal action against the heirs of the extortionist.

This was perhaps the most important legislative contribution of Caesar's consulship. It was no accident that this went to the heart of the vast area of provincial administration. Caesar had direct experience of the harshness and the vices of governors of the provinces. He had been in Spain twice: the first time as *quaestor* to Antistius Vetus, and the second in 61 BC as *propraetor*. As a very young man he had taken his first steps in politics by backing judicial action by oppressed provincials against rapacious governors, in trials which had taught him much. Now, in government, Caesar made great efforts to assert order and discipline in this delicate area, realising full well that this was the foundation and the cement on which was built the entire military and political structure dominated by Rome. The extension of citizenship to the Transpadanians (which came about years later, thanks to his efforts) was another aspect of the same design: to extend citizenship rights and re-establish relations of trust with the peoples of the provinces. It is hardly venturing too far to speak of Caesar's designs, even though we have no text by his hand on which to base our deductions: we have, after all, the evidence of his actions and his legislation, which is broadly consistent within itself and universally regarded as inspired. It is legislation which looks beyond the limits and the political horizon of the city and its conflicts. Besides, it was very plain to him that in order to initiate any far-reaching, long-term plan it was necessary to be victorious in that privileged arena at the centre of power, where the political struggle, the election struggle between factions, would be fought. Hence his extraordinary ability to operate in both planes: as a gifted faction leader in the rough-and-tumble of day-to-day politics, and at the same time as a far-sighted legislator. A mixture of mean-spiritedness and greatness.

Notes

1 Suetonius, *Caesar* 20.1. Despite the way in which Suetonius phrases this information, it seems likely that the novelty introduced by Caesar was the publication rather than the recording. It is certain that *Acta diurna* were already in existence in 59 BC.
2 Suetonius, *Augustus* 36.
3 The law for which Caesar had sought Cicero's support before he took office. See Chapter 9.
4 Plutarch, *Caesar* 14.3–4.
5 ἱερομηνία
6 Suetonius, *Caesar* 20.1: 'obnuntiantem collegam armis Foro expulit'.
7 The senators did not form a politically compact group, but rather a fluctuating mass, subject to guidance by able leaders and pressure groups.
8 Suetonius, *Caesar* 20.1: 'domo abditus' is a deliberately ironic turn of phrase. Bibulus' withdrawal was treated with irony even by those who did not take Caesar's side, such as Cicero.
9 Suetonius, *Caesar* 20.2.
10 They also recited lampoons such as, 'In Caesar's year, not Bibulus', an act took place of late; / For naught do I remember done in Bibulus' consulate.' Suetonius, *Caesar* 20.2.
11 Cicero, *Letters to Atticus* 2.15.2.
12 Cicero, *Letters to Atticus* 2.19.2. The fragment from Ennius is 370 Vahlen = 363 Skutsch.
13 As will be seen, Clodius would soon have him exiled.
14 The earlier legislation had not included these territories. See F. De Martino, *Storia della costituzione romana*, vol. III, 2nd edn (Naples: 1973), p. 169, n. 83.
15 Cicero, *Letters to Atticus* 2.19.3.
16 Dio Cassio, 38.1.6.
17 Appian, *Civil Wars* 2.12.42.
18 Cicero, *Letters to Atticus* 2.18.2.
19 Suetonius, *Caesar* 49.1: 'the Queen of Bithynia [i.e. Caesar] was enamoured of a king, but now of a king's estate'.
20 Suetonius, *Caesar* 20. Other extreme acts by Caesar are also reported. Suetonius devotes much space to such episodes in his account of Caesar's consulship.

CHAPTER 12

An Inconvenient Ally: Clodius

Caesar could not ignore the phenomenon of Clodius. If what he wanted was enduring, stable administration of the provinces, the politics of Rome demanded control over the mood, the spirit and any possible murmurs of unrest among the proletarianised and parasitic urban masses, to whom *déclassé* elements of the ruling stratum not infrequently offered themselves as leaders. In his time Catiline had been one such, and now there was Clodius. Publius Clodius Pulcher, who was born into the patriciate but had become a plebeian[1] – with the authority of Caesar as *pontifex maximus* – with the sole aim of being elected tribune, was the prototypically unprincipled agitator. His case is a striking illustration of the degeneration of the social struggle in the capital of the empire. He had incited mutiny among Lucullus' troops in the East. Then he had appeared as the accuser of Catiline, but later, apparently, changed sides. The most salient fact of his career, before his election as tribune, was an amorous escapade that ended badly in the house of Caesar, not long after the latter had become *pontifex maximus*, on the day of the festival of Bona Dea in 62 BC. In his *Life of Caesar* Plutarch gives a vivid account of this episode, in which Clodius seeks a secret rendezvous with Pompeia, the then wife of Caesar, stressing the fact that according to custom the festival of Bona Dea was celebrated in the house of the *pontifex maximus*, but in the absence of all the men of the house, including the *pontifex*. Here is Plutarch's account, including its political epilogue:[2]

> At the time of which I speak, Pompeia was celebrating this festival, and Clodius, who was still beardless and on this account thought to pass unnoticed, assumed the dress and implements of a lute-girl and went to the house, looking like a young woman. He found the door open, and was brought in safely by the maid-servant there, who was in the secret; but after she had run on ahead to tell Pompeia and some time had elapsed, Clodius had not the patience to wait where he had been left, and so, as he was wandering about the house (a large one) and trying to avoid the lights, an attendant of Aurelia came upon him

and asked him to play with her, as one woman would another, and when he refused, she dragged him forward and asked who he was and whence he came. Clodius answered that he was waiting for Pompeia's Abra (this was the very name by which the maid was called), but his voice betrayed him. The attendant of Aurelia at once sprang away with a scream to the lights and the throng, crying out that she had caught a man. The women were panic-stricken and Aurelia put a stop to the mystic rites of the goddess and covered up the emblems. Then she ordered the doors to be closed and went about the house with torches, searching for Clodius. He was found where he had taken refuge, in the chamber of the girl who had let him into the house; and when they saw who he was, the women drove him out of doors. Then at once, and in the night, they went off and told the matter to their husbands, and when day came a report spread through the city that Clodius had committed sacrilege and owed satisfaction not only to those whom he had insulted, but also to the city and to the gods. Accordingly, one of the tribunes of the people indicted Clodius for sacrilege, and the most influential senators leagued themselves together and bore witness against him that, among other shocking abominations, he had committed adultery with his sister, who was the wife of Lucullus. But against the efforts of these men the people arrayed themselves in defence of Clodius, and were of great assistance to him with the jurors in the case, who were terror-stricken and afraid of the multitude. Caesar divorced Pompeia at once, but when he was summoned to testify at the trial, he said that he knew nothing about the matter with which Clodius was charged. His statement appeared strange, and the prosecutor therefore asked, 'Why, then, didst thou divorce thy wife?' 'Because,' said Caesar, 'I thought my wife ought not even to be under suspicion.' Some say that Caesar made this deposition honestly; but according to others it was made to gratify the people, who were determined to rescue Clodius. At any rate, Clodius was acquitted of the charge, the majority of the jurors giving their verdicts in illegible writing, in order that they might neither risk their lives with the populace by condemning him, nor get a bad name among the nobility by acquitting him.

This took place in 62 BC, when Caesar was still a *praetor* (besides being *pontifex maximus*). He was then sent to the provinces and returned to Rome a year later to take part in the election campaign for the consulship in spring 60, winning it thanks to the triumviral alliance. Clodius, with his men, was a minor figure, but, in view of the new alliances, not a negligible one. As an agitator he carried some weight, and it was therefore inadvisable to have him as an opponent. (Caesar was well aware of this when he gave evidence at his trial.)

Clodius aspired to be a tribune of the plebs, and to achieve this he needed to be formally adopted by a plebeian family. A *transitio ad plebem* was a necessary precondition for his election. It was generally understood that his plan, if successful, would have consequences at many levels: these included the relations of intense personal rivalry between Clodius and Cicero (a result of the trial which followed the scandal of the festival of Bona Dea, in which Cicero was the prosecution's principal witness). According to Suetonius, it was Cicero's imprudent public criticism that spurred Caesar to retaliate by at last approving a *transitio ad plebem* for Clodius, 'a thing for which Clodius had for a long time been vainly striving'.[3] Cicero's attack on Caesar's policies had come during a trial in which Cicero had been defending his former fellow-consul Gaius Antonius,[4] and Caesar's response had its predictable effect. No sooner had Clodius assumed office as tribune of the plebs on 10 December than, while Caesar was relinquishing the office and preparing to take up the difficult administration of his provinces, he prepared a series of measures, grouped in four laws (*Leges Clodiae*), which seemed designed to mesh with Caesar's policy. (One of them provided free distribution of grain to the landless; another forbade senior officials to observe the celestial signs on days when the *comitia* were meeting.)[5] A fifth, a few days later (January 58 BC), affected Cicero directly, though without naming him: 'whosoever may cause the death of a Roman citizen who has not been condemned by a court shall be exiled'.[6] Velleius, who gives us the exact wording of this draft law, says that the triumvirs were not beyond suspicion of having supplied ammunition for Clodius, and further suggests that Cicero had aroused the hostility of the triumvirs by refusing to take part in the commission of the *XX viri* tasked with subdividing the Campanian territory.[7] This version differs from that recorded by Suetonius and Dio, but contains a germ of truth: by refusing any involvement in the policy of the triumvirate, Cicero placed himself in an isolated position, with no protection against the revenge of Clodius. The debate on the *Lex Clodia* was a memorable event: it was held in the Field of Mars, outside the *pomerium*, so that Caesar could take part without being obliged to set aside his proconsular powers. The topic was the fundamental rights of citizens: the *Lex Clodia* was seen as a developed and elaborated form of the *leges de provocatione*; its target was the so-called *senatus consultum ultimum*, an emergency measure by which the Senate arrogated to itself the right to single out 'internal enemies' and take action against them unfettered by any legal constraints, having declared them outside the law. The *populares* had never accepted that the Senate should possess this fearsome prerogative. It implied – and after a Senate debate this was made explicit – that the sentence of death passed on the Catilinarian leaders, endorsed by the Senate and carried out by Cicero as consul in December 63, was to be considered an illegal act because the participants, once accused and *ipso facto* sentenced, were not permitted to appeal to the people (*provocatio*). Isolated, Cicero chose exile, while a further provision introduced by Clodius sanctioned the confiscation of all the property of the exile (who, moreover, was obliged to reside at least 500 miles from Rome). Clodius personally took part when Cicero's house on the Palatine was set alight. (In its place a temple to liberty was erected.)[8] And he 'compared himself to Pompey, who was then the most powerful man in Rome'.[9]

Did Clodius really become a fourth potentate? The assistance he received from Caesar during his year as consul and in the period immediately following should not lead to a simplistic conclusion that Clodius was a creature of Caesar's. Clodius' followers were the lumpenproletariat and slaves who were drawn to him but clearly his subordinates. This allowed him to develop a demagogic policy which showed a certain ability, a policy which was *his own*. This policy was *sui generis* because it was based on the disturbing novelty of the blatant use of armed bands as an instrument of pressure and terror. (Even Pompey thought it advisable to shut himself up in his house when the tribune's bands targeted him.) In the long term this was a counter-productive policy. Eighteen months later, in the summer of 57, when Cicero, thanks to Pompey, returned from his Greek exile,[10] he was welcomed in Italy by large popular demonstrations, proving how unpopular Clodius was with those sections of the population who rejoiced at the return of a 'victim' of his machinations. His failed attempt to prevent Cicero rebuilding his house on the Palatine provoked hostility and revealed Clodius' weakness: he was now confronted by gangs of thugs led by Titus Annius Milo, who would later be his assassin. It is understandable that our sources (almost exclusively Cicero) paint a picture of Clodius which is almost entirely criminal, and scarcely credible in the area of most interest to us: his political programme. When Cicero describes what Clodius did as *praetor*,[11] we may be sure that this is a Catilinarian caricature divorced from reality: 'he created an army of slaves which he used to seize the State and the private property of anyone he chose'. Clodius 'incited the slaves against their masters',[12] and openly promised them emancipation.[13] Clodius' troops were a motley crew (Cicero habitually refers to them as 'dregs', *faex*): lumpen proletarians with no definite occupation, mercenary street fighters, slaves drawn by promises which went no further than personal favours, and gladiators. With followers like these Clodius could certainly influence local politics, and perhaps in certain cases even dictate how the potentates acted. But he could not get far in this way, and was sure to be dropped by all political groupings. With his intrusive presence on the Roman political scene the degeneration of the urban proletariat towards a parasitic state reached its lowest point. This was one of the main reasons why Caesar decided to detach himself from the traditional politics of the *populares* and from the dynamics of these. When the decay of classes reaches the point where they can neither assume a leading role nor adjust to the hegemony of other social strata, one sees a flourishing of blind parasitism and the rise of self-appointed rabble-rousers. This means that the democratic tradition is set aside, often for all too long a period.

Notes

1 On the terms of the *transitio ad plebem* see M. Salvadore, 'L'adozione di Clodio', *Labeo*, 38 (1992), pp. 285–313.
2 Plutarch, *Caesar* 10.
3 Suetonius, *Caesar* 20.4.
4 Dio Cassio 38.10.
5 This was all that Bibulus did during the months of his consulship.
6 Velleius 2.45.1.
7 Velleius 2.45.3.
8 Plutarch, *Cicero* 33.
9 Appian, *Civil Wars* 2.15.58.
10 In Thessalonica and Dyrrhachium (Durazzo).
11 Cicero, *In Defence of Milo* 28.76.
12 Cicero, *In Defence of Sestius* 24.53.
13 Cicero, *Letters to Atticus* 4.3.2.

CHAPTER 13

Semiramis in Gaul

The process of granting to Caesar the provinces of Gaul and Illyricum was not without its difficulties. The Senate's original decision, a provocative one,[1] taken before Caesar had been elected, had to be annulled and a new allocation made in its place. Plutarch's account is eloquent in its brevity:

> Pompey . . . filled the Forum with armed men and helped the people to pass Caesar's laws and to give him, as his consular province to be held for five years, Gaul on both sides of the Alps, together with Illyricum and an army of four legions.[2]

It is here that Plutarch places his report of the ejection of Cato from the Senate, a scene which Suetonius places in another context (following the expulsion of Bibulus from the Forum). On the allocation of the provinces it is Suetonius who provides the most accurate details:

> At first, it is true, by the bill of Vatinius he received only Cisalpine Gaul with the addition of Illyricum; but presently he was assigned Gallia Comata as well by the Senate, since the members feared that even if they should refuse it, the people would give him this also.[3]

This was an exceptional command: the five-year term would end on 1 March 54 BC; moreover Caesar had the right to appoint legates, and could count on an indemnity payable from the treasury. Cicero writes that by his law Vatinius had deprived the Senate of some of its prerogatives, the *aerarii dispensatio* among them.[4]

The long-drawn-out debate on these decisions is recorded with a wealth of detail. Suetonius reports heated verbal clashes. Caesar is alleged to have stated with satisfaction, during a session or on the fringes of one, with the senators present, that he had *'gained his heart's desire* to the grief and lamentation of his opponents' – a declaration which is revealing in what it says about his intention of acquiring precisely these provinces. But then he added that 'he would therefore from that time mount on their heads'.[5] Cary is troubled by

this statement, finding it improbable: 'Truculence was not a characteristic of Caesar.'[6] One might object that there must be some truth in
this if it was said *frequenti curia*, that is, in the presence of many senators. But it is also true that a context may be invented as well as a
sentence. Whatever the case, Suetonius must have had a reliable
source for these pronouncements of Caesar's: the sheer number of
Caesarian utterances, made at critical moments in his eventful life,
recorded by Suetonius with particular care, must in all probability
derive from a witness of considerable stature and astuteness, who
later became the historian of the whole period from the birth of the
triumvirate: Asinius Pollio. The same phrases reappear in other
sources (Plutarch and Appian), who certainly had Pollio's work to
hand, and each of the three (Suetonius, Plutarch and Appian) says
more than once, quite explicitly, that they owe the text of Caesar's
statements to Pollio. For this reason we may be reasonably confident
of the quality of this evidence.[7]

In the exchange with the senators in the assembly, the sharp tone
is no less striking than the cutting coldness of the reply. The threat to
'mount on their heads' is said to have drawn the response that 'that
would be no easy matter for a woman', restating the recurrent allusion to Caesar's well-known bisexuality. Caesar retorted with a laugh,
'Semiramis too had been queen in Syria and the Amazons in days of
old had held sway over a great part of Asia.'[8] The earthy and coarsely
blunt tone makes it easy to believe that Caesar, in a mood to be
provocative, could have uttered the harsh and hyperbolic threat,
'ex eo insultaturum omnium capitibus'. This was far from being an
unrealistic appraisal of the importance of his long and all-inclusive
military command for the growth of Caesar's power *in Rome*.

He had now 'gained his heart's desire'. It is tempting to think that
Caesar really did say this. The choice of Gaul had been a considered
one, which accorded well with his precise calculations. Above all,
there was an emotional angle of great significance, in the form of
Gaius Marius' great victories against the Celtic and Germanic
peoples, victories which had taken such firm hold in the public mind
that they could not be erased. This was why Caesar, as *praetor*, sure
of the emotional effect, had restored the commemorative trophies of
those momentous victories,[9] achieved forty years earlier by the undisputed leader of the *populares*. Moreover, Caesar was related to him,
and proudly mindful of this family connection and the obligations it
imposed. His wish was to be seen by all as the new Marius in the

territory where Marius' greatness was beyond dispute. Seeking a rapprochement with Caesar, Cicero, on his return from exile and feeling somewhat ill at ease under the continuing rule of the triumvirate, would undertake a thorough comparative study (favourable to Caesar) of Marius' and Caesar's campaigns in Gaul. It is found in his speech *On the consular provinces*, which he delivered after the renewal of the triumviral agreement in 56 BC. In this speech Cicero supports the continuation of Caesar's command in Gaul, against the *factio* which urged its termination.[10] He now says:

> Under Gaius Caesar's command, Conscript Fathers, we have fought a war in Gaul; before we merely repelled attacks. Our commanders always thought that those people ought to be beaten back in war rather than attacked. The great Gaius Marius himself, whose divine and outstanding bravery was our stay after grievous disasters and losses suffered by the Roman people, drove back vast hordes of Gauls that were streaming into Italy, but did not himself penetrate to their cities and dwelling-places.[11]

Here Cicero is certainly saying what Caesar wanted to hear. The comparison with Marius, from the mouth of Cicero, is all the more flattering if we remember the special devotion he had displayed, in his poem *Marius*, for example, to his fellow-countryman, the victor over the Cimbri and the Teutoni (despite an inevitable difference of opinion with regard to Marius the faction leader). Gaul therefore served primarily to build Caesar's image as a gifted and effective leader, by referring to a 'better' Marius, who belonged to *all* the 'Roman people'.

There was, however, a more particular reason for Caesar's choice of Gaul: the link with Gallia Transpadana, which should not be underestimated. On his return from his first posting as *quaestor* to Antistius Vetus in Spain, Caesar had upheld the aspirations of the Latin colonists to Roman citizenship.[12] It was said that he had 'plotted' with the Transpadanians in the dark events of the 'first conspiracy'.[13] The defence of the interests of Gallia Transpadana had been a decisive factor when he attacked Gaius Piso for extortion during his governorship of that province.[14] And in 49 BC, at the start of the civil war, when he had only just established himself as dictator, one of his first acts was to grant citizenship rights to the Transpadanians.[15] In the effort to ensure for himself special relations, if not exactly relations of 'clientship', with certain provinces, Caesar had long had his eye on Cisalpine Gaul. He could increase his influence in Rome on the basis of clientship relations developed in the provinces.

Finally, this was a political decision for the long term. To set out, for a long period of time,[16] on a great campaign of conquest and 'colonisation' with a vast army (the number of legions being necessarily proportionate to the scale of the campaign) meant gradually replacing one's narrow, traditional 'urban base' with a sizeable body of military manpower: an increasingly important political factor, which counted for much in the decisions of the potentates (as Caesar himself knew from the time when he had had to fight, as consul, to reward Pompey's veterans as speedily as possible). With his long period of service in Gaul, a *new phase begins in his political biography*. In this phase the most significant fact is the gradual development of a new political base, even though this did not mean a break with his *popularis* power base, left behind in Rome. This was because in Rome, where Clodius was still pursuing a fairly destructive policy, he had his own men in place and the triumviral agreement continued to function, though in conditions of higher risk.

However, a break was made, and Plutarch deals with it in a chapter of his biography of Caesar which functions as a pause in the narrative between the first part, firmly focused on the unscrupulous demagogic leader,[17] and the second, the story of the great conquests (with all their high and low points, which Plutarch does not conceal).[18] The two phases are separated by a kind of watershed, and Plutarch is very conscious of the change:

> Such, then, is said to have been the course of Caesar's life before his Gallic campaigns. But the period of the wars which he afterwards fought, and of the campaigns by which he subjugated Gaul, *as if he had made another beginning and entered upon a different path of life and one of new achievements*, proved him to be inferior as soldier and commander to no one soever of those who have most admiration for leadership and shown themselves greatest therein.[19]

Plutarch places this new life clearly in the context of Caesar's all-important relationship with his legions, and he is right to do so. With the campaign in Gaul everything changes, including – and this is the most important thing – the social reference points of Caesar's political behaviour: the army now replaces the *plebs urbana*.[20]

Plutarch rightly gives much space to the mutual devotion and trust established between Caesar and his soldiers, above all the veterans.[21] It is plain from Plutarch's account that he is well aware of the most salient factor in Caesar's Gallic campaigns: the founding of a new 'base' for his political and military actions. On this subject there already existed a body of literature which went beyond the stories Caesar himself related in his *Commentaries*. The numerous anecdotes collected by Plutarch, as proof of the excellent and enduring relationship of trust and mutual respect between Caesar and his legionaries, demonstrate this. Suetonius writes, 'He valued his soldiers neither for their personal character nor their fortune, but solely for their prowess (*tantum a viribus*), and he treated them with equal strictness and indulgence.'[22] Plutarch comments, after adducing many instances of the soldiers' devotion to their commander,

> Such spirit and ambition Caesar himself created and cultivated in his men, in the first place, because he showed, by his unsparing bestowal of rewards and honours, that he was not amassing wealth from his wars for his own luxury or for any life ease, but that he treasured it up carefully as a common prize for deeds of valour,[23] and had no greater share in the wealth than he offered to the deserving among his soldiers.[24]

The legend of Caesar's style of military command (and not merely as a faction leader in Rome) continued to spread and grow. It was probably founded on events which were not invented, and covered many aspects: his physical stamina, his sense of comradeship, and his ability to accept the harsh conditions of day-to-day army life. A refined and cultured nobleman, with an appreciation of the comforts of a life of privilege, he was yet able to submit with agility and tenacity to the harshest and most dangerous of discipline: frugal with regard to food, or, as Plutarch puts it, 'indifferent in regard to his diet',[25] snatching only a little sleep in uncomfortable conditions such as chariots, able to travel at a pace unheard of for the then means of transport (he was famed for reaching the Rhône from Rome in eight days),[26] and at the same time retaining his clarity of thought and creativity in the most unfavourable physical conditions; he could dictate letters on horseback, keeping two or more scribes busy at the same time.[27]

Another legend concerns Caesar's conduct of war: a happy mixture of caution and boldness. 'He never led his army where ambuscades were possible without carefully reconnoitring the country, and he did not cross to Britain without making personal enquiries about the harbours, the course, and the approach to the island.'[28] At the same time he was capable of assuming daring disguises in order to pass through the enemy lines: 'When news came that his camp in Germany was beleaguered, he made his way to his men through the enemies' pickets, disguised as a Gaul.'[29] 'He joined battle, not only after planning his movements in advance but on a sudden opportunity, often immediately at the end of a march, and sometimes in the foulest weather, when one would least expect him to make a move.'[30] 'When his army gave way, he often rallied it single-handed, planting himself in the way of the fleeing men, laying hold of them one by one, and even catching them by the throat and forcing them to face the enemy', as on one occasion, when he was with his men in close combat, a standard-bearer threatened him with the sharp butt of his standard, and another ran off leaving the standard in his hand.[31]

These are 'Tolstoyan' scenes in the emphasis that emerges on improvisation.[32] Caesar did not draw up plans far in advance, preferring to exploit opportunities as they arose. A further Tolstoyan feature is the personalised nature of the battle scenes, which also show the commanders in close proximity to the fighting men. In this, Caesar's practice directly contradicts Napoleon's pronouncement on Caesar's wars ('The generals of ancient armies were less expert than those of modern armies').[33]

Caesar's physical closeness to his men is related by Caesar himself in a page of his second commentary on the Gallic war. It comes at a critical moment in the battle against the Nervii on the river Sabis (Sambre): the battle is going badly and the soldiers of the Twelfth Legion, having lost many of their centurions as well as their standard and standard-bearer, are hard pressed by the enemy. Then, seeing the danger,

> taking therefore a shield from a soldier of the rearmost ranks, as he himself was come thither without a shield, he went forward into the first line, and calling on the centurions by name, and cheering on the rank and file, he bade them advance and extend the companies, that they might ply their swords more easily.[34]

At this dramatic moment, as C. Marchesi points out, Caesar shows something like genuine personal involvement and himself gives the order to attack; and the army recovers its strength.[35] This is not a case of a godlike power intervening; on the contrary, it rather shows such an absolute fusion of commander and men that it reminds one of Tolstoy's famous reflections on the 'role of the personality in history', where he observes that:

> we need only penetrate to the essence of any historic event – which lies in the activity of the general mass of men who take part in it – to

be convinced that the will of the historic hero does not control the actions of the mass but is itself continually controlled.[36]

None of this, of course, implies that Caesar in any way neglected 'Roman' politics, though far from the centre of power and embroiled in a spreading conflict which was growing in complexity. Even if his deliberate choice of Gaul and his resulting deeper military engagement are to be seen as an extended preparation for the day of reckoning in Rome,[37] it is clearer than ever that Caesar was keeping the political front constantly in view: through his own agents (mainly Oppius and Balbus, not Clodius), and, at the decisive moment of the meeting at Luca (56 BC), by renewing and revitalising the triumviral alliance. From the moment of his departure for the province, Suetonius writes,

> to secure himself for the future, he took great pains always to put the magistrates for the year under personal obligation, and not to aid any candidates or suffer any to be elected, save such as guaranteed to defend him in his absence. And he did not hesitate in some cases to exact an oath to keep this pledge or even a written contract.[38]

But his most decisive and significant step was the meeting at Luca. In spite of the disrepute in which this meeting is held by contemporaries and historians alike, the meeting at Luca preserved peace at home for a further five years. It proved to be another example of Caesar's happy gift for proposing lasting compromise solutions which satisfied all the interested parties. The political scenario in Rome was dominated by the endless struggle between Clodius, backed by his organised gangs, and Pompey. The cause of the trouble was very serious: the insufficient supply of grain. This soon gave rise to the slogan, 'Pompey keeps the people hungry', with corresponding variants favourable to Crassus. A chronology of the ongoing agitation is supplied in an important letter from Cicero to his brother, dated mid-February 56 BC. At this time Cicero himself still had hopes of playing a role in high politics and of driving a wedge between Pompey and Caesar by exploiting, among other things, the undying hostility of Crassus and the constant agitation in the streets against Pompey, who was blamed by Clodius' demagogic supporters for the grain shortage. Even the question of the legitimacy of Caesar's legislation on the Campanian Territory reared its head again, with subtle distinctions being made to placate Pompey, who had become the principal beneficiary of that legislation. The most severe blow, however, was that struck by Caesar's old adversary, Lucius Domitius Ahenobarbus.

Domitius was a candidate for the consulship in 55 BC, and threatened to strip Caesar of his provinces, possibly even before the legal expiry of his five-year term. Everybody knew that the campaign in Gaul was at its height. To terminate Caesar's exceptional command would mean not merely turning that bloody campaign (on which Caesar staked his future) into a failure, but eliminating Caesar for good when he returned to Rome as a private citizen.

But Caesar was geographically not so remotely situated. As usual, he spent the winter in Cisalpine Gaul (Upper Italy), not far from the gates of Rome. In April 56 BC he was in Ravenna, only a few days' march from Rome. At this time both Pompey and Crassus were in difficulty, so this was the right moment to offer them favourable terms for renewing the pact. Furthermore, Caesar was then the only one with an army at his disposal. He invited Crassus to Ravenna. Pompey hesitated, then set out for Tuscany, informing Caesar that he planned to take ship from Pisa for Sardinia to buy some grain. Caesar went to Luca with Crassus, crossing the Apennines and taking a route which would allow a meeting with Pompey without obliging Pompey to deviate from his plan. A group of second- and third-rank politicians accompanied the three 'great ones', no fewer than 120 senators who had no wish to be associated with the virulent revival of the *factio*. These senators did not attend the meeting, which was held in secret, but they soon saw the results: Pompey and Crassus would stand as candidates for the consulship of the following year, with the support of legionaries temporarily made civilians. The electoral illusions of Domitius Ahenobarbus faded to nothing. The new joint consulship of two who had previously, when joint consuls in 70 BC, suppressed the Sullan constitution even had its military component: Pompey would govern the province of Spain, Crassus the province of Syria – with the prospect of dazzling military successes before him, such as a great campaign against the Parthians – and Caesar's governorship of Gaul was renewed for a further five years. Pompey wrote a terse, dry note to Cicero, telling him not to pursue the revision of the agrarian laws. Cicero did as he was bid. Caesar returned to his province. It was clear that he had no intention of trying to unseat the other two. To him, as before, the only practical solution was to share power with them over the republic in a 'protectorate'. Personal power was not on his agenda, nor even on the horizon. Once again what mattered most to him was firm control over the legions fighting in Gaul and the prospect of a long-term provincial command at the gates of Rome.

Notes

1 'Silvae callesque' as a province for the consuls of the year 59 BC. See Chapter 9.

2 Plutarch, *Caesar* 14.10.

3 Suetonius, *Caesar* 22.1. See also Dio Cassius 38.8.5 and Orosius 6.7.1. Appian in his *Civil Wars* 2.13 commits the same error as Plutarch and confuses the two decisions. In fact Vatinius' law gave Caesar three legions. The Senate added a fourth.

4 Cicero, *Against Vatinius* 35–6. (The speech against Vatinius dates from 56 BC, though its publication by Cicero certainly came later.) The reference to 'aerarii dispensationem' is unambiguous, but it is improbable that Vatinius would have legally made it possible for Caesar to access treasury funds to pay for his protracted provincial administration.

5 Suetonius, *Caesar* 22.2: 'ex eo insultaturum omnium capitibus'.

6 H. E. Butler and M. Cary (eds), *Suetoni Tranquilli Divus Iulius* (New York and Oxford 1927), p. 69.

7 Especially in Suetonius, who is the most meticulous in his references.

8 Suetonius, *Caesar* 22.2.

9 Plutarch, *Caesar* 6.6–7.

10 It is known that in private letters Cicero described his position, reversing his anti-triumvirate attitude of the months preceding his exile, as 'somewhat distasteful' ('subturpicula'). Cicero, *Letters to Atticus* 4.5.1.

11 Cicero, *On the consular provinces* 32, but the whole context is significant.

12 Suetonius, *Caesar* 8.

13 Suetonius, *Caesar* 9.3.

14 Sallust, *Catilinarian Conspiracy* 49.2.

15 Dio Cassio 41.36.3: by means of a *Lex Roscia* or a *Lex Iulia de civitate Transpadanorum*.

16 It turned out to be fully nine years.

17 Plutarch, *Caesar* 1–14.

18 Plutarch, *Caesar* 15–27. This is followed by a third part, with much detail on the civil war and the tragic end of Caesar's meteoric career.

19 Plutarch, *Caesar* 15.1–2.

20 Here the key episode from the consular elections for the year 55 has symbolic meaning, as Caesar sends a large part of his army to vote in Rome. These were soldiers who had their civic rights temporarily restored to them. J. Carcopino, *Jules César*, 5th edn (Paris 1968), p. 277.

21 Plutarch, *Caesar* 16–17.

22 Suetonius, *Caesar* 65.1.

23 This did not pre-empt some derision from the ranks on the occasion of the triumph in Gaul: 'Aurum in Gallia effutuisti . . .' (Suetonius, *Caesar* 51)!

24 Plutarch, *Caesar* 17.1.

25 Plutarch, *Caesar* 17.9.

26 Plutarch, *Caesar* 17.5; Suetonius, *Caesar* 57.

27 Plutarch, *Caesar* 17.7: 'as Oppius says' (his devoted *agens in rebus*, the author of a biography of Cassius). See Carisius, in H. Keil, *Grammatici latini*, Vol. I, p. 147.

28 Suetonius, *Caesar* 58.1.

29 Suetonius, *Caesar* 58.1.

30 Suetonius, *Caesar* 60.1.

31 Suetonius, *Caesar* 62.

32 'Tolstoyan' in the sense of resembling Tolstoy the theoretician of war in *War and Peace*.

33 *Précis des guerres de César* par Napoléon, écrit par M. Marchand sous la dictée de l'Empereur [1819] (Paris 1836), p. 205.

34 Caesar, *Gallic War* 2.25.

35 C. Marchesi, *Storia della letteratura latina* [1925–7], 2nd edn (Milan and Messina 1958), p. 345.

36 L. N. Tolstoy, *Voina i mir* (Moscow 1949), vol. 2, p. 458. In English, L. N. Tolstoy, *War and Peace*, book IV, part II, ch. 1, trans. Aylmer Maude (London 1959), p. 1089.

37 Suetonius, *Caesar* 22: 'ex omni provinciarum copia Gallias potissimum elegit'.

38 Suetonius, *Caesar* 23.2. For examples see 29.1 and 73. (On Memmius see Chapter 6.)

CHAPTER 14

The Conquest of Gaul (58–51 BC)

When he departed for Gaul in the spring of 58 BC, Caesar had a clear idea of the movements of the peoples and their tensions; in particular, the German pressure on Gaul. He conceived a long-term strategic plan using up-to-date ethnographic knowledge to which he himself contributed with his *Commentaries*. This is but one example of the way he combined scientific study with imperialism.

Just how dangerous the situation in Gaul really was at that time for the neighbouring Roman provinces cannot be determined, since we rely exclusively on Caesar's version of the facts in his *Commentaries* on the Gallic war, an expertly constructed work in which every statement has been carefully weighed by its author. Many who remembered the Cimbric invasion were conscious of the German threat: fear of a great host of German warriors descending on Cisalpine Gaul or Italy explains the widespread approval of Caesar's campaigns. Varro Atacinus (*Bellum Sequanicum*) and Catullus (Ode 11) celebrated his exploits in verse, and Cicero, whose brother Quintus was Caesar's legate in Gaul following the conference at Luca, also joined the chorus.

The Gallic campaign was conducted on two levels: Caesar's own favourable assessment of sometimes dubious victories; and the reality of an extremely difficult war with an outcome that was uncertain, given the threat constantly posed by the fiercely independent Celtic tribes. The dichotomy (especially in the first two years, 58–57 BC) shows clearly in the disparity between the political and military position and the reactions in Rome to Caesar's skilled reporting of them. Of the first two years of the conflict it has rightly been said that 'Gaul was conquered without being conquered.'[1] Even after the decisive victory over the Belgae, the annexation of Gaul was not on the agenda. For the time being it was a case of 'indirect and tacit protection', through the agency of those tribes which had sought such protection and whose example other tribes had more or less willingly

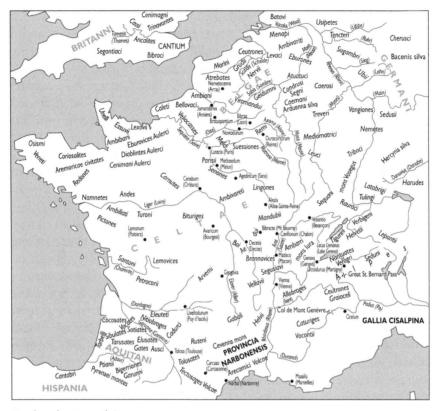

Gaul in the time of Caesar

adopted, 'in consideration of the military strength which was behind such protection and was its foundation'.[2]

The reception of this complicated reality was quite different in Rome. It is vividly expressed by the decision to grant the victor, immediately after the victory over the Belgae (57 BC), on the basis of official correspondence, a *supplicatio* of two weeks, 'an honour that had previously fallen to no man'.[3] Perhaps it is best to see the first two *Commentaries* on the Gallic war, in the form in which they are preserved, as a brilliant and nicely timed tailoring, as works of literary propaganda, of those dispatches that aimed to persuade the city and the Senate of the greatness of the objectives attained.[4]

Naturally, to ensure that the Senate granted ever more disproportionate *supplicationes* to Caesar, action by his men in Rome was necessary (besides the maintenance of a good relationship with Pompey).[5] But not all, obviously, were ready to accept this propaganda. There is a letter from Marcus Caelius to Cicero,[6] of May–June

51 (when almost all of Gaul had been pacified and subdued!), which at one point says: 'As regards Caesar; rumours arrive in plenty about him and they are not pretty [*non belli*] – but only of the whispering sort [about mutinies and setbacks, for example].' And it continues: 'But nothing is confirmed as yet, and even these unconfirmed reports are not bandied about generally but retailed as an open secret among a small coterie – you know who.'[7] This tone is surprising in June 51: the hint by Caelius indicates that knowledge of the manipulative mechanisms adopted by Caesar to promote his exploits and display them in a particular light had led to rejection in limited but well-informed milieux.

When Caesar arrived in the region the monarchic system had given way to a government of the aristocracy in most of the Gallic tribes. Among the Sequani and the Aedui this 'revolution' had occurred a generation earlier. What Caesar says near the beginning of the *Commentaries* about the attempts,[8] incited by the Helvetian Orgetorix, to revive the monarchy among the Sequani and Aedui, makes it clear that, at least among these peoples, the monarchy no longer existed. However, there were still kings among the populations most remote from Roman power: in Aquitania, Britain and North Gaul. In particular, as far as Britain is concerned, it can be seen that the monarchy only gave way to the predominance of the aristocracy much later, in the period between Caesar's testimony and that of Tacitus' *Agricola*.[9] Beyond the Rhine as well this tendency to liquidate monarchies was spread by the influence of Gallic tribes on their German neighbours.[10] Once the aristocracy was established in power, any possible aspiration by an individual to monarchic power was considered high treason: it was believed that anybody guilty of this merited the death penalty. Even where monarchy survived, its weakening is evident; for example, Caesar writes of the Eburones that together the assembled mass of the populace carried a weight equal to that of the sovereign.[11] And the testimony of Dio Chrysostom (AD 40–120), an important source in the time of Flavius, sheds light on another constraint on monarchic power among the Celts, a constraint inherent in its relationship with the priestly caste. Dio writes that Celtic sovereigns could not undertake or decide anything without first consulting the Druids, from which he concludes that, in reality, far from being organs of government, the monarchs tended rather to be 'executive' organs.[12]

It is fair to wonder about the origins of this progressive shift towards aristocratic-collegial administration in the lands of the Celts.

Roman political forms of governance may well have influenced them, being the greatest power with which the Celts were in contact. But probably a different phenomenon should be considered crucial, one that was farther-reaching and concerned the social equilibrium within these communities. An economically strong, enterprising class had come into being, which contributed over several decades to the growth of an urban world. And this phenomenon coincides with the decline of the monarchy and favours forms of government in which the middle and upper classes carry most weight.[13]

At the risk of generalising, it can be added that this process of transformation and greater social organisation may have assisted the policy of Roman penetration. Caesar, as his brilliant account makes clear, always counted on division within – and between – Gallic communities, in his search for collaborationist agreements which he then put to use with consummate ability. (This is not surprising: at the time of the conquest of Gaul, the Romans had almost two centuries of 'imperial' experience.) Caesar was able to secure such understandings by playing on differences, as well as a skilful policy of graded concessions. He was received favourably among the aristocracy, who saw certain advantages in possible *integration*, but encountered hostility among the masses, harshly exploited by the rapacious spirit of the conquerors, and open enmity among the sovereigns and leaders (from Ambiorix to Vercingetorix and Commius, to cite the traditional 'enemies of Rome'). Caesar, by studying the economic and social condition of his enemies, won the most challenging colonial war in the history of Rome.

Military operations began with pressure from the Helvetii, who, confined within their borders and tired of conflicts with neighbouring Germanic peoples, made plans to emigrate to western Gaul. Caesar speaks of 368,000 individuals, amongst whom were 92,000 warriors.[14] This migration, meticulously organised to preclude any possibility of reconsidering or going back, would produce a dangerous situation: the rise of a strong military power on the edge of the Roman province. It was, moreover, easy to foresee that the Helvetii, once they reached the West, would ally themselves with the winning Gallic factions, thus reinforcing them. When Caesar blocked and fortified the Rhône crossings to prevent the passage of the Helvetii, the pressure moved further north, into the territory of the Aedui.

On the pretext of protecting the lands of the Aedui, proclaimed 'allies and friends of the Roman people', Caesar intervened in the summer of 58 BC. He defeated the Helvetii at Bibracte (near Autun) and forced the remnants of the defeated army back to their starting point. From a military perspective it was a most important victory. A single battle broke the military might of one of the most warlike peoples, the Helvetii, in whom lay the hopes of those who supported the unity and independence of Gaul. But it was a two-edged victory. The anti-Roman faction of the Aedui, unenthusiastic participants in the campaign with their cavalry, was already looking to other agreements. Therefore the conditions imposed on the surviving Helvetii were relatively moderate:[15] some were settled in a sizeable area ceded by the Aedui. One motive – the most far-sighted – behind this moderation was strategic: to avoid creating with the collapse of the Helvetii a vacuum that the Germans could attempt to fill.

The Germans had entered with skill and determination into the struggle for hegemony in Gaul between the Aedui on the one hand and the Arverni and Sequani on the other. The Sequani had requested their help. Ariovistus, the German ruler, defeated the Aedui and demanded hostages. In addition he took possession of a third of the Sequani lands. When the Sequani called on the help of other Gauls (including the Aedui), Ariovistus achieved a brilliant victory in pitched battle against them. Thus he consolidated his dominion over the Sequani and encouraged further German incursions into their territory. Caesar decided to mount a frontal opposition to this increasing spread of German dominance across the Rhine. 'The war with Ariovistus', writes Camille Jullian, 'was the natural consequence of the subjugation of the Helvetii.'[16]

Caesar began by reminding Ariovistus of certain indispensable conditions for maintaining the *status* of ally: he must respect the territory of Gaul, stop the passage of Germanic tribes across the Rhine, and return hostages to the Aedui. Ariovistus reacted sharply. As an ally he expected to be treated as an equal, not subjected to injunctions. Caesar's response was an armed attack. He well knew that if he wanted Gaul in his power he had to get rid of Ariovistus, so he penetrated into Sequani territory as far as Vesontio (Besançon), where, without any illusions about the outcome, he held final vain negotiations with Ariovistus. Then he confronted him in battle in what is now Upper Alsace (Mulhouse), forcing him to retreat across the Rhine (September 58).

After this success, which had long-term consequences for the Celtic-Germanic balance on the Rhine,[17] Caesar deliberately proceeded to widen the conflict. To this end, availing himself of the proconsular *imperium*, he raised two additional legions in Cisalpine

Gaul during the winter of 58–57 and re-entered Gaul in the spring of 57 with an audacious scheme that had obvious political consequences: to take the conflict directly into the north of the country, attacking in their own territory the Belgic tribes which were the military core of northern Gaul and which for some time had been ready to attack.[18] He obtained the co-operation of the Aedui, but did not succeed in destroying the unity of the opposing forces. In the decisive battle on the Aisne he found himself facing a coalition of all the Belgic tribes (including the Remi), which he defeated after a bitter clash.[19] However, he met tenacious, heroic resistance from the Nervii, who were finally subdued after a fierce struggle (the battle of Sambre).[20]

The next year the conflict moved west, to Brittany, against the Aremorican tribes and the Veneti. In the meantime Publius Licinius (Crassus), son of the triumvir and Caesar's commander (*legatus*), subdued the Aquitani in the south-west.[21]

Caesar was already looking across the Channel as a result of the close ties between the populations of Normandy and Brittany and those of southern Britain. Crassus was entrusted with a first exploration of the opposite coast in the late summer of 57, while Caesar himself directed operations against the Veneti. This was a totally new military venture. Whereas the Veneti had a powerful fleet, the Romans had none in the Atlantic. There was no choice but to construct one on the Loire (the Liger) during the winter of 57–56, with crews recruited from sailors in the coastal towns. The Veneti had retreated to towns in inaccessible positions on peninsulas which were difficult to approach by land or sea.[22] Battle could not be attempted until the new Roman Atlantic fleet was ready. The clash came in the Bay of Quiberon (Sinus Veneticus). The Veneti had 220 ships of gigantic proportions constructed of oaken beams, with immense sails. The Roman vessels were lighter and flatter, and powered by oars. The greater height of the enemy ships made boarding arduous and javelin-throwing less certain of success. The Roman ruse that confounded the Veneti was to use scythe-blades tied to the end of long poles to cut the ropes supporting their sails (on which these giants of the sea relied for their speed and mobility). With their sails down, the oarless ships of the Veneti fell prey to the Roman triremes. Several were lost in this way; the remnants of the Veneti fleet attempted to flee but were suddenly becalmed. Caesar thus succeeded in seizing almost the entire enemy fleet.

The consequences of this memorable battle transcended the campaign for supremacy in Gaul: the control of the Veneti over navigation in the Bay of Biscay and in the Channel was destroyed. The geopolitical balance was changed in a much greater area, and the Romans could begin in earnest their preparations for expansion in the direction of Britain. Caesar's repression of the defeated was brutal. As a pretext he used a 'violation of international law' (the arrest by the Veneti of Roman officials charged with requisitions). The entire Veneti senate was executed and the mass of the population was reduced to slavery and sold. It is one of the least edifying episodes of this not particularly edifying campaign. The whole area was not under Roman control, however. The Morini took refuge in the forests and turned to guerrilla warfare.

The greatest danger for the precarious Caesarian scheme of new conquests, however, once more came from across the Rhine. In the winter of 56–55 the Usipetes and Tencteri, driven from their centres by the Suebi, crossed the Rhine near Xanten[23] and pushed out the Menapii, who occupied the left bank of the Rhine, downstream from Cologne. Caesar claims that the invaders numbered 430,000 souls.[24] Returning from the Luca meeting, he convened a conference of all the Gallic leaders before attacking the Usipetes and Tencteri in the recently occupied territories. With Gallic contingents as partners, he caught up with the enemy at the junction of the Rhine and the Meuse, a short distance from Xanten. The Germans continued to press for an accord; Caesar, however, sought only a pretext to massacre them. Through deception he got the better of them. The pretext was a sortie of Usipetes cavalry against the cavalry of Caesar's Gallic allies. In the encounter some of the Gallic collaborators dearest to Caesar were killed.[25] Notwithstanding the incident, the German leaders went to the scheduled meeting with Caesar. He received them, but had them treacherously slaughtered. Then he attacked opponents who were disunited, without leadership, and indiscriminately committed an act of genocide against them all, including their women and children.[26]

This massacre was viewed as an inhuman crime even in Rome, where Cato, undoubtedly for reasons to do with the internal political struggle, went so far as to demand that the proconsul be handed over to the enemy.[27] The presumed lack of genuine humanitarian motivation in his proposition is no reason to dismiss the demand of this tenacious opponent of Caesar. It shows that the enormity of the crime was noticed, at least. None the less, the Senate, a prey to 'imperialist intoxication' (in Carcopino's words), decreed a colossal *supplicatio* in honour of the Caesarian carnage.[28]

As for modern historians, the split in their verdicts is significant. Camille Jullian is damning: 'it was the most undistinguished of Caesar's campaigns and the most cowardly of his acts'.[29] 'This deliberate massacre', says the *Cambridge Ancient History*, 'is the most disgraceful of Caesar's actions and the worst example of the atrocities which have often been perpetrated in collisions between civilized and barbarian races.'[30] Napoleon, in his *Précis des guerres de César*, does not even mention the extent of this massacre.[31] Mommsen defends Caesar in almost lawyer-like fashion:

> While negotiations as to this were going on, a suspicion arose in the mind of the Roman general that the Germans only sought to gain time till the bands of horsemen sent out by them had returned. Whether this suspicion was well founded or not, we cannot tell; but confirmed in it by an attack, which in spite of the *de facto* suspension of arms a troop of the enemy made on his vanguard, and exasperated by the severe loss thereby sustained,[32] Caesar believed himself entitled to disregard every consideration of international law.

Mommsen then describes what he defines as 'rather a man-hunt than a battle', and concludes:

> The behaviour of Caesar towards those German immigrants met with severe and just censure in the Senate [in reality by Cato, not the Senate]; but, however little it can be excused, *the German encroachments were emphatically checked by the terror which it occasioned*.[33]

With Olympian detachment, Engels, in an unfinished essay on the Germans, attributes the end of the Usipetes and Tencteri to the highly destructive mechanism of the migrations: 'There were 180,000 Usipetes and Tencteri who crossed the Rhine; almost all perished in battle or during the flight. It is not surprising that, in this long epoch of migrations, entire peoples disappeared without trace.'[34] However, some lines above he records that, in the case of these two tribes, their defeat was not due entirely to the Roman fighting superiority, but also 'to the violation of treaties by the Romans'.[35]

The Italian nationalists adopt quite a different tone. Giulio Giannelli writes:

> It seemed opportune to Caesar to induce a salutary fear of Roman arms in these regions. Caesar first of all turned on the Germanic people of the Usipetes and the Tencteri, who had crossed the Rhine to drive their raids into the territory of the Treviri: once these hordes were wiped out he had a bridge constructed across the river and crossed to the right bank, passing through the country of his allies.[36]

Giannelli expresses disgust, demonstrating once again that in the field of historical research no event can receive a final, comforting and unanimous 'definitive' appraisal. Historiography divides scholars, and its weapon is constant reassessment.

In the summer of 55 BC Caesar opened a new front: Britain. The season was too far advanced for a large expedition that could take full advantage of the explorations carried out earlier by Publius Crassus. This was only an initial foray. As late as the twentieth century, one historian, inspired by British patriotism, writes:

> No military or political interests of the Roman empire were served by this attempt to extend it beyond its natural boundaries,[37] but Roman greed exaggerated the wealth of the unknown island, and a victorious expedition to Britain would be a spectacular success more likely to impress the imagination of Caesar's contemporaries than his great achievements on the continent.[38]

In these words there is an echo of Edward Gibbon, according to whom the expedition had been desired essentially because of a hunger for pearls, as Suetonius attested on the basis of sources hostile to Caesar.

This first expedition, whether because it was late, or because of the shipwreck of the vessels used to transport the Roman cavalry,[39] was on a reduced scale and not very productive. At first the tribes of Kent submitted to the invaders, but when they saw the modest war apparatus and realised the difficulties in which Caesar found himself (in fact he never moved from his camp for fear of having to risk combat without cavalry),[40] they took heart and attacked the Roman camp, only to be defeated decisively.[41] Renewed subjugation followed, and then Caesar withdrew without serious blotches on his balance sheet.[42]

The second expedition set sail early in July 54. Five legions and 2,000 Gallic cavalry constituted a great expeditionary force.[43] Everything pointed to a triumphal march, the more so because the Britons were divided among themselves and far from forming any united anti-Roman alliance like the one then taking shape on the continent. However, once again inclement weather seriously damaged the fleet (which they had made the mistake of not beaching). Caesar was forced to return in haste to the coast where he had disembarked and repair the damage. But much precious time had been wasted: scarcely two months remained before the end of the season favourable for operations. Moreover, the Britons had reunited in the meantime against the invaders under the leadership of Cassivellaunus, the ruler of the region north of the Thames.

On a strictly military level the superiority of the Roman invaders was indisputable. Even the use of war chariots (by now outdated in Gaul) posed no serious difficulties to the Celtic cavalry which was fighting under the Roman colours. However, Cassivellaunus, who did not manage to hold the Romans on the other side of the Thames,[44] resorted to guerrilla tactics.[45] By inflicting a steady trickle of casualties, he made the countryside insecure and any advance futile. As usual it took treachery by some Britons, under the command of Mandubracius, to resolve the conflict. Cassivellaunus, weakened by the defection and disillusioned by a failed attack on the Roman camp, was forced to accept the conditions which Caesar was in a hurry to impose, because alarming news was arriving from Labienus about the danger of a large-scale revolt in Gaul, only recently subjugated. These conditions provided guarantees for Mandubracius, 'protected by the Romans',[46] and the promise of a yearly tribute, which was not taken too seriously by either of the parties. At the beginning of autumn Caesar set sail for Gaul. With the twofold incursion into Britain militarily challenging and in reality hardly profitable, but skilfully promoted in his reports,[47] Caesar's image triumphed. Catullus, in a poem addressed to Furius and Aurelius, the 'comites Catulli', summed up Caesar's great feats thus: 'Caesaris visens monimenta magni / Gallicum Renum, horribile aequor ulti- / mosque Britannos'[48] ('[whether Catullus will] visit the memorials of great Caesar, the Gaulish Rhine, the formidable Britons, remotest of men'). 'Great Caesar', *Caesar Magnus*, is clearly being compared with *Pompeius Magnus* (the title *Magnus* goes back to Alexander). With his thrust into the remotest north, where Romans could only imagine the Britons, the proconsul of Gaul was seeking to lend his endless campaigns an aura of greatness and achievement in foreign lands, an aura equal to that surrounding the figure of Pompey. Bloody battles fought for the sake of prestige exerted a lasting influence on public opinion in Rome and Italy. But the fact remains that, 'No Roman troops had been left behind in Britain to secure the fulfilment of the peace-terms, and it is doubtful whether the tribute was ever paid.'[49]

But the edifice Caesar had built with so little concern for the human cost was at serious risk of being destroyed by the rebellion that smouldered, like embers beneath the ashes, among the tribes of Gaul. It developed fully only when it found in Vercingetorix, the king of the Arverni, a leader capable of unifying, if only temporarily, the many Gallic tribes.

The old disputes were by then all but forgotten in the face of the oppression, economic above all, of the conquering army. Contrary to his law on provincial government, Caesar had squeezed the vast, newly conquered region, convinced, evidently, that those 'rights' which his legislation guaranteed to subjects should become effective only later, when the country had been completely worn down and subjugated. The fact is that Gallic gold had flowed into the hands of the conquerors (including their commander), while immense profits continued to flow in from the sale of prisoners.[50] All this could not but feed rebellion and provide an impetus to one who aspired, with perhaps excessive optimism, to reunite as well as liberate the country.

The revolt developed in a number of stages. The first sign of the impending storm was the assassination by the Carnutes of Tasgetius, a sovereign imposed on them by the Romans, who had co-operated with Caesar in all the campaigns.[51] Then came the turn of the Eburones, instigated by Indutiomarus[52] and led by Ambiorix, who set a deadly ambush for fifteen Roman cohorts under the command of Sabinus and Cotta, and annihilated them. The revolt then extended to the Nervii, who had been summoned to the struggle by Ambiorix. The Roman commander in the region was Quintus Cicero, who, having feared the worst, was saved by Caesar – who arrived with three legions.[53] It is at this point that Caesar, providing us with a fine example of 'secret war', describes the episode of the message sent by javelin into the besieged camp and belatedly discovered by its intended recipients.[54]

The myth of the invincibility of the occupiers began to dispel. In a colonial war there is nothing more dangerous for the occupying power than a defeat. For the first time since the start of the conflict Caesar decided to winter in Gaul. Labienus took on the rebellion in the north-east. He knew very well that Indutiomarus – chief of the Treveri – who opposed him with great tactical ability, avoiding costly encounters, was the only one who could win the sympathies of the restless Gallic community of the Centre and thus expand the revolt. Therefore he determined to liquidate him at any cost. Mustering an enormous Gallic cavalry force in his camp by night, Labienus chose the opportune moment for a sortie against the Treveri: the cavalry-men, attracted by the promise of a large reward, were instructed to capture Indutiomarus even if the others escaped. And this is what happened in a ferocious manhunt which Caesar describes with his customary coolness and elegance on the last page of his *Commentaries*, book 5.[55]

In the winter of 54–53 Caesar, with the legions lent to him by Pompey (which later became involved at the outbreak of the civil war), believed he was in a position to achieve the total pacification of the country.[56] With a force now numbering ten legions, he forced the submission of the Nervii, the Senones and the Carnutes, as well as, for the first time, the Menapii in the north. Meanwhile Labienus defeated the Treveri once more. The Eburones remained unbeaten: Caesar was convinced that he had isolated them, but he was wrong. He decided to put on another demonstration of his strength for the benefit of the Germans. As before, after the massacre of the Tencteri and the Usipetes, he built a bridge across the Rhine in order to be able to swoop more rapidly and menacingly across the border. He hoped for a conclusive encounter with the Germans but this objective eluded him, nor was it prudent to pursue it in the generally uncertain circumstances. This time the bridge was not dismantled. Part of it was left standing, protected by a garrison of twelve cohorts.[57] Having returned to Gaul, Caesar sought to put an end once and for all to the armed hostility of the Eburones and above all to capture the elusive Ambiorix. However, this time the manhunt failed. Despite his aversion to the elusive enemy, there is, in Caesar's description of the failure of this relentless hunt, admiration for the Gallic leader's 'technical' ability and his skill in time and again effecting a narrow escape during the exhausting pursuit.[58]

It was a mistake to punish (by flogging and decapitation) the leaders of the Senones and the Carnutes as if they were provincial rebels. This brutal gesture could only favour the concerted and general insurrection of central Gaul early in 52. The strategic intuition of the revolt's leaders, among whom Vercingetorix was emerging,[59] turned to action while Caesar was still in Cisalpine Gaul and the occupying troops were divided between the north (six legions under Labienus), the East (two legions in the Treveri lands and two on the territory of the Lingones), and the south (the standing troops in the province). Caesar himself, describing the effect of a surprise attack, explains that, faced with the unforeseen situation that was unfolding, he hesitated between two equally risky strategic possibilities: to bring the legions stationed in the north closer, exposing them to the danger of surprise attacks (moreover, without him), or else to cross a territory himself which by this time was far from secure.[60]

With the province and, in particular, Narbonne fortified, Caesar struck the first surprise blow, interrupting the rebels' almost uncontested march. Although the Cévennes were still covered in deep snow which almost blocked the passes,[61] he pushed through a passage that was considered impossible to the heart of the Arverni lands, which he ruthlessly laid waste, forcing Vercingetorix to return to his country. Then Caesar crossed the Aedui territory and rejoined the two legions encamped among the Lingones, thus re-establishing contact with the main part of his army.

At this point the strategy of both sides was changing. For Caesar it was preferable to delay as long as possible the clash with Vercingetorix, in order to be better prepared for it. For the rebels it was necessary to force the Romans into continual skirmishes, while at the same time starving the legions by a policy of scorched earth all around them, thus compelling them to capitulate. But the scorched earth policy was not popular with the rebels themselves, as may be seen from the fact that Vercingetorix was unable to pursue his proposal to abandon and lay waste the town of Avaricum – under attack from the Romans, who planned to occupy it and use it as a base. Vercingetorix was thus forced to defend it, at great cost in resources, from a fortified position to the north-east of the town. In the end, by exploiting their superior military technology with a huge earthwork, which made possible a surprise attack,[62] the Romans seized the town and proceeded to another total and indiscriminate massacre, as part of a new strategy of terror.[63] For Vercingetorix this was a severe blow, which confirmed – too late – that his strategy, rejected by his own side, had been correct.

Now the initiative passed to the Romans. Caesar's plan was to strike at the enemy in the heart of the Arverni lands. Vercingetorix did not succeed in blocking this by cutting one of the bridges over the river Allier: the Romans repaired it, and at that point all the Gallic army could do was withdraw into the fortified town of Gergovia and prepare for a long siege. However, Vercingetorix had the cunning and presence of mind to station part of his forces on the hills to the south and east of Gergovia, where the enemy could be expected to attack. Caesar realised at once that it would be impossible to storm the town. Gergovia would not be easy prey. For the Romans, with a total of six legions, it was not possible to encircle completely and besiege all the fortified points, including those on the nearby hills. Caesar first considered withdrawing, but then he noticed a gap in the enemy lines and launched a successful assault on the defensive positions on the heights close to Gergovia. The false move was an attack on the town itself (blamed by Caesar on an unauthorised initiative from his own men), which resulted in a rout with over 700 dead (including many officers).[64]

The defeat, suffered this time by Caesar in person rather than his commanders, led to the immediate defection of the Aedui. But by going over to the rebels they upset the internal balance of their forces: the very leadership of Vercingetorix was called into question, and he had to have his command confirmed at a general assembly in Bibracte.[65] Encouraged by this success, he increased his cavalry to 15,000 men, and then sought to shift operations towards the Roman province. Caesar moved promptly, and not without risk, to defend it. It was at this stage that the battle with the gravest consequences took place: the German cavalry came to Caesar's rescue and forced Vercingetorix to fall back on Alesia.[66] There the leader of the Gauls took up position and prepared for a siege, while managing to send his cavalry into the surrounding country to bring the maximum forces to his relief.[67] His plan was to mount an assault in the rear of Caesar's besieging forces.

Compared to the siege of Gergovia, the situation here seemed more favourable to the besiegers. The fortified area (Mont Auxois) was smaller, and Caesar now had ten legions at his disposal. But it was clear that the reinforcements called out by Vercingetorix would arrive long before the besieged gave any signal of capitulation. Caesar therefore decided upon a most ambitious feat of military engineering: a double line of trenches and bastions – the inner one for the assault on Alesia, and the outer one to repel the impending attack by the relieving army raised in the rest of Gaul.[68]

According to Caesar's estimate, the Gallic army which came to relieve Alesia numbered 250,000 foot soldiers and 8,000 cavalry.[69] This was a powerful and disciplined force, well able to coordinate its actions with the operations of Vercingetorix and his men from inside Alesia, especially against the Roman positions to the south. Caesar fought against Vercingetorix, Labienus against the relief force, which sought to encircle the besiegers. The final victory of the Romans was due partly to the strength of Caesar's double ring, but also to his decisive move at the height of the battle: he sent part of his Roman cavalry to attack the newly arrived relief army from the rear, and succeeded in dispersing it.[70]

Vercingetorix, who enjoyed the standing of a great leader, resolved to avoid a massacre of his forces. On the day after the defeat he gave himself up to Caesar, in order to spare his people the suffering of a debilitating siege and merciless plunder. He addressed his people and explained that 'he had undertaken that campaign, not for his own occasions, but for the general liberty'.[71] He left Alesia alone, on horseback, and resplendent in his finest suit of armour. And alone he presented himself to Caesar, rode once round the chair on which Caesar was sitting, dismounted, took off his armour, and sat down on the ground in front of the proconsul, before being led away.[72] His fate was appalling. For six long years he was kept in captivity for the triumphal procession marking the end of the Gallic war, a procession which Caesar held only when the long civil war was over, or rather, when he thought it was over. In August 46 BC, after the victory of Thapsus, when he celebrated four triumphs – the first being the Gallic war[73] – Vercingetorix was paraded as the victor's prisoner through the streets.[74] Shortly afterwards he was executed,[75] a few months before Caesar himself was assassinated.

From the moment of the brave and tragic capitulation of Vercingetorix the final 'pacification' of Gaul began. Caesar had at last triumphed, with the aid of groups of collaborators and important families. The Germans too had played their part whenever the opportunity offered. Along with his uncommon gift for strategy, these factors were a vital element in his victory. With his pitilessness, his paternalism and his shrewd mind, but also his willingness to study and understand the object – or victim – of his actions, he possessed all the qualities of a great colonialist. It is no accident, for example, that his long excursus on the customs and religions of the Celts and the Germans, which occupies much of his *Commentaries*, book 6, appears where it does:[76] as if he were seeking by ethnographic and sociological analysis to find the reasons for the defeat of those peoples in the moment their great but ill-starred rebellion began. As a colonialist he made a serious study of the peoples he had to fight against, live among, and reign over for so long.

The year following the defeat of Vercingetorix, 51 BC, was given over to re-establishing effective control over the territory as far as possible. To this end it was necessary to deal with or eliminate those second-rank leaders who still retained followers and prestige. Even with Commius, the king of the Atrebates, Caesar came to an understanding. (It was Commius who had launched ferocious attacks on Roman convoys in the area of Arras.) But Commius did not stay long in one place.[77] He fled to Britain,[78] where he was joined by other Atrebates and established an independent kingdom. As long as he remained on Gallic soil he made difficulties for the Romans, but the Romans held control. Caesar did not show the same bitter hostility towards him as he had towards Ambiorix.[79] He describes subsequent events in *Commentaries*, book 8,[80] only up the point where Commius and Antony reach accord concerning his personal safety.[81] In the case of Ambiorix the tone of his writing is furious. Ambiorix never gave up guerrilla action, and Caesar seethes with uncontrollable rage when he relates how, having failed to catch him,

> he deemed it the best thing, out of regard for his own prestige [*proximum suae dignitatis esse ducebat*], so completely to strip his territory of citizens, buildings, and cattle as to make Ambiorix hated by any of his subjects who might chance to survive, and to leave him no return to the state by reason of disasters so grievous.[82]

These tactics, aimed at discrediting a rebel in the eyes of his own people by laying upon him the blame for crimes committed by the occupier, is a time-honoured one, still practised today. What is striking is that Caesar boasts about it.

It was in Caesar's interests to push ahead with pacification as speedily as possible, not only because it was the only way to consolidate his rule after such a merciless genocide, but also for policy reasons: given deteriorating relations with the Senate, and presumably with Pompey too, it was vital not to have a restless and rebellious province at his back.

It would be wrong to suppose, however, that at this point the conquest of Gaul was complete. The modern notion of colonial conquest may be helpful here. The conquest of an entire territory is a prolonged process, lasting centuries. The colonial power gradually takes control of the conquered country. After the military phase, or while it is still in progress, fortresses, streets, towns and ports are occupied; communication routes are taken under firmer control, resistance movements suppressed, and local elites, where possible, co-opted. The countryside at this point is not under complete control. One example which demonstrates this well comes from Caesar's own career. As *propraetor* in Spain, Plutarch writes, he had conducted campaigns 'subduing the tribes *which before were not obedient to Rome*'.[83] Yet Spain had been a province since 197 BC, almost a century and a half before Caesar arrived as governor (61 BC), and the last revolt was put down, after a savage war, when Numantia fell in 133. But twenty years after Caesar's governorship, Asinius Pollio, governor of Further Spain, writes to Cicero complaining that bandit attacks are making it virtually impossible for Roman *tabellarii* (dispatch-carriers) to travel through certain mountainous regions of Baetica.[84]

This analogy may help us understand the extent to which we may speak of the 'Romanisation' of Gaul in the long period of Caesar's reign over it. It is a phenomenon which has its beginnings here and was reinforced primarily thanks to increasing participation by local ruling groups, and would bear visible and significant results only a century later, in the reign of the emperor Claudius. If one loses sight of this long-term aspect, one runs the risk of mythologising the works of Caesar. The comparison with Alexander the Great and the Hellenisation of the East, so beloved of his admirers (and still found in the young Droysen), confuses different realities. We can say with sober realism that in his nine-year Gallic campaign Caesar 'contrived with rare success, except in the two expeditions to Britain, to reconcile the interests of the empire with his own'.[85] The glory he had won was beginning to outshine that of Pompey the Great. And above all he had succeeded in assembling and leading a large army, of whose total devotion he could be quite sure. This is the basis on which he could launch his later career.

Notes

1 J. Carcopino, *Jules César*, 5th edn (Paris 1968), p. 252.
2 Ibid.
3 Caesar, *Gallic War* 2.35.4: 'Ob easque res ex litteris Caesaris dies quindecim supplicatio decreta est, quod ante id tempus accidit nulli.'
4 The episode narrated by Dio Cassius (39.25) gives some idea of the number and scale of these. According to Dio Cassius, Pompey once asked the consuls in the Senate to postpone the reading of a letter from Caesar regarding certain difficulties, and wait until the next report arrived, announcing the successful outcome of the operations.
5 The episode recorded by Dio Cassius is also an indication of this (see preceding note).
6 Later we shall see M. Caelius' activities as an anti-Caesar agitator (see Chapter 22).
7 Cicero, *Letters to his friends* 8.1.4.
8 Caesar, *Gallic War* 1.3.
9 Tacitus, *The Life of Julius Agricola* 12.1: 'Originally the people were subject to kings: now the quarrels and ambitions of petty chieftains divide them.'
10 Twentieth-century French scholars speak of a 'Gallic revolution' (occurring shortly before the invasion of Caesar) that was similar in all respects to the French Revolution of the end of the eighteenth century, even as regards its capacity to spread beyond the Rhine. But this is an analogy imposed with the benefit of hindsight.
11 Caesar, *Gallic War* 5.27.3 (Ambiorix speaks): 'ut non minus haberet iuris in se multitudo quam ipse in multitudinem'.
12 Dio Chrysostom 49.8.

13 See A. Demandt, *Die Kelten* (Munich 1998), pp. 78–9. An apt and well-informed summary.

14 Caesar, *Gallic War* 1.29.2–3. These statistics are based on *tabulae* written in Greek letters which were found by Caesar's men in the Helvetii encampment.

15 Approximately 200,000 died. It was an early 'genocide', with repeated massacres brought about by the Roman conquest.

16 C. Jullian, *Histoire de la Gaule*, vol. III, 5th edn (Paris 1920), p. 221.

17 At the news of Ariovistus' defeat the approximately 100,000 Germans who were hastening to cross the Rhine changed course and withdrew to the interior of the country (Caesar, *Gallic War* 1.54.1).

18 Caesar, *Gallic War* 2.1.1.

19 Caesar, *Gallic War* 2.3–5; 10–11.

20 Caesar, *Gallic War* 2.18–27.

21 Caesar, *Gallic War* 3.20–7. Only a quarter of the 50,000 Aquitani and Cantabri who fought against Crassus survived.

22 Caesar, *Gallic War* 3.12.1.

23 Caesar, *Gallic War* 4.4.2–7, with commentary by Jullian, *Histoire de la Gaule*, vol. III, p. 325, note 3.

24 Caesar, *Gallic War* 4.15.3; Appian, *Gallic History* 18; Plutarch, *Caesar* 22.

25 Among others Piso of Aquitania and his brother (Caesar, *Gallic War* 4.12.4–6).

26 Caesar, *Gallic War* 4.14.5. Caesar noted complacently that the Romans suffered only a few wounded.

27 Plutarch, *Caesar* 22; *Cato the Younger* 51. Caesar responded with a savage document that was to be read aloud in the Senate.

28 Caesar, *Gallic War* 4.38.5.

29 Jullian, *Histoire de la Gaule*, vol. III, p. 326.

30 *Cambridge Ancient History*, vol. IX, *The Roman Republic*, eds S. A. Cook, F. E. Adcock and M. P. Charlesworth (Cambridge 1951), p. 558. (The chapter on the conquest of Gaul is by C. Hignett.)

31 *Précis des guerres de César* par Napoléon, écrit par M. Marchand sous la dictée de l'Empereur [1819] (Paris 1836), p. 57.

32 In reality seventy-four knights of the allies of Gaul.

33 Theodor Mommsen, *The History of Rome*, trans. William Purdie Dickson (London 1894), vol. 5, pp. 60–1.

34 F. Engels, *Zur Urgeschichte der Deutschen* [1881/2], in *Marx – Engels – Werke*, vol. XIX (Berlin 1976), p. 431.

35 Ibid. p. 430.

36 G. Giannelli and S. Mazzarino, *Trattato di storia romana*, vol. I (Rome 1953), p. 428.

37 In reality this idea of the 'natural boundaries' of the empire was bizarre: Gaul was included, but not Britain.

38 *Cambridge Ancient History*, vol. IX, p. 559.

39 Caesar, *Gallic War* 4.28–9.
40 Caesar, *Gallic War* 4.30.1.
41 Caesar, *Gallic War* 4.34–5.
42 Caesar, *Gallic War* 4.36.
43 Caesar, *Gallic War* 5.8. The account of the second expedition comprises chs 8–23.
44 Caesar, *Gallic War* 5.18.
45 Caesar, *Gallic War* 5.19.1.
46 Caesar, *Gallic War* 5.22.5.
47 For example his *Commentaries*, book 5, on The *Gallic War*.
48 Catullus 11.10–12.
49 *Cambridge Ancient History*, vol. IX, p. 562.
50 Hignett, exaggerating, writes that 'every needy adventurer in Rome who could win Caesar's favour went to Gaul to restore his fortunes' (in *Cambridge Ancient History*, vol. IX).
51 Caesar, *Gallic War* 5.25.
52 Caesar, *Gallic War* 5.26.2.
53 Caesar, *Gallic War* 5.39–52. Caesar dedicated much space in the commentaries to the episode of Quintus Cicero and to praising his bravery on this occasion. He clearly had reasons for doing so.
54 Caesar, *Gallic War* 5.48.
55 Caesar, *Gallic War* 5.58.6: 'cum unum omnes peterent, in ipso fluminis vado deprehensus Indutiomarus interficitur caputque eius refertur in castra'.
56 Caesar, *Gallic War* 6.1: 'Quod cum Pompeius et rei publicae et amicitiae tribuisset.'
57 Caesar, *Gallic War* 6.29.3.
58 Caesar, *Gallic War* 6.43.3–5.
59 Whose father had been put to death for seeking to be king (*Gallic War* 7.4.1).
60 Caesar, *Gallic War* 7.6.
61 Caesar, *Gallic War* 7.8.
62 Caesar, *Gallic War* 7.24.
63 Caesar, *Gallic War* 7.28.4: 'nec fuit quisquam qui praedae studeret'.
64 Caesar, *Gallic War* 7.50–1.
65 Caesar, *Gallic War* 7.63.5–6.
66 Caesar, *Gallic War* 7.68.
67 Caesar, *Gallic War* 7.71.1–2.
68 Caesar, *Gallic War* 7.72.
69 Caesar, *Gallic War* 7.75.
70 Caesar, *Gallic War* 7.87.2.
71 Caesar, *Gallic War* 7.89.
72 Plutarch, *Caesar* 27. The words cited by Florus as being uttered by Vercingetorix, 'You are the best of men, and you have defeated me'

(1.45.26), are most probably the stereotypical product of imagination.

73 Suetonius, *Caesar* 37.1; Livy, *Periocha* 115.

74 Dio Cassius 43.19.4.

75 Ibid. It seems from Josephus' *Jewish War* 7.154 that he was throttled. See also M. Gelzer, *RE*, 'Vercingetorix', col. 1007, 12–14.

76 Caesar, *Gallic War* 6.11–28. With the second, this is one of the briefest of the eight *Commentaries*.

77 His adventures are very much in evidence in *Commentaries*, book 8.

78 Frontinus, *Stratagems* 2.13.11.

79 Caesar, *Gallic War* 8.24.4.

80 I have elsewhere shown that this is by Caesar up to ch. 8.48.9; see 'La lettera a Balbo e la formazione della raccolta cesariana', *ASNP*, ser. III, 23, 1 (1993), pp. 79–103, esp. pp. 94–5.

81 Caesar, *Gallic War* 8.48.8–9.

82 Caesar, *Gallic War* 8.24.4.

83 Plutarch, *Caesar* 12.

84 Cicero, *Letters to his friends* 10.31.1.

85 Hignett in *Cambridge Ancient History*, vol. IX, p. 573.

CHAPTER 15

The Black Book of the Gallic Campaign

We have become too humane not to be repelled by Caesar's triumphs.
Goethe

Caesar's Gallic campaign was not exactly viewed with enthusiasm by his contemporaries. This must be taken into account when estimating its 'long-term effects', whose 'inevitability' is often teleologically overestimated. There is doubtless a risk of adopting a colonialist view. The campaign was unprovoked and there was no real menace; it led to the destruction of the old civilisation, which was gradually replaced by a Romanised one; and Pliny and Plutarch agree that it was an act of genocide of monstrous proportions. It was all for one end: it is clear that the protagonist and instigator of the venture cynically used the genocide in the political struggle at home. Part of his objective was also to capture a huge number of slaves (according to Plutarch, one million), who were useful for demagogic purposes (one thinks of Caesar granting at least one slave to each of his soldiers). Caesar knew well that, without a counter to Pompey's military glory, an equal division of power with him would be impossible,[1] especially after Crassus' death.

Thus the impressive military achievement in Gaul in the years 58–51 BC (thanks to the renewal of the triumviral pact at the Luca conference and consequent extension of Caesar's provincial command) reveals itself as a twofold triumph: it was the vehicle of Romanisation of a large part of the North European West (as Mommsen observes with genuine enthusiasm, while suggesting a questionable comparison with the conquests of Alexander the Great); and at the same time it provided the aspiring *princeps* with the authority, military and legal, that he needed, as part of a long *praeparatio* for the day of reckoning and civil war.

The subsequent widespread enthusiasm for Caesar's conquest of Gaul, often viewed as another of the 'traces' which a kind of historical providence left on the world by means of its intermediary

Caesar, risks being truly misleading. It affected great historians like Mommsen and many others after him. These historians not only ennobled a ferocious conquest, placing it on a par with Alexander's Hellenisation of the East, but above all they credited to Caesar a *weltgeschichtlich* intention which perhaps was far from the mind of the proconsul of Gaul, and of which there is no indication in his elegant and elaborate *Commentaries* on that almost ten-year war. In the heat of the factional struggle, Cato, Caesar's most stubborn and consistent adversary, denounced the proconsul in the Senate for violation of the national rights of the Gallic tribes of the Usipetes and the Tencteri.[2] He knew it was unlikely that he would be heeded. Perhaps Cato was motivated by humanitarian feeling (his Stoic mentality could entertain such sensitivity; however, it was certainly lacking in most of his colleagues). The move was inspired by domestic politics, and it failed.

But even when Cicero, in his overall assessment of Caesar's career at the end of the *Second Philippic* – one of the orator's most truthful appraisals after many months spent mouthing fulsome praise during the dictatorship – conceded much to him after his death, he gave little consideration to that prolonged and ferocious war: 'res bello gesserat, quamvis reipublicae calamitosas, at tamen magnas'.[3] Great enterprises certainly – who could deny it? – but 'harmful to the republic'. Harmful because all prolonged, senseless wars are harmful, or because in the end this war was used *against* the republic? Perhaps both.

It is not a kind judgement, but neither is it reductive or one-sided. It is *necessarily* balanced by virtue of being presented in this dazzling *peroratio* as a counter to his devastating judgement of the still living Antony, the menacing political heir of the assassinated dictator. It is a well-crafted and wisely nuanced judgement. It is certainly not a sympathetic portrait. Cicero in almost everything he says maintains a distance. In particular he makes it very clear that Caesar's main gift to the people of Rome was to deter them forever from elevating a single individual to power[4] (here the orator was wrong); however, he does not overlook any of the strong endowments of the deceased. Yet on this balance sheet the great conquests do not figure in the 'column' of positive actions; certainly they are 'great', but *harmful*. Gaul as such is not even mentioned: the long Gallic campaign is included, to be sure, in Cicero's recollections of *labor* and *pericula*, but as one aspect within the factional struggle and in Caesar's irresistible rise to the *regnum*: 'for years he conceived the plan of *ruling*', yet 'magno labore, magnis periculis quod cogitarat effecerat'. Nothing else, not one word on the *fines imperii* in Gaul, Germany and Britain. Cicero knew how much it would have pleased Caesar had he struck that chord.

At the very beginning of *In Defence of Marcellus* (summer 46), he turned to the dictator and exclaimed:

> It is my practice to let my vision dwell upon the fact – aye, and to maintain it eagerly in daily converse – that all the achievements of our generals, of foreign nations and sovereign peoples and of the most renowned kings, can be compared with your own neither in the importance of the issues involved, nor in the multitude of engagements they comprise, nor in the diversity of battle-grounds nor in the manifold variety of warfare they present; and that lands the most widely severed could have been traversed by the footsteps of none in shorter time than they have been traversed I will not say by your marches but by your victories.[5]

Shortly before this he had proclaimed that nowhere in the world did there exist an intellectual force or an orator capable of recounting in detail the feats of Caesar, let alone exalting them adequately. And as he moved towards his conclusion, he offered an even clearer prophecy:

> Doubtless generations yet to come will stand aghast when they hear and read of the commands you have held and the provinces you have won – the Rhine, the Ocean, the Nile – your countless battles, your amazing victories, your largesses, and your triumphs.

This hyperbole captures the whole military career of the dictator, his victories in the four corners of the empire. One can say, however, that despite the panegyrical and in no way critical tone, on the whole the achievement in Gaul is overshadowed by those of Alexandria, Pharnakes and Thapsus, as well as his conquests during his long consulship. And even these do not rate an adequate mention, even in this context. An understanding of the epoch-making significance of the conquest of Gaul developed slowly and became established only in modern times.

The 'Black Book' of the conquest of Gaul by Rome was written by Pliny the Elder in the seventh book of his *Natural History* (91–9). It is a 'Black Book' – to use a modern expression – of extraordinary harshness, in which Caesar's crimes are set against the vastly different balance sheet of Pompey's long political and military career. As well as the many deaths resulting from the ferocious fratricidal war provoked by the ambition of one man when he crossed the Rubicon, we need, Pliny writes, to recall the 1.2 million people massacred by Caesar simply because he wanted to conquer Gaul. 'I would not myself count it to his glory that in addition to conquering his fellow-citizens he killed in his battles 1,192,000 human beings, a prodigious even if unavoidable wrong inflicted on the human race.' In addition he accuses Caesar of having concealed the huge number of those slaughtered in the great massacre: 'He himself confessed it by not publishing the casualties of the civil wars' (7.92). More indulgent historians, like Velleius Paterculus, speak of 400,000 deaths in Gaul and as many or more prisoners (2.47.1). Plutarch knows the 'round' figure of a million victims and a million prisoners (*Pompey* 67.10; *Caesar* 15.5), and in his biography *Cato the Younger* he speaks of 300,000 Germans being killed (51.1). And Appian, in his fragmentary *Gallic history* (1.12), tells of 400,000 dead in the campaign against the Usipetes and the Tencteri (55 BC) alone.

Plutarch furnishes these figures without criticism. On the contrary, they are an essential part of the Greek historian's comparison between Caesar and all other Roman leaders – to Caesar's advantage. These massacres and the masses of prisoners killed by Caesar are a sign of his greatness in Plutarch's eyes. It is Pliny who condemns with the greatest *moral* indignation what he calls Caesar's *crime against humanity*. Caesar himself, moreover, did not attempt to conceal the details. Here, to give but one example, is how he describes the carnage wrought upon the fleeing Belgae: 'Thus without any danger our men slew as great a host of them as daytime allowed, and, ceasing at sunset, retired according to orders into camp.'[6] With excessive aestheticism, Concetto Marchesi comments:

> One sees the sunny day rather than the bloody day: and the soldiers who returned at dusk to the calm of their camps, after massacring so many, were more like tired peasants returning to their village at the end of the day.[7]

Gaul, the Celtic world, was thus, through violence and genocide, brought into the realm of Roman 'civilisation'. Only a Napoleon III could praise Caesar (almost identifying with him) and at the same time raise monuments to Vercingetorix. The human and cultural loss which this genocide represented was recognised and denounced by, among others, the great historian Camille Jullian, who emphasised how Caesar's conquest of Gaul brought the autonomous development of Celtic civilisation to an abrupt end. Confirmation of the

Celts' cultural independence comes from recent excavations of Bibracte. We should not invent any 'other history' which did not happen, but we should guard against reducing the history of the Roman conquest to a paean on the inevitability of imperialism. On this Caesar's defenders and critics agree. With every report of a bloody victory by the proconsul, the acquiescent Senate decreed days of *supplicatio*. When, at the end of *Commentaries*, book 2, Caesar recalls the fortnight of *supplicatio* decreed by the Senate following victories over the Bellovaci, he notes complacently: 'quod ante id tempus accidit nulli' (2.35.4). After the massacre of the Usipetes and Tencteri there were twenty days of *supplicatio* (6.38.5). The proof of the senators' acquiescent enthusiasm was that the masses of slaves who thus reached the Roman market were coveted equally by Caesar's supporters and republican loyalists. Cato opposed the *supplicatio* after the victory over the Usipetes and Tencteri and suggested handing Caesar over to them as a perjurer, because the victory had been won through betrayal (evidently 'barbarians' were not to be credited with a sense of honour and loyalty – just as the Spanish conquistadores did not accept that the American Indians possessed a soul), but this idea is rather the fruit of Cato's irreconcilable political enmity, paradoxically expressed (Plutarch, *Caesar* 22.4; *Cato the Younger* 51). This became clear in what followed: Caesar responded with a very harsh letter against Cato, and Cato used this to launch an attack on Caesar in the Senate, which centred on the theme: 'it was not the sons of the Britons and the Celts whom they must fear, but Caesar himself'.[8]

The Romanisation of Gaul is a phenomenon of such historical magnitude, however, that one wonders whether Pliny's precise account-keeping of the casualties (and his searing allegation that Caesar had concealed the figures) should not take second place, on the historical balance sheet, to what can be regarded as the crucial event in the shaping of medieval and modern Europe: the Romanisation of the Celts, which resulted from Caesar's conquest.

The savage conquest of the New World, achieved through the convergent actions of conquistadores and missionaries on behalf of Old Europe, still raises the question of its human cost. Here, too, there have been attempts to write a 'Black Book', which have usually been pushed aside by the argument of the historical necessity of the conquest. However, while today it is possible to ask 'what would history have been like without Pizarro?', one still cannot pose the question 'what would Europe have been like without Julius Caesar?'

It seems as though such an accusation, in the long time that separates us from those events, has diminished and faded in view of the comprehensive historical balance sheet.

The debate on the figure of Caesar really revolves around a completely different problem: the question of whether he was in fact driven by personal ambition rather than the intention of opening a new page of history. As if the two can so easily be separated in the actions of a great politician! In Caesar's case the argument over decades and centuries has centred on the theme of the destruction of the old republic, for which he is either praised or blamed, not on the human cost of the Romanisation of Gaul. Centuries later Simone Weil, in her writings from the late 1930s on *Hitler and Roman Foreign Affairs*,[9] puts the accent back – in the wake of Jullian's studies – on that massacre, and on the different history of that brutal conquest which might have been written by historians of Gallic origin (if there had been any), not subservient, like the Greeks of the time, to Rome. Goethe, however, had already voiced the now requisite 'repugnance' of modern scholars, who have 'become too humane' for 'Caesar's triumphs'.

Notes

1 R. Syme, *The Roman Revolution* [1939] (Oxford 2002), p. 47, suggests that the 'maximal' programme of Caesar had to be to share power in the republic with Pompey for some considerable time. This cannot be ruled out, but it is at odds with Cicero, who saw Caesar from the very beginning as a claimant to the *regnum*, which necessarily entailed a collision with the other *princeps in re publica*. It is certain, however, that a politician's plans are never fully formed at conception, just as a chess-player's moves are only conceived in the course of the game and cannot be predicted more than three or four moves ahead.

2 It is related by Tanusius Geminus, who was certainly a witness to the proposal in the Senate. See Chapter 14.

3 Cicero, *Philippics* 2.116. On this passage, see below, Chapter 42.

4 Cicero, *Philippics* 2.117: 'of very many evils which he has inflicted on the Commonwealth, there has emerged this much good: quod didicit populus Romanus quantum cuique crederet a quibus caveret!'

5 Cicero, *In Defence of Marcellus* 5.

6 Caesar, *The Gallic War* 2.11.

7 C. Marchesi, *Storia della letteratura latina*, 8th edn, vol. I (Milan and Messina 1959), pp. 345–6.

8 Plutarch, *Cato the Younger* 51.4.

9 Published in a collection of essays by Gallimard in 1960.

Part III

The Long Civil War

CHAPTER 16

Towards the Crisis

Without doubt the most dangerous moment for Caesar in the political crisis which erupted in Rome, while he was occupied with the revolt of Vercingetorix, was the designation of Pompey as 'consul without colleague' (*consul sine collega*) at the end of February 52 BC. This happened in a most traumatic way from the point of view of the triumvirate (which had been strengthened at Luca but 'decapitated' by the death of Crassus at Carrhae, in Syria, in the catastrophic campaign against the Parthians). The destructive and uncontrollable street fighting which led to the assassination of Clodius at Bovillae (18 January 52) was diametrically opposed to Caesar's interests. It was not in his interest to appear as the instigator of a subversive faction such as Clodius', nor was it in his interest that the deleterious activities of that faction should push Pompey to seek the backing of the *factio* (and vice versa). What most conflicted with his intention never to break with Pompey was the street fighting: it could lead to a state of emergency (*senatus consultum ultimum*), with effective power in the hands of the proconsul stationed at the gates of Rome – Pompey.[1] And this is precisely what happened, precipitated by the murder of Clodius. The Senate resorted to emergency powers and charged Pompey himself ('qui pro consule ad urbem erat', as the *senatus consultum* said),[2] together with the tribunes of the plebs and the *interrex*, with 'assuring the salvation of the republic'.[3] The outcome of this extreme step was the weighty decision, from the constitutional, to say nothing of the political, point of view, to nominate Pompey (without elections, of course) *consul sine collega*: a form analogous to dictatorship, and which emerged from a not dissimilar procedure. On the political level it was an affront to Caesar, who had no part in the decision. For as long as the triumviral pact had functioned, the designation of consuls, and particularly the awarding of a consulate to one of them, had been the result of meticulous accords between the potentates. This time it was the *factio* which awarded Pompey his third consulate, in addition giving him a position of total

constitutional preponderance, adding these powers to his proconsular authority. The fact that, with his usual gift for maintaining
appearances, Pompey would share the consulate for the last months
of the year with his father-in-law Quintus Caecilius Metellus Pius
Scipio Nasica did nothing to diminish the gravity of the change.[4]

Caesar's response reflected his realism and constant striving for
compromise. He stopped 'his' tribunes, who were pressing for him to
be designated Pompey's colleague, and instead authorised a counter-
proposal, which was accepted by Pompey:

> that he be permitted to stand for a second consulship without coming
> to Rome, when the term of his governorship drew near its end, to
> prevent his being forced for the sake of the office to leave his province
> prematurely and without finishing the war.[5]

This highly controversial accord, which Pompey later attempted –
after some indecision – to repudiate, became a fixed point in Caesar's
strategic design from that moment on. His overriding imperative was
not so much to join Pompey, except in a purely nominal way, in the
quasi-dictatorship of 52, but rather to assure himself a return to the
consulship, not as *privatus*, on the expiry of the second five-year
period in Gaul. In the meantime he continued to manifest his presence
in Rome by means of widespread involvement in economic concerns
individually and with others, setting up public utilities and prestigious
works like the *Forum Iulium*, whose site cost more than a hundred
million sesterces.[6] At the same time, on his own initiative and counting on very lavish Gallic plunder, he increased his legionaries' pay.
And, as we know, he gave each soldier a slave as war booty.[7]

Caesar, when he mentions these events, does not fail to note at the
beginning of his seventh *Commentary* that the essence of the *senatus
consultum ultimum* was that Pompey – though pro-magistrate in Spain
(but in reality firmly encamped at the gates of Rome) – had been permitted to recruit in all of Italy.[8] He used an expression, probably drawn
from the text of the Senate opinion: 'that all the inhabitants of Italy of
military age should take an oath'.[9] After which he added that for his
part he 'would arrange for recruiting in the province' (that is, in Gallia
Cisalpina and Narbonensis). This is a very important passage, in the
first place for the confidence with which Caesar lets it be understood,
by the casual reader, that his recruitment in Gallia Cisalpina was a way
of complying with the Senate opinion! Obviously it was not: for the
simple reason that the Senate's peremptory and dramatic order was
addressed to Pompey alone and concerned Italy, understood *stricto*

sensu.[10] In fact it was Caesar's response to the reality of Pompey's military reinforcement, in a situation which, moreover, could only euphemistically be defined as being within the limits of legality. Thanks to a very strained interpretation of the constitution, Pompey holds the proconsular *imperium* (applied to crucial provinces endowed with legions, such as Spain) and at the same time the consular (he is moreover the sole consul!), and is invited to undertake mass recruitment throughout Italy: thus to promote a sort of *coniuratio Italiae* in his name.[11] For this reason Caesar responds with his own recruitment, but does not hesitate to place it confidently under the aegis of the Senate opinion. It was the only response which he could give while formally stressing his own loyalty and rejecting the impolitic pressure of his own men to put himself, as a colleague of Pompey, in an equally illegal position. To proceed with new recruitments signifies instead his drawing the only possible effective advantage from the fast-developing crisis.

These recruitments on the spontaneous initiative of the proconsul (with only specious reference to the Senate opinion) already overstepped the bounds of legality. When Suetonius speaks of the 'spontaneous' recruitments for example of the *Alaudae* legion (added to the legions allocated to him by the Senate) by Caesar in Gaul, he stresses that the proconsul was raising them 'privato sumptu'.[12] The *Alaudae* legion, being meritorious and very faithful, was granted Roman citizenship en bloc by Caesar. In this climate it clearly made good tactical sense for both sides to continue to profess loyalty to the legitimate authorities of the republic.

It is probable that the *factio*, as Caesar called it, did not think that he would go so far as the 'Sullan' choice of marching against the republic: they insisted that he should return to Rome as *privatus* and hedged him in with a range of judicial measures from which it would not be easy to escape, convinced that he would not dare to risk armed conflict with the Senate and against the most influential potentate, who had behind him a solid clientele stretching to the East and West. The disconcerting novelty of Caesar's move was to employ Sulla's extreme tactic against the 'party' which had been Sulla's with the support of the forces which Sulla had attempted to humiliate.

Marcus Claudius Marcellus (the consul of 51) announced in an edict to the Senate that he was bringing before it a proposal of extreme importance for the security of the republic. His proposal was to relieve Caesar before his mandate as proconsul in Gaul and Illyricum expired.[13] His argument was irresistible: it was clear from the dispatches and from Caesar's own 'victory bulletins' that by this time the Gallic war had been victoriously concluded, so it remained only to disband the army.[14] But his frontal attack did not stop here. He went on to tackle the thorniest question: Caesar's request that he be allowed to stand for office *in absentia* at the next consular elections. He argued that, now that the war was over, the recall of the proconsul of Gaul was necessary precisely because he wished to stand.

This candidature had been the subject of negotiation between the rulers. In 55 BC, when the triumviral pact had been renewed and Pompey and Crassus were once again joint consuls, the *Lex Pompeia Licinia* had prolonged the proconsular *imperium* of Caesar for a further five years. Caesar would be 'protected', endowed with *imperium*, and therefore unassailable by political adversaries, until the end of 49, and in that year would obtain the consulate for 48, observing the ten-yearly interval required for the highest office of the republic. Contrary to the rule dating from 63 BC, the year of Cicero's consulship, forbidding candidates to stand *in absentia*, that is, far from Rome, a plebiscite moved by the tribunes in the year of uncontrolled disturbances, the year of Pompey's consulship *sine collega*, 52 BC, expressly permitted Caesar to put his own name forward even if absent. But Pompey, master of the corrosive double game and always able to place himself in a position which appeared most 'respectful of legality', attempted to undermine this strong point in Caesar's favour by passing a *Lex de imperio magistratuum*, which reasserted the candidates' obligation to be present in Rome, and did not signal any exemption for the proconsul of Gaul. Caesar voiced his disappointment and Pompey sidestepped by declaring that he had 'forgotten', and adding that anyway he could not put it right 'until the law has been inscribed on a tablet of bronze and deposited in the Treasury'.[15] Caesar thus had an opportunity to start a dispute, and did so, pointing out the contrast between the new rule and the tribunal plebiscite. But his position was weakened, not only by the increasingly complex legal situation, but because Pompey was clearly becoming more and more distant. Nor did it escape him that the attack on him was gaining strength and things were moving towards a showdown. The action of the consul Marcellus in instituting an unprecedented measure to deprive of citizenship the colonists installed by Caesar at Como by the *rogatio Vatinia* could only be understood as signalling a frontal assault, aimed at demolishing Caesar's position. Marcellus' explanation was a clear provocation: that the concession of citizenship had been motivated *per ambitionem*;[16] that is, in order to win votes.

Caesar used to repeat a sentence which should have thrown light on his true intentions for his adversaries: 'Now that I am the leading Roman of my day, it will be harder to pull me down from first to second place than degrade me to the ranks.'[17] In this case Suetonius does not say whence he drew this saying of Caesar's: he confines himself to saying: 'it was said that he often repeated it'. Considering the assiduity with which Suetonius references Caesar's words and expressions drawn from the *Histories* of Asinius Pollio, we may take it that here, too, the information comes from him. And that would be entirely in accord with the attention Asinius pays to the motives by which Caesar himself explains his actions, beyond what is written in his *Commentaries* where everything is suffused with propaganda, as Asinius emphasises.

Whether or not this indiscretion can be attributed to Asinius, it gives us a clear idea of the state of mind in which Caesar was preparing to resist the concerted attack on him. As a programmatic declaration it says clearly that he would not step back, precisely because he well knew that the real defeat lay in stepping back 'from first to second place', and losing 'first place' in reality meant losing everything. The explanation for this seemingly cryptic observation came with the utmost brutality at the battle of Pharsalus, with victory won and thousands of dead strewn on the field. And it is Asinius Pollio who reports this explanation, as both Suetonius and Plutarch attest in concord. We shall return to this point. For the moment it is clear that Caesar did not intend to retreat so much as one step, that he was ready for the struggle. If understood rightly, this phrase signified that not even the prospect of civil war frightened him.

For the moment, however, he put to work all of the 'constitutional' weapons at his disposal: from the tribunal veto (*intercessio*) to provoking the other consul, Servius Sulpicius Rufus. Even Pompey could do nothing but make a show of distancing himself from the extremism of Marcellus.[18]

The following year the anti-Caesar banner passed into the hands of the cousin of Marcus Claudius Marcellus, Gaius Claudius Marcellus, who was consul together with Lucius Aemilius Lepidus Paullus for the year 50. This time too Caesar had recourse to the classical methods of Roman politics: he bought Aemilius Lepidus 'by a heavy bribe',[19] thus creating once again a situation of paralysis in the friction between the two consuls. Most importantly, he also bought a lasting alliance and the devotion of Gaius Scribonius Curio, 'the most reckless of the tribunes', until his tragic death at the start of the civil war,[20] by freeing him from crippling debts. According to Velleius Paterculus it was an amount of approximately ten million sesterces; according to Valerius Maximus – another historian from the time of Tiberius – it was sixty million.[21]

The situation changed radically with the consuls of the following year, who took office on 1 January 49. Gaius Claudius Marcellus and Lucius Cornelius Lentulus Crus were both Caesar's personal enemies and determined to deprive him of his command before he stood as a candidate for the consulship.

Faced with the new situation, Caesar proved the extent of his pliability, a quality that is indispensable for the politician who has no intention of giving in on the main thing. Pliability and inflexibility are inseparable qualities, except in the doctrinaire or the opportunistic. Caesar was neither one nor the other; he was a great tactician who never lost sight of the stakes and the various priorities, and above all the balance of forces. Therefore he made a series of conciliatory proposals. He asked the Senate not to deprive him of a privilege granted by the people,[22] but declared himself ready to renounce it, provided that the other pro-magistrates who had been given commands also surrendered them. In relating this proposal Suetonius does not fail to observe that Caesar knew very well that he could – in case of need – 'more readily muster his veterans as soon as he wished, than Pompey his newly levied troops'. He devised still more attempts at compromise: he would renounce Transalpine Gaul and as many as eight legions, retaining for himself, if he were not elected consul, only Cisalpine Gaul and two legions. A further proposal contemplated the renunciation of both Gauls: he would keep only Illyricum and one legion.[23] The presumption, generally shared, was that one could engage in politics only if one had troops at one's command.

He also exploited the notorious inclination for compromise of an old and respected consul (whom he had not hesitated to see off ten years earlier), the never completely defeated Cicero, who had returned to Rome from Cilicia in the final days of the conflict. Cicero had returned on 4 January 49 to the city which he had left on 1 May 51.[24] In governing the difficult Asiatic province, which bordered on restive Syria, he had shown his ability, not without a sense of self-irony, in military exploits that were not at all negligible, against local rebellions; but he had, as it were, lost his feel for the situation. The very fact that he thought he could mediate is proof of this. Thinking that he could still exert some influence over Pompey, Cicero vainly tried to put Caesar's proposals to him – an unforgivable error of judgement, primarily because Pompey 'the Great' was impervious, convinced he was already the protector of the republic, or would be once the field was cleared of the wearisome proconsul of the Gauls. A simple calculation shows that he must have approached Pompey on 6 January, that is, on the eve of the session so catastrophic for the peace and the very lives of the citizens: that of 7 January, described by Caesar in chapters 3–5 of his *Civil War*. This was the session in which nothing that Caesar suggested was even considered, the tribunes were blocked, their prerogatives trampled upon, while the faction (which now had a firm hold on Pompey himself) shared out the provinces with an eye to an approaching time when 'the enemy' would be completely obliterated or removed. Dismayed by his burning failure, and especially by the dramatic turn of events, Cicero anxiously withdrew (in so far as he was able) to the position of an aloof observer, terrified by the arrogance of those who should have been his 'natural' friends, who now were intent on war. He was wooed at all levels, including that of cultural affinity, by Caesar, who was unwilling to lose a single possible ally and was in any case interested in increasing the number of neutrals, especially from the rank of consul. But this still lay in the months ahead. Faced with the rigidity of his adversaries Caesar knew what to expect. He had known it for some time: some of the legions which should really have been in Belgium were unexpectedly in Rimini, which shows that he had taken the necessary steps for the coming armed conflict in good time.[25] He knew with whom he was dealing and never seriously believed that it was possible to come to an accommodation with a Cato.

But before proceeding according to an established scenario, Caesar turned a coldly ironic eye on his enemies and depicted them in the incisive opening pages of his *Commentaries* on the civil war, not as a record for the future, but as propaganda for the present. The account can only have been based on the reports of others. Its sources were certainly the tribunes – Antony, Quintus Cassius Longinus, Scribonius Curio, Caelius Rufus – driven to flee from Rome by the extremist threats during the night of 7–8 January 49. Antony and Quintus Cassius were those who were most exposed in the Senate in this dangerous game. But they were not the only informants, and certainly not the ones who provided Caesar with details of what was happening in the opposing camp. Of much greater significance were the figures of Balbus and Oppius, two names which are important, yet are not to be found in the *Commentaries* (except once,[26] and for a minor detail). Caesar, like any true party leader, tended not to name his real agents, and not to reveal precisely who belonged to his inner circle.

Thus it is that Asinius Pollio, who had followed Caesar from the very start in the civil war,[27] and held command at Pharsalus,[28] never appears in the *Commentaries*: yet we are indebted to him for the detailed testimony of declarations made by Caesar to his inner circle at crucial moments of the battle. He sets forth his account in his historical work on the civil war, and Appian, Plutarch and Suetonius make use of it. The so-called stylistic 'canon' which forbade quoting directly from substantial prepared speeches by prominent individuals already in circulation evidently did not extend to single often illuminating declarations by the same protagonists. At least that was Asinius Pollio's view. Which is not surprising: in the case of Caesar's statements, he was relaying real revelations of the deepest motivation behind certain decisions.

A direct witness to the battle of Pharsalus, which sealed the fate of Pompey in the summer of 48, Asinius not only gives a conservative figure for the losses on Pompey's side (6,000 dead),[29] but records for posterity the words uttered by Caesar at the sight of the field covered by thousands of bodies of the defeated enemy: 'They would have it so. Even I, Gaius Caesar, after so many great deeds, should have been found guilty, if I had not turned to my army for help.'[30] Asinius Pollio writes about twenty years after Pharsalus and records these words because they reflect a crude attitude on the part of Caesar: had I not had recourse to insurrection, had I yielded and 'not turned to my army for help', I would have been hauled before a tribunal – as a *privatus* – and judicially destroyed. From Asinius Pollio, certainly, comes the statement which we read in Suetonius that these were Caesar's exact words (*ad verbum*) – a statement which is clarified by the emphasis which Asinius Pollio places (not incorrectly) on that *authentic declaration*, made in a solemn tragic moment before a field strewn with dead, his fellow citizens. And indeed that harsh declaration provides a key to the understanding of Caesar's decision to accept the challenge and take it to the limit, to the point of insurrection against the republic: it was, for him, the only way to avoid the certainty of judicial persecution – most likely disastrous – which his opponents had been steadily preparing for nearly ten years.

Thus Asinius Pollio, an unexpected source,[31] twenty years later reveals the real reason, declared by Caesar himself, why he decided on the break in January 49. And he thus contradicts, obviously, the Caesarian propaganda set down in the *Commentaries*, where Caesar presents the defence of the rights of the tribunes[32] and the defence of his personal wounded *dignitas* as the cause of the conflict.

Suetonius, who carefully recorded Asinius Pollio's text and took from it, not only here, valuable information on what Caesar actually said at pivotal moments, made skilful use of this revelation of Caesar's on the decision to force the crisis to the limit. In fact he places it in a kind of panorama of various theories and hypotheses formulated about it. And at the same time he provides facts that complete the picture and help to clarify it. He tells us, for example, that Cato had repeatedly promised, 'and took oath too', that he would impeach Caesar, 'the moment he had disbanded his army', and would have tried him for illegal acts committed during the consulship of 59.[33] At that time it had not been possible: Caesar had gone without interruption from the consular *imperium* to his extended proconsulship. In fact (for a time with Pompey's agreement) he was pressing for an election *in absentia* in order to step straight from proconsulship to the second consulship and thus remain judicially unassailable. 'It was openly said too', wrote Suetonius, 'that if he was out of office on his return, he would be obliged, like Milo, to make his defence in a court hedged about by armed men.'[34] And here he adds that the testimony of Asinius Pollio – who related those blunt, crude words uttered by Caesar in a small circle at the very moment of victory – seems to confirm that that widespread version of the real cause of the civil war was completely correct.

Notes

1 This decision by Pompey not to return to his province (Spain) after the consulate of 55 BC, but to remain with proconsular *imperium* at the gates of Rome, was not exactly reassuring.

2 Asconius, p. 35 Clark; cf. Dio Cassius 40.49.5.

3 The *interrex* had been nominated because of the impossibility of proceeding to consular elections, in the climate of total illegality.

4 At the Ides of September: *CIL* I². 2.933. Scipio passed a law that abrogated the Clodian reform of censorship (earlier supported by Caesar).

5 The exact formulation we owe to Suetonius, *Caesar* 26.1. For further details see Dio Cassius 40.50–1.

6 Suetonius, *Caesar* 26.2.

7 Suetonius, *Caesar* 26.3.

8 Caesar, *Gallic War* 7.1.1.

9 Asconius, p. 35 Clark paraphrases: 'that Pompey should recruit in all of Italy'.

10 Compare the pertinent comment in F. Kraner, W. Dittenberger and H. Meusel, *Commentarii de bello gallico*, 17th edn, vol. II (Berlin 1920), p. 237 (note to VII.1).

11 A *coniuratio Italiae* was promoted by Octavian in order for him to be accredited as *dux* in the war against Cleopatra (and Antony) in 31 BC: it was also an act of institutional breakdown if one considers that the other consul in office at that time was Antony, against whom the *coniuratio* was directed.

12 A type of initiative which in Roman politics generally foreshadowed dramatic consequences.

13 Suetonius, *Caesar* 28.

14 Ibid.: 'Quoniam bello confecto pax esset ac dimitti deberet victor exercitus.'

15 Suetonius, *Caesar* 28.3 ('mox lege iam in aes incisa et in aerium condita').

16 Suetonius, *Caesar* 28.4.

17 Suetonius, *Caesar* 29.1.

18 Plutarch, *Pompey* 56.1–2.

19 Suetonius, *Caesar* 29.2.

20 Suetonius, *Caesar* 29.2; Plutarch, *Caesar* 29.3.

21 Vellius 2.48.4; Valerius Maximus 9.1.60.

22 Suetonius, *Caesar* 29.3: 'ne sibi beneficium populi adimeretur'.

23 Suetonius, *Caesar* 29.4.

24 Cicero, *Letters to Atticus* 7.7.3; 8.2; *Letters to his friends* 16.11.2.

25 Compare P. Fabre, Introduction to Caesar, *La Guerre civile*, vol. 1 (Paris 1936), p. xxvii. Thus the phrase in *The Civil War* 1.8.8: 'reliquae [scil. legiones] nondum convenerant' is rather suspicious.

26 Caesar, *Civil War* 3.19.

27 He said as much to Cicero (*Letters to his friends* 10.31.2) in March 43. But see also Plutarch, *Caesar* 32.7 (on Asinius being present at the crossing of the Rubicon).

28 Appian, *Civil Wars* 2.82.346.

29 Appian, *Civil Wars* 2.82.346.

30 Suetonius, *Caesar* 30.4: 'haec eum ad verbum dixisse: Hoc voluerunt tantis rebus gestis, Gaius Caesar condemnatus essem, nisi ab exercitu auxilium petissem.'

31 Caesarem [. . .] dilexi summa cum pietate et fide', he would write to Cicero (*Letters to his friends* 10.31.3) exactly one year after the death of the dictator.

32 Suetonius dismisses this version of the facts, dear to Caesar, as 'praetextum' (*Caesar* 30.1).

33 Suetonius, *Caesar* 30.3.

34 Milo's trial had had a disastrous outcome.

CHAPTER 17

Striving after Tyranny?

Sullam nescisse litteras, qui dictaturam deposuerit.
[Sulla was ignorant when he renounced dictatorship.]

Caesar

Suetonius rejected all other explanations, including the one 'frequently repeated' by Pompey, which was, however, rather unlikely. According to Pompey – and one would like to know Suetonius' source for this interesting information – Caesar could not complete what he had undertaken; that is, finish the monuments and public works he had begun and satisfy the expectations he had aroused in the people; therefore he took the path to revolution.[1] If Pompey really did say this – Butler and Cary facetiously observe – it is clear that he understood nothing about his adversary's character.[2] In reality, Pompey's remark was far less an attempt at analysis than a contemptuous judgement which reduced the figure of his opponent to the level of a party leader without prospects who was tormented by a pressing need for money, or rather, who was crushed by enterprises that were too great for him. This could describe 'Catilinarian' characters, and probably Clodius as well, but not an able career-builder like Caesar, who had derived an uncommon economic strength from the Gallic campaign. We do not know *when* Pompey made his polemical judgement ('omnia permiscere voluisse'): certainly it does not fit Caesar's behaviour in 51–50 BC, which seems, on the contrary, obstinately bent on compromise.

There is another explanation for Caesar's decision to face the risk of a breach: the 'teleological' image of a Caesar who from the outset of his career had one aim – a Caesar striving tirelessly to achieve 'tyranny'. Suetonius puts forward this theory too, but, while not directly critical of it, he treats it implicitly as being of secondary importance. 'Some think', he writes, 'that habit had given him a love of power,[3] and that weighing the strength of his adversaries against his own,[4] he grasped the opportunity of usurping the despotism[5] which had been his heart's desire from early youth.' Suetonius offers no *corroboration* here; rather he says that this is also what Cicero thinks. He cites a well-chosen passage from *On duties*,[6] in which Cicero puts forward this hypothesis and attempts to support it. The version of *On duties* available to us dates from after the death of Caesar, so it reflects Cicero's thinking once he was freed from 'affectionate' co-existence with the dictator. Naturally he tries to adopt a neutral tone, preferring to speak of Caesar without naming him, as he does in the second book, when he makes a heavy allusion to the involvement, in his own lifetime, of the deceased dictator in Cato's plot.[7] However, on this page not even Pompey is spared; he is unnamed, but is clearly 'he who wanted to have for father-in-law one [Caesar] whose unscrupulousness served his own power'. As for Caesar (the father-in-law), Cicero's judgement is implicit, but no less clear none the less. It is expressed in a 'revelation': '[Caesar] loved to repeat the verse from Euripides' *Phoenician Women*, in which Eteocles says: "If wrong may e'er be right, for a throne's sake were wrong most right." '[8] Cicero renders the equivalent of 'for a throne's sake' as 'for the *regnum*', a judicious translation in accordance with the Roman political lexicon of republican times, in which *regnum* was equivalent in meaning to *tyrannis*.[9] Cicero explains that Caesar would also repeat the second part of Eteocles' speech: 'be God in all else feared'.[10] Cicero's knowledge of Caesar went back a long way, possibly to his years of study in Greece. Therefore there is no reason for not believing him when he reveals such a significant *constant* in Caesar's thinking – better, in his mental make-up, the deep structure of the political sense of the man whom Cicero characterises a little later in the words 'he who wanted to be king of the Roman people and sole ruler of all peoples' ('rex populi Romani dominusque omnium gentium')'.

It goes without saying that the 'deep structure', the intellectual predilection (expressed in a provocative quotation), is one thing, and the plan for *regnum* is another: a plan for definitive personal power, which he had harboured all his life. It was a project that was not foreign to Pompey either, as Cicero well knew ('occultior non melior', according to Tacitus' famous definition). Titus Ampius Balbus cites another no less revealing line spoken by his enemy Caesar: 'Sulla revealed himself as ignorant when he renounced the dictatorship.'[11] This, too, whether the claim is true or false, has an air of 'provocation', since Caesar had risked falling victim to Sulla when he had very few weapons and men to defend himself.[12] However, Cicero changed his attitude towards Caesar several times and repeatedly revised his judgement of the man and his aspirations. According to Plutarch,[13] Cicero had raised the alarm long before the 'posthumous' verdict in *On duties*: he does not say precisely when, but claims that Cicero was the first to understand it, and 'fear his public policy as one might fear the smiling surface of the sea'.[14] But one should not place too much emphasis on these extempore assessments: when Cicero returned from Cilicia, he committed himself *in extremis* to supporting the proposals of compromise which Caesar continued to make in order to avoid conflict.

Thus it is risky to see Caesar as a man implacably intent on conquest of the *regnum* from the outset to his assumption of perpetual dictatorship at the beginning of 44 BC. Such an image, if taken seriously, gives a misleading picture of the frantic negotiations which preceded the crossing of the Rubicon and the opening of hostilities, by suggesting a game, privately not believed in, which concealed *from the start* the 'true' intentions of the proconsul who clashed with the Senate. Suetonius also presents this reading of the conflict with the Senate, in which Caesar 'grasped a propitious opportunity' in order to implement a plan which had been harboured for a long time. But Suetonius himself seems – to judge from Asinius' precise testimony – to prefer a more clearly defined, more concrete analysis, and refers to the reprisals and judicial 'persecutions' which Caesar's adversaries had long since prepared for him, and which he had no intention of enduring. From this decision, the most critical of Caesar's career and the one with the most significant consequences, one can see just how abstract the monist and mystical 'Übermensch' interpretations of Caesar's political actions are: 'as though Caesar set the tune from the beginning, in the knowledge that monarchy was the panacea for the world's ills'.[15]

Notes

1 Suetonius, *Caesar* 30.2.
2 H. E. Butler and M. Cary (eds), *Suetoni Tranquilli Divus Iulius* (Oxford 1927), p. 84.
3 'Captum imperii consuetudine' – an apt psychological comment.
4 'Pensitatisque suis et inimicorum viribus' – this is the kernel of the whole sentence.
5 'Usum occasione rapiendae dominationis' – the term *dominatio* means more than 'power', it is almost tyranny (in the classical Greek sense).
6 Cicero, *On duties* 3.20.82.

7　Cicero, *On duties* 3.24.84. On this passage see E. Gabba, 'Per una inter-pretazione politica del "de officiis" di Cicerone', *Rendiconti Accademia dei Lincei*, S. VIII, 34 (1979), pp. 126 and 139.

8　Euripides, *Phoenician Women* 524–5 (Suetonius, *Caesar* 30.5). In some recent editions (J. Diggle, *Euripidis Fabulae* [Oxford 1994], p. 111) this early reference to Euripides is completely ignored.

9　Cicero's following comment is very significant. It echoes the anti-Euripides current of classical criticism established by Aristophanes' *Frogs*, and accuses Euripides of having brought that terrible precept onto the stage under the mask of Eteocles.

10　E. Narducci (Milan 1987) translates this as 'i santi doveri': in Greek εὐσέβεια, which Cicero translates as *pietas*. But it is clear that this is a judicious reference to politics, not a general ethical judgement. Caesar would not have intended it otherwise.

11　Suetonius, *Caesar* 77: 'Sullam nescisse litteras qui dictaturam depo-suerit.' After the death of Caesar, Titus Ampius Balbus, tribune in 63, *praetor* in 58, and a supporter of Pompey, published a damaging bio-graphy of the late dictator.

12　See Chapter 1.

13　Plutarch, *Caesar* 4.4–9.

14　Plutarch, *Caesar* 4.8.

15　R. Syme, *The Roman Revolution* (Oxford 1939), p. 47. This idea, already dear to Mommsen, had its most eloquent proponent in Carcopino (*Points de vue sur l'impérialisme romain* [Paris 1934], pp. 89–155). But the most reasonable response, with a wealth of con-crete experience, which can address these mythicising theories is found in Napoleon I's *Précis* (p. 214: 'Les Romains étaient accoutumés à voir les rois dans les antichambres de leurs magistrats').

CHAPTER 18

Attacking the World with Five Cohorts

> Le véritable auteur de la guerre n'est pas celui qui la déclare, mais celui qui la rend nécessaire.
>
> Montesquieu

On the eve of civil war, in December 50 BC and the first week of January 49, illegality became official where one would least expect it: in the Senate. On 1 December Gaius Scribonius Curio, a tribune of the plebs whose support had been bought by Caesar,[1] said openly what nearly everyone else was thinking:

> that, if any person suffered from apprehension of Caesar's arms, and as the armed tyranny of Pompey was creating considerable alarm in the Forum, he would move that both leaders should give up arms and disband their armies. He held that by this means the state would be free and independent.[2]

It was obvious that both powerful men threatened the republic and the freedom of its institutions, and this statement *made it official in the place of greatest authority*. Curio's proposal was accepted decisively, with 370 votes in favour and only 20 (or 22) against.[3] Considering that everyone knew who he was and on which side he stood, it is clear from this episode how narrow was the 'parliamentary' base of the *factio*, now that it rested more and more on Pompey. It should not be forgotten either that the senators en masse were unstable and little inclined to factional alignment[4] – it was not easy to predict their behaviour. On this occasion the spectacularly defeated *factio* could think of no better solution than to dispatch the consuls-designate for the year 49 (both personal enemies of Caesar) to Pompey, who was encamped outside the *pomerium*, to ask him to intervene to defend the city 'menaced by Caesar's legions'! This was the first serious threat to the tribunes, and a more provocative initiative than this appeal to Pompey – in defiance of Curio's (Senate-sanctioned!) motion – is difficult to imagine.

It was the new consuls who, immediately on taking office, personally sanctioned the break with legality. In their start-of-year report on the state of the republic they spoke as if Caesar had already been proscribed. Lentulus Crus (Clodius' principal accuser in 61)[5] declared that:

> he will not fail the republic if the senators are willing to express their opinions with boldness and resolution; but if they pay regard to Caesar and try to win favour with him as they have on previous occasions, he says he will consider his own interests and *will not obey their authority*.[6]

The same threat was made by his colleague Scipio (Pompey's new father-in-law, co-opted *sine collega* in the last months of the consulate), who said that Pompey was not inclined to desert the republic if the Senate followed him; but if it did not back him, it would in vain solicit his aid should it wish to do so in the future.[7] When Caesar recounts these details – undoubtedly based on reports by his informants – he selects his material carefully, to make clear that his enemies have violated the law. Naturally, his enemies' (unprovable) assumption was *that he was already outside the law*: this alone would justify such harsh words and actions. Although he attempts to maintain his usual objective tone, Caesar does permit himself some sharp comments in his memorable account. Of Scipio, he says that it was as if Pompey spoke directly through his mouth,[8] and of the stormy debate, at the conclusion of which the tribunes' right of veto was trampled upon, he says: 'The more harsh and cruel the speech, the more it is applauded by the personal enemies of Caesar.'[9] When he describes the 'real' reasons for the hostility of Cato, Scipio and Pompey himself, he concludes: 'For these reasons [that is, highly egoistic reasons] everything is done in hurry and confusion.'[10] And when he finally refers to the *senatus consultum ultimum* issued in the Senate when it sat on 7 January – without giving precise details of its contents[11] – he comments:

> So on the first five days on which a meeting of the Senate could be held after the date on which Lentulus entered on his consulship, except two election days, decrees of the severest and harshest character are passed affecting Caesar's imperial command and those highly important officials, the tribunes of the people.[12]

Mark Antony and Quintus Cassius Longinus had led the battle against the *factio*; at the end of that day, deprived of the right of *intercessio*, they began to fear for their safety.

Caesar had followed the progress of negotiations with the Senate from Ravenna, the city in Cisalpine Gaul closest to Italy. His even tone is in reality heavy with irony: 'He was at that time in Ravenna and was awaiting a reply to his very lenient demands, in the hope that by some sense of equity a peaceable conclusion might be reached.'[13] In fact he had no illusions about the possibility of a compromise, because he was being kept constantly informed. Between 10 and 11 January, before his tribunes fleeing from Rome had reached him, he made up his mind, and the news of the Senate's serious decision to quash the tribunes' right of veto removed any doubts. The fact that the news reached him before the fleeing tribunes is reported by Suetonius.[14] Caesar's decision was swift. He 'sent ahead'[15] – meaning, to the border, that is, the river Rubicon – several cohorts, and then 'in order to arouse no suspicion' he himself spent a normal evening. This indicates that his cohorts had already been alerted to take, should the need arise, the step of no return: insurrection against the established authority. They could not have gone so far had they not understood this. It is clear, then, that there was a very small circle whose members knew what was about to happen. It also implies that Caesar suspected enemy agents could infiltrate even his closest entourage.[16]

So Caesar went to the theatre.[17] After that he busied himself with something he was known to enjoy: his plans for a new gladiator school.[18] After he and his followers had examined the sketches of this new killing school, he took care to dine, as he usually did, in the presence of a large company.[19] Then, when it was dark,[20] he took the most unlikely form of transport: instead of his favourite, almost legendary horse,[21] as a means of camouflage he rode in a cart pulled by two mules which had been borrowed from a local mill.[22] Caesar on horseback, especially on *that* horse, was recognisable even at night, whereas an apparent miller on a mule-drawn cart did not attract attention. Caesar had few men with him, and he chose a little-known secondary route[23] to join the cohorts he had sent on ahead. But, in an incident that could have ruined all his plans, he got lost and spent the night wandering in the woods. It was only at dawn that they encountered someone who could guide them to the river. The scene has something of the surreal about it: the proconsul of Gaul, ready to lead an insurrection against the republic, finds himself depending on an obscure shepherd, who was unaware of the true identity of these night wanderers who had lost their way in the woods. By then the cart had been left behind and they continued on foot. It was thus that Caesar and his faithful companions at last reached the Rubicon, where the cohorts had been waiting for many hours, having expected him since the previous evening.

Because the nocturnal incident had affected the men's morale, a *coup de théâtre* was required. Suetonius' reliable witness reports that Caesar, having reached the limit of the province, consulted his most trusted men, telling them that it was not too late to turn back.[24] This source is clearly Asinius Pollio: Plutarch explicitly declares as much when he recounts the moment of final hesitation on the bank of the Rubicon.

> Then, halting in his course, he communed with himself a long time in silence as his resolution wavered back and forth, and his purpose then suffered change after change. For a long time, too, he discussed his perplexities with his friends who were present, among whom was Asinius Pollio, estimating the great evils for all mankind which would follow their passage of the river, and the wide fame of it which they would leave to posterity.[25]

As they hesitated, a man of imposing stature appeared, sat down near the group, and began to play his flute. Many ran to hear him, shepherds and soldiers, among whom were the trumpeters. Suddenly the taciturn musician seized a trumpet from one of them, and, taking a deep breath, sounded the advance and dashed across to the opposite bank. Caesar used the moment of excitement to launch his cause in the most favourable circumstances. According to Suetonius, he ordered: 'Take we the course which the signs of the gods and the false dealing of our foes point out. The die is cast!'[26] After this he crossed the river with his men. Plutarch does not explain the 'sign', but describes Caesar's sudden call in a similar way to Suetonius. In Plutarch's version there was a moment of paralysis when Caesar expressed his doubts, after which, 'with a sort of passion, as if abandoning calculation and casting himself upon the future', he pronounced the words used by many who risk everything in an audacious venture ('Let the die be cast!') and rushed towards the ford.[27] The 'sign' of which Suetonius speaks is in Asinius Pollio's account and all the evidence suggests that that is where Suetonius found it. The story of the giant flautist who suddenly transformed himself into a trumpeter and gave the signal to cross the river cannot have come from nowhere. Rather, the whole episode seems to be a carefully crafted device. It would not have been difficult, with so many prisoners, to find a giant Gaul to act out such a scene. Pisistratus had done something similar,[28] and Caesar was certainly no less imaginative than he.

During the night of 7 January, the tribunes of the plebs, Antony and Quintus Cassius, accompanied by Curio and Rufus Caelius, fled Rome. They were led to Caesar's camp. Before they left, Rufus Caelius had sought out Cicero, who, in a letter to Tiro some days later,[29] set out the chronology of events, a chronology which somewhat contradicts the picture of their flight created by Caesar's account.[30] Asinius, too, was influenced by Caesar (in fact his observation point for these events was Caesar's camp): this can be deduced from the way in which Suetonius speaks of the 'expulsion from Rome'[31] of these tribunes. Cicero, on the other hand, writes to Tiro that the tribunes fled from Rome 'without any violence having driven them to this'.[32]

Where did they flee to? At first Caesar wrote: 'The tribunes at once flee from the city and betake themselves to Caesar. He was at that time at Ravenna.'[33] Later he stated that he had encountered the tribunes fleeing from Rome *at Rimini* – that is, *after* he had crossed the Rubicon.[34]

In the account in the *Commentaries*, Caesar addresses his troops at *Ravenna*, that is, before the crossing of the Rubicon, describing in dramatic terms the grave violation of rights suffered by the tribunes, and he obtains their consent to open rebellion against the Senate (guilty of trampling on the tribunes).

> Thereupon the men of the Thirteenth Legion, which was present (he had called this out at the beginning of the disorder; the rest had not yet come together) exclaim that they are ready to repel the wrongs of their commander and of the tribunes.[35]

All of this contrasts with the precise testimony of Asinius, as found in the various narratives that derive from his account. It was at Rimini that Caesar addressed the soldiers, parading before them the humiliated fugitive tribunes. 'By these means he most of all incited his soldiers, showing them men of repute and high office who had fled the city on hired carts and in the garb of slaves.'[36] Suetonius is the most thorough: not only does he describe in detail the night of subterfuge and mistakes which preceded the dawn in which the Rubicon was crossed by a few cohorts, but he then describes in detail Caesar's rally at Rimini following the crossing of the river: 'Crossing with his army, and welcoming the tribunes of the plebs, who had come to him after being driven from Rome, he harangued the soldiers with tears, and rending his robe from his breast besought their faithful service.'[37] This scene with its carefully calculated pathos took place outside his province, at Rimini, with the tribunes who had just joined him dressed as befitted fleeing refugees. A fragment from Livy, preserved by his later admirer Orosius, confirms that Livy too knew this sequence of events: 'As soon as Caesar had come to Ariminum, he told the five cohorts, which at that time were all he had, and with which he was attacking the whole world, what it was necessary to do.'[38]

The reason for the falsification[39] of events by Caesar is obvious. According to the account in his *Commentaries*, it was with the unconditional prior assent of his men that he crossed the Rubicon.[40] But in reality the entire operation was conducted in a way that presented the men with a fait accompli. They were dispatched to the river with little explanation, but perhaps not entirely unaware of what was about to happen. Caesar wanted to join them without being seen, and had to resort to a ruse in order to lead his most faithful cohorts, those of the Thirteenth Legion, to take the unlawful step. When they reached Rimini, and the tribunes, disguised as victims of political persecution, had arrived with immaculate timing, Caesar resorted to his most 'soldierly' rhetorical skill (as he himself ironically described it),[41] with a maximum of brutality ('protect your commander!'), theatrical gestures (tears and tearing of garments) and persuasive skill. The *mise-en-scène* was designed to parade the fugitive tribunes, then stir up the troops with tears and torn garments and ask them to reaffirm their *personal* loyalty. Suetonius once again provides the most realistic detail:

> he often pointed to the finger of his left hand as he addressed them and urged them on, declaring that to satisfy all those who helped him to defend his honour he would gladly tear his very ring from his hand.[42]

Evidently Asinius' account did not make 'allowances'[43] and concealed nothing, not even the rather unedifying aspects of the event. Caesar spoke clearly to the troops and tempted them with concrete promises, *when they reached Rimini*, and going back was more difficult. In the account in the *Commentaries* everything is rewritten according to a sequence of events that ennobles – and almost manages to justify – the decisions made by the commander and his soldiers. It is clear that the reconstructed order of events places the role of the tribunes in the correct light. They went straight to Rimini because they already knew in advance that Caesar would cross the border of the province and would go on to open war. A decision that certainly grew firmer in Caesar's mind following the brutal conclusion of the Senate sitting of 7 January, but was already foreseen and considered inevitable. Therefore the tribunes dramatised the circumstances of their flight to the maximum: because Caesar's propagandist line was directed at placing responsibility for the split as far as possible on the *factio*-dominated Senate.

It is understandable why Pollio, writing to Cicero (after Caesar had been dead for almost a year), insisted on the justice and necessity of Caesar's decision in that January of 49.[44] But in his *Histories* he claims that the *Commentaries* are 'not truthful', that Caesar had been 'deliberately' inaccurate, and that 'he would have rewritten and corrected them', if he had had time.[45] This constituted a radical devaluation of that testimony, quite the opposite of the judgement of Cicero in *Brutus*, who considered them so faultless that nobody else should now attempt to recount these same facts (he was, however, writing under Caesar's dictatorship).[46]

Everything suggests that the account Suetonius used was that of an eye-witness: this is evident from the detail concerning the soldiers who can see Caesar but not hear his words.[47] It is reasonable to suppose that that eye-witness, who later became the historian of those events, is Asinius; and that therefore, thanks to Suetonius, we have Asinius' account of the crucial moment, not only emblematic but politically decisive, of the crossing of the Rubicon. Suetonius had rightly understood that the event would have an important place in the narrative. And Asinius had wanted to correct the *Commentaries* on that particular point: the purely military account of what followed perhaps offered fewer opportunities for significant variation.

Notes

1 Caesar paid all Curio's debts, which amounted to sixty million sesterces.
2 Caesar, *Gallic War* 8.52.4. From 8.48.10 on, book 8 is not by Caesar but by an anonymous author, whom modern historians, without firm grounds, have chosen to identify as Hirtius. See L. Canfora, 'La lettera a Balbo e la formazione della raccolta cesariana,' *ASNP*, Ser. III, 23, 1 (1993), pp. 79–103.
3 Plutarch, *Pompey* 58.5; Appian, *Civil Wars* 2.30.119; according to Plutarch there were twenty-two votes against.
4 From the time of Sulla to that of Augustus the Senate was repeatedly purged and forcibly reconstituted.

5 Clodius was accused of profaning the festival of Bona Dea.

6 Caesar, *Civil War* 1.1.2–3.

7 Caesar, *Civil War* 1.1.4.

8 Caesar, *Civil War* 1.2.1.

9 Caesar, *Civil War* 1.2.8.

10 Caesar, *Civil War* 1.5.1.

11 For example, he says 'de imperio Caesaris', but does not explain what the decision was.

12 Caesar, *Civil War* 1.5.4.

13 Caesar, *Civil War* 1.5.5.

14 Suetonius, *Caesar* 31.1: 'Cum sublatum tribunorum intercessionem ipsoque urbe cessisse nuntiatum esset . . .' The record of these hours, splendidly synthesised by Suetonius (*Caesar* 31–3), is certainly drawn from Asinius Pollio, who was a member of the intimate circle surrounding the proconsul. See also Plutarch, *Caesar* 32.7.

15 Suetonius, *Caesar* 31–33.

16 And in fact, hardly had they crossed the Rubicon before Labienus, Caesar's stalwart commander in the Gallic War, went over to the other side.

17 Suetonius: 'spectaculo publico interfuit'.

18 We know of his almost obsessive enthusiasm for this *ludus*: Suetonius, *Caesar* 26.3.

19 Suetonius: 'ex consuetudine convivio se frequenti dedit'. The subject of the evening's table-talk is tantalisingly unknown.

20 'Post solis occasum'.

21 Suetonius, *Caesar* 61.

22 Suetonius, *Caesar* 31: 'mulis e proximo pistrino ad vehiculum iunctis'.

23 'Occultissimum iter modico comitatu ingressus est.'

24 Suetonius, *Caesar* 31.2: 'reputans quantum moliretur, conversus ad proximos: "Etiam nunc", inquit, "regredi possumus".'

25 Plutarch, *Caesar* 32.7. It is noteworthy that the wording coincides fully with that of Suetonius ('reputans quantum moliretur, conversus ad proximos . . .'). Suetonius, Plutarch and Appian repeat nearly identical passages from the same account.

26 Suetonius, *Caesar* 32. On the basis of comparisons with the corresponding passages in Plutarch, *Caesar* 32 and *Pompey* 60, Erasmus upheld the form 'Iacta alea esto.' This fixed Greek expression is noted also by Menander (Fr. 59.4 Koerte-Thierfelder): *est* for *esto* is clearly a simplification.

27 Plutarch, *Caesar* 32.7. Plutarch's description in *Pompey* 60.4 is essentially the same, adding only that these words were said in Greek, a clarification which is typical of Asinius; cf. Caesar's statement following the battle of Pharsalus, for example (Plutarch, *Caesar* 46.1–2).

28 On his return to Athens for his 'second' tyranny he placed in his cart a

statuesque and beautiful Thracian, making it seem as if a woman of Athens were conducting him into the city (Herodotus 1.60; Aristotle, *Athenian Constitution* 14.4). One is tempted to believe that Caesar had heard the well-known story of the 'democratic tyrant', as Aristotle calls him. 'A curious and very striking story', observe Butler and Cary. 'If true, it must have been prearranged by Caesar.' H. E. Butler and M. Cary (eds), *Suetoni Tranquilli Divus Iulius* (Oxford 1927), p. 95.

29 A letter meant to remain in the family.

30 Caesar, *Civil War* 1.5.4: 'de amplissimis viris, tribunis plebis, gravissime acerbissimeque decernitur'. And a little later the soldiers vow to be ready to avenge the shame inflicted on the tribunes of the plebs (1.7.8).

31 Suetonius, *Caesar* 33.1: 'Adhibitis tribunis plebis, qui *pulsi* supervenerant.'

32 Cicero, *Letters to his friends* 16.11.2: 'nulla vi expulsi'. The tone here is amicable: Cicero calls Antony 'our Antony' and Caesar 'our friend'.

33 Caesar, *Civil War* 1.5.5.

34 Caesar, *Civil War* 1.8.1.

35 Caesar, *Civil War* 1.7.8. Detail about the movements of the legions is extremely scant here.

36 Plutarch, *Caesar* 31.3.

37 Suetonius, *Caesar* 33.1.

38 Livy, fr. 32 (= Orosius 6.15).

39 It is accurately described as such by Eduard Meyer, *Caesars Monarchie und das Principat des Pompeius* (Stuttgart and Berlin 1918), p. 291.

40 The Rubicon is not named, but it is implied in a hurried line of narrative in his *Civil War* 1.8.1: 'Seeing the enthusiasm of his men, he set out to Ariminum [Rimini] with that legion.'

41 Plutarch, *Caesar* 3.4.

42 Suetonius, *Caesar* 33.

43 According to Suetonius (who is probably also following Asinius), the soldiers in the back rows could see Caesar holding up his ring, but could not hear what he was saying. Many believed he had promised them a ring, that is, the right of the knight's ring, with the estate that went with it.

44 Cicero, *Letters to his friends* 10.31.2.

45 Suetonius, *Caesar* 56.4.

46 Cicero, *Brutus* 262.

47 Suetonius, *Caesar* 33.

CHAPTER 19

Caesar's 'Programme': In Search of Consensus

Caesar to Oppius and Cornelius Balbus, Greetings. I am very glad to hear from your letters how strongly you approve of what happened at Corfinium.[1] I shall follow your advice with pleasure – with all the more pleasure, because I had myself made up my mind to act with the greatest moderation, and to do my best to effect a reconciliation with Pompey.

Let us see if by moderation we can win all hearts (*omnium voluntatem recuperare*) and secure a lasting victory, since by cruelty others[2] have been unable to escape from hatred and to maintain their victory for any length of time except L. Sulla, whose example *I do not intend to follow*.

This is a new way of conquering, to strengthen one's position by kindness and generosity. As to how this can be done, some ideas have occurred to me and many more can be found. I should like you to turn some attention to the matter.

I have taken N. Magius, a prefect of Pompey. Of course I kept to my policy and set him free at once. So now two of Pompey's prefects of engineers have fallen into my hands and I have set them free. If they have any gratitude, they ought to exhort Pompey to prefer my friendship to that of men who were always the bitterest enemies both to him and to me. It is their machinations that have brought the State into its present plight. (Cicero, *Letters to Atticus* 10.7C)

It is thanks to Cicero's correspondence with Atticus, which has survived only in part, all the letters of Atticus being missing, that we know of this letter, written by Caesar on the march towards Rome shortly after the capitulation of Corfinium.[3] On 13 March 49 BC Cicero writes to Atticus, who is advising him not to break with Caesar.[4] Cicero essentially agrees with Atticus that such an approach should be taken, but weakness undermines his resolve. As confirmation that this is the correct approach, Cicero informs his friend of the content of the lively correspondence between him on the one hand and Oppius and Cornelius Balbus, Caesar's agents in Rome and his political advisers, on the other. He also attaches Caesar's letter to

Oppius and Cornelius Balbus, the latter having sent him a copy: a letter, he adds, 'which is sane enough considering these mad times'.[5] The letter disturbs Cicero's precarious balancing act. In his commentary to Atticus, he writes that he is astonished at 'how Pompey desires to imitate Sulla's reign'. While Cicero is sometimes inclined to place the two adversaries and their ambitions on an equal footing, here, with Caesar solemnly declaring that he intends to seek a consensus and, in particular, not to adopt Sulla's methods, he has to admit that it is Pompey who means to follow in the footsteps of the hated dictator and friend of the *optimates*. Hence, in this letter to Atticus, he summons up all his courage, adding in Greek,[6] 'I know what I am saying', and then in Latin, 'He has made no secret of it.' The ground had long been prepared to transmit to Cicero a copy of Caesar's letter, an 'open letter' designed to make Caesar's plans widely known. First of all Oppius and Cornelius Balbus informed him of their expectation and prediction that Caesar was resolved to seek compromise ('At this time one can at best presume, though not be sure, what Caesar has resolved'[7]). So they played him adroitly, writing to him, 'If you wish it, however, we will write to Caesar to ascertain his intentions in this matter.' So the letter which Caesar sent to the pair was at the same time also a positive answer to Cicero, who had to reply to them that, naturally, he opposed war and favoured a solution through conciliation.[8] The pair used the same strategy to approach other prominent citizens who, despite Pompey's threat that anyone remaining in the capital by doing so became Caesar's 'accomplice', were waiting it out in Rome. In this way Caesar's 'open' letter to his agents became in a sense a proclamation of his next steps,[9] but also a declaration of his long-term and enduring aims. Basically it anticipates the line which Caesar adheres to throughout the endless civil war that began with the crossing of the Rubicon. What is of fundamental importance here is his decision not to follow in Sulla's footsteps, that is, not to persecute his opponents, as had happened previously in the history of the republic, when, in the so-called 'proscriptions', Sulla declared his enemies outlawed, with all the familiar consequences. Whoever was placed outside the law lost all rights and, as an outlaw, could be killed by anyone. Sulla had believed that he could thus through terror consolidate the victory he had won by force of arms.[10]

In this significant 'open letter', Caesar *inter alia* writes that he has had 'some ideas'[11] as to how his programme of reconciliation (his 'new way of conquering', as he calls it) might be implemented. We do not know what he means by this – over and above the practice he has followed at Corfinium of letting his opponents go, once beaten (even high-ranking opponents like Domitius Ahenobarbus), at the risk of facing them again later. He is aware of the huge propaganda value of this approach and realises the necessity of achieving an objective which for him is decisive – consensus, the greatest possible degree of consensus. Consensus means not only favourable public opinion, but also the rapid integration of Pompey's disbanding legions in his own army. This was of great importance not only militarily (it yielded splendid results), but also politically, given the short- and long-term privileges reserved for the legions.

Immediately upon the outbreak of hostilities, Caesar asked himself the question of questions: *how does one get out of a civil war?* Or better: how is a *political* exit from a civil war to be found? And he resolved on a strategy diametrically opposed to Sulla's: no proscriptions, but amnesty. In a flash he recognised that to impose 'martial law' on an enemy beaten both militarily and politically would be a mistake. Nor did it escape him that there was a huge difference between Sulla, who had triumphed over a popular 'party', and himself, seeking to overcome a handful of *optimates*, even if they did possess clienteles and armies.[12] The defeat of the *optimates*, so Caesar calculated, would entail the disbanding of their armies and the dissolution of their client network. That in turn would facilitate the strategy of further reconciliation and the possible absorption of the more ambitious and least compromised among them, above all those who were young and still had a political career before them.

That is why Caesar would adopt the relatively neutral method of dictatorship, while disdaining proscriptions. But in the fierce struggle which broke out after his death, his heirs would solemnly abjure the dictatorship, while pursuing proscriptions on a much greater scale than Sulla. The opponents whom Caesar had defeated and co-opted resorted to the extreme means of conspiracy and assassination and thus certainly contributed to this tragic outcome.[13] Despite this dramatic and grave series of developments, the possibilities of a political solution to the civil war other than Caesar's amnesty seem not to have been considered.[14]

In the political polemics of the later Roman republic, that is, thirty years after Sulla's death, the term 'Sullan' was still current as a synonym for radical struggle. Caesar makes use of this term in the beginning of his *Commentaries* on the civil war: the coalition of his opponents, trampling upon the tribunes' rights, went further than

Sulla and did what Sulla had not once dared to do; they denied the tribunes their right of veto and issued threats against them when they had been in office for only seven days. Shortly thereafter, in his speech to the Thirteenth Legion, Caesar repeats this accusation and leads with the classic attack of the populares: 'novum in re publica introductum exemplum!'[15] 'The tribunes' right of intervention, which in earlier times had been restored by arms, was now being branded with ignominy and crushed by arms.' While Sulla had in every regard undermined the tribunes' power, he had at least respected their right of veto. Pompey, by contrast, who boasted of having restored the tribunes' rights, had now deprived them even of the right of *intercessio*.[16] Caesar from the outset deftly launched the characterisation of his opponents as 'Sullan', using the words of one of them: 'Lentulus . . . boasts among his friends that he will prove a second Sulla to whom shall fall the supreme command.'[17]

Since this was recorded following the end of the civil war, these polemics are retrospective and have the aim of labelling the opposing coalition as 'Sullan'. The assertion that Sulla's coup was the direct forerunner of Caesar's coup belongs to Cicero. The reply to this charge was Caesar's 'manifesto', which he circulated as the open letter to Oppius and Cornelius Balbus.

In the first months of the civil war, Cicero expresses in his almost daily letters to Atticus the fear that Sulla's order could return. The conflict then under way seems to him to be almost a repetition of the conflicts of thirty years earlier. He had heard that Caesar was threatening to avenge the murder of the leading Marians,[18] and that he would, as soon as possible, demand official recognition from the Senate. Here also the closest precedent is Sulla: 'If Sulla could arrange to be named dictator by an *interrex*, why should not Caesar?'[19] Caesar's watchword (*liberalitas*) did not convince Cicero. He feared that 'all his kindness' amounted to 'Cinnanam illam crudelitatem' ('cruelty like Cinna's').[20] Nevertheless, Cicero perceives the greatest danger in Pompey's camp and its nostalgia for old times. On 27 February he writes: 'A sort of Sulla's reign has long been his object, and is the desire of many of his companions.'[21] And a month or so later, on 20 March, he reports the impressions of his friend and former son-in-law Crassipes, who has returned to Brindisi from Pompey's camp: 'Nothing but proscriptions, nothing but little Sullas.'[22] Even Pompey, who had begun thirty years earlier with a private army on Sulla's side, appears resolved to resort to these methods: '*sullaturit* animus eius', as Cicero sarcastically puts it, coining a new expression, '*et* proscripturit *iam diu*' ('so long has he been eager to play at Sulla and proscriptions').[23]

The Sullan temptation was an old demon: 'It is wonderful to see how Pompey desires to imitate Sulla's reign. I know what I am saying.'[24] Cicero's perceptive assessment of the intentions of Pompey and his allies is revealing: for one thing, it was made in private (his official appraisal was quite different: 'quos civis, quos viros!' – 'what citizens, what men were they!');[25] for another, it deplores tendencies which could not be openly admitted, showing that at the propaganda level the oligarchy rejected the term 'Sullan'. Lentulus' remark ('se alterum fore Sullam', 'that he will be a second Sulla'), if authentic, was merely a boast, and Caesar himself understood it as such. Moreover the term 'Sullan' retained its negative connotation – *proscriptio Sullana, saeculum Sullanum, Sullana tempora* (Sullan proscriptions, Sullan age, Sullan times)[26] – until the Sullan age came to an end with the great 'Sullan' massacre at the end of 43.

The capitulation of Corfinium had provided Caesar with a fresh opportunity to realise his programme. When Publius Cornelius Lentulus Spinther,[27] unable to hold Corfinium against Caesar's siege, sued for surrender negotiations to begin, Caesar exploited the opportunity – inevitably, given the circumstances – to make Lentulus spokesman for his propaganda directed at the city and the beleaguered troops. His account of events follows. It is no accident that in his *Commentaries* the details receive such emphasis.

[1] About the fourth watch Lentulus Spinther confers with our outposts and sentries from the wall, saying that he would like to have an interview with Caesar if the opportunity were granted him. [2] Permission being given, he is escorted from the town, nor do the Domitian soldiers leave him till he is brought into the presence of Caesar. [3] He pleads with him for his own safety, begs and beseeches that he will spare him, reminds him of their old-standing friendship, and sets forth the benefits that Caesar had conferred on him – and they were very great, [4] for through his means he had been admitted to the College of the Pontifices, had held the province of Spain after his praetorship, and had been assisted in his candidature for the consulship. [5] Caesar interrupts his speech, observing that he had not quitted his province with any evil intent, but to defend himself from the insults of his foes, to restore to their position the tribunes of the people who at that conjuncture had been expelled from the state, to assert the freedom of himself and the Roman people who had been oppressed by a small faction. [6] Lentulus, encouraged by his speech,

begs permission to return to the town, saying that the fact that he had gained his point about his own safety would comfort the rest in their hope for theirs; 'some of them,' he added, 'are so terrified that they are being forced to adopt harsh measures against their own life.' Receiving permission, he departs.[28]

But this was by no means the end. As we know from Caesar's letter to Oppius and Cornelius Balbus, among the leaders of Pompey's forces taken at Corfinium was Numerius Magius, an engineering officer.[29] Caesar writes in his letter of 5 March, 'I have taken N. Magius, a prefect of Pompey. Of course I kept to my policy and set him free at once.' In reality everything happened differently. After the surrender of Corfinium, some cohorts went over to Caesar, others were caught as they attempted to break through to Pompey in Apulia, but then set free again. Numerius, by contrast, was taken, brought to Caesar and dispatched with pressing proposals for compromise to Pompey, who had already gone to ground in Brindisi and was preparing to cross the Adriatic.

In his *Commentaries* Caesar maintains that Pompey did not send Numerius back to him, and certainly not with a reply.[30] However, among Cicero's letters to Atticus there happens to be a noteworthy missive from Caesar to Oppius and Cornelius Balbus, a copy of which Balbus sent to Cicero (on 22 March) together with a brief commentary.[31] It runs: 'On the 9th of March I reached Brindisium, and under its walls pitched my camp. Pompey is at Brindisium. He sent N. Magius to me to talk of peace.' A condensed form of words this, since 'misit ad me N. Magium de pace' might mean either 'with peace proposals' or 'with a reply to my peace proposals'.[32] It goes on: 'I replied as I thought fit (*quae visa sunt respondi*). I wanted you to know this at once. When I have hopes of settled terms, I will inform you immediately.' The contradiction could only be resolved if one were to take it[33] that Magius had first conveyed proposals which were unacceptable to Caesar, so that talks had been broken off, whereupon Magius remained in Pompey's camp and shortly afterwards took ship for the further shore of the Adriatic. The fact remains that Caesar in the *Commentaries* presents the affair in the most favourable light possible[34] and is silent on the negotiation phase (which certainly took place), during which Caesar resolved to reject proposals which for him represented more a surrender than a favourable outcome.

What Caesar wrote to his two agents revealed great irritation. Though not in so many words, Caesar made it clear that he had rejected his opponent's proposals: 'quae visa sunt respondi', which could be construed as 'I have given him an appropriate response.' The subsequent sentence then makes sense: 'I wanted to let you know at once.' The final sentence not only accords with the disappointment evident in the previous sentences, but expresses Caesar's scepticism over the prospect of a settlement: 'When I have hopes of settled terms, I will inform you immediately.' Hence Balbus attaches an almost sorrowful commentary to these sentences (in a last attempt to keep alive his contact with Cicero): 'If I were there with him, perhaps I might succeed in seeming to be of use.' In reality this meant breakdown. On 14 March, a few days after Caesar's letter to Oppius and Cornelius Balbus, Caesar told Quintus Pedius, his nephew and ally, that the siege of Brindisi would be long and that, above all, he had 'no better course'.[35] This sentence is all too significant: it implies not only that there was no alternative to Caesar's blockade of the port, but that there was no alternative *to war*, which had already broken out, since the frail thread of negotiations had been snapped. Numerius had not returned. Cicero understands that the hour of decision has struck for him also, giving vent to: 'Where is the peace about which Balbus wrote that he was tormenting himself?'[36]

The subsequent course of events we know.[37] The game of last-minute negotiations was risky. Caesar spared no effort to reach a settlement, but could not let himself be driven into a corner before it came to a fight. Therefore he had to venture much, but at the same time show firmness and withdraw in time. For their part, his opponents could hold Caesar responsible for the breakdown. Hence the proposals of Numerius, rejected by Caesar as unacceptable. That is also why Caesar, in his *Commentaries*, passes over the negotiation phase in silence, in order better to set off his own version of events – that it was his opponents who were to blame for the breakdown of negotiations.[38]

Notes

1 On 21 February 49 BC at Corfinium Pompey's garrison surrendered, including Domitius Ahenobarbus, who held the city against Caesar. Caesar set them all free. In this letter he explains why.

2 He has in mind particularly Gaius Marius.

3 Meanwhile correspondence flowed in both directions: news of the capitulation of Corfinium reached Rome, and Caesar received from Rome the letter of Oppius and Cornelius Balbus approving his strategy of being open to dialogue even after hostilities had begun.

4 This emerges from Cicero's reply, which runs: 'You advise me to ask Caesar to allow me to pay Pompey the same homage as I did to him' (Cicero, *Letters to Atticus* 9.7.3.)

5 Ibid.: 'sana mente scriptas litteras quo modo in tanta insania'.

6 A very common precaution for significant statements.

7 Cicero, *Letters to Atticus* 9.7A.2 (Oppius and Balbus to Cicero).

8 In which Atticus also encouraged him.

9 On 17 March Pompey would flee Brindisi, making Caesar's siege of the port unnecessary.

10 In the bloody battle at the gates of Rome.

11 'Nonnulla in mentem veniunt.'

12 This decisive difference was pointed out by Napoleon, who repeatedly referred to Caesar's having 'le peuple' on his side.

13 Hence, following the Ides of March, Sallust writes a demonic history, packed with allusions, of a *coniuratio* as *precedent* (*Catilinarian Conspiracy* 4.3: 'sceleris novitate'). In it the Catilinarians are the forerunners of the 'liberators', Caesar appearing as the one who presses for *clementia*.

14 Another possibility (to take an example from another age) is 'posthumous antifascism', which, practised by subsequent generations, is ultimately no more than a literary attitude.

15 'Novum illud exemplum!' Sallust has Caesar say in his speech in the Senate against the execution of the Catilinarians (*Catilinarian Conspiracy* 51.27).

16 Caesar, *Civil War* 1.7.

17 Caesar, *Civil War* 1.4.2.

18 *Letters to Atticus* 9.14.2 (25 March 49): 'Cn. Carbonis, M. Bruti se poenas persequi omniumque eorum in quos Sulla crudelis hoc [= Pompey] socio fuisset.' 'Moreover someone told me with authority that Caesar said in conversation he was the avenger of Cn. Carbo, M. Brutus [the father of his future assassin!], and all those on whom Sulla with Pompey to help him wreaked his cruelty.'

19 *Letters to Atticus* 9.15.2 (25 March 49). The appointment of an *inter-rex*, whom Sulla proclaimed *dictator*, had become necessary since both consuls had been killed by Sulla's followers.

20 *Letters to Atticus* 8.9A (25 February).

21 *Letters to Atticus* 8.11.2: 'Genus illud Sullani regni iam pridem appetitur multis, qui una sunt cupientibus.'

22 *Letters to Atticus* 9.11.3: 'meras proscriptiones, meros Sullas' (Crassipes had left Pompey's camp on 6 March). Cf. 9.10.2. 'How often do we hear this: "Sulla could do it, and shall not I?"'

23 *Letters to Atticus* 9.10.6 (18 March). 'Il a son coeur depuis longtemps déjà prurit de syllanisme et de proscriptions' (J. Bayet trans., *Cicéron, Correspondance*, vol. V [Paris 1964]). The unusual *sullaturit*, which

textual tradition sees as corrupt, is restored on the basis of Quintilian (*Institutio Oratoria* 8.3.32.)

24 *Letters to Atticus* 9.7.3 (13 March).

25 Cicero, *Phillipic* 13.29.

26 Seneca, *On anger* 1.20.4. 'Qualis illa [vox] dira et abominanda "oderint dum metuant": Sullano scias saeculo scriptam'; 2.34. 3. 'Inter Sullanae crudelitatis exempla est quod ab re publica liberos proscriptorum submovit'; Pliny, *Natural History* 9.123: 'Sullana tempora'.

27 He had been consul in 57 and had worked for Cicero's return from exile (see F. Münzer, s.v. *Cornelius, RE*, IV, 1, no. 238).

28 Caesar, *Civil War* 1.22.

29 This is also mentioned in Caesar, *Civil War* 1.24.4.

30 Caesar, *Civil War* 1.26.2: 'Magnopere admirabatur Magium [. . .] non remitti.'

31 Cicero, *Letters to Atticus* 9.13A (Balbus to Cicero).

32 Balbus also bemoans the vagueness of the letter, thinking Caesar must be very occupied 'that he has written *tam breviter* on such a significant matter'.

33 See P. Fabre (ed.), César, *La Guerre civile*, vol. 1 (Paris 1936), p. 22, note 1.

34 See F. Münzer, s.v. *Magius, RE*, XIV, 1, no. 9.

35 Cicero, *Letters to Atticus* 9.14.1. Caesar's words as Cicero reports them are: 'Nihil est quod potius faciamus.'

36 *Letters to Atticus* 9.14.2.

37 See Chapter 21.

38 I fear that it will never be possible to ascertain who Numerius really was and why Caesar conveyed his proposal to Pompey through him, of all people, while setting all the others free. The only inference we can draw is that Caesar knew him.

CHAPTER 20

'Amicitia'

The functioning of Roman public life depended on *amicitia*. The fulcrum of the political groups, *amicitia* also humanised and strengthened relations between representatives of different alignments. According to some, it explains Roman politics: it was certainly a determining factor also because the political class had a single provenance.[1] Indeed, 'the conservative Roman voter could seldom be induced to elect a man whose name had not been known for centuries as a part of the history of the Republic'.[2] Cicero reflects on *amicitia* in a famous treatise, in which he asserts categorically (rather in contrast with his experience of life) that true *amicitia* must be disinterested. He fails to acknowledge that *amicitia* founded on mutual interest and benefit may be in every sense perceived as *amicitia* and to all intents the same. One should look therefore not to Cicero's *De amicitia* for an understanding of *amicitia*, but rather to Caesar's *Commentaries* on the civil war. Years later, Asinius Pollio would write that the 'amicitiae principum' were inextricably intertwined with the causes of the civil war.[3]

There exist two letters, both addressed to Cicero,[4] written after the death of Caesar, in which his correspondents, Asinius Pollio and Gaius Matius, who had followed Caesar in the civil war, explain with some embarrassment why they did so. In both cases the choice of side was determined by *amicitia*. Matius writes in August 44 BC: 'It was not Caesar I followed in the civil conflict, but a friend.'[5] Asinius says: 'Since I could not remain neutral because I had powerful enemies on both sides, I avoided the camp where I well knew I should not be safe from my enemies' plots.'[6] The discussion between Matius and Cicero concerns the role of *amicitia* in testing times such as civil war. Cicero recalls in minute detail how their *amicitia* had remained firm throughout and been demonstrated (especially by Matius, who had been on the winning side) while the two of them took different paths. He goes into detail: 'As far back into the past as my memory extends, no friend of mine is older than yourself.'[7] The sense of the long recollection,

scarcely hinted at, but still evident, is that politics is something cor-
related to but distinct from *amicitia* (he says his own painful and long-
delayed decision to follow Pompey was determined by 'my sensitivity
to criticism or by obligation or by Fortune').[8] Matius replies:

> I acknowledge that I have not yet arrived at that philosophical level
> [i.e. to be able to forget that he had chosen to back Caesar out of
> friendship]. They say [i.e. Cicero says] that country should come
> before friendship – as though they have already proved that his death
> was to the public advantage.[9]

In these letters Cicero's position is in line with his thinking in *De
amicitia*, written in the same period, while that of Matius reflects a
widespread view. Matius, who Cicero says was the inspiration for his
philosophical treatises, first of all states with good-natured irony that
he is not so advanced in philosophy as to have forgotten that *amicitia* comes first in their public behaviour. For this reason the choice
made by Brutus, the son of Servilia, Caesar's most devoted mistress,
caused a sensation at the outbreak of hostilities. Everyone knew that
Brutus' father had been brutally done away with by Pompey during
the Sullan civil war,[10] and they expected Brutus to opt for Caesar.
Instead, under the influence of his uncle Cato, the sworn enemy of
Caesar and ally against his will, *obtorto collo*, so to speak, of
Pompey, he chose Pompey's camp, convinced that Rome, in Matius'
words (though Matius did not share this view), 'came before *amicitia*'. Cicero, moreover, when he wrote to Tullius Tiro in mid-January
49 on the movement of events towards conflict, speaks of Caesar as
the author of 'letters menacing to the Senate', but does not forget to
call him 'our friend'.[11] In reality 'the wise one', Matius, adhered
much more closely to accepted Roman political practice. When
Publius Cornelius Lentulus Spinther, incapable of further resistance
to the siege of Corfinium, requested and obtained an audience with
Caesar, he first 'reminded him of their long-standing *amicitia*' and,
more significantly, began to enumerate not only the services he had
performed for Caesar, but also Caesar's services for him.[12] This indicates that the ties of *amicitia* were of value not only in reciprocity but
in their own right: an *amicus* was in some measure believed to remain
one, even in the extreme situation of Caesar and Lentulus, the
besieger and the besieged, in a war which had recently progressed
from words to arms. The reflex mechanisms of *amicitia* prevailed, or
one expected them to prevail, over those of the civil war. So Caesar
interrupted him and explained that 'he had not quitted his province

with any evil intent, [Lentulus therefore had nothing to fear] but to defend himself from the insults of his foes',[13] and furthermore, (but this is put after the personal aspect of the conflict), 'to restore to their position the tribunes of the people who at that juncture had been expelled from the state, to assert the freedom of himself and the Roman people who had been oppressed by a small faction'. Lentulus, who should have been there to oppose the orders of such a *factio paucorum*, is more than cheered: he returns to Corfinium with Caesar's leave and reassurances for the other besieged. Very soon they were free.

Nothing is more inaccurate, then, than to imagine there is a sort of reflex mechanism to the civil war, at least until the lines are clearly drawn between the victors and the vanquished. Marius, no less than Sulla, was considered *ferox* for applying this logic and severing the other threads that held the network of Roman political society firmly together.

Caesar remains *pontifex maximus* during the civil war. At no time in the crisis do his opponents ever think to remove him from this office, not even at the deadly, and in some ways tragicomic, sitting of 7 January 49. This does not depend on the improvidence of his opponents. Rather it was not politic to undermine prerogatives that had to do with bodies (priestly colleges, etc.) other than political ones, such as the Senate.[14] The zeal with which Sulla had tried to remove Caesar when he was very young from the position of *flamen Dialis* had disgusted even his supporters.[15] The sacred offices could not be taken away by any political act, only by a clear abuse of power, like Sulla's attempt to oust Caesar as *flamen*. Caesar remained *pontifex maximus* even when he was *hostis*. And his main opponent and 'persecutor', Lucius Domitius Ahenobarbus, remained in the pontificate until he died at Pharsalus. Not until then did Caesar replace him with his own great-nephew, the fifteen-year-old Octavius.[16]

Only on the eve of Pharsalus, when it was thought that Caesar had only hours to live, did various people (Domitius Ahenobarbus, Lentulus Spinther and others) contest the position of *pontifex maximus*, which he still held.[17] It is obvious that they believed that Caesar would either be dead or fleeing, and therefore unable to exercise his priestly function. He was not deposed from his priesthood; the problem of replacing him only arose when it appeared (in this case wrongly) that soon he would no longer be there.

Counter-evidence of the working of *amicitia* is the implacable, irremediable character of *inimicitia*. '*Amicitia* presupposes *inimicitia*, inherited or acquired: a statesman could not win power and influence without making many enemies.'[18] Labienus' head would be brought to Caesar after his last stubborn battle against his ex-general in the Gallic campaigns, because Labienus betrayed *amicitia* by changing sides shortly after the crossing of the Rubicon. It is probable that he had infiltrated Caesar's side from the start, and climbed steadily through the hierarchy.[19]

Titus Labienus had begun his career as a tribune of the plebs (63 BC) alongside Caesar. He had also lent him powerful backing in the highly political trial of the killer of the *popularis* Saturninus decades earlier. He had smoothed Caesar's election to the *pontificatus maximus*, restoring the awarding of this important position to the vote of the *comitia*. Caesar had therefore named him *legatus pro praetore* in Gaul, a post Labienus held from 58 to 50 BC.[20] Even on the eve of the civil war Caesar had entrusted Labienus with military assignments of great responsibility.[21] But scarcely had hostilities begun than Labienus went over to Pompey's side, in obedience to a secret but ancient 'loyalty', which he could not – and would not – avoid. Pompey with great emphasis informed the senators of Labienus' change of side at his meeting with them on 17 January 49. There was exaggerated enthusiasm: it was almost as if Caesar's forces were about to disintegrate. Labienus hastened to reveal everything he knew of Caesar's most secret plans, beginning with the disposition of his forces. It can easily be seen that Caesar was forced to revise much of his strategy in great haste, because we know that his movements continued to surprise his adversaries.

From that moment Labienus was placed in the most precarious position, and resisted all attempts to reach agreement. He had fought in every campaign in the civil war, and at Munda almost won. He could not hope for the *clementia Caesaris*, but only for a good funeral – which he received.

The position of Cato was no different. In the brief description of his opponents at the start of the civil war Caesar says of Cato simply that his spiteful envy was provoked by the 'old enmity'[22] (there was the painful scene of the note to Caesar intercepted by Cato in the sitting which was to decide the fate of the Catilinarians), and by his stunning defeat in the election to the consulship.[23] Cato disembowelled himself at Utica, to the astonishment of his associates, after he learned of the disastrous outcome of the battle of Thapsus. Caesar mentions Cato in the *Commentaries* only to make him look ridiculous in the description of his ignominious flight from Sicily (the province entrusted to him on 7 January). Caesar's short, savage portrait of his enemy is enhanced not only by his paraphrase of a speech by Cato explaining this flight, and blaming Pompey for 'an unnecessary war',[24] but also by its vivid conclusion with the words: 'After making these complaints in the assembly he fled the province.'[25]

In the speech that Caesar, still deprived of any official power, would give in the Senate shortly after he reached Rome following the invasion of Italy, he would attack *only Cato*, singling him out from the group of his *inimici* (personal opponents).

> A proposal had been carried by the ten tribunes while Pompey himself was consul that he [Caesar] should be allowed to compete in absence, though his enemies spoke against it, while Cato opposed with the utmost vehemence and after his old habit spun out the days by obstructive speech.[26]

With these hints at Cato's political activity Caesar meant to make clear how unexceptional and obtuse he considered him to be as a politician.

It is not known from whom he had obtained the account of Cato's words against Pompey and the 'unnecessary war'. It is certain, however, that those words, spoken by one who was about to 'flee the province' entrusted to him at the time of the division of responsibilities *in preparation for the conflict with Caesar*,[27] amounted to political suicide.[28]

Notes

1 This also applies to a large extent to modern parliamentary systems.
2 R. Syme, *The Roman Revolution* (Oxford 1939), p. 11.
3 Horace, *Odes* 2.1.1–3.
4 And therefore preserved.
5 Cicero, *Letters to his friends* 11.28 (Matius to Cicero).2.
6 Cicero, *Letters to his friends* 10.31 (Asinius to Cicero).2. This may refer to Cato.
7 Cicero, *Letters to his friends* 11.27.2.
8 Cicero, *Letters to his friends* 11.27.4: 'sive pudor sive officium sive fortuna': a somewhat puzzling form of words which does not express enthusiasm for the decision.
9 Cicero, *Letters to his friends* 11.28.2.

10	The father of Marcus Brutus was the same Marcus Brutus whom Caesar wished to punish, according to rumours reported by Cicero (*Letters to Atticus* 9.14.2), when he opened hostilities against Pompey.

11	Cicero, *Letters to his friends* 16.11.2. It should be borne in mind that, after deciding to publish some of his letters, Cicero selected those which showed him in the best light. Of these he collected some seventy, which we now have in book 13 of the collection *To his friends*.

12	Caesar, *Civil War* 1.22.3–4.

13	Caesar, *Civil War* 1.22.5.

14	Considering *how* Caesar succeeded in being nominated as dictator in spring 49, Cicero canvasses the possibility of an initiative by the college of augurs.

15	See Chapter 1.

16	Velleius 2.59.3: 'pontificatusque sacerdotio puerum honoravit'; Nicolaus of Damascus, *Life of Augustus* 1 and 4; Cicero, *Philippics* 5.46 and 53.

17	Caesar, *Civil War* 3.83.

18	Syme, *Roman Revolution*, p. 13.

19	R. Syme, 'The Allegiance of Labienus', *JRS*, 28 (1938), pp. 113–25 (esp. p. 121).

20	It is also likely that Labienus accumulated his enormous wealth in Gaul: Cicero, *Letters to Atticus* 7.7.6 (where Labienus is compared in this respect to Mamurra!). Caesar hints very clearly at the wealth of his erstwhile alter ego (*Civil War* 1.15.2).

21	See Caesar, *Gallic War* 8.52.2. Here Syme, rather than Mommsen, is correct.

22	Caesar, *Civil War* 1.4.1, 'veteres inimicitiae'.

23	When Caesar was certainly not the only one to bar his way.

24	Caesar, *Civil War* 1.30.5.

25	Caesar, *Civil War* 1.30.5: 'ex provincia fugit'. La Penna gives a good appreciation of this passage in 'Tendenze e arte del Bellum civile', *Maia*, 5 (1952); also in *Aspetti del pensiero storico latino* (Turin 1978), p. 149.

26	Caesar, *Civil War* 1.32.3.

27	Caesar, *Civil War* 1.30.2: 'Sardiniam obtinebat Cotta, Siciliam Cato.'

28	The author of the *African War* speaks of Cato in very different terms. One thinks of the improvised address to Pompey the Younger, the commentary immediately following it, and the description of Cato's suicide in Utica. This respect for Cato is at odds with Caesar's polemical presentation of him. Perhaps an indication of different authorship?

CHAPTER 21

From the Rubicon to Pharsalus

The start of the civil conflict is a kind of 'phoney war'. After the occupation of Picenum, Umbria and Etruria, and the humiliation of L. Domitius Ahenobarbus, who expected to succeed Caesar as governor of Gaul (and instead was ridiculed after his unsuccessful defence of Corfinium), Caesar hastened down the Adriatic coast as far as Brindisi to attempt to block Pompey's flight from Italy. When this failed – Pompey successfully crossed to Durazzo (Dyrrhachium) on 17 March 49[1] – Caesar 'lost' his enemy for some time. He hurried back to Rome to consolidate, first, the conquest of Italy. This hectic start was followed by a period of deadlock, or rather, of waiting: the fast-moving 'mobile warfare' so dear to Caesar gave way to a tedious and lasting standstill. Strategic objectives were temporarily changed. Caesar busied himself with consolidating his hold on Italy and the West, while Pompey set about building a great army in Greece and Macedonia.

How did this paradoxical situation come about? Pompey had deceived his friends when he said, with his usual air of superiority towards the rest of the world, that he had only to give the signal by stamping his foot and 'whole armies would rise up out of the ground'.[2] After this he decided to leave Italy to his enemy and try to build an 'invincible' army in Greece. Favonius, a loyal Catonian, did not hesitate to remind him of that rash and self-satisfied pledge when it became clear that nothing at all would rise up out of the ground, at least in Italy.[3] Napoleon considered Pompey's strategy to be suicidal. Despite an evident liking for Caesar, which occasionally clouds his judgement, and despite a habit (formed during his days at military college) of viewing the military campaigns of history as 'war games', the Emperor of the French does have a point this time. His criticism is at once military and political: being a good general, a child of the Revolution and of the renaissance in the art of war, Napoleon Bonaparte knows that war and politics are inextricably linked. So the first mistake – in order of gravity – with which he charges the

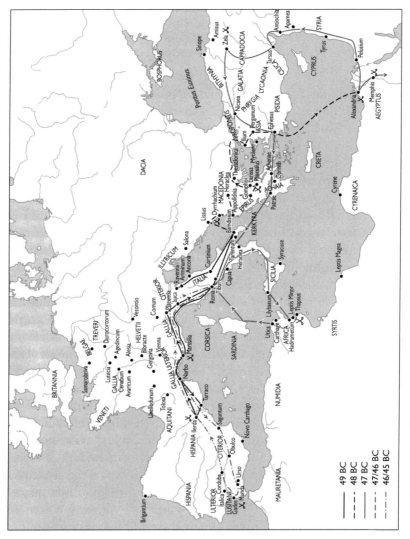

The campaigns of Caesar during the civil war

inadequate imitator of Alexander the Great, at the end of the ninth chapter of his *Précis*, lies in failing to appreciate that 'the people' were with Caesar. Pompey miscalculated, because he associated only with great men and senators 'qui parlaient très haut', and whose 'deafening' voice concealed from him the fact of greatest political significance: 'the people were irresistibly inclined towards Caesar'. At first this produced the illusion of being safe in Rome, then came the panic and the search for a secure base far from Italy. His second mistake was not even to consider the possibility of making the six most loyal legions he had in Spain converge on Rome (he was still proconsul of Spain, even if he never moved from Rome while Caesar was building his future in Gaul). The legions stationed in Spain, had they set out from Valencia, Cartagena and Tarragona, could have landed at Ostia and Naples within a few weeks, Napoleon calculates correctly.[4] These, moreover, were highly effective, battle-hardened legions, even though they had mediocre commanders (Afranius, Petreius, and the great writer but modest fighting man Marcus Terentius Varro), which is why Caesar called them 'an army without a leader'.[5] In short, concludes Napoleon, 'It was Rome that should have been defended; that was where Pompey should have concentrated his forces at the very beginning [of the civil war].' And then he observes, somewhat magisterially, 'It was necessary to keep all the forces together, so that they should feed one another's fighting spirit[6] and gain confidence in their strength. This is how soldiers are bound together and remain true.' And here he puts forward his own strategy, which he would have put into effect had he been in Pompey's position: if the thirty cohorts of Domitius Ahenobarbus (instead of trying in vain to defend Corfinium in order to bar Caesar's way to Picenum) had been camped at the gates of Rome with Pompey's two legions, and if the Pompeian legions from Spain, Africa, Egypt and Greece, in a coordinated converging manoeuvre, had all come by sea to join up in Italy, Pompey would have fielded against Caesar an army that was larger than that of his enemy.[7]

Mommsen has Bonaparte's observations in mind when he writes about Pompey's baffling move in his *History of Rome* (book 5, ch. 10). Mommsen, too, acknowledges that Pompey would quickly, at the latest by the start of the spring, have had at least 60,000 men, whose core would have been the seven ultra-loyal legions in Spain. He considers the two legions ceded to Pompey, which were garrisoned at the gates of Rome, highly untrustworthy, nostalgic – he observes (or rather, imagines) – for the personal rewards that Caesar lavished on his men as 'an advance' on the celebration of the triumph. He observes, furthermore, that initial defeats in Picenum had thrown Rome into panic and convinced Pompey of the advisability of withdrawing, accustomed as he was to fighting only when sure of overwhelming superiority. Pompey, besides, was used to adhering to tactics that were slow and sure, not swift or reliant on sudden, unpredictable manoeuvres. The great German historian, who did not hide his liking for the third Napoleon, here questions, without naming it, the military theory of the first Napoleon, but he overlooks the most important point. The vain defence of Picenum, according to Napoleon, had been a serious mistake: Domitius Ahenobarbus should not have been sent to certain defeat alone; his troops should have joined with the other Pompeian forces in the defence of Rome, but this did not happen.[8]

Actually, Domitius himself had pointed out to Pompey the folly of his strategic decision. Caesar relates this in the *Commentaries*, relying on information gained during and after the campaign.[9] Domitius, when besieged by Caesar at Corfinium, tried to persuade Pompey to abandon his plan, even when he was already in Puglia (Apulia). Caesar says: 'Domitius offers a large reward to some men acquainted with the district, and sends them with dispatches to Pompey in Apulia to beg and beseech him to come to his assistance.'[10] Those envoys brought this strategic proposal: 'pointing out that [if Pompey immediately turned north and joined Domitius in the defence of Corfinium] Caesar could easily be cut off by two armies operating in the narrow passes and so be prevented from foraging'.[11] Otherwise, Domitius argued, he himself, with more than thirty cohorts, 'and a great number of senators and Roman knights', would be in great difficulty.[12]

Pompey ignored the appeal. Corfinium surrendered. Caesar takes pleasure in describing in great detail the scene of the surrender and humiliation of his fiercest enemy. First of all Caesar had all the senators, senators' sons, knights, and military tribunes who had led the besieged army brought before him. It was revealed that there were only five members of the senatorial order,[13] two of whom were Domitius Ahenobarbus and Lentulus Spinther (who had gone to Caesar the previous evening to discuss the terms of the surrender). There were two other senators, plus Domitius' son, some knights, and a handful of decurions summoned by Domitius from the neighbouring towns. They were conducted into Caesar's presence amidst volleys of abuse. 'All those when brought before him he protects from the clamorous insolence of the troops.'[14] He addressed them briefly, reminded them all of the ingratitude each of them had returned for the favours he had bestowed on them. After this he sent them away: they departed unharmed. The *duumviri* of Corfinium came with the enormous sum of almost six million sesterces that Domitius had deposited in the public treasury of the city. Caesar ordered it to be restored immediately to Domitius.[15] Commenting on his own gesture, Caesar writes that he did this 'in order that he may not be thought more self-controlled in dealing with men's lives than with their property', although, he goes on, 'there was no doubt that this money belonged to the state'. His choice of words is deliberate: this is a reply to the accusations levelled against him of seizing the public treasury in Rome a few days later. (An incident that is not to be found in the *Commentaries*,[16] although Lentulus, the consul, is ridiculed for failing to bring that money to Pompey, as he should have done *ex senatus consulto*.)[17]

Rome had been left in total chaos. Plutarch describes very well the general confusion, the quarrels between citizens of opposite persuasions, and the Senate sitting (17 January) at which Pompey was the object of the bitterest recriminations: from those, for example, who reproached him for having rejected Caesar's offers, or Favonius, who sarcastically asked him to stamp his foot and make all the soldiers he had promised appear.[18] After this distressing sitting the consuls fled with Pompey to the south. Caesar's final peace proposals reached them at Teanum, but were once again rejected. Before leaving Rome, somebody remembered that the consuls should have (or at least could have) put the public coffers in a safe place. When they were asked to do so, they replied that they would 'deem it safer' if Pompey first occupied Picenum.[19] The panic was due to the fact that nobody had a clear idea of Caesar's imminent movements, and some visionaries were already claiming they had seen his cavalry at the gates of Rome. This kind of rumour, in spite of Labienus, who had only just fled from the Caesarian camp and would have brought important secret information,[20] produced the chaos that characterised the flight of the consuls, Pompey, and part of the Senate southwards, and then directly to Brindisi.

Now the Senate found itself being blackmailed: to remain in Rome meant to collaborate with Caesar. Many are doubtful when Pompey replies, 'Places and houses are not strength and freedom to men; but men, wherever they may be, have these qualities within themselves, and by defending themselves will recover their homes also.'[21] This was the strategy of Themistocles: to abandon Athens, because the city was its people. Cicero, in one of his regular troubled letters to Atticus in these months, recalls the Themistoclean precedent and calls Pompey's entire strategy a 'Themistocleum consilium'.[22] He is not really fully convinced of what he writes: he discourses on strategy, interpreting Pompey's decision in his own way. Of course he lost Spain – he explains to Atticus: he concentrated all his forces in the fleet, just like Themistocles.[23] There was also another precedent, another famous commander in Athenian history who had voiced a similar thought: Nicias, who, before the Sicilian catastrophe, had said 'it is men that make a state, not walls nor ships devoid of men'.[24] But this was a disturbing precedent best passed over in silence.

We do not know exactly how many senators actually followed Pompey to Brindisi, Durazzo, then Greece, and how many remained in Rome. It is a fact that, after his attempt to stop Pompey at Brindisi failed, Caesar, on returning to Rome, convened the Senate outside the *pomerium* on 1 April and spoke at length and in a spirit of skilful conciliation to those senators who had stayed. One prominent figure, Cicero, would sail from Formiae *only on 7 June*, after countless doubts and much mental wavering, and after an exchange of letters with Caesar filled with mutual amiability.[25]

The thorny problem that worried Cicero was this: why should he set out to take direct part in Pompey's war? He was seized by nagging doubts, which no amount of rational thought could resolve. On 12 March, while Pompey was in Brindisi and Caesar was outside the port, intent on preventing his rival's escape and possibly inducing him to parley,[26] Cicero wrote Atticus a fundamentally self-mocking letter, in which the alternatives appear as so many themes of *declamationes*. He writes of himself and his own dilemmas in an exercise in rhetoric designed to bring out the ambivalence and problematic nature of both possible alternatives. With meticulous precision he constructs his debate with himself – in Greek, to accentuate his detachment from the topic (and perhaps as an extra precaution):[27] (a) should one remain in one's country even when that country is under the rule of a tyrant; (b) should one do all one can to overthrow that tyranny, *even when this could place the city in grave danger*; (c) should one who plans to overthrow the tyrant *also look to his own safety*; (d) should one aid the country oppressed by a tyrant by timely political words and action, *rather than by recourse to arms*; (e) may it be considered a political act to leave one's country when it is oppressed by a tyrant, or should one instead confront all dangers for the sake of liberty; (f) should one bring war upon one's own country, and is it legitimate to lay siege to it when it is oppressed by a tyrant (this is exactly what Pompey claimed to be doing against an Italy that was occupied by Caesar); (g) should one still enlist with the *optimates, even if one does not approve the overthrow of a tyrant by force of arms*; (h) should one, in political life, face danger beside one's friends and benefactors, *even if it seems utterly impossible to share their political preferences*, etc. The series rises in a crescendo to the ninth and last: ought a person who has suffered so much for his country still willingly expose himself to danger? This last is the most explicit of all in explaining Cicero's reluctance to join with Pompey and his current influential advisers in a new civil war. He goes on in his letter to say that these are the questions he has been inwardly debating *in utramque partem*, that is, seeking answers to each, pro and contra, in both Greek and Latin. On 5 March Caesar had written to him asking to see him 'and employ your advice, favour, *position* and help of all kinds'.[28]

These words are not intended merely as compliments. It is true that Cicero exerted influence, in particular on that not insignificant part of the Senate that constituted a malleable and suggestible mass. Caesar knew well the mechanisms of senatorial politics: a powerful clique, the *factio*, especially if furnished with an 'armed wing' in the person of Pompey, could dominate the Senate, and intimidate and blackmail it. But now these people were fleeing. Certainly they had tried to blackmail the others (by saying that anybody who stayed must be on Caesar's side), but many had stayed all the same,[29] and men like Cicero could offer a behavioural model for many in this 'malleable mass'. Hence Caesar's pertinent judgement, and hence his determined 'courtship' of Cicero in the hope of keeping him in Rome to 'legitimise' the rump of the Senate, the part remaining after the flight of the consuls. And Cicero is kept informed by Caesar's main political collaborator, Balbus, of the secret final proposals put to Pompey, who was barricaded in Brindisi: we have, in his correspondence with Atticus, a copy of the letter from Balbus to Cicero about Magius' mission.[30] On 18 March Cicero explains to Atticus in a long letter why he had not followed Pompey.[31]

> Pompey was slipping or rather rushing towards ruin. I saw he was terrified on the 17th of January:[32] on that day I felt what he would do. Since then I have never approved his course, and he has never ceased to commit one blunder after another.

And here the recriminations are as stinging as the wound itself: he did not attempt to reach me, not even by letter. He makes a comparison: 'Just as in love affairs[33] men are repelled by untidiness, stupidity and indelicacy, so the ugliness of his flight and his carelessness have estranged my love.' And his judgement could not be clearer: 'He has done nothing of a kind to induce me to share his flight.'

Caesar, for his part, writes again and again to Cicero, gets his followers to write to him, and even involves him in the final negotiations. And Cicero replies (among the *Letters to Atticus* is Cicero's long letter to Caesar, of which he sent a copy to Atticus).[34] He replies on 19 March with great embarrassment, asking questions such as: what do you mean by 'my advice and my position'? He then accepts the role of adviser, at least for the moment, and sets out for Caesar his thoughts regarding the final negotiations with Pompey. There was nothing remarkable in the substance, except for the very fact that he appeared to be beginning to 'gravitate' towards Caesar, while still proclaiming friendship and loyalty to Pompey (about whom he had written to Atticus the previous day). He also stresses his own neutrality ('since the outbreak of hostilities I have not taken any part in the war').[35] This shows a significant shift in attitude towards the person whom, in his rhetorical *declamationes*, he had called 'the tyrant'. Caesar circulated Cicero's letter,[36] evidently because it helped and supported him. Many disapproved of Cicero's more than conciliatory initiative towards the 'tyrant'. Cicero, writing to Atticus, is greatly put out by these negative reactions,[37] and devotes an entire letter to the defence of his own actions.

In the meantime, Caesar stepped up the pressure, seeking a firmer commitment from the respected and indecisive consul. On 16 April, two weeks after the Senate sitting at which he at last spoke, in the absence of the fugitive extremists, not as a bandit but as a pro-magistrate, he wrote once more to Cicero: 'Although I had concluded that you would do nothing rashly or imprudently, nevertheless I have been so stirred by what people say that I thought it best to write to you . . .'[38]

Caesar was on his way to Marseilles when he wrote these words. In view of Pompey's flight and the new situation in Italy (a power vacuum and duplication of authority at the same time), he had decided to adopt a new strategy. He would not immediately pursue Pompey: he understood that Pompey would reinforce his army and attempt to return to Italy, as Sulla had done before him, thus catching Caesar's legions in a pincer movement by means of an attack on Italy from Spain and Greece at once. To avoid this trap, he decided to press on to Spain and there confront Pompey's most faithful troops.

At this point the civil war assumed almost global proportions. Cicero understood this very well, as we see from his dismay at Pompey's decision to leave Rome:

> Pompey has not abandoned Rome because it was impossible to defend, nor Italy on forced compulsion; but it was his idea from the first to plunge the world into war, to stir up barbarous princes, to bring savage tribes into Italy under arms, and to gather a huge army.[39]

Pompey's strategy is well described here: mobilisation of his clients and the impressive resources which he could count on in the East, while postponing the decisive battle until he was able to deploy all of these, perhaps to return to Italy, replicating in grand style the victorious movement once made by Sulla. Caesar's response was strategically flawless, and he was much quicker to implement it than his enemy could have foreseen: to neutralise Pompey's Spanish and African forces in his rear. In Spain he succeeded brilliantly, but in Africa Curio suffered a punishing defeat and lost his life. Surrounded by the focal points of Pompey's clienteles, Caesar resolved to break the encirclement where it was weakest, in Spain. (Pompey's network of clienteles in Spain remained in place for years after his death, at the time of the Spanish revolt organised by his sons, and even later; in Africa, Juba was the focus of a Pompeian revival after Pharsalus.) Pompey's activities in the West were beginning to cause Caesar particular concern. Two of the nobles whom he had 'pardoned' after the surrender of Corfinium (21 February 49) and sent back to Pompey's camp as a calculated gesture of magnanimity, Domitius Ahenobarbus and Vibullius Rufus, had promptly returned to 'active service'. Pompey had sent Vibullius Rufus to Spain and Domitius to Marseilles to organise the counter-offensive and bar Caesar's way. Domitius had occupied a fortified position in Marseilles with a private army of slaves and colonists recruited on the island of Giglio (Igilium) and in the area of Cosa. Furthermore, Pompey had already sent back to Marseilles a group of his clients from among the local nobility, with a message for the city: 'not to let Caesar's fresh services drive from their minds the memory of his own earlier kindnesses'.[40] This is an eloquent example of the role of 'foreign clienteles' during the civil war. Caesar too, as a benefactor of the citizens, had claims on them, which he now sought to make good.[41] But all he received was an equivocal response, 'it is our duty to show them equal good-will, and not to receive either within our city or ports',[42] which permitted Domitius Ahenobarbus to enter the city with his fleet, take firm hold there and organise strong resistance to a potential siege by Caesar. Caesar replied by laying siege to the city with three legions by land and a newly built fleet blockading the port, under the command of Decimus Brutus and Trebonius.[43] This took place in May 49. Until the beginning of December, when Caesar finally returned to Rome, assumed the dictatorship and crossed the Adriatic to confront Pompey in the Balkans, six months passed in hard-fought campaigning against Afranius and Petreius in Spain, and against Marseilles, which capitulated at the end of October.[44]

It was anything but a triumphal march. Not only were the forces in the field well balanced; so were the tactical abilities of the generals. Throughout his Gallic campaign Caesar had had a veritable alter ego in Titus Labienus. At Caesar's side, Labienus had assimilated his tactical style to the point of becoming his double. Now this man, who perhaps had always been a Pompeian infiltrator at the apex of Caesar's general staff,[45] went over to the other side. And this added to the complexity of the long war. No one could be sure of victory, but, until Pharsalus, Pompey stood the better chance. But even later, right up to the last and fiercest battle, against the sons of Pompey at Munda, Caesar was faced with the possibility of defeat and the temptation of suicide. One factor in his victory was his good relationship with his troops. Even anti-Caesar historians such as Adcock allow him that trump card which all his numerous opponents lacked: 'In the magnetism which inspires troops to fight to the death for their leader Caesar had not to fear a rival in the enemy camp.'[46] Caesar had built up the precious capital of his charisma day by day during the long years of the Gallic campaign, for use as the decisive weapon on the field of battle.[47] In this area Pompey, being far from his Spanish legions, could not compete, sure though he was of broad consensus at the four corners of the Roman world, but for years no longer in direct contact with his men. Hence Caesar's indestructible, sometimes triumphalist self-confidence, and his contempt for opponents incapable of appreciating the 'human factor', a contempt which is visible on every page of his *Commentaries*, especially those on the civil war. And hence the new political mood engendered by 'Caesarism': the new phenomenon of Caesar's wars gave rise to citizen-soldiers as the product of that extended symbiosis with the troops.[48]

The hardest part of the Spanish campaign was the forty-four-day siege of Lérida (Ilerda), where Afranius and Petreius held a defensive position after an astutely fought campaign on difficult terrain. In the end Varro, Pompey's legate in Further Spain, surrendered to Sextus Julius Caesar, a cousin of Caesar designated to represent him on this important occasion: the capitulation of Pompey's feared and powerful Spanish legions.[49] At the same time, Curio's operation in Africa ended in defeat for him and the triumph of Juba, king of Numidia and Pompey's faithful client.[50] But this setback, which had no immediate military consequences (a landing by Juba in Sicily was hardly likely!), did not deflect Caesar from the main lines of his strategy. Having returned to Rome, where he had already been named as dictator and was elected consul for 48 (between 2 and 12 December 49),[51] he at once set about seeking an opportunity for a decisive confrontation with Pompey. On 22 December he was in Brindisi, and on 4 January 48 he crossed the Adriatic.

From the constitutional point of view, the situation was now reversed. The consuls of 49, the real authors of the final clash which had led to open war, were now ex-consuls. To the few surviving offices (to call them 'legal' in a situation of civil war, with two opposing codes, makes no sense), Caesar had in the course of his brief and violent halt in Rome made his own appointments: himself and Publius Servilius Isauricus as consuls; Antony as *magister equitum* for the few days until the end of 49 when Caesar was dictator (the dictatorship would pass to him again after Pharsalus); then Caelius Rufus, Quintus Pedius, Sulpicius Rufus, Trebonius and, possibly, Pansa as *praetors*. He had his men also in the provinces which he controlled: Lepidus in Hispania Citerior; Decimus Brutus in Gallia Transalpina; Aulus Albinus in Sicily; and Sextus Peducaeus in Sardinia. Meanwhile the pro-magistrates loyal to Pompey, having taken up their positions in the provinces allocated to them through the influence of the *factio* in January 49, had not been replaced for 48 and in fact continued in office. Hence there was a duality of power: the *orbis romanus* was divided between two conflicting 'legitimate authorities'. For a time in this phase of the long civil war there came to be a schism between East and West.

In 48, the pro-magistrates who had lost their provinces through the de facto division of the empire came to join those 'Pompeian' pro-magistrates in office in 49 whose appointments had been 'prolonged'. Domitius Ahenobarbus, Caesar's 'fiercest' enemy, is one of them. His nomination amid turmoil on 7 January 49, vainly declared invalid by the tribunes of the plebs, sheds light on his subsequent fortunes during the civil war. He had been allotted Gaul, where he was to replace Caesar. He resolved on Gallia Cisalpina, but became trapped in the web of Caesar's siege of Corfinium.[52] Humiliated, and then freed, by his 'enemy', he promptly took ship to Marseilles and took charge of the months-long resistance to Caesar's siege. When the city could no longer be held, he escaped by sea, evading pursuit by Decimus Brutus' ships.[53] As a proconsul expelled by force from his province, he fled to Pompey. On the eve of the battle of Pharsalus, in the somewhat premature allocation of post-war offices, he laid determined claim to the post of *pontifex maximus*.[54] He fell at Pharsalus.

It was the Balkan campaign that sealed Pompey's fate. It began with the failed blockade of Durazzo, which occupied the first six months of the year, and ended with the battle of Pharsalus on 9 August 48.[55]

The original plan was to bottle up and destroy Pompey in the bay of Durazzo, but not all went according to Caesar's plan. The part of the fleet under Mark Antony's command was to arrive at a set time to enable the complete occupation of the strategic points in the bay (Durazzo, Apollonia, Oricum), but was held off at sea by Bibulus, Caesar's fierce, but luckless, colleague in the consulate of 59. Caesar could only occupy Apollonia and Oricum, while Pompey was able to set up camp at Petra with unhindered access to the open sea. Even in these circumstances, with the two forces in almost direct confrontation, Caesar did not relinquish the hope of bringing Pompey to negotiation. At the outset of the campaign he had sent Vibullius Rufus to him. Now, with signs of reconciliation appearing among the soldiers of both camps,[56] he sought a meeting with Pompey through the intervention of Vatinius, but an abrupt rejection by Labienus destroyed all possibility of further negotiations.

For months Caesar had to face this difficult situation alone, while Bibulus and his fleet held Antony at Brindisi.[57] Not until 27 March[58] did Antony succeed in evading the blockading force, to reach the port of Durazzo following risky and daring manoeuvres and aided by an unexpected change in wind direction.[59] Then fortunes changed. Until now Caesar's troops had endured inhuman conditions. Their provisions were exhausted, while Pompey could obtain supplies by sea and by land. Caesar's troops lived on a kind of bread made of herbs. Coming across this 'bread' by chance, Pompey declared that he was fighting wild beasts and ordered that it be shown to no one, so as not to undermine the morale of his forces.[60] At the siege of Durazzo,

Caesar resolved on a supremely reckless scheme: to encircle a numerically superior army. Of this Napoleon writes:

> a rash manoeuvre, and justly punished. How could he ever hope to hold a fortified line six leagues in length and reduce an enemy who had the advantage of a central position [Petra,[61] where Pompey had his camp] and command of the sea?[62]

Pompey broke through the blockade and retired towards Macedonia. Caesar gave chase until finally the two armies faced each other on the Haliakmon river. Following marches and counter-marches, the two forces took up their final positions on the plain of Pharsalus in Thessaly. Caesar had under his command legions consisting predominantly of veterans of his Gallic campaign. At first Pompey was reluctant to give battle here, but his commanders were impatient and restless. Labienus, who had already shown how harshly he could treat prisoners,[63] was instrumental in bringing Pompey to change his mind. In a council of war, described in great detail by Caesar, Labienus said, *inter alia*, that few of Caesar's veterans, the victors of Gaul, were still alive and that, as a result, Caesar's legions consisted entirely of raw recruits.[64] Once they had persuaded one another that this was indeed so (a classic example of a ruling group falling victim to its own propaganda), they all followed Labienus in swearing that they would return to camp only as victors.[65] Too late did Pompey recognise his mistake in giving battle in such a disadvantageous position and so far from the fleet, his mainstay.[66]

At Pharsalus too Caesar was at a numerical disadvantage. He even says that he fought with half the numbers that Pompey had. One might ask whether he exaggerates to enhance the brilliance of his victory. Auxiliaries and followers must, after all, be taken into account to gain some notion of how many men were involved in a campaign of this nature.[67] Caesar's address to his troops before the battle began was again in a tone of moderation.[68] Having first recounted all that he had done for his men, he recalled his persistent efforts to arrive at a peaceful outcome. He listed his attempts at negotiation up to the very last and ended thus: 'He had never, he said, wished to squander the blood of his soldiers, *or to deprive the republic of either of its armies.*' He had not forgotten the spontaneous impulse of the troops on both sides to fraternise at the bay of Durazzo. While Labienus had had Pompey's prisoners put to death, Caesar right to the last was pointing out to his troops the horrors of civil war. Inspired by his words, the troops demanded battle, and

Caesar had the signal given. Caesar reports that a man of the Tenth Legion named Crastinius, the first from the right wing to hurl himself into the fray, had shouted to the others, 'This one battle alone remains; when it is over he will recover his dignity (*suam dignitatem*) and we our liberty (*nostram libertatem*).'[69] We do not know if this is a genuine episode or an edifying insertion from a later date, but it takes up precisely the slogan launched by Caesar at the crossing of the Rubicon – restoration of the general's honour (*dignitas*), slighted by his opponents, and of the Roman people's freedom, threatened by the clique which had driven out the tribunes of the plebs. In addition to being brave, Crastinius had about him much of what we might term the 'political commissar'.

In his description of the battle of Pharsalus, Caesar launches into an examination of the psychology of men at war. These are the perceptive reflections of a man for whom the terrible reality of war had for years been part of his intellectual experience. Caesar begins with a discussion of a strategic detail which must have puzzled him at the outset. Pompey had given orders that his troops were to await Caesar's attack without moving from their position, calculating that Caesar's ranks would be dispersed during their attack and his troops breathless at the end of their charge (a longer one than intended) when they reached Pompey's lines.[70] 'Now this seems to us to have been an irrational act on the part of Pompey', Caesar comments, 'because there is a certain keenness of spirit and impetuosity[71] implanted by nature in all men which is kindled by the ardour of battle.' He refers to the old custom of sounding trumpets and shouting war cries in massed chorus. Here Caesar has grasped the animal nature of battle and sees clearly that the energy latent in each individual must be released in exertion, and in moments of violence and psychological tension each is capable of much more than under normal circumstances. Caesar here gives Pompey a lesson in the psychology of war and demonstrates its immediate implications for winning battles: the human factor versus the arithmetical factor.

None of the classical moves brought success to Pompey and his officers. Caesar had taken some cohorts from the Third Legion and formed them into a fourth line.[72] This 'extra' legion engaged Pompey's cavalry and prevented them from outflanking Caesar's right wing, before finally putting them to flight. And with the flight of the cavalry, the rest of Pompey's army also crumbled and fled the field. The casualties were unevenly divided: 200 on Caesar's side (half of them officers); about 15,000 dead and wounded on Pompey's. Commenting on these figures, Napoleon correctly observes that this was a relatively normal proportion 'in the battles of ancient times', while the proportion is one to three in modern times and 'the great difference is in the number of prisoners'. Napoleon goes on to say that it is a fact that modern armies suffer heavy losses before coming to close quarters, whereas an ancient battle was man to man almost from the first moment. In the countless duels which made up an ancient battle, the proven discipline of the battle-hardened veterans of the Gallic war gave them a decisive advantage over Pompey's troops, whose experience did not go beyond 'Asian wars': so was it at Pharsalus.[73]

In the light of the total defeat and flight of the enemy commanders, Caesar quickly resolved that his first priority must be to pursue Pompey.[74] There has been much discussion of this decision, which, as we know, led Caesar into the near death-trap of Alexandria. Napoleon castigates Caesar,[75] his main charge being that, 'immediately after Pharsalus Caesar proceeded at once to the African coast to forestall Cato and Scipio'.[76] In my view, Caesar's hot pursuit of Pompey as he fled to Egypt, as impetuous as it was rash,[77] once again had a political reason. Caesar could certainly not have foreseen that Pompey would be murdered by his own client, Ptolemy. His intention was to seize the defeated Pompey before the latter could reform his scattered troops and his entourage, temporarily in disarray. Caesar was attempting, from a position of strength following a victorious battle, to bring about a favourable new political order and to put an end to the ongoing conflict and Cato's determined opposition. If, as I believe, this was Caesar's plan, then it foundered in surprising fashion. When Caesar reached Egypt, a few days after Pompey, the unforeseeable had happened. Pompey had been killed in Alexandria at the height of the civil war.[78]

Notes

1 All dates up to 45 BC are from the pre-Julian calendar.
2 Plutarch, *Pompey* 60.3 (and 57.7); Plutarch, *Caesar* 33.2; Appian, *Civil Wars* 2.37.
3 See also F. Münzer, s.v. *Favonius*, RE, VI, 2, col. 2076, 1–2.
4 *Précis des guerres de César*, par Napoléon, écrit par M. Marchand sous la dictée de l'Empereur [1819] (Paris 1836), p. 125. Napoleon writes of 'six legions', rather than seven. Cf. Mommsen (below).
5 Suetonius, *Caesar* 34. He called Pompey and the others who had fled to the East 'leaders without an army'.

6 In French, *s'électriser*.

7 The first rule of ancient warfare was, as we know, to outnumber the enemy in troops (or ships). This is why Caesar, when forced by the Senate to cede two legions to Pompey on the pretext of a campaign against the Parthians, had speedily moved to boost his forces by levies in his province.

8 J. Carcopino, in *Jules César*, 3rd edn (Paris 1968), pp. 370–1, aligns himself explicitly with Bonaparte's *Précis*, but, following Mommsen, confines himself to the observation that the troops under Pompey in Italy were 'neither homogenous nor reliable'.

9 Collaborators on both sides played a decisive role, and also served historians well.

10 Caesar, *Civil War* 1.17.1. Caesar had detailed knowledge of his enemies' most secret plans.

11 Ibid.

12 Caesar, *Civil War* 1.17.2. To win over the soldiers he promises each one four *iugera* of his own land. Details of this nature are an indication of the importance of land-ownership at the period.

13 Caesar, *Civil War* 1.23.1–2.

14 Caesar, *Civil War* 1.23.3.

15 Caesar, *Civil War* 1.23.4.

16 The anti-Caesarian tradition, starting with Lucan's *Bellum civile* (*Pharsalia*), treats it at length.

17 Caesar, *Civil War* 1.14.1.

18 Plutarch, *Caesar* 33.3–4.

19 T. Mommsen, *Römische Geschichte*, 4th edn (Munich 1986), book V, ch. 10, p. 51 (= III, 385). In English, *The History of Rome*, trans. William Purdie Dickson (London 1908), vol. 5, p. 208.

20 Pompey was greatly relieved when Labienus changed sides. See Cicero, *Letters to Atticus* 7.13a.3.

21 Appian, *Civil Wars* 2.37.147.

22 Cicero, *Letters to Atticus* 10.8.4 (2 May 49, Cumae): '[eius] omne consilium Themistocleum est'. Themistocles had ordered that Athens be evacuated and left for the Persians to occupy, but had achieved victory at sea, driven out the Persians and recaptured the city.

23 Pompey, however, was not preparing for a naval battle.

24 Thucydides 7.77.7.

25 Preserved in his *Letters to Atticus* (9.6A; 9.11A etc.). It is unlikely that he went to the Senate on 1 April.

26 This was when Caesar made one more attempt to reach a settlement with Pompey. The intermediary was Numerius Magius (see Cicero, *Letters to Atticus* 9.13A). Pompey took refuge behind a need to 'first consult the consuls!' (Caesar, *Civil War* 1.26.3–5). On this episode see Chapter 19.

27 Cicero, *Letters to Atticus* 9.4.2. Note that in 10.8 (2 May 49) he considers the possibility that these letters may be intercepted, and that it could be dangerous to write too openly of events still in train.

28 Caesar's letter is transcribed in Cicero, *Letters to Atticus* 9.6A. It was written en route from Arpi to Brindisi.

29 It was hardly easy for members of the land-owning class to detach themselves from their daily material interests and follow the example of a 'fanatic' like Cato.

30 Cicero, *Letters to Atticus* 9.13A.

31 Cicero, *Letters to Atticus* 9.10.

32 This refers to the Senate sitting in which Favonius mocked Pompey.

33 ἐν τοῖς ἐρωτικοῖς (Cicero, *Letters to Atticus* 9.10.2).

34 Cicero, *Letters to Atticus* 9.11A.

35 Cicero, *Letters to Atticus* 9.11A.2.

36 See Cicero, *Letters to Atticus* 8.9.1.

37 Cicero, *Letters to Atticus* 8.9 (29 or 30 March 49).

38 Cicero, *Letters to Atticus* 10.8B: written on the march to Marseilles.

39 Cicero, *Letters to Atticus* 8.11.2. He continues: 'A sort of Sulla's reign [*regnum Sullanum*] has long been his object'!

40 Caesar, *Civil War* 1.34.3.

41 Caesar, *Civil War* 1.35.1–2.

42 Caesar, *Civil War* 1.35.5.

43 Caesar, *Civil War* 1.36.

44 Caesar, *Civil War* 2.22.

45 See R. Syme, 'The Allegiance of Labienus', *JRS*, 28 (1938), pp. 113–25.

46 *Cambridge Ancient History*, vol. IX, 'The Roman Republic 133–44 BC', eds S. A. Cook, F. E. Adcock and M. P Charlesworth (Cambridge 1951), p. 647.

47 It did not prevent attempts at mutiny: the four legions which had come to Spain and were stationed in Placentia were bent on plundering the local population, as the prize of victory. Caesar reacted by threatening *decimatio* (which he did not carry through; he merely punished the twelve ring-leaders). See Appian, *Civil Wars* 2.191–6; Dio Cassius 41.26; Suetonius, *Caesar* 69. The last states that mutinies against Caesar were extremely rare (and occurred only during the civil war), and that he 'never gave way to them when they were insubordinate, but always boldly faced them'. In his previous chapter (68.3) Suetonius describes a typical case: at the outset of his Balkan campaign Caesar failed in an attempt to hold Pompey at Durazzo (Dyrrhachium); 'When his men suffered their sole defeat before Dyrrhachium, they insisted on being punished, and their commander felt called upon rather to console than to chastise them.' The *Commentaries* are silent about the incident at Placentia.

48 This symbiosis and its results were fundamental to the ancient city, but

should now be seen against a broader background, involving other forms of political synthesis.

49 Caesar, *Civil War* 2.20–1. Varro's war in the service of Pompey ended here. Some time later, when the African campaign was over, Caesar assigned to him the project of establishing a Greek and Latin public library in Rome. Making use of those with the best talents regardless of their political affiliations was the central pillar of Caesar's political practice.

50 Curio's ill-starred campaign is recounted (on the basis of his reports) in Caesar's *Civil War* 2.23–44.

51 For more detail see Chapter 32.

52 There for a while Domitius Ahenobarbus contemplated suicide with poison, but the doctor gave him a sleeping potion. When he learnt that Caesar was not executing his opponents, 'he rose up overjoyed and went to Caesar, the pledge of whose right he received, only to desert him and go back to Pompey' (Plutarch, *Caesar* 34.6–8). Once released, however, Domitius Ahenobarbus continued to fight against Caesar.

53 Caesar, *Civil War* 2.22.2–4.

54 Caesar, *Civil War* 3.83.

55 By the Julian calendar, 29 June.

56 Caesar certainly saw this as positive.

57 In this predicament Caesar is said (Plutarch, *Caesar* 38) to have boarded a boat, secretly and dressed as a slave, to sail along the river Aous. The voyage was disastrous, and despite Caesar's own efforts at the tiller, they were forced to turn back. The end of this anecdote is of interest: 'When he came back, his soldiers met him in throngs, *finding much fault and sore displeased with him* because he did not believe that even with them alone he was able to conquer' (38.7). An important indication of Caesar's relationship with his soldiers: a band of comrades with their own laws.

58 By the Julian calendar, 16 February.

59 Caesar, *Civil War* 3.25.30.

60 Suetonius, *Caesar* 68.2.

61 Now known as Sasso Bianco.

62 Napoleon, *Précis des guerres de César*, p. 149.

63 Caesar, *Civil War* 3.71.4. Caesar's comment here is brilliant and politically incisive: Labienus vented his hatred on Caesar's followers in order to 'increase his own credit as a traitor'. He knows the mind of his one-time comrade perfectly: his extremist stance stems from his inner sense of insecurity and a wish to be accepted.

64 Caesar, *Civil War* 3.87.1–4.

65 Caesar, *Civil War* 3.87.5–7.

66 Plutarch, *Pompey* 76.2–3: 'On hearing, too, that his fleet still held together, and that Cato had taken many soldiers aboard and was crossing the sea to Africa, he lamented to his friends, blaming himself for

having been forced to do battle with his land forces, while he made no use of his navy, which was indisputably superior, and had not even stationed it at a point where, if defeated on land, he might have had this powerful force close at hand by sea to make him a match for his enemy. And in truth, Pompey made no greater mistake, and Caesar showed no abler generalship, than in removing the battle so far from naval assistance.'

67 See Napoleon's observations in *Précis des guerres de César*, p. 146.

68 Caesar, *Civil War* 3.90.

69 Caesar, *Civil War* 3.91.2. Caesar delivers a funeral oration for him (Crastinius died at Pharsalus from a sword thrust to the face). In his *Commentaries* he remembered to express his gratitude to this soldier (*Civil War* 3.99).

70 Caesar, *Civil War* 3.92.1–3.

71 Caesar, *Civil War* 3.92.4: 'Animi incitatio atque alacritas naturaliter innata omnibus.'

72 Caesar, *Civil War* 3.89.4.

73 Napoleon, *Précis des guerres de César*, pp. 152–3.

74 Caesar, *Civil War* 3.102.1.

75 Napoleon, *Précis des guerres de César*, p. 163.

76 While Caesar was campaigning in Alexandria, they organised a republican rising in Africa with the help of Juba, king of Numidia.

77 With only two legions!

78 This theory contradicts Adcock's hypothesis, no less founded on conjecture, that Caesar was glad that Pompey had been murdered by Ptolemy's counsellors: 'After Pharsalus no composition was possible. Pompey stood too high even for Caesar's clemency, and his death, by his own hand or another's, was necessary. Now Caesar's good fortune had removed his rival without Caesar's act' (*Cambridge Ancient History*, vol. IX, p. 669). In my reading, this hypothesis is countered by the *Commentaries* to the civil war, which emphasise throughout the pressure exerted on Pompey from outside, constantly obstructing a settlement with Caesar at the last moment, even at the siege of Durazzo. Caesar composed the *Commentaries* not for abstract reasons of scholarship: his motives were political. He wanted to place on record that a settlement with him was feasible to the end, and that Pompey was not to be equated with the *factio*, or with Domitius Ahenobarbus, for example.

CHAPTER 22

Against Subversion

While Caesar was occupied with the difficult campaign in the Balkans, two episodes of particularly dramatic social unrest occurred in Rome; each ended in repression. The main player in the first was Marcus Caelius Rufus, one of the tribunes who in January 49 BC had found refuge with Caesar. Caelius Rufus, much of whose correspondence with Cicero has been preserved,[1] had, on his return from the Spanish campaign against Afranius and Petreius, received the praetorship from Caesar for 48, but not the urban praetorship, which Caesar entrusted to Trebonius. This humiliated Caelius and increased his sense of disillusionment. The fact that Caesar, at the start of *Commentaries*, book 3, on the civil war gave a full polemical account of Caelius' action indicates that the *praetor*, by making himself the interpreter of the debtors' needs, had made considerable difficulties for the distant dictator.[2] Caelius Rufus' action was meant to support the debtors' requests: he considered the Caesarian legislation on that issue disappointing.[3] He himself, like Catiline fifteen years earlier, had personal reasons for warmly supporting a radical remission of debts. Caelius did not accept the principle of the valuation of property in Caesar's legislation (a prior condition for any partial reduction of debt). In his *Commentaries* Caesar perceives the need to argue directly and forcefully against the radical programme of Caelius: 'for persons who admit their indebtedness to cling to the whole of their possessions, what an audacious, what a shameless spirit does that mark!'[4] Caelius, he continues, 'proved himself harder to deal with than the very persons whose interests were concerned'. The argument here is that of an expert from the party of the *populares* against the demagogue who has turned against him. Caesar has a thorough knowledge of populist rhetoric and is well able to use its linguistic devices and flourishes: he comes from that tradition. Given his familiarity with its weaponry, it was less easy for his opponents to play the same game against him.[5]

Hence the sharp words Caesar employs in this account to demonstrate that Caelius had no one (or almost no one) behind him. 'His next step was to promulgate a law that money owed shall be paid without accumulation of interest on that day six years hence.'[6] Such proposals were easily blocked, and this is what happened. Caelius made others (suspension of the payment of rent for a year; new cancellation of debts). The Senate, in agreement with the consul Servilius, was heavy-handed: Caelius was suspended from office and pulled forcefully down from the rostra from which he harangued the crowd. At this point Caelius moved to openly illegal conflict and established ties with none other than Milo, who had re-emerged after his exile in Marseilles. Milo, who controlled bands that operated much like the strong-arm men of the anti-popular *optimates*' circle, had disappeared from circulation following his condemnation in 52, when he murdered Clodius. Caesar, in his detailed account of the movements of Caelius Rufus, places clear polemical emphasis on this unusual alliance between the one-time thug who had murdered Clodius (and still maintained bands of gladiators) and the restless neo-Catilinarian Caelius Rufus. 'Caelius summoned him to Italy, associated him with himself and sent him on in front to the Thurine district to raise the farmers.'[7] Meanwhile Caelius was trying to recruit gladiators in Campania, but at Capua the Roman citizens chased him away, taking up arms and proclaiming him *hostis publicus*. The paradox reveals the special character of this improvised movement: Caelius repeated that he was appealing to Caesar and was going to talk to him; Milo sent proclamations to the debtors telling them he was acting in the name and under the mandate of Pompey! This brought meagre results. He then tried to liberate the prisoners serving life sentences at Cosa in Irpinia, but was killed by a stone thrown from a wall. As for Caelius, he attempted to raise the Thurii in rebellion (in the name of Caesar), offering money to some knights of Gallic origin who made up the garrison of the town. But they killed him.[8] Caesar, with the evident intention of playing down the drama despite all the space he gives to the event, comments: 'Thus the first outbreak of a serious movement, which kept Italy harassed by the burden of work imposed on the magistrates by the crisis, came promptly and easily to an end.'[9]

The second 'sedition' was that of Dolabella some months later, on the eve of Pharsalus. Dolabella, a tribune of the plebs, took up the matter of the remission of debts, but the proposal was defeated by Antony, Caesar's *magister equitum*. At the time Caesar was occupied first with the difficult Alexandrian conflict, and then in Asia.[10]

Plutarch's account is highly coloured. Antony appears first as a 'friend' of Dolabella; then he becomes his enemy for purely personal reasons. The political situation faced by Antony at the start of 47 was made critical by the division among the tribunes, although all of them had been Caesar's men. Dolabella clashed with Trebellius and Asinius Pollio,[11] who were hostile to his proposals.

Dolabella occupied the Forum with his followers to force the approval of his proposed law. The Senate did not hesitate to take extreme measures that had already been used on other occasions: they declared the *senatus consultum ultimum*, proclaimed the country in danger, and charged Antony (who held the highest authority in the absence of the dictator) with the task of suppressing the rebellion. The fighting that resulted was fierce, leaving about a thousand dead on the rebel side.[12] Judging from Dio Cassius' account, the troubles did not end until Caesar returned to Rome in August 47.[13] Caesar, however, had a more flexible attitude towards the rebels. He 'pardoned' Dolabella (he facilitated his career) and distanced himself from Antony, whose position of *magister equitum* he gave to Lepidus for 46.[14] Caesar did not change his policy on the vexed question of debts, but he sent a signal to the rebels of his 'understanding' by sacrificing Antony, who had been responsible for a too brutal repression. His view on the scanty political prospects of rebellion among the urban plebs did not change. It was also clear to him that the effects of the mood of this class (dangerous to the rulers owing to its privileged position close to the seat of power) were not to be ignored. Irritating though it was, and however disproportionate to its actual weight, Caesar was fully aware of the influence and the political role of this 'subject' class. He would not make the mistake of ignoring it or trampling on it, but he could not be, nor did he want to be, *their* dictator.

Notes

1 In *Letters to his friends* we have their correspondence from the years 51–48: in the second book the letters from Cicero to Caelius (2.8–16), while the entire eighth book is composed of seventeen letters from Caelius to Cicero.

2 Caesar, *Civil War* 2.20–22.3 (see also Dio Cassius 42.22.1–25, with different details).

3 See Caesar, *Civil War* 3.1.1–3 (and Chapter 32 below).

4 Caesar, *Civil War* 3.20.3.

5 In this part of the *Commentaries* Caesar takes issue with the extremist wing: their language and their manoeuvrings hold no mysteries for him.

6 Caesar, *Civil War* 3.20.5.
7 Caesar, *Civil War* 3.21.4.
8 March 48.
9 Caesar, *Civil War* 3.22.4.
10 Plutarch, *Antony* 9–10.2.
11 Compare the doubts of J. André and B. Haller, in their respective biographies of Asinius, with Broughton, *MRR*, vol. III, p. 26; Asinius was a tribune in that year. (J. André, *La Vie et l'œuvre d'Asinius Pollion* [Paris 1949]; B. Haller, 'Caius Asinius Pollio als Politiker und zeitkritischer Historiker', dissertation, Münster 1967.)
12 Livy, *Periocha* 113.
13 Dio Cassius 42.33.
14 Plutarch, *Antony* 10.2.

CHAPTER 23

Alexandria

> Caesar, when that the traitor of Egypt
> With th' honourable head did him present,
> Covering his heart's gladness, did represent
> Plaint with his tears outward, as it is writ.
>
> Petrarch, *Canzoniere* 102

When Caesar reached Alexandria on 2 October 48 BC, he certainly did not expect to be greeted by the embalmed head of Pompey, but even less did he expect to be bogged down for all of nine months in a local conflict which almost cost him his life, until 28 June 47, when he finally sailed from Alexandria for Syria. Suetonius writes, correctly, that in that lengthy period Caesar found himself fighting

> a war in truth of great difficulty, convenient neither in time or place, but carried on during the winter season, within the walls of a well-provisioned and crafty foeman, while Caesar himself was without supplies of any kind and ill-prepared.[1]

It was a paradoxical war, in effect a trap of gigantic proportions: the victor of unforgettable wars and battles was besieged, with no chance of rapid reinforcements, by a very well-advised client king. The most ancient kingdom of the Mediterranean was taking its revenge on the last of many Roman generals accustomed to telling the Alexandrians what to do. Certainly there was, in the minds of Ptolemy's shrewd 'counsellors', an 'Egyptian' perspective on the episode that the Romans regarded as an interminable and inexplicable interlude in the civil war. Cleopatra, installed on the throne of Egypt by Caesar at the end of the Alexandrian war, achieved increased prestige and political influence while Caesar was still alive, and more so later, thanks to her alliance with Antony. If we bear this in mind, an Egyptian perspective seems not only legitimate, but valuable in helping us to understand this period of Hellenistic Egypt's history – the last flourish of the great Macedonian dynasty, which was the most enduring of those established since the death of Alexander.

The background to the Egyptian dynastic crisis in which Caesar became entangled in the middle of the civil war was the operation managed by Pompey, but also supported by Caesar, which, thanks to the 'protection' of Aulus Gabinius, had restored Ptolemy XII Neos Dionysos, popularly known as Auletes, on the throne in 55 BC. But the crisis lay further in the past. When Auletes had first ascended the throne (80 BC), there hung over him a handicap that exposed him to blackmail by the powerful and unscrupulous Roman pro-magistrates in Syria (the Roman province bordering Egypt). The danger lay in the will of his predecessor, Ptolemy XI, pompously self-styled the 'Second Alexander', who had effectively permitted the Romans to annex not only Cyprus but also Egypt. Cyprus was ruled by Auletes' brother. But in 58 the Roman Senate arranged the liquidation of the autonomous 'Ptolemaic kingdom' in Cyprus, and Auletes' brother preferred to die rather than live out the rest of his days in the service of the Romans.[2] In the same year Auletes was driven out by his Alexandrian subjects who were tired of his total subjection to the Romans, from whom, after two decades of painful humiliation, he had obtained recognition of his sovereign status. Guessing who would have the lucrative role of restoring Auletes to the throne was one of the political 'games' played in the first year of the triumvirate. In the end it fell to Aulus Gabinius, governor of Syria in 55: Gabinius was one of Pompey's followers, but Caesar also gave his blessing and support to the operation. From that point on, Egypt became a Roman protectorate, and not merely a de facto protectorate: a *dioiketes* (minister of finance) was placed, or imposed, at the sovereign's side, so the whole financial system of the extremely rich kingdom was in the hands of the Romans. The Roman legionaries who had come to the mythic land of the pharaohs and Ptolemies settled permanently and established themselves in the country. These *milites Gabiniani* were part of the Egyptian army when Caesar landed in the great and enchanting city. Moreover, Egypt was invaded by swarms of hungry creditors of Auletes, who had lived in Rome for three years and run up debts. It is indicative of the situation that the chief of these creditors, Gaius Rabirius Postumus,[3] was imposed on Auletes as the *dioiketes*. We know of Rabirius' further adventures thanks to Cicero's bold speech in his defence. The fact that Rabirius was very close to Caesar, especially financially (he falsely claimed at the trial that he was a ruined man), must not be ignored. Ptolemy Auletes would probably not have kept his formal independence had the struggle between the potentates in Rome not gradually worsened as it focused on other objectives. When he died (51) he was succeeded on the throne by the eighteen-year-old Cleopatra together with her husband and brother Ptolemy XIII, who was nine years younger. She was called Philopator, and probably meant to follow her father's politics, but her actions met with strong opposition from the closed 'Council' of her brother-husband-king, composed of the eunuch Potheinus, a capable and audacious politician, Achillas, commander of the troops, and Theodotus, a rhetor of Samian origin, to whom the king's education was entrusted. It is clear that Cleopatra aimed to deprive her brother of power, if only from the royal seals of the epoch, on which the name 'Cleopatra' appears alone, contrary to the Ptolemaic tradition of portraying both members of a royal couple formed by two siblings.

Adept at following the interests and networks of Roman politics, Cleopatra was increasingly unpopular with her Alexandrian subjects, who were exasperated by the oppression of the Roman 'protectors'. This was apparent when the queen wished to deliver the assassins of Bibulus' two sons to a Roman tribunal (51 BC).[4] It was apparent when she received Pompey's older son, who sought her help at the start of the civil war, and she opted to back the Pompeian cause (nearly every-one in the East was certain that Pompey would win); she sent sixty ships laden with grain and 500 *milites Gabiniani*[5] to the great father of that enterprising son, who, according to Plutarch, immediately became her lover.[6] The gift of grain was a mistake at a time when, for at least three years, the harvests had been poor because of modest Nile floods, and the population was starving. Cleopatra had to flee from Alexandria and take refuge in Syria among a friendly population, and there she raised troops for a return to the capital. In the summer of 48, when Pompey was defeated, the armies of Cleopatra and Ptolemy (the latter under the command of Achillas and Potheinus) met: Ptolemy's troops were at Pelusium when the fleeing Pompey's ship reached that port.

What happened next is told by Plutarch with the inevitable senti-mentalism notable in him when he recounts the experiences of the defeated. Pompey heaves to outside the port of Pelusium, where Ptolemy is camped with his advisers, and sends a messenger to ask for refuge. On land a consultation takes place. Theodotus of Chios, the 'hired teacher of rhetoric' according to Plutarch's contemptuous description, wins the day: Pompey is not to be either received or turned away, he is to be killed; eloquently, and with great political sagacity, he explains why the other courses of action must be rejected, concluding: 'a dead man does not bite'.[7]

Pompey's ambush was incomparably easy: also involved was an officer called Septimius,[8] who had at one time served under Pompey. In his account Plutarch stresses how at every step disaster was almost avoided. Pompey considered fleeing to the Parthians, or straight to Juba in Numidia (where Cato had made for after the rout of Pharsalus), but instead Theophanes, Pompey's historian, urged him to go to Egypt. Then, when only a small fishing boat came out from Pelusium, which suggested less than royal treatment, somebody said to Pompey that they ought to alter course to stay outside the range of arrows. But by then the fishing boat was drawing close to the fugitives' vessel, and Septimius hailed Pompey in Latin, calling him *imperator*: a reassuring title in a moment of doubt. Achillas greeted him in Greek and explained that the seabed was sandy and the water too shallow for a trireme. Meanwhile, on the shore, troop and ship movements were occurring, which might have been seen as ominous. Pompey ceased hesitating and stepped into the boat below, with two centurions, a freedman and a slave. Bidding farewell to his wife, who was overcome by anguished foreboding, he recited a line from Sophocles:

> Whenever man unto a tyrant takes his way,
> His slave he is, even though a freeman when he goes.[9]

On the boat the few words Pompey tried to say were greeted with chilly silence. Pompey gave up talking and began to re-read the words he was to say to Ptolemy, which he had prepared, in Greek, on a little scroll. When he rose to step onto the shore, first Septimius, then Achillas ran him through. From the ships the fugitives from Pharsalus saw and understood. They barely managed to escape pursuit by the Egyptian ships.

Caesar explicitly states that he 'learned of the death of Pompey' at Alexandria[10] at the very moment when he disembarked,[11] hearing the cries of the soldiers posted by Ptolemy for guard duty, and of the citizens, who were indignant because Caesar was preceded by the *fasces*,[12] the symbol of the authority of the Roman consuls. As usual, his words are carefully weighed. Caesar does not betray any emotional reaction to Pompey's death, nor does he give any detail about that unforeseeable turn of the civil war. His silence is not to be taken for granted. It is not enough to observe that Caesar's style is 'lapidary': when he wants to, he gives accurate information of what happens in the opposing camp and furnishes details of the behaviour and incidents in the lives of his main rivals. Against this extreme restraint, other accounts exist of the emotions Caesar displayed when Pompey's head was brought to him by Theodotus,[13] or by others.[14] Lucan's account, which is the most analytical and interesting, besides being closest to the facts,[15] dwells on one detail. The 'servant', as he calls him, of King Ptolemy, who brings the macabre gift of the severed head of Pompey to Caesar, delivers a long speech in which the murder of Pompey is presented as the final and conclusive act of the civil war,[16] so Ptolemy is placed in a positive light as the one who rendered to Caesar, 'in his absence', the great service of concluding the civil war; and this act is presented as a 'token' (*pignus*) of firm alliance between Ptolemy and Caesar, sealed with the blood of Pompey.[17] The quid pro quo demanded is the acceptance of Ptolemy among Caesar's clientele.

> We give you the kingdom, to be yours without bloodshed; we give you power over the Nile's waters; we give you all that you yourself would have given for Pompey's head; reckon us then as worthy clients [*dignumque clientem*] of your army, because Fortune willed that we should have such power against your kinsman.[18]

The proposal to formalise a client relationship – in which Caesar 'receives' Egypt but the Egyptian sovereign remains on the throne – is soon afterwards argued and developed. Caesar is invited to consider how much this gesture has cost Ptolemy: 'Pompey was our friend of old; he had restored the throne to our king's banished father [Auletes].' Ptolemy had, after all, been in a client relationship by virtue of his father's links with the *bâtisseur d'Empire*. Therefore the eloquent 'servant of the king' concludes his well-constructed speech with the reflection: do not imagine that it did not cost much to carry out this sudden and traumatic change of clientele.[19] Lucan is certainly not a source favourable to Caesar; nevertheless he is to be taken very seriously because he reflects a 'republican'-inspired historiographical tradition that might have its starting point in the historical work of Seneca the Elder on the civil wars. Here, as elsewhere, the *Pharsalia* is historiography in verse, not mere poetic invention. So Lucan describes in precise detail Caesar's reaction to the display, so well-prepared politically, of Pompey's head: and it is a shrewd, calculated and only seemingly emotional reaction. Before belatedly giving vent to tears, Caesar closely scrutinises the cruel offering, and only when he is quite sure that it is Pompey does he give way to tears that are largely feigned.[20] These crocodile tears – Lucan points out bluntly – *are all Caesar has to prevent himself showing enthusiasm*, the feeling of joy that the macabre spectacle aroused in him: tears that must conceal 'his delight'. Besides – Lucan continues – in that melodramatic mode Caesar frees himself, or thinks he frees himself, from any obligation to the aspiring client. 'By his tears he belittles the king's horrid service, preferring to mourn the severed head of his kinsman rather than owe obligation for it.'[21]

Lucan's account is confirmed by a historiographically important source which goes back to Livy: Dio Cassius' history of Rome.[22] Dio's account is even more disturbing, as it indicates (with what foundation we do not know) that Ptolemy, or rather his ministers, acted in collusion with Caesar. Caesar reached Alexandria before Ptolemy and his retinue had returned from Pelusium (where Pompey was liquidated), but,

> on discovering that the people of the city were in a tumult over Pompey's death he did not at once venture to go ashore, but put out to sea and waited till he saw the head and finger-ring of the murdered man, sent to him by Ptolemy.[23]

If we re-read Caesar's laconic and far from transparent report of his arrival at Alexandria – in which the news of Pompey's death and the Alexandrian uproar over the consular *fasces* are recounted in somewhat confusing fashion[24] – we can see that some elements of Dio's account coincide with Caesar's unforthcoming lines. It is, however, evident that for Dio there was a preliminary agreement: how else could Caesar *expect* to be shown the head, and go ashore only when that display has taken place?[25] But Dio takes further the unmasking of Caesar the 'actor' faced with the macabre trophy: when they brought it to him he burst into tears, began to call Pompey his son-in-law, and started enumerating all the things they had done to help each other. At this point, says Dio sarcastically,

> As for the murderers, far from admitting that he owed them any reward, he actually heaped reproaches upon them; and he commanded that the head should be adorned, properly prepared, and buried. For this he received praise, but for his hypocrisy he incurred ridicule.[26]

After this Dio lets himself go in a veritable peroration against Caesar's hypocrisy: how could he be believed, in that exhibition of grief and regret, when he had done everything to destroy that rival, when not even the threat of civil war had swayed him from his course, and 'he had but now been hurrying to Egypt in pursuit of Pompey, with no other end in view than to overthrow him completely *if he should still be alive . . .*'.[27] By adding 'if he should still be alive', Dio lets it be understood once again that, in his view, Caesar knew that Pompey was going to his death when he placed his trust in Ptolemy.

Modern scholars have wondered whether Ptolemy had spies in Caesar's entourage, or if Caesar had his own agents close to Ptolemy:[28] certainly Theodotus' well-timed move, with his macabre trophy, from Pelusium to Alexandria, to meet Caesar and offer him the brutal agreement, can only be explained if one imagines the infiltration (perhaps reciprocal) of the two camps. It is curious that Velleius is silent about Caesar's reactions, even though he dedicates a lot of space to deploring the treacherous murder of Pompey.[29] But what seems improbable, and contrasts with Caesar's usual practice of leaving open several ways out, is that Caesar really put himself in Ptolemy's hands, propitiating his criminal action, while reserving the right to turn down any binding agreement.[30] As for Plutarch's touching, and not at all malicious, reconstruction of Caesar's reaction when confronted with the display of his rival's head,[31] it is certainly motivated by the desire to offer the reader a vivid scene of great pathos, which may, however, descend into the general and fanciful: such as when it presents the subsequent physical liquidation of Achillas and Potheinus, and of Ptolemy himself, by Caesar as punishment for their crime against Pompey.[32]

How was it, though, that Caesar became embroiled in the Alexandrian conflict with so few troops at his disposal?[33]

How Caesar came to fall into the trap of the Alexandrian war was a topic of debate and conjecture even for the ancients (nor was it all clear to contemporaries, even the most discerning).[34] Plutarch reports that, according to some, Caesar brought that 'unnecessary' war upon himself 'for love of Cleopatra', and that, therefore, the war brought him only 'shame and dangers'. In the view of others, the responsibility belonged to the Ptolemaic court, in particular Potheinus, who had deluded himself, in a sort of delirium of omnipotence, that he could liquidate both Pompey and Caesar.[35] Inclining towards this second explanation, Plutarch maintains that Caesar spent 'whole nights at drinking parties in order to protect himself' (in that first phase of the Alexandrian sojourn Cleopatra was still far away).[36] Plutarch comments that this should not be seen as a foolish or romantic formulation: in fact it was during one of these nocturnal revels, during which the rivals continued to spy on one another, that Caesar attempted to capture and destroy Potheinus and Achillas together. He seized the former and put him to death, but the latter escaped and hastened to stir up revolt.[37] However, even in recent times, academic historians, their imagination fired by the figure of Cleopatra, repeat that 'Caesar's relationship with the "provocative Levantine" was the cause of the Alexandrian War.'[38] Napoleon, more elegantly, evades the relationship with 'la belle Cléopâtre' and simply 'suggests' belatedly that Caesar should have been satisfied with Ptolemy's sham submission and 'postponed his punishment for a year'.[39]

More faithful to reality, Theodor Mommsen points out that at Alexandria Caesar remained 'faithful to his custom – wherever he found himself in the wide empire – of finally regulating matters at once and in person . . .'.[40] He recognises, though, that Caesar acted in the light of a calculation that proved wrong: namely, that although he had only 3,000 men, he would have no trouble from either the Roman garrison (the famous *milites Gabiniani*) or the court. He failed to realise that those *milites Gabiniani* were by then settled in the Alexandrian world, thanks to marriages with local women: therefore they no longer felt bound by the authority of Rome. Moreover, their ranks had been filled with bandits and pirates of Syrian and Cilician origin:[41] in short, that army had become a potential and dangerously unpredictable powder keg.

Besides, Caesar's intention in the negotiation with Ptolemy's guardians and protectors was, in the first place, financial. Egypt's sovereigns had compromised themselves by their association with Pompey in the civil war (and Cleopatra was even more 'guilty' than her odious brother). The action of Potheinus and his comrades in assassinating Pompey and making a virtue of this to Caesar may be explained as an attempt to cancel out the memory of that embarrassing compromise in the eyes of the victor of Pharsalus. Caesar was well within his rights to impose a war contribution in recompense for the help given to Pompey; but instead he chose another way. He reminded his hosts that only half of the money promised by the restored Auletes had been paid (partly because the country was financially exhausted), and declared that he would remit a large part of the outstanding Egyptian debt, and instead seek a final instalment of ten million *denarii*. A corollary of this injunction was the order to the brother and sister to cease hostilities. As a consul in office he could demand that his directives and requests be acted upon. He had paraded the *fasces* and axes from the moment he landed at Alexandria because he considered it was urgent, and fitting, to impose his authority, by then formalised and duly accepted by the client king Ptolemy. He intended to bring order at last to the confused Egyptian situation, and at the same time draw from it appropriate sums for the possible (foreseeable) continuation of the conflict.

In Caesar's *Commentaries* and their sequel, dedicated to the Alexandrian war, Cleopatra is virtually absent. Her name appears for the first time when the background to the dynastic crisis is related,[42] and then when Caesar gives his directions for the future of the kingdom:

> he declares that it is his pleasure that King Ptolemy and his sister Cleopatra should disband the armies that they controlled, and should settle their disputes by a process of law before himself rather than by armed force between themselves.[43]

Finally, in the *Alexandrian War*, the name of Cleopatra appears only at the end of the account,[44] where the reader is informed of Caesar's decision to entrust the kingdom to her, now that her rival, Ptolemy XIII, is dead. Here, however, the writer of this continuation of the *Commentaries* explains that during the conflict Cleopatra had remained faithfully 'on Caesar's side'. Thus, in the 'official' history, of Caesarian origin, Cleopatra was a pale and fleeting presence. Caesar wanted this figure, who was as important for the history of Egypt as for that of Rome, to remain in the margins of his own self-portrait: he had had a son by her, and Cleopatra was in Rome, in Caesar's villa on the other side of the Tiber, from 46 until his death in March 44, when she fled back home; and yet, in Caesar's public life, she is an invisible presence.

Other accounts offer a radically different presentation of the facts.[45] Cleopatra returns to the stage when Caesar formally requests the two sibling-rivals to appear before him to settle their differences in the presence of the highest authority of the Roman republic. According to Plutarch, at that point Caesar 'secretly sent for Cleopatra from the country'.[46] Obviously it did not escape him that, in that particular situation, Ptolemy and his advisers, who found themselves in a position of strength with regard to Cleopatra, would not readily accept a forced reconciliation. He was under no illusion that Cleopatra's return to the capital would be simple or straightforward, and therefore felt that it would be logical to play the local powers one against the other. Cleopatra was also well aware of the risks of returning to court: those who had not hesitated to stab Pompey would certainly have no regard for her. So she accepted Caesar's invitation but took precautions.

At nightfall a little boat drew near the palace (which looked over the sea) unobserved. Shortly afterwards a man who looked like a carpet merchant asked to be conducted to Caesar. His name was Apollodorus, he said, and he came from Sicily. When he was in Caesar's presence, he unrolled his bundle before the amused eyes of the Roman general. From it there emerged, lying at full-length, the not very tall Cleopatra, clad, to disguise herself, in one of the linen sacks that was used to carry carpets. Caesar was 'captivated, for she showed herself to be a bold coquette'.[47] According to Plutarch, Caesar 'succumbed to her grace and conversation'. Plutarch pays a great deal of attention to her and her resourcefulness, and she appears again as a protagonist in the *Life of Antony*:

> There was a sweetness also in the tones of her voice; and her tongue, like an instrument of many strings, she could readily turn to whatever language she pleased, so that in her interviews with Barbarians she very seldom had need of an interpreter.[48]

It is obvious that Cleopatra, then aged twenty-one, counted on the effect that she was certain to have on a man advanced in years, like Caesar, then over fifty:[49] her immediate objective was, as is easily imagined, to make the conqueror forget the aid that months before she had offered to Pompey. However, as a prudent sovereign and already an experienced politician, Cleopatra did not venture into a relationship such as this without making some preliminary enquiries. According to a source who was certainly not kindly disposed to Caesar, but was always well informed, Dio Cassius, Cleopatra first attempted through intermediaries to find out about the Roman general, above all about his character:

> As soon as she discovered his disposition (which was very suscept-ible, to such an extent that he had his intrigues with ever so many other women – with all, doubtless, who chanced to come in his way) she sent word to him that she was being betrayed by her friends and asked that she be allowed to plead her case in person. (ἐρωτικώτατος)[50]

This was an elegant way to let the Roman dictator know that she trusted him alone. It was only after these preliminaries (a good example of the secret behind-the-scenes activity which lies behind visible events), that Cleopatra staged the *coup de théâtre* of her arrival at the palace by night disguised as a carpet.

During this troubled period on the eve of war, Caesar, with his 3,000 men and hardly any ships, installed himself in the palace of Alexandria. To understand this fact better, it must be explained that the royal palace in Alexandria was actually an entire quarter: the Brucheion, which overlooked the great harbour and on the south-west abutted the shipyards. Two travellers, Diodorus Siculus, a contemporary of Caesar, and Strabo, in the time of Augustus, have left us vivid and valuable descriptions of this unique site.[51] From them we learn that the palace had been gradually extended over the years, as each sovereign had added new buildings: in Strabo's day the palace complex occupied 'one-fourth or even one-third of the whole circuit of the city'.[52] Within this great complex lay the so-called 'inner royal palaces',[53] which included various buildings and gardens as well as the theatre. This was the *pars oppidi* where Caesar installed himself when he realised that the situation was coming to a head.[54] Caesar expresses himself with all due precision when he uses the term *pars oppidi* for the inner palace (*oppidum*). Being in a strategic position, jutting out over the sea, it was unassailable from that side and easily defensible on the landward side because of the maze of alleys surrounding it, which allowed the position to be defended – as Caesar does not fail to point out – with very few men.[55] Then there was a system of secret tunnels and underground channels, as well as an elaborate system of water pipelines that the besiegers attempted to disable.

Lucan conveys the situation accurately when he writes that Caesar 'distrusted the city walls and defended himself by closing the gates of the palace'.[56] The poet-historian adds that, in that situation, Caesar appeared to 'submit to an unworthy hiding-place'. In Lucan there is already a marked tendency to emphasise the 'unworthy' nature, for Caesar, of the Alexandrian campaign. One aspect of this *strategic humiliation* was his being forced to barricade himself in a place which was considered a den of vice,[57] besieged, moreover, by the 'rabble' of 'inferior creatures', as Egyptians and Orientals in general were thought to be in the eyes of Roman racism. In reality, Caesar again displays the extreme flexibility of his strategic inventiveness, which could adapt to a situation that was decidedly anomalous compared to any previously known strategy. During the first phase of the operations he pursued two objectives that seemed contradictory but

were, in reality, convergent: on the one hand advancing from one
building to the next, seizing ground, little by little, from the enemy;[58]
on the other constantly keeping the *pars oppidi* he controlled separate from the rest of the city by gradually moving the fortification
works forward.[59]

The drift into armed conflict and this unexpected strategic situation
occurred because the reconciliation Caesar tried to impose once
he had the rival brother and sister rulers beside him in the palace
failed almost from the start. There was, in fact, no chance of a real
agreement, because Ptolemy (and his advisers) had absolutely no
intention of sharing power with Cleopatra, whom they considered –
not without reason – to be without any following among the
Alexandrians. However, Caesar's astute move calmed feelings when
he proclaimed the restitution of Cyprus to Egypt, appointing Arsinoe
and their other brother (the future Ptolemy XIV) to reign over the
island. By annulling in this way the Roman annexation of Cyprus,
which had so outraged the Alexandrians, provoking the banishment
of Auletes, Caesar soothed, for a time at least, the growing restless-
ness of the population, incited by Achillas.

Beyond the subjective reasons, which are so often given prominence,[60] to explain Caesar's preference for Cleopatra, it is evident
that underlying this choice was an obvious calculation: to prevent the
kingdom falling into the hands of a strongly nationalistic anti-Roman
leadership, such as that of Ptolemy's entourage, who might exploit the
difficulties created by the Roman civil war. And to this end a diarchy,
with the unpopular Cleopatra under Roman control, seemed a viable
solution; still better would be the liquidation of Ptolemy and his
backers, which Caesar could not but see as an almost unavoidable
outcome of an armed conflict that was likely to eventuate. In a civil
war situation that was still unresolved and was paralysing the hegemonic power, the only wise policy for Caesar was to maintain at all
costs a volatile country such as Egypt in a position of effective subjection to Rome; and this could be achieved only by imposing
Cleopatra from the start. The extent of the local reaction, the degree
of perversion of the function of the *milites Gabiniani*, who had the
task of keeping Egypt under control – these were imponderable
factors and in no way predictable. They would soon put Caesar in a
critical situation.

Mommsen, with a touch of anti-revolutionary conservatism,
writes that the people of Alexandria had 'a turbulent spirit, which

induced them to indulge in their street riots as regularly and as heartily as the Parisians of the present day'.[61] He recognises, however, that the plundering of wealth, private as well as that which belonged to the temples, caused by Caesar's order to pay the last instalment of Gabinius' large debt, must have provoked exasperation, and the exasperation was ably exploited by Achillas and his 'nationalist' supporters. The revolt broke out because of an almost unavoidable train of events. Faced with the reconciliation contrived by Caesar, Achillas secretly summoned Ptolemy's fleet from Pelusium (while the king was still in the palace). When informed of this, Caesar ordered Ptolemy, his 'hostage', to send two messengers – Dioscorides and Serapion, old friends of Rome – to tell Achillas to countermand his order; instead the messengers were immediately killed on Achillas' orders.[62] On the arrival of Egyptian troops in Alexandria, Achillas occupied the entire city except for the *oppidum*, where Caesar had retreated, taking Ptolemy with him as hostage.

Achillas attempted to win a quick victory: he attacked the inner palace while at the same time trying to take possession of all the ships in the great harbour (the fifty sent by Pompey and the twenty-two permanently stationed there).[63] Caesar was able to halt the land attack; the attempt on the harbour was more dangerous, as it would have totally deprived Caesar of the possibility of receiving aid from the sea. Once in control of those seventy-two ships and access to the harbour, Achillas and his troops would have prevented any fleet from coming to the aid of the besieged. This is when Caesar made his most daring and successful move: incendiary projectiles, 'brands steeped in resin',[64] hurled from the top of the palace set the Egyptian fleet completely ablaze,[65] depriving the besiegers of their only truly formidable weapon. Thanks to the wind, the fire on the ships at their moorings caused a further unforeseen effect, a conflagration in the whole harbour area, which eased the pressure of the siege. The wind, writes Lucan, from whom we have the best account of the incident, 'fanned the conflagration, till the flames, smitten by the eddying gale, rushed over the roofs as fast as the meteors that often trace a furrow through the sky'. The disaster drew the attackers away from the palace to the defence of the city. The harbour area was the worst affected. Dio informs us of the destruction, among other things, of some stores of grain and some books.[66] This does not mean the books in the valuable and famous library, which was inside the palace. But Plutarch,[67] and indeed a number of modern historians, mistakenly perpetuated the misunderstanding that it was indeed the 'Great Library' that had been destroyed. George Bernard Shaw's joke, when his Caesar says, 'I am an author myself; and I tell you it is better that the Egyptians should live their lives than dream them away with the help of books', is therefore misplaced.[68]

When the assault failed and Achillas was killed on the order of Arsinoe, the vivacious younger sister of Cleopatra, Ganymede, the new leader of the Egyptian forces, devised a new scheme: to cut the water supply to the palace and force Caesar to surrender. The implementation was a stroke of technical genius: huge quantities of sea water were pumped into the supply to the higher parts of the city, and very soon the entire Brucheion quarter had only salt water to drink.[69] Caesar's legionaries panicked and were ready to rebel: they wanted to climb onto the ships in the roadsteads below the palace and escape. Caesar flatly refused to allow them: he was sure – and it was quickly confirmed – that the entire coastal zone held plentiful spring water. After a night spent digging, the soldiers found abundant spring water and water-bearing strata.[70] In the meantime, Caesar had arranged to send out a call for help, through trustworthy channels, to all of the neighbouring zones.[71] He turned to his Oriental clienteles and sent his most trusted client, Mithridates of Pergamon, who was probably at his side from the start of the civil war, to Syria and Palestine: a move that proved decisive for the subsequent development of the conflict. Meanwhile, Domitius Calvinus' fleet had arrived off Alexandria, carrying the Thirty-Seventh Legion, made up of Pompeian legionaries who had surrendered after Pharsalus.[72] The wind prevented their entry into the harbour. Caesar went out with his own ships to meet Domitius' fleet, taking fresh supplies of water, and on the return he repelled an attack by Ganymede and Arsinoe, whose remaining ships were scattered.[73]

This was the moment when the Alexandrians, a trading and seafaring people, as the author of the *Alexandrian War* describes them,[74] called on all their resources: in a few days twenty-two quadriremes and five quinqueremes were fitted out, besides a sizeable number of small boats without decks, all with experienced crews. The new fleet put the Egyptians in a position to provoke Caesar's legionaries to do battle at any convenient moment. For Caesar it was necessary to occupy Pharos, the little island connected to the mainland by the heptastadium mole: only in this way could he regain control of the harbour and oversee the arrival of reinforcements. For this reason he decided to accept a naval battle with the renewed Egyptian forces. It would be a very difficult battle, during which, at one point, he had to swim to safety.[75] Pharos was finally taken, along with the mole, but Caesar's losses were heavy (400 men drowned).[76]

Frustrated by this outcome, the Egyptians tried to resort to subterfuge to free King Ptolemy, who was still Caesar's prisoner. They asked Caesar to return Ptolemy as a precondition for their surrender. Caesar agreed,[77] calculating that the return of Ptolemy to his people would create sharp dissensions and further divisions in the enemy camp, and this is exactly what happened. Seeing the comic side of the situation, Caesar agreed to play along. He took part in a poignant farewell, heavy with hypocrisy on both sides. Caesar exhorted the boy-king to take care of his kingdom, declaring his confidence in the maturity of the very young sovereign: 'he had so much faith in him that he was sending him to join an enemy under arms'. And the shrewd young boy, 'schooled in all the lessons of utter deceit',[78] clung to Caesar's hand, pretending to implore him not to leave his side. Naturally, once he was released from his gilded cage, Ptolemy took good care not to do what was promised and, if anything, he exacerbated the conflict as much as possible. But only naïve people, comments the writer of the *Alexandrian War*, believed that Caesar had allowed himself to be deceived.[79] Just then, news arrived of the approaching reinforcements mustered by Mithridates of Pergamon, then a short distance from Pelusium.

The end of all the Egyptians' illusions about their rebellion came with the arrival of the Jewish contingent led by Antipater, with other forces which he had raised by skilfully exploiting ties of loyalty. Mithridates of Pergamon had been held up with his reinforcements at Ascalon, six days march from Pelusium, because the local tribes would not grant him passage. Here the intervention of Antipater, the Idumaean leader and *curator* of Judea, proved decisive.[80] At this point Antipater really did decide the fortunes of his family by taking Caesar's side and permanently binding the Jewish ruling class to the dictator's family.

Antipater brought with him 1,500 hoplites;[81] furthermore, he had won over to his cause the leaders of the Arab tribes, and thanks to him all the dynasties of Syria elected to join the expeditionary force that was hastening to Caesar's aid. With the arrival of this seasoned army, Mithridates was able to storm Pelusium. Antipater was the author of the victory and above all the author of valuable efforts among the Jewish communities of the Delta, won over to the Caesarian cause by the gifted Idumaean, backed by the prestigious name of the high priest Hyrcanus. Antipater continued to win increasing support: when Memphis also went over to him, Mithridates and Antipater were strong enough to take on the Egyptian army in the field, at the so-called 'Jewish Camp', and defeat it.[82]

The final act of this strange and dangerous 'colonial' war followed.[83] The march of Mithridates and Antipater on Alexandria robbed the Egyptians of their last chance of maintaining the initiative in the city (as they had until then). Ptolemy and his commanders took the desperate decision to attack the reinforcing army in strength. But Caesar was swifter, and on 27 March 47 – together with Antipater and Mithridates – he confronted the Egyptian army on the Nile. His legionaries and the men of the allied armies attacked the Egyptians in their camp and routed them. Ptolemy, weighed down by a suit of armour made of gold, fell into the water and drowned. For an Egyptian sovereign this was a propitious death: whoever drowned in the Nile could count on the favour of Osiris and would be resurrected. Caesar, attentive as always to the *idola tribus*, to use Francis Bacon's term, ordered the body to be recovered from the river and displayed in public in Alexandria, rendering to it the honour expected by the people of the capital. As he prepared to decide the fate of the restive and unreliable kingdom, he could hardly have hit upon a better way to make his decisions accepted.

Alexandria capitulated on 27 March. Arsinoe was immediately sent to Rome, a prisoner queen to be company for the defeated Vercingetorix. Auletes' youngest child, a boy who was given the name Ptolemy XIV, was proclaimed Cleopatra's husband and sovereign, with her, of Egypt. In the meantime, Cleopatra was expecting Caesar's child; the baby, when he was born, was called by the Alexandrians 'Caesarion' (Καισαρίων), the diminutive of Καῖσαρ.

The administration of Egypt was clearly established, without doing violence to Auletes' will.[84] Caesar did not make the mistake of transforming the kingdom into a province. The governors of such a province might have been tempted into ill-considered actions.[85] In some ways the most practical solution was to maintain the status of client kingdom, under strict supervision. Suetonius says explicitly that Caesar had no wish to transform Egypt into a province, 'fearing that if he made a province of it, it might one day under a headstrong [*violentiorem*] governor be a source of revolution'.[86] This is why a figure with reduced political power, like Cleopatra in her own country, was indispensable to him. For her part, Cleopatra firmly bound the fate of the dynasty to that of the victor of the civil war (who would presumably remain victorious). The blood tie represented by Caesarion was, so the audacious queen imagined, a weapon in her hands.

The principles of the system imposed upon Egypt are clearly explained by the author of *Bellum Alexandrinum*.[87] Caesar left the main body of his troops in Egypt as an occupying force. When he set off for Syria he took with him only one legion of veterans, the Sixth. The reason for such a massive army of occupation is set forth in this way:

> all the others he left there, the more to bolster up the dominion of the said rulers, who could enjoy neither the affection of their people, inasmuch as they had remained throughout staunch friends of Caesar [*in amicitia Caesaris*], nor the authority of a long-established reign, it being but a few days since they came to the throne. At the same time he deemed it conducive to the dignity of our empire and to public expediency that, if the rulers remained loyal,[88] they should be protected by our troops: whereas if they proved ungrateful, those same troops could hold them in check.

He says *reges* in the plural each time, but it is clear that he means Cleopatra alone, the child placed at her side as her husband having no significance. This statement provided the political frame of reference for Caesar's relations with the queen, over and above personal tenderness.

Before taking leave of Cleopatra, we must give some general consideration to the figure who, after the death of Caesar, dominated the political scene to the point of assuming the role (to a large extent created by hostile propaganda) of the 'enemy of Rome':[89] the woman responsible for a last attempt to secure the triumph of the East over the West.

But had not Caesar already, in the last months of his life, given thought to the model of Hellenistic monarchy that was embodied by Cleopatra, as a way out of the constitutional uncertainty in which he was placed after the victory? Caesar died too soon for us to say with any assurance what path he would have taken to legitimise his authority. But it is probable that he had in mind, if only vaguely, a structure influenced by the Hellenistic model. Years later, Octavian presented the war against Antony, leader of the opposing party in a civil conflict, as an 'external' war against an enemy queen, Cleopatra (and Antony as *pars adiecta*, or at best, an imprudent accomplice). And he presented his victory, the victory of Actium, as the victory of the West, and Italy in particular, over the East. In this way the break with Caesar's policies, which he had effected, could be downplayed. What is more, at Actium he had defeated one of Caesar's heirs, the triumvir Antony, who had inherited the murdered dictator's military charisma and much more.

Of course, the *personal* picture of Cleopatra that emerges from the sources known to us, which give prominence to vices and crimes, may also have much truth in it. It is no secret that the standard of personal morality of the potentates and the leading figures of the upper classes in general was somewhat perplexing. When the upholders of the ancient Roman tradition railed against the spread of 'corrupt' customs imported with the conquest of the East, they meant that the moral standards of the ruling classes had undergone disturbing changes as a result of this mingling with a more ancient civilisation. In this connection, we should not forget the gallery of portraits of Roman emperors that Suetonius left for us. On the level of personal morality, scarcely any of them escape his critical scrutiny, but this in no way detracts from the political greatness of some of them. So it is with Cleopatra, the capable last inheritor of a Hellenistic model of monarchy that, centuries later, would prevail – but nobody could foresee this at Actium – over the bellicose Westernism of the Augustan model.

Notes

1 Suetonius, *Caesar* 35.1.
2 What Roman domination meant for the island is well illustrated by the usury of Marcus Junius Brutus. See Chapter 5.
3 Cicero, *In defence of Rabirius* 22 and 28.
4 Valerius Maximus 4.1.15.
5 Appian, *Civil Wars* 2.71.296.
6 Plutarch, *Antony* 25.
7 Plutarch, *Pompey* 77.4.
8 In his brief account of this episode, Caesar (*Civil War* 3.104) says that Septimius had served under Pompey in the war against the pirates, and that Pompey recognised him when he came before him.
9 Plutarch, *Pompey* 78.4 (= 873 Radt; *fabulae incertae*).
10 Caesar, *Civil War* 3.106.4: 'Alexandriae de Pompei morte cognoscit.'
11 Ibid.: 'e nave egrediens'.
12 Ibid.: 'quod fasces anteferrentur'.
13 According to Plutarch, *Caesar* 48.2.
14 The Roman custom of cutting off the head of the vanquished foe and presenting it to the 'authority' was extensively practised at the time of the triumviral proscriptions.
15 Lucan 9.1010–46.
16 Lucan 9.1018: 'absenti bellum civile peractum est'.
17 Lucan 9.1021: 'hoc tecum percussum est sanguine foedus'.
18 Lucan 9.1022–6.
19 Lucan 9.1026–7: 'nec vile putaris hoc meritum, etc.'.

20 Lucan 9.1037–8: 'lacrimas non sponte cadentis effudit'.
21 Lucan 9.1041–3.
22 Dio Cassius 42.7–8.
23 Dio Cassius 42.7.2.
24 This detail too is in Dio Cassius 42.7.3.
25 From Dio's account it is possible to deduce that Pompey's head was taken to Caesar *on the ship* from which he hesitated to disembark. This is also the logic of the facts known to Lucan (9.1011). Caesar, on the other hand, states clearly that he learned of Pompey's death *in Alexandria*.
26 Dio Cassius 42.8.1.
27 Dio Cassius 42.8.2–3.
28 J. Brambach, *Kleopatra* (Munich 1991), p. 66.
29 Velleius 2.53.
30 The question posed by Brambach (why did Caesar make for Alexandria, not Pelusium?) is not well founded. Caesar's 'wrong' choice suggests that at the time he was less well informed about the Egyptians than Ptolemy and his advisers were about him. It is not surprising, however, that Pompey made straight for Pelusium: Cleopatra had chosen his side, and he was certainly well informed on the situation in Egypt.
31 Plutarch, *Caesar* 48.2; Plutarch, *Pompey* 80.7.
32 Plutarch, *Pompey* 80.6. Plutarch even writes that Theodotus (who did not fall in the Alexandrian war) 'escaped the vengeance of Caesar'.
33 In his *Civil War* 3.106.2, Caesar says that he had with him only 3,200 men, which is far less than two legions. After Pharsalus the pursuit had begun at once and it was not possible to replace the dead and wounded.
34 Cicero speaks of Caesar in Alexandria almost with irritation, while he himself awaited 'pardon' in Brindisi (*Letters to Atticus* 11.15.1).
35 Plutarch, *Caesar* 48.5.
36 Plutarch, *Caesar* 48.6.
37 Plutarch, *Caesar* 49.4–5.
38 H. Bengston, *Römische Geschichte*, 2nd edn (Munich 1970), p. 227.
39 *Précis des guerres de César*, par Napoléon, écrit par M. Marchand sous la dictée de l'Empereur [1819] (Paris 1836), p. 163.
40 T. Mommsen, *Römische Geschichte* [1856], III, 4th edn (Munich 1986), vol. 5, p. 103. In English, *The History of Rome*, trans. William Purdie Dickson (London 1908), vol. 5, p. 274.
41 Caesar, *Civil War* 3.110.2–3.
42 Caesar, *Civil War* 3.103.2.
43 Caesar, *Civil War* 3.107.2.
44 Caesar, *Alexandrian War* 33.2. The rest of the book deals with other campaigns; the title is inappropriate.
45 In Shakespeare's *Julius Caesar*, for example, which is set in the days immediately before and immediately after the murder, Cleopatra does not appear at all.

46 Plutarch, *Caesar* 48.9. This is Caesar's reaction to the arrogance of Potheinus, who had suggested that he leave Egypt and devote himself to his great enterprises.

47 Plutarch, *Caesar* 49.1–3.

48 Plutarch, *Antony* 27: Cleopatra could converse with Ethiopians, Troglodytes, Jews, Arabs, Syrians, etc. without an interpreter, but may not have known Latin. Other sources let their imagination run riot. Dio Cassius, for example, maintains that Cleopatra 'possessed ... a knowledge of how to make herself agreeable to everyone' (42.34).

49 Brambach (*Kleopatra*, p. 78) underscores this with fine irony. We shall refrain from participating in the still ongoing debate as to whether Cleopatra possessed only charm or charm with beauty. Even Blaise Pascal ventured an unhelpful and obscure observation on the political and historical effects of the shape of the queen of Egypt's nose.

50 Dio Cassius 42.34.3–4.

51 Diodorus Siculus, *Historical Library* 15.52; Strabo, *Geography* 17.1.8.

52 Brucheion was destroyed at the end of the third century, under the emperor Aurelian (AD 270–5), together with the old royal palace, built in the days of Alexander the Great.

53 Strabo (17.1.9) called it τὰ ἐνδοτέρω βασίλεια.

54 Caesar, *Civil War* 3.111.1: Achillas occupied almost all of Alexandria 'praeter eam oppidi partem quam Caesar cum militibus tenebat'.

55 Caesar, *Civil War* 3.111.1–3.

56 Lucan 10.439–43.

57 We have only to think of Lucan's description of the banquet held to celebrate the short-lived reconciliation. Here the poet dwells on Cleopatra's provocative dress (Lucan 10.140–1).

58 *Alexandrian War* 1.2: 'per foramina in proxima aedificia arietes immittuntur'.

59 *Alexandrian War* 1.4.

60 With professorial naïveté, Adcock bases his account on the 'fiery' temperament of Cleopatra and Caesar himself (*Cambridge Ancient History*, vol. IX, 'The Roman Republic 133–44 BC', eds S. A. Cook, F. E. Adcock and M. P. Charlesworth [Cambridge 1951], p. 669). Brambach (*Kleopatra*, pp. 81–2) takes his cue from Lucan and describes Cleopatra's transparent veils.

61 Mommsen, *Römische Geschichte*, vol. 5, p. 103. In English, *History of Rome*, vol. 5, p. 274.

62 Caesar, *Civil War* 3.109.5.

63 Caesar, *Civil War* 3.111.1–3.

64 Very well described in Lucan 10.491–2.

65 Caesar, *Civil War* 3.111.6. Caesar's ships, lying at anchor close to the palace, escaped damage.

66 Dio Cassius 42.38.2. The books were being stored for export, as may be seen from a valuable fragment of Livy, which has reached us thanks to Seneca (*Tranquillity of the Soul* 9.5). See L. Canfora, *La biblioteca scomparsa* (Palermo 1986), pp. 139–43.

67 Plutarch, *Caesar* 49.3.

68 George Bernard Shaw, *Caesar and Cleopatra*, Act II.

69 *Alexandrian War* 5–6.

70 *Alexandrian War* 7.

71 Caesar, *Civil War* 3.112.6 (= *Alexandrian War* 1.1).

72 *Alexandrian War* 9.

73 *Alexandrian War* 10–11.

74 *Alexandrian War* 12.

75 Caesar's daring leap into the water is linked with the (perhaps apocryphal) story of his rescue of some valuable notes (Plutarch, *Caesar* 49.8; Suetonius, *Caesar* 64; Dio Cassius 42.40.8), which some have taken to be the notes for his *Commentaries*.

76 The naval battle for Pharos occupies much of the *Alexandrian War* 14–22. Caesar's swim in the harbour is recorded in sober, factual manner (21.1) but without the detail of the notes being saved.

77 *Alexandrian War* 23–4.

78 *Alexandrian War* 24.3.

79 *Alexandrian War* 24.6. Brambach (*Kleopatra*, p. 94) observes that, by releasing Ptolemy, Caesar was preparing to remove him from the reorganised Egypt to be established as soon as the rebellion was put down. In the new system only Cleopatra would have a role, and she would be utterly dependent upon him.

80 The father of the future Herod the Great.

81 The account which follows is based on the only serious source to deal with these events: Josephus Flavius, *Antiquities of the Jews* 14.128–36. The figure of 1,500, however, comes from a document cited in *Antiquities of the Jews* 14.193. Josephus himself speaks of 3,000 hoplites.

82 On this the *Alexandrian War* is not forthcoming. See Chapter 24 below.

83 From this point on the *Alexandrian War* again becomes richer in details (chs 27–32).

84 *Alexandrian War* 33.1.

85 It would become a province after the battle of Actium (31 BC), but held a special position; serious rebellions were not avoided.

86 Suetonius, *Caesar* 35.1. This did in fact happen several times, before and after Suetonius wrote these words. There is no reason to suppose that Caesar did not fear such an event. See also Suetonius, *Caesar* 76.3.

87 *Alexandrian War* 33.1.

88 'Si permanerent in fide'.

89 The poetry of Horace (*Odes* 1.37) is a faithful reflection of this propaganda.

CHAPTER 24

Caesar Saved by the Jews

Caesar owed his salvation to the Jews, and this he never forgot. The decisive battle that lifted the siege in which he was trapped in Alexandria was the battle of Pelusium, followed immediately by that of the Jewish Camp. Here Antipater decided the battle against the Egyptians in Caesar's favour, after the Egyptians had overwhelmed the flanking force commanded by Mithridates. According to Josephus Flavius it was Antipater who forced the surrender of Pelusium and entered the city first.[1] Brandishing the directives of Hyrcanus he secured the support of the Jews from the Memphis area.[2] In the battle of the Jewish Camp (in the Nile Delta) Antipater, with his Jewish troops, not only saved those who survived the battle, but lost scarcely fifty men, compared with Mithridates' 800 killed.[3] There is a letter from Mithridates to Caesar acknowledging Antipater's decisive role in the battle and in the whole campaign. It is clear that Josephus is quoting a document, a letter to Caesar which he knew of directly.[4]

The author of the *Alexandrian War* also says – admittedly by hints – that the battle of the Delta was the decisive moment.[5] According to that account, Ptolemy dispatched a great army to face Mithridates in the Delta, convinced that his best option would be to defeat him, but adding that it would suffice (*satis habebat*) if he could prevent Mithridates from linking up with Caesar (*interclusum a Caesare a se retinere*).[6] Thereafter the battle went entirely in Caesar's favour. Caesar staged a sortie in strength in order to link up with Mithridates and cut off Ptolemy, who was leaving Alexandria in force. They met on the Nile. Caesar launched a surprise attack on the enemy camp and in the end won.[7] The decisive role of the Delta battle is also clear from the account in the *Alexandrian War*. It induced Ptolemy to make the mistake of placing a large part of his troops outside and at a distance from the city, allowing Caesar to make the unexpected move of attacking the enemy camp. Naturally in Josephus' version attention is focused on the battle as seen from the standpoint of Mithridates' force, and therefore on the Delta encounter, rather than the one between Caesar and the Egyptian troops which resulted from it.

Non-Jewish historiography makes little mention of it. Asinius' account is rather confused because he speaks of Hyrcanus (and not Antipater) joining Mithridates' troops.[8] Strabo tells us much more and explains details that are almost all found in Josephus.[9] He says that Antipater was the only one who acted (ἐξελθεῖν μόνον);[10] that Antipater was summoned to Ascalon by Mithridates; that he brought 3,000 men with him; that he had involved other rulers; and that Hyrcanus had lent his support to the expedition.[11]

In his account of Mithridates of Pergamon's advance to Pelusium and beyond, the author of the *Alexandrian War* credits Mithridates with achievements[12] that, according to Josephus, belong to Antipater:[13] the involvement of local rulers and the Nabataeans ('the leading figures of Arabia' must refer to Malchus Nabataeus), as well as that of the Jews who lived around Memphis in the Delta, after the obstacle of the resistance of Pelusium had been overcome. The reference to the request for aid sent to Malchus is given straight away at the beginning of the *Alexandrian War*[14] (and it is almost certainly Caesar who makes the request). This completes our information: *Caesar had summoned Malchus, but Malchus acted only on the request of Antipater.* Asinius Pollio provides the necessary acknowledgement of Antipater's intervention, but in a confused way. Pollio at least makes it clear that 'after Mithridates, Hyrcanus, the high priest of the Jews, also invaded Egypt' (quoted by Strabo, who was in turn quoted by Josephus).[15] It is plain here too that Asinius 'corrected' the account given in the *corpus Caesarianum*.

The acknowledgement by Caesar of the undisputed services (in the case of Antipater they were decisive) rendered to him by the Jews in battle may be seen in the decrees that Josephus Flavius, almost a century and a half later, went to look for in Rome 'on the Capitol'.[16] For Josephus, Caesar's statement had a certain protective value as proof of long-standing collaboration between Rome and the Jews, and a partisan spirit lay behind much of his research. While Josephus looked favourably on the Jewish establishment, he clearly condemned the (Messianic?) rebellion of Ezechias,[17] even if he had reservations about the brutality of Herod's repression. However, it is to his credit to have located in Rome what he could no longer seek in Jerusalem, since at the beginning of the revolt of AD 69 he had committed treason by going over to the Romans and into the service of the Flavian family. It is easy to imagine that even before being 'transplanted' to Rome, he knew of the existence of these documents attesting to the ancient friendship with Rome at the time of Julius Caesar, and that such documentation existed in copied form in Jerusalem as well.[18]

The total secularity of Caesar's cast of mind points to this complete openness towards the Jews, who were despised by 'middle Rome'.[19] Caesar, who had no prejudices in his dealings with the Jews, was inwardly sceptical, secular, and open to all faiths out of intellectual curiosity. Although he had Epicurean sympathies, he was aware of the political role of religion in Rome (he was *pontifex maximus* from 63 to the end of his life and in his final years he was also an *augur*). At the same time, having far fewer clients in the provinces than Pompey, he sensed the political potential of having connections with the Jewish community as a possible 'client' link to use against Pompey. The community was on Tiber Island in Rome from 63 BC. It comprised prisoners of war taken by Pompey, who had given deep offence to the Jewish people by taking advantage of the feast of the Sabbath to invade the Temple. Faced with the powerful position of Pompey in the East, the possibility of a fruitful and mutually helpful relationship with the Jews is a step that Caesar took without any anxiety. This relationship proved valuable when the Jewish contingent led by Antipater made it possible for Caesar to break the siege at Alexandria: not only because of the courage of Antipater's men in the siege of Pelusium and the battle of the Delta, but also because of the ability of Antipater to channel other assistance from local populations, to whom Caesar had turned in vain in his moment of greatest need.

Hence the gratitude which can be seen again and again in Caesar's official documents. He made sure that the Roman Senate also endorsed the decrees, while very probably enjoying riding roughshod over the anti-Semitism of the Romans, cultured or uncultured. In some of these documents Caesar writes sometimes as the dictator, sometimes as the *pontifex maximus* of the Romans, to Hyrcanus, the high priest of the Jews.

When at last in control of the situation in the East after the perilous adventure at Alexandria, the first thing he did was to order the reconstruction of the walls of Jerusalem, destroyed by Pompey,[20] and he bade the consuls inscribe an appropriate decree on a plaque to be fixed in the Capitol. The Senate approved.[21]

Dictator for the second time in 47 BC, Caesar requested the Senate and the people of Sidon to display the following inscription, engraved in Greek and Latin:

> Gaius Julius Caesar, Imperator and Pontifex Maximus, Dictator for the second time, to the magistrates, council and people of Sidon, greetings. [. . .] It is my wish that this be set up on a tablet of bronze in both Greek and Latin. It reads as follows. 'I, Julius Caesar, Imperator and Pontifex Maximus, Dictator for the second time, have decided as follows with the advice of the council. Whereas the Jew Hyrcanus, son of Alexander, both now and in the past, in time of peace as well as in war, has shown loyalty and zeal toward our state, as many commanders have testified on his behalf, and in the recent Alexandrian war came to our aid with fifteen hundred soldiers, and being sent by me to Mithridates, surpassed in bravery all those in the ranks, for these reasons it is my wish that Hyrcanus, son of Alexander, and his children shall be ethnarchs of the Jews and shall hold the office of high priest of the Jews for all time in accordance with their national customs, and that he and his sons shall be our allies and also be numbered among our particular friends; and whatever high-priestly rights or other privileges exist in accordance with their laws, these he and his children shall possess by my command. And if, during this period, any question shall arise concerning the Jews' manner of life, it is my pleasure that the decision shall rest with them. Nor do I approve of troops being given winter-quarters among them or of money being demanded of them.[22]

Most probably in the year 46 BC the *senatus consultum* was announced, with Caesar's approval, concerning the opening of negotiations on the status of Judea[23] as an 'ally and special friend' of Rome.[24] This *senatus consultum*, engraved in Greek and Latin on a bronze plaque, was displayed not only in the Capitol, but also in Tyre, Sidon and Ascalon. Besides other provisions highly advantageous for the Idumaean dynasty of Hyrcanus, we should note the honorific decree passed when Caesar was 'dictator for the fourth time' and 'dictator for life',[25] which bound the Senate and the people to ensure that Hyrcanus and his sons would always receive adequate recompense 'for their loyalty to us *and the benefits which they have conferred upon us*'.

The mass of documents collected by Josephus attests objectively to Caesar's careful management of this important eastern clientele in an area of great strategic importance, in view of future military developments envisaged by the dictator. In these documents the dominant motif is gratitude for what Hyrcanus and his family have done for Caesar. The figure of Hyrcanus is central to the relationship with the strong ally, even if, in Josephus' account, the military merit is accorded to Antipater and his men. But the choice is probably justified. Antipater had acted in the name of Hyrcanus and under his direction. The emphasis on him and his authority (even if Sextus Caesar, then *in loco* as the new governor of Syria, tightened the bonds with Antipater and his son Herod, who would later become famous) must have had positive consequences for the Jews in Jerusalem and Palestine and – not least – the Jewish community in Rome. When Caesar was murdered on 15 March 44 and his body, following days of mass unrest, was cremated publicly with displays of great mourning, 'at the height of the public grief a throng of foreigners went about lamenting each after the fashion of his country, above all the Jews, who even flocked to the place for several successive nights'.[26]

The precise and literal transcription of 'gentile' histories (not a common phenomenon in Josephus) serves a clear polemical purpose. He was concerned to counter that much larger historiographical tradition which concealed the Jewish contribution.[27] We return to Josephus' account:

> Moreover, when Caesar in the course of time concluded the war and sailed to Syria, he honoured him greatly; while confirming Hyrcanus in the high-priesthood, he gave Antipater Roman citizenship and exemption from taxation everywhere. It is said by many writers that Hyrcanus took part in this campaign and came to Egypt. And this statement of mine is attested by Strabo of Cappadocia, who writes as follows, on the authority of Asinius. 'After Mithridates, Hyrcanus, the high priest of the Jews, also invaded Egypt.' And again this time Strabo in another passage writes as follows, on the authority of Hypsicrates.[28] 'Mithridates went out alone, but Antipater, the procurator of Judaea, was called to Ascalon by him and provided him with an additional three thousand soldiers, and won over the other princes; and the high priest Hyrcanus also took part in the campaign.'[29] These are Strabo's own words.[30]

And on the chief merit of Antipater at Pelusium and in the battle of the Jewish Camp, Josephus mentions, but unfortunately does not quote, a letter from Mithridates to Caesar.[31]

On the other hand, the origin of the tradition that conceals the contribution of the Jews is the author of the *Alexandrian War*, who, as we know, allocates the credit to Mithridates alone – for mobilising the *civitates* of the region, raising suitable troops, storming Pelusium, winning support after the storming of Pelusium, and winning the battle of the Delta against the Egyptian troops. Josephus gives the alternative version of all these points,[32] and he provides minute details, in particular, for the battle of the Jewish Camp, where Mithridates was defeated and Antipater rescued him when his men had fallen back.[33] Josephus bases his account on a letter from Mithridates to Caesar, which recognises these decisive services of the Jewish leader and his troops, but he does not provide the text of the letter (as he does for Caesar's decrees and the passages from Strabo). Evidently he no longer had these pages when he was writing in Rome.

Was this letter known to Antipater and his descendants? Did it form part of the 'family history' of the heirs of Herod the Great? Was it mentioned by other authors like Hypsicrates? We cannot say for certain. One can only remark the care with which the author of the *Alexandrian War* obscures all the facts relative to the Jewish role in Caesar's victory. This author is not Caesar himself. The unknown writer's part begins, it appears, with chapter 26 and is characterised by high praise for Mithridates of Pergamon. The writer is an officer very close to Caesar who probably also knows the letter from Mithridates to Caesar – which would have been known among Caesar's staff – but he deliberately distorts the facts (misleading most later writers). It can be supposed that he wrote very soon after the events: from his silence on the death (not long afterwards) of Mithridates and Sextus Caesar it may perhaps be deduced that he was writing before the end of 46.[34]

Among those later writers, once again Asinius Pollio stands out. He was not kind to manipulations in the Caesarian corpus, which he ascribed to Caesar himself.[35] In this case Asinius – who had returned with Antony to Rome after Pharsalus, and thus was not present at Alexandria[36] – simply states, in evident denial of what had been written by the author of the *Alexandrian War*, that 'after Mithridates, Hyrcanus, the high priest of the Jews, also invaded Egypt'.[37] If Strabo (who concludes his *Histories* in 27/25 BC) is able to give all those other details based on Hypsicrates, this means that a tradition survived that was not infected by Roman anti-Semitism, and that Strabo, made aware by Asinius' admonitions of the little faith that could be placed in the *Commentaries*, had also preferred to stick to sources that provided different versions. If he did so for the Alexandrian episode, it means that he was well aware of the significance of that passage in the career of Julius Caesar, because it was clear that Caesar had risked losing everything, including his life, at Alexandria, and it was historically important to establish how he had extricated himself from that deadly trap. This led Strabo to report the various versions of that extremely delicate moment. It seems obvious that the Cappadocian historian transplanted to Augustan Rome provided in his account a variety of voices and versions. Josephus took from him two quotations, from Asinius and Hypsicrates, which seemed most useful to his case. It must not be forgotten that Asinius had Timagenes in his house, and that Timagenes, hated by Livy and Augustus for his scant 'Roman patriotism', knew a great deal about the history of his country, which was Alexandria.

The exact reconstruction of the intervention of Mithridates in the Alexandrian War was thus provided by two historians who came originally from Pontus: Hypsicrates of Amisus and Strabo of Amasea. Strabo's family on his mother's side was related to Mithridates V (the father of Mithridates VI Eupator, who was defeated in 66 BC by Pompey and committed suicide the same year). Mithridates of Pergamon was the 'pupil' of Mithridates VI Eupator, and in 47 BC, after Caesar's victory over Pharnakes, he obtained the Bosphorus kingdom.[38] The possibility cannot be excluded that Hypsicrates took directly from Mithridates of Pergamon the information on the Alexandrian campaign, and that Strabo took it from Hypsicrates, partly out of respect for this Pontic historian who was well informed about personages of whom Roman historians knew little. Hypsicrates must have been a contemporary of these events and personages (and older than Strabo). Varro (116–27 BC) argued against his grammatical writings.[39]

Josephus relied heavily on Strabo, who placed the greatest trust in Latin and 'Augustan' historiography. Almost all of the fragments of Strabo's *Histories* have reached us from Josephus Flavius.[40] Livy, however, relied largely on the Caesarian corpus, as is evident also from the correspondences between Dio Cassius and Livy's *Periochae* on the one hand and Caesar's *Commentaries* on the other.

Notes

1 Josephus Flavius, *Antiquities of the Jews* 14.130.
2 *Antiquities of the Jews* 14.131–2.
3 *Antiquities of the Jews* 14.133–5.
4 The existence of this letter is confirmed in the *Alexandrian War* 28.1: 'mittitur a Mithridate nuntius Caesari qui rem gestam perferret'.

5 The author of the *Alexandrian War* mentions the aid requested from the Nabataeans (ch. 1) but is silent about the Jews. (In 26.3 he attributes one of Antipater's achievements to Mithridates.)

6 *Alexandrian War* 27.4–5; 28.1.

7 *Alexandrian War* 28.2–32.

8 *Antiquities of the Jews* 14.138.

9 *Antiquities of the Jews* 14.139.

10 This sentence could, however, mean that Mithridates acted on his own. (Cf. *Alexandrian War* 26.1.)

11 Strabo and Josephus both say that he 'took part', and in Caesar's decrees in favour of the Jews all the credit is attributed to Hyrcanus; but the intention may be to say that Hyrcanus supplied all the help that depended on his authority. Josephus is citing two 'gentile' authors, passing on a valuable fragment from Asinius and one from Strabo. Strabo had detailed knowledge of the position of the local rulers: we need look no further than the details he supplies on Caecilius Bassus.

12 *Alexandrian War* 26: 'cum magnis copiis, quas celeriter [. . .] sua difugentia confecerat'.

13 *Antiquities of the Jews* 14.128 and 131–2.

14 *Alexandrian War* 1: 'equites ab rege Nabataeorum Malcho evocat'.

15 *Antiquities of the Jews* 14.138. A fragment not present in H. Peter, *HRR*.

16 He tells at length of this, giving numerous quotations, in book 14 of the *Antiquities of the Jews*, as well as in *Against Apion* (2.61).

17 He thus provides valuable information about the Jewish unrest while Caesar was governor of Syria.

18 See *Antiquities of the Jews* 14.191, where Caesar writes to the Jews: 'I am sending you a copy of the decree . . . in order that it may be deposited among your public records.'

19 See for example the anti-Semitic sallies of Horace (*Satires* 1.4.143; 5.100; 9.70), but Cicero also called Jewish monotheism 'barbarous superstition'. There are sarcastic remarks in his *Defence of Flaccus*, the proconsul of Judea, whom Cicero was defending against a charge of embezzlement. Tiberius exiled 4,000 Jews to Sardinia, and Tacitus reflects the view of the Senate when he observes, 'If they all died of malaria it would be no great loss' (*Annals* 2.85.4).

20 *Antiquities of the Jews* 14.144; the text is in 14.200.

21 *Antiquities of the Jews* 14.189, 199 and 212.

22 *Antiquities of the Jews* 14.191–5.

23 A significant honour.

24 *Antiquities of the Jews* 14.197.

25 *Antiquities of the Jews* 14.211–12.

26 Suetonius, *Caesar* 84.

27 This tradition began with the *Alexandrian War* 26 and continued with Livy's *Periocha* 112; Dio Cassius 42.40–1; Plutarch, *Caesar* 58, etc.

28 A contemporary of Strabo.

29 This is also confirmed by Caesar in his decree (*Antiquities of the Jews* 14.193).

30 *Antiquities of the Jews* 14.137–9.

31 *Antiquities of the Jews* 14.136.

32 *Antiquities of the Jews* 14.128–36.

33 Here too Asinius rebuts the falsehoods in the *Commentaries*.

34 The most likely hypothesis is that there were several reports which after Caesar's death were assembled, with brief linking passages, to form a corpus covering these events.

35 Suetonius, *Caesar 56*.

36 See B. Haller, 'Caius Asinius Pollio als Politiker und zeitkritischer Historiker', dissertation, Münster 1967, p. 30.

37 See *Antiquities of the Jews* 14.138.

38 The connection between Mithridates of Pergamon and Eupator is mentioned by Strabo in his *Geography* 13.625, and in the *Alexandrian War* 78.2.

39 See Varro's *De lingua Latina* (dedicated to Cicero in 44 BC).

40 *FGrHist* 91: eleven out of nineteen, but it would be more accurate to say 'out of sixteen' since nos. 1–3 come from Strabo himself.

CHAPTER 25

From Syria to Zela

By regarding the Alexandrian war as a not very serious 'diversion' or a 'distraction' for Caesar from his primary goal of concluding the civil war we may overlook a significant fact. While risking a great deal, with that conflict Caesar had added an important element to his clientele: Egypt, which for a long time had been feudally subject to Pompey and his associates.[1] Now, however, all his efforts were directed towards the rearrangement of the eastern clientele, disrupted by the death of Pompey. From Syria to Pontus this was Caesar's priority, despite urgent calls for him to return to Rome,[2] and although he knew that Cato was reassembling the remaining Pompeian forces in Africa. The confirmation of this is in the fact that, once Alexandria was dominated, Caesar did not march against Juba but towards Syria.

In Syria the reaction to Pompey's defeat at Pharsalus had been so swift and well-organised (Antioch had taken up arms, menacing any supporters of Pompey who approached the city),[3] that the suspicion arises that Caesarian elements must have been active there. Caesar is well informed, down to the slightest details, about the expulsion of Pompey from Syria after the defeat, which also seems to confirm that his men were operating there. When he found himself in difficulties in Alexandria he was able to rely on elements that came primarily from Syria.[4] With regard to the province of Syria (in this period, at least), the two antagonists exhibited quite different behaviour: Pompey thought (wrongly) that he could cross the province he had created and return with the help of a Parthian expeditionary force. Caesar consolidated the old and new Syrian and Palestinian clienteles and put the entire region in order for a campaign *against* the Parthians.[5] If Pompey did not return with Parthian support (and it would certainly have embarrassed Caesar not a little while other Pompeian forces were regrouping in the West), this was due essentially to the fact that 'his' province had closed its gates to him. He had therefore renounced the audacious project and made for Egypt, towards the trap of which we know. Caesar meanwhile presented

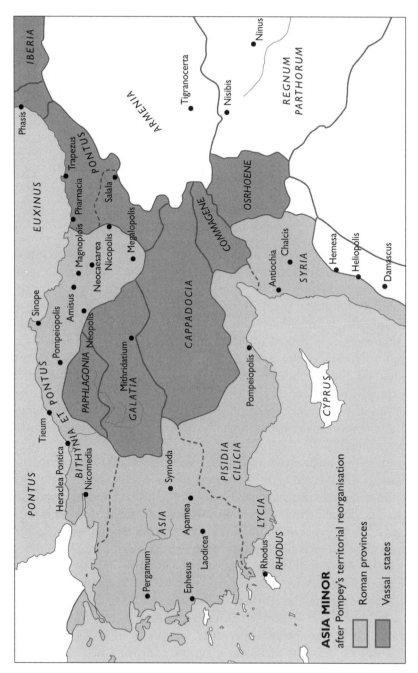

ASIA MINOR
after Pompey's territorial reorganisation

☐ Roman provinces

☐ Vassal states

Asia Minor

himself as the 'saviour' of the treasure of the temple of Artemis at Ephesus,[6] and in Syria, Antioch, Ptolemais and elsewhere in Asia there were reports of 'miracles' coinciding with Caesar's expected arrival. Caesar is singularly meticulous in recording these 'supernatural' phenomena.[7] By the end of 48 BC he had proceeded to acknowledge the high priest Hyrcanus at Jerusalem.[8] Recognition of him as ethnarch and high priest was confirmed after the war ended,[9] when Caesar went to Syria and proceeded to reorganise the region in person, giving firm support to his old and new clients.

In the meantime Caesar's troops entered Syria. One of his legions had already halted here when Caesar was still fighting in Alexandria.[10] Then in June (April) of 47 BC Caesar himself, back from Alexandria, halted in Syria,[11] bringing with him the Sixth Legion, a legion of veterans.

Caesar's sojourn in Syria lasted only a few days,[12] mainly to consolidate ties with the cities actively pledged to help him, and to make clear the position of the patchwork of local rulers scattered throughout the province. Given the urgency of intervening against Pharnakes, king of the Bosphorus, who had just defeated Domitius Calvinus at Nicopolis and was menacingly expanding his influence, Caesar had to restrict himself to receiving the hasty submission en masse of these rulers, who had rushed to render homage to him. They were *recepti in fidem* (welcomed into his clientele) by him,[13] and he promised them his *amicitia* – the formula of acceptance into the clientele – in exchange for their commitment to support the Roman administration in the border zones.[14]

Among the most favoured rulers were certainly Antipater and Hyrcanus. They were weighed down by a pro-Pompeian past, but they had changed sides in time. Their intervention in the Alexandrian war had cemented their relationship with the victor. The latter had to rid himself – not without pain – of a rival to Hyrcanus and Antipater, another aspirant to a client relationship, the Maccabaean Antigonus, son of the Aristobulus who was taken as a prisoner to Rome by Pompey in 63 and was then put to death by the Pompeians: 'for his allegiance to Caesar' according to his son.[15] Of the cities to which prizes fell *publice et viritim* (to all the communities together, but also to particularly deserving individual communities), Antioch was singled out on account of its early support for the Caesarian side.[16] Caesar felt particularly grateful to that city, *post eventum*, given the effects of Pompey's failed flight to the East. And Antioch rewarded its benefactor by instituting a new historical era, measuring time from the date of the battle of Pharsalus.[17]

The most important measure was the appointment of a relative who had close ties to Caesar as governor of Syria. Sextus Julius Caesar had been committed to his side in the civil war from the outset. The writer of the *Alexandrian War* emphasises this appointment and describes Sextus as not only a 'relative' but also a 'friend' of Caesar.[18] Sextus was entrusted with Syria and the command of the legions[19] (but not the Sixth, which followed Caesar into battle against Pharnakes).[20] His rank was that of *proquaestor propraetor*, which puts his birth around the year 80 BC (and not later than 78).

Sextus Julius Caesar was descended in a direct line (the son or grandson)[21] from Sextus Julius Caesar, the consul in 91 BC, who was the brother of Caesar's father. Caesar's father, who died in 85, never attained the consulship but only the praetorship; the grandfather (or father) of Sextus, however, had reached the summit of the *cursus honorum*. In the family's recent history, then, Sextus' branch was the one that had achieved the greatest renown. This could explain Caesar's regard for his younger relative, a regard that one sees from the roles held by Sextus at various points in the civil war, but also from Cicero's very solemn and circumspect words in his speech in defence of Deiotarus,[22] if – as seems likely – he was referring to Sextus Caesar: 'one whom you selected as the most loyal and universally respected of your adherents'.[23] Caesar, as *pontifex maximus*, had nominated him *flamen Quirinalis* as early as 57 BC. In 49 Sextus is with Caesar in Spain as his military tribune and receives, on behalf of Caesar and as his right-hand man, the capitulation of Varro after the rout of the Pompeian legions.[24] Since Sextus is mentioned in an eminent position close to Caesar both in the campaign against Afranius and Petreius, and during the reorganisation of Syria, the only reasonable conclusion – given the rapid and uninterrupted course of all Caesar's campaigns from the crossing of the Adriatic to the subjugation of Alexandria – is that Sextus followed the dictator for all of that crucial and perilous sequence of events. We should either picture him together with Caesar in Alexandria, or suppose that he arrived with the Thirty-Seventh Legion under the command of Domitius Calvinus,[25] unless he remained in Syria with the legion that had stayed there, while Domitius continued by sea to Alexandria. Most information on Sextus' government in Syria comes from Josephus Flavius in the fourteenth book of *Antiquities of the Jews*.[26]

There is a marked familiarity evident almost from the start between Sextus and the family of Antipater (in particular with the rising and unscrupulous Herod). This means that Sextus, when he took office in the province assigned to him, already had good contacts there. Perhaps his links with the family of Antipater were already strong in the period when Mithridates of Pergamon was seeking allies and support in Syria to take to Caesar's aid. It is a fact that, from that moment on, Sextus protects the Idumaeans and even the criminal actions of Herod,[27] and Antipater and his sons commit themselves to Sextus. When Sextus is killed by mutinous troops, his sons want to avenge him 'out of devotion', as Josephus says – 'to Caesar alive' (the dictator) and 'to Caesar dead' (Sextus).[28] But this, we shall see, happens later. For now, one of the tasks, and not the easiest, assigned to the new governor of the sensitive border province would be that of preparing the ground for the campaign that Caesar planned against the Parthians.[29]

To carry forward his reorganisation of the East, now bereft of its great protector Pompey (murdered by one of his clients), Caesar hastened by sea to Tarsus in Cilicia.[30] Here he was rejoined by Gaius Cassius,[31] who had attempted several times, it seems from some hints in Cicero,[32] to join Caesar at Alexandria. Cicero seems somewhat surprised by his old friend's intention. 'To go to Caesar', as Quintus Cicero did with his son Quintus, usually meant to seek his 'pardon'. Later, in August 47 BC, Cicero would write to Cassius acknowledging that it was he who had promoted the abandonment of the 'war spirit'[33] and the attempt to come to an arrangement with Caesar. But in March, when everything pointed to imminent defeat for Caesar in Alexandria, things no doubt looked very different. What really happened in Cilicia, when Cassius presented himself to Caesar and became a legate,[34] is not at all clear. Three years later, when Caesar had just been assassinated on the initiative and by the hand of Cassius, Cicero would claim that Cassius was in Cilicia to make an attempt on Caesar's life, and that this failed by sheer chance. Caesar was supposed to land on one of the banks of the river Cydnus and instead, unexpectedly, he landed on the opposite one.[35] According to some modern historians,[36] Cicero was confused by a naval encounter in the Hellespont between Caesar and *Lucius* Cassius in 48 BC,[37] shortly after the battle of Pharsalus, but this opinion does not seem tenable. Any confusion of these two episodes, very different in all respects, is impossible. Besides, Cicero was very close to Cassius and had the information directly from him. The facts are: (a) Caesar had a narrow escape from an attempt (which normally happens thanks to a tip-off); (b) this attempt was organised by Cassius; (c) Caesar did not take Cassius in his entourage as a legate (despite having named him as such) in either the African campaign or the Spanish. And this could not have been a matter of chance.

At Tarsus Caesar proceeded to formalise his new hegemonic role by calling together the notables of the cities of the province and the nearby province of Asia.[38] By holding a general meeting he could avoid a long detour while it was urgent to settle accounts with Pharnakes. He preferred to deal with all contentious matters in Tarsus, and then move on at once to the new campaign in Pontus. He crossed Cappadocia and reached Mazaca, where he even found the time to give Lycomedes of Bithynia charge of the temple of Bellona and confer upon him the role of priest, making him the second most important figure in Cappadocia after the sovereign.[39]

On the border with Galatia, Deiotarus, the tetrarch of Galatia, appeared before Caesar in garments of supplication. Deiotarus at that time was under attack by Pharnakes. He was prepared to be of service and had already tried to gain acceptance when he gave money to Caesar's envoy (perhaps Sextus) at a difficult moment in the Alexandrian campaign.[40] He wanted to keep the kingdom for himself, but knew he was in danger for having chosen to support Pompey's forces until the defeat at Pharsalus. A dialogue took place, which the writer of the *Alexandrian War* concisely summarises.[41] It is instructive because it throws light on Deiotarus' position: what else could he have done, 'situated as he was in a part of the world which had no garrisons of Caesar's to protect it?'[42] Acting under duress, 'compelled by orders backed by armed force', he had no choice but to fight on Pompey's side: 'for it had been no business of his to act as judge in the disputes of the Roman people, but only *to obey the commands of the moment*'.[43] A very interesting expression: a client of the dead Pompey explains to his presumed new *patronus*, on whose protection he expects to rely, how the mechanism of the clientele functions on the periphery of the empire. Of course Deiotarus has no intention of behaving imprudently or arguing with the individual into whose grace he meant to enter. A client cannot reason in terms of *melior causa*, he can only conform to the authority that is present and visible. Caesar's reply does not question these assumptions, which he certainly shares. He points out, however, that the benefits from which Deiotarus had profited could not be forgotten;[44] and he stresses above all that at the time of the battle of Pharsalus his judicial and constitutional position was the other way about: Caesar was the legitimate authority, his adversaries the law-breakers. Who had been consul after the year of Lentulus and Marcellus? And where was the Senate? In Greece or Thessaly, perhaps?[45] (Most of it had remained in Rome.) This reply constitutes a valuable piece of information that complements the account of the civil war. It has already been said that at the beginning of the year 48 BC the judicial position of the two sides was reversed and the full gravity of Pompey's error in wanting to take the state with him to the Balkan peninsula became apparent. From this brief, important dialogue between Caesar and Deiotarus we learn that Caesar was able to exploit this advantage on the propaganda level too, just as he had taken care to consolidate steadily his position from the moment when, observing all proper procedure, he had first assumed the dictatorship. Clearly Deiotarus was pardoned and invited to provide troops against Pharnakes immediately.[46]

Pharnakes II was the son of Mithridates VI the Great, the fearsome and implacable enemy of Rome. When Mithridates was defeated by Pompey in 63 BC, Pharnakes rebelled against his father and thus obtained a tiny kingdom, while Pontus became a Roman province. He was given the Cimmerian Bosphorus (the present-day Crimea). But during the civil war, prior to Pharsalus, Pharnakes had occupied Sinope, on the coast of his father's old kingdom; he had then invaded Colchis, Armenia Minor and Cappadocia. And when Domitius Calvinus, Caesar's representative in Asia Minor, attempted to stop him, in response to an appeal from the local rulers overthrown by the advance of the ambitious Pharnakes, he suffered a serious setback in December 48 BC at Nicopolis, on the border between Pontus and Armenia Minor. This was not a good start for Caesar's 'new order' in the region. Pharnakes pressed on, invading Pontus and pushing still deeper into Cappadocia. Caesar urgently needed to stop him, and above all to restore his own prestige, after the defeat of Domitius, in the eyes of that vast Pompeian clientele which needed reassurance.

Pharnakes immediately tried to parley. He counted on the incontrovertible fact that he had not sent any forces to assist Pompey, whereas Deiotarus – he recalled – 'who had provided them, had none the less given Caesar satisfaction'.[47] Caesar quickly dismissed this logic, stressing his own natural inclination to treat suppliants well, and pointing to his own victory at Pharsalus, which owed nothing to the neutrality of people like Pharnakes. However, he showed that he took seriously Pharnakes' conciliatory attitude and laid before him conditions for a peaceful settlement, despite the grave wrongs done to the Roman citizens killed or exiled from Pontus. These conditions were: immediate withdrawal from Pontus, the return of Roman and allied prisoners, and as a sign of homage 'the tributes and gifts which triumphant commanders are in the habit of receiving from their friends'.[48] Pharnakes thought he could gain time with delaying tactics, presuming that the situation in Rome would force Caesar to return in haste.[49] It was a catastrophic miscalculation; perhaps Caesar's artfully chosen words had – it is difficult to tell how consciously – instilled in Pharnakes a disastrously false belief. Pharnakes occupied Zela (the scene of the victory of Mithridates over Triarius).[50] Caesar moved up in a rapid overnight march, rendering a battle inevitable.[51] Between them lay a narrow valley, and Caesar began to prepare earthworks and fortifications. On 2 August (12 June) Pharnakes made a surprise attack, deploying chariots with scythe-blades fitted to the axles, but was unable to retain the initial advantage of surprise. At first there was panic in Caesar's ranks. Once again it was the Sixth Legion that won through in close hand-to-hand combat. The victory started there. Pharnakes' soldiers were thrown down the ravine, and the setback became an uncontrolled rout. The battle was swift and decisive.[52] Pharnakes fled with some of his cavalry, successfully evading capture (he was not part of the triumphant procession of defeated chiefs), but was killed at home, by the rebel Assandrus who had once been his most loyal follower. Caesar awarded the Bosphorus kingdom to Mithridates of Pergamon.[53]

Caesar's satisfaction with the speed of this victory was expressed afterwards in the triumph with the famous notice carried in the procession, on which were the three words VENI VIDI VICI.[54] According to Suetonius, Caesar repeated more than once afterwards that from this battle against Pharnakes he had learnt to reappraise the military glory of Pompey, who had 'gained his principal fame as a general by victories over such feeble foemen'.[55] These were not casual words: this was a further opportunity to cancel out the memory and the myth of Pompey in the very place where it was strongest.

The reordering of Asia occupied him until the end of that summer. On 26 September he embarked at Tarentum,[56] and a few days later he finally entered Rome, whence he had set out in December 49.

Notes

1 It was no accident that Cleopatra's first choice fell on Pompey.
2 *Alexandrian War* 65.1.
3 Caesar, *Civil War* 3.102.6.
4 Thanks to Mithridates of Pergamon and to Antipater's good connections.
5 Appian, *Civil Wars* 3.77.312.
6 Caesar, *Civil War* 3.105.2.
7 Caesar, *Civil War* 3.105.4–5.
8 Josephus Flavius, *Antiquities of the Jews* 14.199: '[He] has granted that both Hyrcanus and his sons shall be high priests and priests of Jerusalem and of their nation.' The dates may be established from the orders. See A. Momigliano, 'Ricerche sull'organizzazione della Giudea sotto il dominio romano (63 a.C.-70 d.C.)', *ASNP* (1934), p. 194. Other dates have been cited for this decree.
9 Josephus Flavius, *Antiquities of the Jews* 14.192–3.
10 *Alexandrian War* 34.3: 'quarum altera in bello Alexandrino non occurrit'.
11 The exact date of Caesar's arrival in Syria may be established indirectly by a *terminus ante quem*. The decree on the autonomy of Antioch, by the Syrian-Macedonian lunar calendar, is dated 23 Artemisios, which corresponds to 16 April by the Julian calendar and 28 June by the pre-Julian calendar. See W. Judeich, *Caesar im Orient* (Leipzig 1885), pp. 106–9.
12 *Alexandrian War* 66.1: 'paucis diebus in ea provincia consumptis'. By 16 July Trebonius had met Caesar at Antioch (Cicero, *Letters to Atticus* 11.20.1).
13 *Alexandrian War* 65.4: 'reges, tyrannos, dynastas provinciae finitimos, qui omnes ad eum concurrerant, receptos in fidem'.
14 Ibid.: 'condicionibus impositis provinciae tuendae ac defendendae, dimittit et *sibi* et *populo Romano* amicissimos'.
15 Josephus Flavius, *Antiquities of the Jews* 14.140.
16 Johannes Malalas, *Chronographia*, ed. L. Dindorf, part of the Corpus Scriptores Historiae Byzantinae (Bonn 1831), p. 216.
17 Malalas, p. 217: 'In honour of Gaius Julius Caesar, Great Antioch counts the years from his time.' See also G. Downey, *A History of Antioch in Syria* (Princeton 1961), pp. 157–8.
18 *Alexandrian War* 66.1.
19 It is not advisable to correct *legionibus* to *legioni*. When Dio Cassius and Appian speak of *one* legion which mutinied against Sextus, this does not mean that in June 47 BC he had less than two legions. The redeployment of troops after the mutiny is not fully clear.
20 *Alexandrian War* 66.1.
21 The information on the genealogy of Sextus is taken from my *Storici della rivoluzione romana* (Bari 1974), p. 14 and n. 9.

22 This speech was delivered in Caesar's house at the end of 45 BC, in defence of the tetrarch of Galatia, who stood accused of having conspired against the dictator.

23 Cicero, *In defence of King Deiotarus* 14: he cannot be referring to Domitius Calvinus, who is named a moment later, and these words cannot refer to anybody else from Caesar's entourage at the time of the Alexandrian War.

24 Caesar, *Civil War* 2.20.7. Varro had already stated that he was prepared to hand over his legion to the person designated by Caesar.

25 As ex-consul (in 53 BC he was the colleague of Valerius Mesalla Rufus) Domitius enjoyed greater authority than Sextus, who was *quaestor* in 47.

26 This also contains revealing details (see 14.180, on the 'sale' to Herod of a high office).

27 For example, the liquidation of Ezechias in blatant defiance of the Sanhedrin.

28 Josephus Flavius, *Jewish War* 1.217.

29 This is asserted by Appian, *Civil Wars* 3.77.312, referring to a source which merits attention but is to be treated with caution.

30 *Alexandrian War* 66.1.

31 His assassin-to-be.

32 Cicero, *Letters to Atticus* 11.13.1; 11.15.2.

33 Cicero, *Letters to his friends* 15.15.1.

34 Cicero, *Letters to his friends* 6.6.10.

35 Cicero, *Philippics* 2.26.

36 See P. Wuilleumier (ed.), Cicero, *Discours*, vol. XIX (Paris 1959).

37 A well-known event, thanks to Suetonius, *Caesar* 63.

38 *Alexandrian War* 66.2.

39 *Alexandrian War* 66.3–4.

40 Cicero, *In defence of King Deiotarus* 14.

41 *Alexandrian War* 67.

42 *Alexandrian War* 67.1.

43 *Alexandrian War* 66.2.

44 During Caesar's first consulship.

45 *Alexandrian War* 68.

46 *Alexandrian War* 68.2.

47 *Alexandrian War* 69.3.

48 *Alexandrian War* 70.

49 *Alexandrian War* 71.1.

50 *Alexandrian War* 72.2.

51 He occupied exactly the same position in which Mithridates had successfully fought against Triarius (*Alexandrian War* 73.2).

52 The author of the *Alexandrian War* stresses that, without the help of the gods, victory would have been difficult to achieve (75.3).

53 *Alexandrian War* 78.1–2.

54 Suetonius, *Caesar* 37.2. According to Plutarch, *Caesar* 50.3, these words constitute the message sent by Caesar to Gaius Matius. Appian, *Civil Wars* 2.91.384, is less specific, saying that Caesar addressed these words 'to Rome'.
55 Suetonius, *Caesar* 35.2.
56 'Faster than expected', says the author of the *Alexandrian War*, concluding his commentary.

CHAPTER 26

The Long Civil War

Il a été six mois maître du monde.

Napoleon

One could argue that the reason the civil war did not end at Pharsalus was precisely because Pompey died so unexpectedly. The distinguishing feature of this civil war, different from all the others between the first century BC and the third century AD, was that it never ended. The forces in the field remained in balance, neither side able to achieve conclusive military success. For Caesar, the most urgent imperative each time was to achieve decisive victory on the field of battle, and, immediately or at the same time, to seek a political solution that would re-establish the balance of power. Hence his policy of *clementia*, and hence his chosen solution: 'Caesarism' (dictatorship) plus accord with the aristocracy.

Napoleon's apparently paradoxical observation was well aimed. The 'six months'[1] are those between the return to Rome after the very difficult and protracted Munda campaign against Pompey's sons (the end of August 45 BC) and the fatal attack of 15 March 44. Napoleon saw the civil war as a unique, uninterrupted and long-drawn-out conflict that began at the end of December 50 and ended (if this term is not too optimistic) with the conclusion of the Spanish campaign, in the late summer of 45. In the middle there were very brief intervals. At the beginning of October 47 Caesar returned to Rome from the East, after the series of battles at Pharsalus, Alexandria and Zela, but by the beginning of December he was already leaving for Africa, setting out from Lilybaeum, to confront the 'republican' forces that had regrouped in Tunisia under the protection of Juba, the king of Numidia. He returned from Africa to Rome on 25 July 46 but at the beginning of November departed again for Spain, where he stayed until the end of August the following year.[2] The delayed triumphal celebration of four victories (over Gaul, Egypt, Pontus and Numidia), held only on his return from Africa in August 46,[3] provides a clear indication of the provisional nature of his long period of rule, which began with his appointment as dictator in November 49 and ended in an unbroken series of campaigns to the four corners of the empire.

Nevertheless, depending on the various contenders, the 'long civil war' may be divided into separate periods, corresponding to Caesar's various opponents. First came the 'Pompeian' war, which ended with the death of Pompey and was reactivated by his sons nearly three years later. Then came Cato's 'republican' war. How separate these two perspectives are – although this is partially obscured by the fact that the opponent to be beaten is always Caesar – may become clearer if one considers that, subsequently, no *common* front was ever formed between Sextus Pompey and the 'liberators' (as Caesar's assassins called themselves). And from 43 onwards the Caesarians fought the two wars separately. Thus, in a certain sense, the war against Sextus Pompey would be an *Octavian* war, a continuation of the *Pompeian* war in which the respective fathers had clashed.

The letter written to Cassius by Cicero in August 47 helps to provide a clearer picture of the stages of the long civil war.[4] By that time not only had Cassius and Brutus gone over to Caesar about a year earlier (August 48), but Cicero was stuck at Brindisi awaiting Caesar's return from the campaigns against Alexandria and Pharnakes. In the meantime Cato had reorganised the 'Pompeians' in Africa, but Cassius and Cicero voiced disapproval of this unforeseen extension of the civil war, which they had hoped to see ended in a single battle. If, however, we adopt the viewpoint of Cato, Juba or the sons of Pompey, then Cassius and Cicero and their ilk are simply traitors who had given up too readily. For them the game with Caesar was far from over.

For Cato, in particular, Pompey's war had not really been *his* war: that had been a war between two aspirants to the crown.[5] Now, however, in Africa, with Pompey out of the way thanks to an unforeseen chance, the real war of the republic against the usurper was being fought, and Cicero and the others were on the opposite side.[6] To Cato this was a separate war, not a single long war.

The vast extent of the area over which the civil war was fought also played its part: Spain, Marseilles, Illyricum, Macedonia, Alexandria, Pontus, Numidia, while a flashpoint reignited in Syria at Apamea. It ranged from the far West to the far East and included the failed endgame in Syria. It was the most spectacular and long-lasting civil war in Roman history, including the conflicts that broke out at the end of the Julio-Claudian dynasty and at the end of Commodus' reign. One wonders to what extent the decision to have a *great* Parthian campaign (the dates of whose planning are not clear) was also aimed at putting a match once and for all to the potential fire represented by the Pompeian mutiny in Syria.

Caesar's progress was no triumphal march: it was rather a constant drive to obstruct the continuous reorganisation of a faction that had deep roots, and not only in the provincial clienteles. Without them the choice of Africa first, then Spain as the venue for the return match, cannot be explained.

The vitality of the side that we may for convenience call the Pompeian bloc is impressive. Even after Pharsalus, the death of Pompey, the rout and the mass defection, it continued to regroup and fight. Thapsus was a crucial confrontation, and it was strategic superiority that saved Caesar, not a real political victory.

On his return to Rome in October 47 BC Caesar was forced to deal with urgent internal problems. After Pharsalus, Antony had returned to Italy and had effectively governed as the dictator's *magister equitum*. He had had to confront serious difficulties, not all of them political. On the institutional level he had had to adopt an extreme measure, reconfirming Caesar as dictator for 47 BC and himself as *magister equitum* (the augurs had protested because the appointment was not limited, as was usual, to six months).[7] On the level of public order, Antony had had to deal with the inflammatory activism of Publius Cornelius Dolabella (Cicero's son-in-law). A wholehearted supporter of Caesar's cause, which he understood in the old terms of *popularis* agitation, Dolabella was playing on his position of tribune of the plebs for the year 47 to seek the cancellation of debts. First the tribune's colleagues, Pollio and Trebellus, opposed him, then Antony intervened – as the highest authority present in Rome – with an iron hand to crush the rebellion. On the social level, Dolabella's activism was able to evoke a response because the economic situation was worsening, above all for the weakest social groups. Moreover, Africa, in the hands of the Pompeians, represented a dangerous crescent of potential attack – by his opponents – on the provinces that supplied grain to Italy. On the military and social levels, the legions, especially those stationed in Campania, were complaining about the delay in holding the triumph (with attendant benefits for every legionary) and were demanding their discharge. When Caesar returned to Italy the first signs of mutiny in the legions were already in evidence. Gaius Sallustius Crispus,[8] sent to Campania to quell them, was stoned and barely escaped with his life. The troops marched on Rome and camped on the Field of Mars. Caesar had to employ his charisma and with it the coarseness that he could produce when necessary. He addressed his men, calling them 'citizens' rather than 'fellow soldiers',[9] an alarming indication (be it noted in parenthesis) of the disrepute into which the key concept of the republic had fallen. Caesar made plain his contempt for them and roused them to anger by letting it be understood that they would not participate in the triumph. It was precisely the Tenth Legion, the only one free of unrest during the campaign against Ariovistus, that was now the most troublesome: in order to be admitted to the triumph they had to have fought in the most difficult campaigns of Africa and Spain. All the legions involved in the attempted mutiny had been formed for the imminent campaign against Africa, which was firmly in the hands of the Pompeians. Antony and Dolabella also received their deserts: Dolabella for his irresponsibility and Antony for the excessive harshness of his repression. The (partly) suppressed vexation of Antony, who would soon lose the office of *magister eqitum*, dates from this time: among other things he had to pay the money he had offered for Pompey's confiscated possessions.[10] He had gone so far as to have Pompey's house demolished in order to rebuild it in even grander style.[11] This greatly annoyed ordinary people, who saw the eager beneficiaries of the regime taking up position even before the regime was established.

At Lilybaeum, the furthest point of western Sicily, a natural embarkation point for Africa, Caesar gathered a force of six legions and 2,600 cavalry men in the month of December 47.[12] Against all advice to the contrary, he put to sea in the depths of winter, on 25 December.[13] The advantage of such a move was obvious, despite the risks, because his opponents did not have a fleet capable of blocking his armada at sea. Nor did they imagine he would move so swiftly.

The Pompeian forces had been consolidating in the long time that had elapsed since the defeat at Pharsalus, and the province of Africa was an obvious choice, as it had been a Pompeian stronghold without interruption from the start. At the beginning of the civil war, Caesar, who was fighting in Spain, had sent Curio to Africa, where he had been killed.[14] After Curio's defeat, Africa remained firmly in the hands of Attius Varus, Pompey's lieutenant, with three legions, two of them raised locally, at his command. After Pharsalus, the first to reach Africa was Quintus Metellus Scipio, Pompey's father-in-law, whose authority over the remaining troops was due largely to that family connection. Then Cato arrived. In Corfu, soon after the rout, he had assembled a council of war that crumbled in his hands as authoritative senators (beginning with Cicero) defected, convinced that all was lost.[15] From the Adriatic Cato reached Cyrenaica,[16] and after a thirty-day march across the desert he reached the province of Africa with fifteen cohorts and 1,600 cavalry, as well as a group of veterans who had survived Pharsalus thanks to Labienus and Afranius.[17] A stickler for form, Cato declined the supreme command: in the *cursus honorum* (thanks to the combined boycott of Caesar and Pompey) he had remained barred from the praetorship. He never attained the consulate, and with his rank of *propraetor* he certainly could not dream of commanding proconsuls. He ordered that the command go to Scipio – whose name had an effect in an African campaign. Pompey's father-in-law was not renowned as a strategic thinker, but he was supported by capable generals like Labienus, Afranius, Petreius, Varus, Pompey the Younger and Cato himself. While Caesar was dealing with the child-sovereigns of Alexandria, Africa was being militarised, becoming an armed camp with a strength of ten legions and 14,000 horsemen. In addition there were four legions belonging to Juba, the king of Numidia, with sixty elephants and a substantial and well-trained force of light infantry. Furthermore, requisitions of food had enabled this strong army to count on unlimited supplies. The leaders were again in the arrogant state of mind that preceded Pharsalus. But the troops were not all hand-picked. In particular the combat-readiness of the legions left something to be desired, as these were composed of local elements and freed slaves.[18]

For Caesar the campaign had a far from brilliant opening. Since the bulk of the republican forces were at Utica (on the Tunisian coast), Caesar landed further to the south, towards Hadrumetum; however, a storm surprised the fleet off Capo Bon and scattered a large part of his force. No more than 3,000 men and 150 horses reached Hadrumetum. This initial disaster settled the course of the campaign: Caesar remained on the defensive, renouncing an offensive strategy and instead securing and fortifying positions, and awaiting reinforcements in order to provoke his adversary into combat. Caesar had fortified Ruspina and without encountering resistance had occupied nearby Leptis. Here some of the ships that had been scattered in the storm found shelter with about 5,000 men.[19] They were still about 13,000 men short, and their fate appeared to hang by a thread: for reasons of security Caesar had told only his commanders that the landing was not at Utica (closest for those who were leaving from Lilybaeum) but at Hadrumetum. There was the risk that by mistake those who had been 'shipwrecked' would fall into the hands of his opponents. However, the worst was avoided, and at dawn on 3 January 46 BC these boats, for which the worst had been feared, appeared off the peninsula of Monastir. Caesar's army, though rather battered, was now able to defend itself and hold its own fortified camps. But only a day later the extreme delicacy of the situation became clear, when Labienus, with 10,000 horse, encircled – and almost overcame – a contingent of cohorts and cavalry led by Caesar, surprised while requisitioning grain. The battle was very fierce and it took great tenacity to avoid annihilation. Caesar managed to control his men and break out of the encirclement, then make an orderly withdrawal to Ruspina.[20] The author of the *African War* describes individual encounters as well, and above all he focuses attention on Labienus' error: once again he was quite sure (as he had been in Thessaly) that he was facing raw recruits instead of veterans of the Gallic campaign. Hence the space given to an exchange between Labienus and a soldier of the Tenth Legion. The two recognise each other from the time of their service in Gaul,[21] and talk as they fight. Labienus first mistakes the legionary for a recruit, and the soldier exploits his error, aiming to give heart to the frightened recruits, who 'kept looking round for Caesar and contented themselves with dodging the enemy javelins'.[22] With Caesar in his sights and within earshot, Labienus – himself a defector – vented his hatred by addressing the soldier: 'What are you up to, recruit? Have all of you been made fools of by that fellow's words?' This harsh initial experience was very instructive for Caesar: it made clear that he could count only on a strategy of attrition. For the moment there was nothing for it but to settle into secure positions and await reinforcements.

At this time (January 46 BC) Caesar began to work on the psychological motivation of his men while they waited for the delayed reinforcements.[23] At the same time, by intensive interrogation of deserters, he formed a clear picture of his opponents' plans.[24] An unexpected element was the mass desertion by troops from Numidia and Gaetulia, who remained faithful to the memory of Gaius Marius: nurturing memories of Marius' benevolence sixty years earlier, during his campaigns against Jugurtha, these native soldiers sought refuge with Caesar, having heard that Caesar was related to the great Marius![25] This significant fact reduced the chronological distance between the protagonists of the 'Sullan century' in the minds of witnesses and victims alike. In the meantime Caesar 'day and night kept his eyes and attention bent and riveted upon the sea', waiting for help to arrive.[26]

Finally the arrival of Sallust, from Cercina, with the Thirteenth and Fourteenth Legions, 800 cavalrymen, and 1,000 archers, returned the initiative to Caesar (22 January). Caesar advanced as far as Uzitta, but did not attempt to capture the town: he preferred to wear down Scipio's forces, thrown into crisis by the steady flow of desertions.[27] Leaving the area of Uzitta, Caesar made for Aggar, repeatedly challenging Scipio to battle. On the night of 6 April he attacked Thapsus. Here Scipio could no longer avoid combat, which proved catastrophic for him. Caesar's psychological remotivation of his men had been so effective that, when the battle began, the Ninth and Tenth Legions did not even wait for the signal: they attacked the enemy without encountering serious resistance, and Scipio promptly took flight. The high mortality among the republican leaders is noteworthy. Cato, who had remained in Utica as governor throughout the campaign and applied a restraining hand in a city strongly in favour of Caesar, killed himself as soon as he received word of the defeat. Juba and Petreius killed each other in a duel when they realised that there was no way out.[28] Scipio, surprised in the port of Hippo, threw himself into the water and drowned. Afranius and Faustus Sulla were captured and executed. The following weeks allowed Caesar to impose a new order on the province: the eastern part of the kingdom of Juba became the province of *Africa nova*, while the rest of the kingdom was divided between Bochus II of Mauretania and the formerly Catilinarian adventurer Sittius, who had loyally served Caesar in this bitter campaign.

Caesar returned to Rome on 25 July 46 BC. Although he was looking forward to the enjoyable celebration of four triumphs, and to joining Cleopatra and the newborn Caesarion,[29] whom he had installed in a sumptuous villa across the Tiber, Caesar was far from considering the chapter of civil conflict closed. At the end of 47, Pompey the Younger had left Africa for Spain, called there by two legions that had just rebelled against Quintus Cassius, the Caesarian governor who had been succeeded – without any improvement in the situation – by Gaius Trebonius. Having been ill for a while in the Baleares, Pompey the Younger finally reached Spain at about the time when Scipio was being defeated at Thapsus (early in April 46). In Spain rebellion was spreading fairly rapidly. Joined first by his brother Sextus, then by the indestructible Labienus and Attius Varus, Pompey the Younger was welcomed enthusiastically in Further Spain, which was oppressed by the swingeing taxes imposed by Caesar's governors. In a short time young Pompey controlled the whole province.

News that was no better came from the other end of the empire. While the African campaign with its highs and lows was in full swing, the government of Sextus Caesar in Syria was afflicted by crisis: the legions rebelled,[30] and Sextus was murdered by his own legionaries. Considering the synchrony of these events, it can be said that the Caesarian order had reached crisis point in two nerve centres. To complete the picture there was also the murder of Mithridates of Pergamon by Assandrus (the rebel who had already eliminated Pharnakes). With him passed an important pillar of Caesar's policy in the East; he had been a very loyal client, as well as one with valuable connections.[31] It can also be added, anticipating events that were yet to come, that Caesar's victory, won at high cost over Pompey the Younger at Munda, did not really pacify Spain (where Pompey's other son would continue to engage Caesar's governors in a never-ending conflict), nor would the large-scale counter-attack put down the mutiny of the Syrian legion. The crises that opened up at the two farthest points of the empire would remain unresolved even after the death of Caesar, and even deepen. Thus at no point in his extended rule did Caesar achieve a full pacification.

The events of the Syrian crisis were closely linked to the course of the campaign in Africa. The trigger of revolt here was a knight who had fought under Pompey, Quintus Caecilius Bassus, whose operational base was the free city of Tyre,[32] which gave him great freedom of action. He gathered about him others of Pompey's veterans, and succeeded in a subtle propaganda campaign among Sextus' legionaries, who steadily passed through Tyre, assigned to the defence of the city.[33] The most likely explanation is that Sextus commanded a legion recruited from the Pompeians who had surrendered at Pharsalus. This would account for Caecilius' persistence in urging these troops to mutiny; clearly he knew them well and was confident of a favourable response. Caecilius' influence on the troops increased when false reports reached them of defeats suffered by Caesar in Africa.[34] When exposed, Caecilius said he was raising troops for Mithridates of Pergamon (which he was). Shortly afterwards he forged letters from Scipio claiming that Caesar was dead and entrusting the province of Syria to him, Caecilius. He exploited this forgery to raise more troops, but was defeated in a clash with Sextus' legionaries.[35] It is clear that the (false) news of Pompeian victories provided him with his most effective weapon. In the end he organised a successful conspiracy against Sextus, who was murdered by some of the men of his own legion.[36] At this stage some of Sextus' troops fled to Cilicia. The rebels put themselves under the command of Caecilius Bassus, obtaining help from various local rulers and even the Parthians,[37] while the most faithful of Caesar's clientele, above all Antipater and his Jewish dynasty, opposed them.[38]

The most striking feature of this event (which lasted from the spring of 46 to the arrival of Cassius in Syria early in March 43)[39] was the determined and uncompromising mutiny of this Syrian legion. In Caesar's army nothing of the kind had ever happened. In both Gaul and Campania things had gone differently, thanks, it seems certain, to the *personal* intervention of Caesar. The unprecedented and scarcely credible new fact was that the rebellious troops not only did not seek 'the pardon of Caesar' – who was no longer a mere party leader experiencing local difficulties, but master of the empire – but chose 'to make war on Caesar' *sine die*.[40]

This decision to fight to the last probably resulted from the knowledge that in Sextus they had killed someone who was too close to Caesar's heart for them to hope for an acceptable settlement. The manner of the mutiny and its continuation to the bitter end are themselves an indication of Sextus' elevated position in the dictator's mind and in his practical considerations. It is difficult to imagine that Caesar would have left a particularly untrustworthy legion in Syria of all places,[41] while 'contemplating an expedition against the Parthians'.[42] Apart from anything else, Syria and the Roman troops stationed there had always had the role of 'guarding' Egypt: one more reason to put loyal troops there. The crisis must have exploded not only thanks to the able leadership of Caecilius Bassus, but above all in reaction to the measures taken by Sextus Caesar, whom the troops hated.[43] But to kill this relation who was so dear to the dictator meant to embark on a conflict with no way out.

As for Caecilius, it is clear that his tactics have much of Sextus Pompey about them,[44] for example his recourse to native support,[45] and the recruitment of slaves to fill the gaps in the mutinous legion. This can also be inferred from the good-will that Deiotarus, although Cicero denied it, appears to have shown him.[46]

Caesar heard about the serious crisis unfolding in Syria in the late summer of 46, while he was preparing to intervene in Spain at the urging of his governors – one of whom was his nephew Quintus

Pedius – shaken by the overwhelming advance of Pompey's sons.[47] He entrusted the task of putting down the rebellion to Quintus Cornificius, governor of neighbouring Cilicia. In mid-September Cicero wrote to Cornificius: 'Reports of disturbances have reached us from Syria.'[48] In December he received a letter from Cornificius telling him that he had received from Caesar the task of dealing with 'the present war in Syria'.[49] Allowing time for the letter to travel, this means that Caesar had given this order to Cornificius in October,[50] at the moment he decided to intervene personally in the Spanish rebellion. He was confronted by the 'loss' of two provinces, both fallen into the hands of Pompeians:[51] Syria and Further Spain. For a number of reasons, including the enormous degree of support enjoyed by Pompey's sons, he opted for Spain. And in the meantime he sent legions to Cornificius, who lacked the resources for his *bellum Syriacum*.[52] But these legions would depart only with the new governor of Syria for 45, Gaius Antistius Vetus, who would suffer a resounding defeat through the intervention of Alchaudonios the Arab and the Parthian king Pacorus, who was supporting rebels dug in in Apamea.[53]

The unexpected death of Sextus Caesar must have brought to a head another aspect of the Caesarian order. Here one can only conjecture, but the evidence is substantial. We know for certain that Caesar made two wills: one in favour of Pompey, valid 'from his first consulship until the beginning of the civil war',[54] the other, described by Suetonius as 'the last will' of Caesar (that is, the most recent), written on 13 September 45 in Caesar's villa on the Via Labicana after his return from Spain, and entrusted to the highest Vestal priestess. This 'last' will was opened after Caesar's murder and declared his three nephews to be his heirs: Octavius to receive three quarters, and Lucius Pinarius and Quintus Pedius the remaining quarter. The first will – when Caesar annulled it – was made public by Caesar himself in front of his troops,[55] so that it would be clear to all how much – and this was true – he had counted on his stable alliance with Pompey. One notes that at the beginning of 49, when Caesar 'denounced' this will, Julia had been dead for years, and Pompey had remarried, and yet Caesar kept the designation of Pompey as his heir for the clear implication of political alliance that this entailed.

What cannot be denied is that a Roman will can be annulled 'only when replaced by a subsequent valid will'.[56] Even the destruction of the document is not enough to invalidate its contents, 'because the contents cannot be identified with the document, but with the *nuncupatio*, the oral statement contained in it'. Hence, when Caesar announces that the will in favour of Pompey is no longer in effect, there is already a succeeding will that has annulled the previous one.[57]

If we consider the principle that governs the two wills we know about – the first in favour of his son-in-law, the last in favour of his three nephews – it is clear that the one between them, about which we have no direct information, must have been for the benefit of the nearest (relevant) adult male in the family. We are bound to think of Sextus Julius Caesar, a cousin, or second cousin, son (or grandson) of the only consul the Julian family had recently produced. The tone in which the writer of the *Alexandrian War* and, it seems to me, Cicero in his defence of Deiotarus,[58] refer to Sextus Caesar is such as to render highly probable this identification of the designated heir with that 'amicus et necessarius' who had followed Caesar from Spain to Syria, receiving from him more and more rewarding and responsible tasks. The war with no exit that the rebel legion was waging against Caesar, after murdering Sextus, seems to offer further confirmation. The Syrian revolt thus struck a very serious blow at Caesar on a level that is political no less than personal: it had struck down his 'heir'. For a potentate who was occupying the dictatorship permanently and hoping to contrive new forms of personal power that might find acceptance in the Roman political culture, this was a significant gesture, rich in possibilities. With Sextus dead, Octavius, notwithstanding his more distant relationship to Caesar, would gain the place of heir through the same process: he went to Spain as quickly as possible to take part in that punishing campaign.

The Spanish campaign was the most dangerous of all Caesar's military ventures, and the only one in which he gave serious thought, at the height of the battle of Munda, to suicide. Napoleon himself was strongly drawn to this extreme option, to which his hero and archetype went so close. But he objects: kill oneself one can, perhaps one must, if there is no hope, 'but who can ever be without hope? How is it possible in a changing theatre, in which the death of a single man may instantly transform the destiny of so many?'[59] He is speaking of himself, emperor in exile, wondering, perhaps, in the dismal exile of St Helena, while being slowly poisoned by the English, why he had to live on after his defeat. As a good Roman aristocrat, Caesar, on the other hand, had a quite different view of suicide. And at Munda, writes Florus, he seemed almost to want 'to end his life by his own hand'.[60] Mommsen was wrong to omit the Spanish campaign from his admirable, perhaps unsurpassed history of republican Rome. For him the republic ends with Cato's death at Utica, and with the related deaths of the republican leaders; what happened later concerns Caesar the monarch, and is another story that Mommsen proposed to tell, but did not.[61] In this way one loses sight of the unity of the civil conflict, which extends beyond Munda and has as its last act – as Livy knew[62] – the conspiracy and murder of Caesar.

With the arrival of Labienus, the great organiser and tenacious tactician, the situation in Spain worsened dramatically for Caesar's legates Quintus Pedius and Quintus Fabius. In the meantime, Pompey the Younger had assumed the title of *imperator*.[63] At the end of 46 BC he had under his command no fewer than thirteen legions, two of which constituted the garrison of Corduba, the provincial capital. Pompey's superiority was becoming overwhelming, and for Caesar there was no other choice, in the light of the dramatic appeals his legates sent him, than to meet Labienus once again – after the harsh African experience – in a decisive battle.

Caesar left Rome at the beginning of November, and in twenty-seven days reached Obulco,[64] that is, according to our calendar, at the beginning of December. The campaign began, for Caesar, with the liberation of the city of Julia, the only one to remain loyal to the dictator, from Pompey the Younger's siege. He relieved the pressure on Julia by threatening Corduba and thus forcing Pompey to hasten to the defence of his brother Sextus.[65] Caesar's aim was to force the leaders of the Pompeian army to give battle. To this end he continued to menace cities that they would have sought to defend. He attacked Ategua, but Pompey made little effort to defend it, and Ategua passed into the hands of Caesar.[66] Failures of this kind, added to the extreme harshness with which the young Pompey dealt with all Caesarian sympathisers, began to cause defections. To withdraw no longer seemed an appropriate tactic. Pompey established himself in a fortified site between Urso and Munda: an elevated position protected by a river. Here the young *imperator* declared to his followers that this time it would be Caesar who would renounce the fight. He was mistaken. On 17 March 45, Pompey and the other leaders saw Caesar's troops advance and take up positions that were strategically highly unfavourable. Once the river was crossed they would have to scale the heights to make contact with the enemy. Caesar was no novice at taking tactical risks based on a combination of favourable timing (when the enemy's guard was down) and unfavourable terrain. The balance gave him the advantage. This time, however, the risk cost him dearly in human lives. The commander who in somewhat pedestrian fashion recorded the course of this battle in the *Spanish War* (*de Bello Hispaniensi*) wrote that that day, 17 March, was 'a calm, sunny day [. . .] a wonderful, longed for and well-nigh heaven-sent opportunity for engaging battle',[67] but acknowledged that the hill-top position gave the enemy an extraordinary defensive advantage.[68] Once again the Tenth Legion, which had already been immortalised in Africa, distinguished itself in the ferocious battle, as if seeking forgiveness for the perilous mutiny put down by Caesar on his return from Zela. Thanks to the resistance of the Tenth Legion to attempts to surround them, Caesar was able to throw his cavalry into the fray, and at the same time Bogud's African soldiers. Labienus sensed the danger and moved his troops to the opposite flank, but this move led to a misunderstanding. The others took it to be the start of a withdrawal and fell back. An unforgivable error: Caesar's men savaged them pitilessly as they retreated. About 30,000 men were killed, including at least 1,000 in Caesar's own ranks: a very high figure if one considers that the majority of the casualties in ancient battles occurred at the moment of defeat, and thus almost exclusively on the losing side. Labienus, who harboured in his heart the implacable bitterness of the defector and had now fought his last battle against his erstwhile commander in the Gallic war, died fighting. Caesar, the expert manager of the deaths of others, gave him a splendid funeral.

Notes

1 *Précis des guerres de César* par Napoléon, écrit par M. Marchand sous la dictée de l'Empereur [1819] (Paris 1836), p. 207: 'six mois maître du monde'.

2 On 31 January the new calendar was introduced. This must be borne in mind in calculating the duration of the Spanish campaign.

3 Livy, *Periocha* 115; Dio Cassius 43.19–23.

4 Cicero, *Letters to his friends* 15.15.

5 We should bear in mind that Caesar in his *Civil War* 1.30.5 has Cato say during the flight from Sicily that Pompey has dragged everybody into an unnecessary war and without proper preparation. For a Cato who is neither Pompeian nor Caesarian, but 'republican', see Seneca, *Letters to Lucilius* 104.29–33 and 95.70. See also above, Chapter 20.

6 Hence the tone of the letter from Cassius to Cicero (*Letters to his friends* 15.19) in which Cassius gives vent to all his loathing and contempt for Pompey the Younger.

7 A sign of the institutional confusion during Caesar's long Alexandrian 'adventure' came in the events of 47 BC: the consuls were elected only at the end of the year, when Caesar returned to Rome, and remained in office only for a matter of two months. They were extremely contentious figures, one of them the egregious Vatinius.

8 The future historian.

9 As was customary; see Suetonius, *Caesar* 67.2. It is significant that Augustus banned the use of the term 'citizen' as it was excessively redolent of the civil war (Suetonius, *Augustus* 25.1). On the mutiny, see Plutarch, *Caesar* 51.2; Appian, *Civil Wars* 2.92–4; *Dio Cassius* 42.30; 52–5.

10 If only nominally (Cicero, *Second Philippic* 64).

11 Plutarch, *Caesar* 51.3.

12 *African War* 1.1.

13 31 October by the Julian calendar.

14 Caesar, *Civil War* 2.23–44.

15 Dio Cassius 42.10.1–2; Plutarch, *Cicero* 39.1–2; *Cato the Younger* 55.

16 Dio Cassius 42.13.3.

17 Plutarch, *Cato the Younger* 56. On the crossing of the desert the best account is Lucan 9.371–949.

18 *African War* 20.4.

19 *African War* 7.3.

20 The detailed account of this battle occupies chapters 12–18 of the *African War*.

21 The soldier recognised Labienus because he had served under him. He took off his helmet so that Labienus could recognise him.

22 *African War* 16.

23 *African War* 26.

24 *African War* 19.

25 *African War* 32.3.

26 *African War* 26.4.

27 *African War* 56–7; Dio Cassius 43.5.

28 The details of this duel may be found in the *African War* 94.

29 Dio Cassius 43.27.3; Cicero, *Letters to Atticus* 14.20.2: 'De regina velim atque etiam de Cesare illo', i.e. the infant Caesar.

30 Perhaps only one rebelled, but it met no resistance.

31 Deiotarus was another who from the beginning paid hopeful attention to the news coming from Africa.

32 On the status of Tyre see O. Eissfeldt, *RE*, s.v. *Tyros*, no. 3.

33 Dio Cassius 47.26.4. Dio's testimony is the fullest and most reliable; that offered by Appian in two places (*Civil Wars* 3.77 = 4.58) is paradoxically misleading.

34 Cicero, *In defence of King Deiotarus* 25: 'graves de te rumores, qui etiam furiosum illum Caecilium excitaverunt'.

35 Dio Cassius 47.26.6–7.
36 Livy, *Periocha* 114; Appian, *Civil Wars* 3.77 (= 4.58); Dio Cassius 47.26.7. See H. Botermann, *Die Soldaten und die römische Politik in der Zeit von Caesars Tod bis zur Begründung des Zweiten Triumvirats* (Munich 1968), pp. 207–8.
37 Dio Cassius 47.27.5: Pompeian alliances!
38 Josephus Flavius, *Jewish War* 1.217.
39 Cicero, *Letters to his friends* 12.11.
40 Their behaviour makes the version given by Appian of this episode (*Civil Wars* 3.77 = 4.58) all the more suspect. According to Appian, Caecilius Bassus was a good officer of Caesar's who was disgusted by the unseemly behaviour of Sextus and for this reason impelled to lead the mutineers. If this were really so, the determined resistance of the mutineers to Caesar's envoys would be difficult to understand. The only valid element in Appian's account (aimed at demolishing the figure of Sextus Caesar) appears to be the realistic portrait of Sextus, whose lack of scruple is also indicated by Josephus.
41 When one remembers the links between the Parthian rulers and Pompey it is even more unlikely.
42 Appian, *Civil Wars* 3.77.
43 On this point it is helpful to remember the cautiously deferential circumlocution by which Cicero may be referring to Sextus Caesar (by now deceased) in his *In defence of King Deiotarus* (§ 14).
44 In the confusion following the Ides of March, Decimus Brutus thought that the 'liberators', then under pressure, might flee either to Sextus Pompeius or to Caecilius Bassus (Cicero, *Letters to his friends* 11.1.4).
45 Strabo, *Geography* 16.753.
46 Cicero, *In defence of King Deiotarus* 23.
47 Dio Cassius 43.31.1.
48 Cicero, *Letters to his friends* 12.17.1.
49 Cicero, *Letters to his friends* 12.19.1: 'Bellum quod est in Syria Syriamque provinciam tibi tributam a Caesare ex tuis litteris cognovi.'
50 The journey from Cilicia to Rome took about a month.
51 Cicero, *In defence of King Deiotarus* 23. Cicero, addressing Caesar, links Caecilius with the defeated 'illa causa'.
52 Cicero, *Letters to his friends* 12.19.2: 'legiones quas [ad te] audio duci'.
53 Cicero, *Letters to Atticus* 14.9.3 (probably reflecting a dispatch from Antistius to Caesar, of which Balbus held a copy; R. Syme, 'Observations on the Roman Province of Syria', in *Anatolian Studies presented to W. H. Buckler*, eds W. M. Calder and J. Keil [Oxford 1939], p. 320); Dio Cassius 47.27.4.
54 Suetonius, *Caesar* 83.1. The first-class source on which Suetonius relied was the jurist and friend of Caesar, Quintus Aelius Tubero, also the author of a historical work (see Gellius 7.3 and 4).

55 Ibid.: 'pro contione'.
56 See P. Voci, *Diritto ereditario romano*, vol. II, 2nd edn (Milan 1963), pp. 488ff. I am grateful to Mario Bretone for his illuminating comments.
57 We cannot be sure of the exact date. Pompey died in September 48, and after this date another will was in effect (and Tubero, according to Suetonius, refers to the will in favour of Octavian as *novissimum* – the last).
58 If the 'fidelissimus et probatissimus ex tuis omnibus' in *In defence of King Deiotarus* 14 is Sextus.
59 Napoleon, *Précis des guerres de César*, p. 206.
60 Florus, *Epitoma* 2.13.83: 'quasi occupare mortem manu vellet'.
61 Mommsen's lecture notes, published by Barbara and Alexander Demandt under the title *Römische Kaisergeschichte* (Munich 1992), begin with the last year of Caesar's life.
62 A consistent view of the unity of the civil war emerges from the tradition which derives from Livy. Judging by his *Periochae* and Florus' Livian *Epitoma* (2.13), the idea which Livy wished to communicate was that the civil war began with the crossing of the Rubicon and ended with the murder of Caesar. In the *Periochae* we learn of some *inscriptiones* to books 109–16 ('qui est civilis belli primus [. . .] octavus'). These books treat the whole period from 'causae civilium armorum' up to Caesar's funeral and Amatius' revolt. We do not know if the description of books 109–16 as books 1–8 of the civil war dates back to Livy himself, or if it was added later when the *Periochae* were written. If the former, we can say that the idea of the conspiracy as part of the civil war is as old as Livy. Book 8 *Belli civilis* begins with the triumph *ex Hispania*, that is, Caesar's return to Rome in September 45. It contains no war episodes, yet it is designated *Belli civilis* on account of the event which takes up the whole of it: the conspiracy (its beginnings, its development, its immediate consequences right up to the funeral and the execution of Amatius by Antony). This presentation of the material in the *Periochae* must be derived from the books themselves. It is notable that the conflict in the years 43–31 BC is not treated in the same way, judging by the *Periochae*, at least.
63 CIL I². 2.885. See *Spanish War* 42.6: 'fasces imperiumque sibi arripuit'.
64 Appian, *Civil Wars* 2.103.429; Suetonius, *Caesar* 56.5, says twenty-four days.
65 *Spanish War* 3–4.
66 *Spanish War* 6–19.
67 *Spanish War* 29.4: 'mirificum, optandum tempus [. . .] ad proelium committendum'.
68 *Spanish War* 31.1.

CHAPTER 27

The Shoot of a Palm Tree: The Young Octavius Emerges

Octavius, the future Augustus, was the son of a certain Octavius (of an equestrian family, of Velitrae/Velletri) and Atia. Atia was the daughter of Marcus Atius Balbus of Aricia, who had married Caesar's sister, Julia, and perhaps because of this he had forged ahead in his public career, attaining the praetorship. The kinship, then, between Octavius and Caesar was not close. Sources like Dio Cassius who describe Octavius (the later Octavian) as the son of a *sister* of Caesar (43.41.3) simplify too much, or are lying in order to bring Octavius and Caesar closer together, like the historical myth-maker Nicolaus of Damascus, who declared, 'Octavian was Caesar's closest relative.'[1]

Sextus Caesar, as we know, was a much closer blood-relation to the dictator. He was a son of the Julian family, Octavius was not. Octavius was *adopted* into the Julian family, becoming Gaius Julius Caesar Octavianus.

Sextus Caesar, however, described by the author of the *Alexandrian War* as 'a friend and relation' of Caesar, was removed from the political scene by his unexpected death.[2] This happened, as we know, in the summer of 46 BC, when Caesar's men were appealing to him to make haste to Further Spain, where the rebellion fomented by Pompey's sons was spreading alarmingly with every passing day. In that summer of 46 Caesar found himself once again facing the need to make rapid and difficult choices between the rebellion in Syria and the rebellion in Spain. The latter was dramatic in its implications because it risked carrying to victory the direct heirs of Pompey; the former was disturbing because it created a threatening void on the eastern frontier. Moreover, it unexpectedly took from him a 'relative and friend' who had had a promising future.

Whether a simple coincidence, a matter of pure chance, or a far-seeing calculation, the fact is that, with the death of Sextus Caesar, the young Octavius emerges. He hurries to Spain, not without some difficulty, to join Caesar in the field at any cost. It is indicative, and must be pointed out here, that not one of the surviving sources, however much influenced by Octavian (as the emperor Augustus), goes so far as to say that Caesar had *summoned* him to Spain. The most audacious, Nicolaus of Damascus, instead invents the story that Octavius had some months earlier expressed the desire to enlist with Caesar for the African campaign, but that Caesar had tried to dissuade him, showing a fatherly concern for his welfare and seeing that his mother was anxious. Antony,[3] on the other hand, some time later heavily insinuated that the young man had seduced his great relation into deflowering him, in exchange for that adoption on which he then based his future.[4] While this charge constitutes a *topos* and Caesar was certainly neither blameless nor moderate in his sexual habits, we have no means of ascertaining whether or by how much Antony was exaggerating, or whether he was close to the mark. It is certain that the planned 'adoption' of Octavius must have been fully developed by then. It clearly owed nothing to any martial deeds of the young man, since in his *Memoirs* Augustus produces only one such episode, which proves nothing, but does suggest that Caesar's regard for him increased while he was in Spain. Augustus claimed that Caesar sent him from Spain to Apollonia 'in expectation' of the campaigns in Dacia or Macedonia and Parthia, or all three together (here the sources are contradictory). Essentially, then, it is not his deeds in Spain that are outstanding, but rather his prospects for the future.

It is well known that Octavius, when he became Augustus, was always happy to have others highlight the epoch-making points of his career. His example has gained a following. The '*Duce*' of Italian fascism also spoke with some restraint (even reluctance!) of his own beginnings. It was the official and semi-official biographers who threw restraint to the winds.

The comparison will not seem far-fetched if one considers the chapter Suetonius dedicates to 'the house where Augustus was born', the modest suburban house in which the future Augustus had been raised: 'a small room like a pantry is shown to this day as the emperor's nursery in his grandfather's country house near Velitrae, and the opinion prevails in the neighbourhood that he was actually born there'.[5] Suetonius goes on, 'No one ventures to enter this room except of necessity, since there is a conviction of long-standing that those who approach it without ceremony are seized with shuddering and terror.' It is the archetype of the humble proletarian dwelling of the 'blacksmith of Predappio', the *Duce*.

So the task of inflating the deeds of the young Octavius from these obscure Spanish beginnings fell to others. It is not surprising that Dio

Cassius (perhaps from the Livian tradition) goes furthest in his account of the Spanish *initia* of the future *princeps*, telling a story well suited to hagiography. Here, not only are his martial deeds set forth in a general way; it is also presented as established fact that he fought at Caesar's side συνεστρατεύετο, and that there in Spain, in that dawning of a great future, *the miracle* occurred: a miracle which contained, in the symbolic language typical of miracles, his entire future development. On the battlefield of Munda, as Dio tells it, scarcely had the din of the victorious battle died away when a palm tree suddenly put forth a shoot. It was a clear portent of future victories. But, Dio explains, no longer the victories of Caesar, who was approaching (unknowingly) his unforeseen and tragic end, but of Octavius, who there and then, in that same battle at Munda, covered himself with glory. As Dio Cassius, the historian of Septimius Severus, reports:[6]

> Caesar, too, would doubtless have chosen to fall there, at the hands of those who were still resisting and amid the glory of war, in preference to the fate he met not long afterward of being murdered in his own land and in the Senate at the hands of his dearest friends. For this was the last war he carried through successfully, and this the last victory that he won, in spite of the fact that there was no other project so great that he did not hope to accomplish it. In this hope he was confirmed especially by the circumstance that from a palm that stood on the site of the battle a shoot grew out immediately after the victory. Now I do not assert that this had no bearing in some direction, yet it was no longer for him, but for his sister's grandson, Octavius; for the latter was making the campaign with him, and was destined to gain great lustre from his toils and dangers. As Caesar did not know this, and hoped that many great successes would still fall to his own lot, he showed no moderation, but was filled with arrogance, as if immortal.[7]

If in conclusion Octavius emerges at Caesar's side with a certain 'delay', the most respectful sources took pains not only to explain this, to justify it, but also to transform this initial disadvantage with regard to other 'rivals' in the dictator's heart into an effective primacy.

In Suetonius' account,[8] the way the 'miracle' happened is quite different. *Before the battle of Munda*, that is, well before young Octavius arrived in Spain, Caesar had had a small wood cut down near Munda, the better to set up camp. Among the trees that were being cut down was a palm tree, and Caesar ordered it to be spared as a portent of victory.[9] A shoot appeared, which in a few days caught up with its mother-plant and overshadowed it, and many doves came to build their nests in it – a most unusual occurrence. And Suetonius explains how this 'miraculous' event related to Octavius; not to his supposed Spanish deeds, however, but to his *adoption*. 'Indeed, it was that omen in particular, they say, that led Caesar to wish that none other than his sister's grandson should be his successor.'[10]

The mythologising processes at work in Dio's story are plain to see:[11] a palm puts forth a shoot 'on the battlefield' of Munda (no longer in the Roman camp), and moreover, 'straight after the victory'; Caesar hoped that the portent was *for him* 'and that many great successes would still fall to his own lot', but instead the marvel concerned Octavius, '[who] was making the campaign with him' (we know, however, from a source above suspicion, Nicolaus of Damascus, that Octavius arrived in Spain for a campaign that was already over) 'and was destined to gain great lustre from his toils and dangers'. This latter expression seems to imply a continuity of military glory, passing directly from Caesar to Octavius. We are witnessing the 'adaptation' of a 'miracle' which originally must have had a different purpose: to place Caesar's adoption of Octavius in a symbolic and 'supernatural' temporal framework, and establish that Caesar had made him his heir not for want of other possible heirs (as other versions may have suggested) but *in conformity with divine signs*.[12] The Suetonian 'phase' of this military-botanical fable built around the germination of a palm tree is thus older than Dio's.

Velleius offers a clever presentation of Octavius' Spanish adventures:

> Gaius Octavius, his father,[13] though not of patrician birth, was descended from a very prominent equestrian family, and was himself a man of dignity, of upright and blameless life, and of great wealth. [. . .] He was returning [from Macedonia] to sue for the consulship when he died on the way, leaving a son still in his early teens. Though he had been reared in the house of his step-father, Phillipus, Gaius Caesar, his great-uncle, loved this boy as his own son. At the age of eighteen Octavius followed Caesar to Spain in his campaign there, and Caesar kept him with him thereafter as his companion (*Hispaniensis militiae adsecutum se postea comitem habuit*), allowing him to share the same roof and ride in the same carriage, and though he was still a boy, honoured him with the pontificate.[14]

What exactly is meant by 'Hispaniensis militiae adsecutum se postea comitem habuit'? We shall try to translate, paying attention to the position and value of *postea*. It can be understood in two ways:

1. He was his *comes* in the *militia Hispaniensis*, but it is admitted that Octavius joined the campaign only at a later stage.[15] This is in line with Dio's συστρατευόμενος αὐτῷ (43.41.3), and therefore far from Nicolaus, according to whom, 'Octavian arrived when Caesar had already achieved victory in a seven-month campaign.'
2. Caesar *later* regarded him as his *comes militiae Hispaniensis*, that is, the young man had in fact only been a follower of his up to this point.

It is inconceivable that Nicolaus would have omitted any of Augustus' achievements. It is therefore beyond doubt that Octavius arrived 'after *seven* months of Caesar's campaign in Spain (and when the war was over)', well after Munda,[16] which was on 17 March; that is, in the *fourth* month of that long campaign. Thus Octavius was in Spain only in the period June to August, and it was then that he accompanied Caesar in his carriage, and so on, and won his favour.[17] And on 13 September 45 Caesar, back in Rome, adopted him.

Nicolaus said simply that Octavius had taken part in Caesar's 'pacificatory' operations in Spain. The other accounts, on the other hand, emphasise Octavius' Spanish experience and tend to transform it into *participation in the campaign* (implying that he was present at Munda!).[18] This is evident both in Velleius[19] and in Dio Cassius,[20] and the latter may again be relying on Livy.

Velleius continues:

> When the civil war was over, with a view to training his remarkable talents by liberal studies, he sent him to Apollonia to study, with the intention of taking him with him as his companion in his contemplated wars with the Getae and the Parthians.[21]

Here too we are faced with a daring 'teleological' elaboration of the Apollonian episode.

Dio accentuates the Spanish period in the life of Octavian. He speaks of it as the *glorious dawn* of a military career: 'For Octavius was making the campaign with him,[22] and was destined to gain great lustre from his toils and dangers.'[23] This sentence is totally deceptive: both in claiming a long and constant military collaboration between Caesar and the young Octavius in Spain (which did not happen); and in the skilful 'translation' of Augustus' lack of any record of military glory into a positive phenomenon, which leads to a unique continuity of military glory redounding to *both* from Caesar's deeds, thanks precisely to that long collaboration. 'Making the campaign with him' goes beyond the generous, but not unrealistic, reconstruction of Nicolaus of Damascus.[24]

The most 'daring' element in the manipulation is the *miracle*. It would not be imprudent to wonder if Dio took from Livy the part in which the Caesar-Octavius nexus is accentuated and sealed with a miracle that would ratify the continuity between the two.[25]

Livy wrote this part (book 115) some time after Nicolaus, and yet he brought Octavius onto the scene at the moment of the opening of the will (book 116). From the *periocha* of book 117 one infers that Livy returned to earlier events concerning the young Octavius, recalling that Caesar had sent him to Apollonia, in Epirus, 'bellum in Macedonia gesturus' (because he intended to wage war in Macedonia). Livy, then, dedicated much space and attention (books 116 and 117) to the *initia* of Octavius.

Nicolaus, who published around 20 BC, already assumed familiarity with Augustus' *Memoirs*. Livy wrote many years later (and there may be no reason to alter the generally accepted date of his death from AD 17). In any case, from book 121 onwards he is writing *post excessum Augusti* (after the death of Augustus), and thus long after the circulation of the polemical *Memoirs* (and Nicolaus' hagiographical *Life*), so can permit himself much freedom with respect to that 'constrictive' model.[26] He writes when the Augustan 'truth' was no longer sought so much in the *Memoirs*, but more in the *Res gestae*, which begin in 44 with the 'liberation' of the republic from the domination of the tyrannicide faction. On the earlier events Livy could allow himself more freedom, since the argument over who Sextus Caesar and Caecilius really were was no longer of interest; and, furthermore, he could freely establish a *thread* that linked Octavius and Caesar, beginning with the Spanish experience, by mythologising the story.

A signal of the emphasis placed by Augustus on the crucial (for him) Spanish campaign may be provided by a carved stone, once studied by Ludwig Curtius. It portrays a very young Agrippa with the emblems of the *legio VI Ferrata*, one of the legions that had fought in Spain.[27] Doubts raised about the identity of the figure, proposed by Curtius, do not appear well founded. Roddaz's objection, 'There was no reason to commemorate Agrippa's presence', is particularly weak.

There was a reason, and a very powerful one: it was the intention of placing Octavius, with the figure of his closest and most loyal 'comrade-in-arms', in an enterprise in which he had *not* participated.

Despite the exaggerations put about by Augustus regarding his own presence in Spain in 45 BC, his name does not figure in any part of the *Spanish War*. For one thing, he did not arrive until that war was over. Octavius went to Spain on his own initiative and arrived, as Nicolaus of Damascus says, 'when Caesar had already achieved victory in a seven-month campaign'. He was not involved – nor could he be – in any military operations. Nor could he allow his name to appear in 'official' reports like the *Bella*. Their value as 'official' texts derives from their anonymity and the fact that they were circulated *together with Caesar's writings*. This aspect of the Caesarian corpus needs to be emphasised, whatever may be the value of individual contributions.

Instead, it is the task of 'government' historians – at once more servile and freer to indulge their fantasies – to circulate hyperbolic or downright miraculous details. As we know, this applies to the source used by Dio Cassius (43.41.3), for example, which invents accomplishments for the young man, along with miracles pointing to his future greatness.

The *Memoirs* are a somewhat different matter. Here, plainly, Augustus was relating private details for that period, the most significant of which was that Caesar, feeling confidence in him, had sent him forward to Apollonia for the Parthian campaign (the implication being that the dictator meant to avail himself of his services in that great martial enterprise).[28] These personal details, of course, had no importance *for the Spanish campaign*, but they were suggestive, hinting that in the course of that campaign the young Octavius had attracted the attention of the dictator for his merits, for his conduct (as a soldier), and *therefore* Caesar had sent him on a reconnaissance mission to Apollonia. Thus there was free rein for the imagination of servile historians: if he had distinguished himself so much as to be engaged for the coming enterprise, he must have accomplished notable feats of arms. Here is Dio's report: 'For Octavius was making the campaign with him, and was destined to gain great lustre from his toils and dangers.' Almost a legitimate invention, overlaid on the introductory remarks neatly put by the *princeps* in his famous *Memoirs*. The fact that for these years Dio relied on Livy brings us back once again to the Paduan 'Augustan' historian, tormented and often naïve though he was. Is it to him that we owe the fable of the palm shoot on the field of Munda, a symbol of the sprouting on that battlefield of the radiant future of Octavian? As the foregoing paragraph has shown, there is much to suggest that it is. Intimacy with the power-wielders of this world plays disagreeable jokes, especially on the naïve.

If we reconsider the entirety of the historiographic tradition surrounding Octavian, we can see that it breaks down into various 'stages'. It runs from the 'official' collection, which purports to have *documentary* force (the Caesarian corpus guarantees the 'truth' about the father of the *princeps*), to the personal memoir of the *princeps* (which allowed him notable freedom of movement but did not permit anything grossly improbable, especially when verification was possible), to 'government' history (which only in extreme cases arises as such en bloc, and then descends into partisan politics, adopting a position on individual issues, however, case by case).[29]

This phenomenon has been apparent in other eras in which the rulers have exerted powerful pressure upon the work of historians, seeing their work as politically influential.

The skill with which Augustus created the impression that Caesar 'chose' him at a very early stage (well before the adoption of 13 September 45) needs to be acknowledged. This is the purpose served by mentioning even the smallest acts of recognition which prepare the ground for his adoption.

The two biographers thanks to whom we can retrieve the autobiographical story of Augustus are Nicolaus of Damascus and Suetonius (with contributions from Velleius, Appian and Dio). But on the *'first steps'* of the future *princeps*, Nicolaus and Suetonius are the most detailed, and it is Nicolaus who presents the fullest picture. Although largely fragmentary, it is nevertheless entirely preserved for the first stage, up to the conclusion of Caesar's Spanish campaign.

The individual stages of the rise of Octavius in this description seem to correspond to the reality. It is a fact that, at the end of the two-year period 47–45, Octavius was adopted and proclaimed 'heir for two thirds', and that, as such, following the Ides of March, he was projected into high politics as a principal protagonist. These stages thus acquire significance as *preparatory steps* towards a great future. This is where the 'manipulation' takes place, set in train and certainly approved by the interested party, and carried further by the admiring writers. For example, the task of acting as urban prefect for short periods, while the consuls were away, or as *praetor* for the *Feriae*

Latinae, was a small and purely symbolic privilege. Fathers who held Senate seats would confer them upon their sons who were still minors, so unable to sit in the Senate.[30] This honour was bestowed upon Octavius in October–November 47, but it has no significance as a 'sign' for the future. This precocious debut by the fifteen-year-old is recorded only by Nicolaus.[31] Suetonius, though alert to these first steps, notes a rather more significant event, from the following year: 'Four years later, after assuming the gown of manhood, he received military prizes at Caesar's African triumph, although he had not taken part in the war on account of his youth.'[32] And immediately he reports the news of the departure of Octavius for Spain (spring 45), 'in pursuit', so to speak, of Caesar who was engaged in the war with Pompey's sons. It is fair to regard these *dona* as a kind of 'compensation' – and an indication of 'family' concern – for the young man, who was disappointed at not having participated in the campaign (as he had wished, according to all the sources). In reality it is with the decision to go to Spain that Octavius takes the decisive step and attracts the favour of the dictator, who adopts him, makes him his heir (with the will of 13 September 45) and names him *magister equitum destinatus* in 44.[33]

The earliest dating of these first steps is thus by Nicolaus, who manages to take the so-called *praefectura* episode back to the end of 47 BC, during the *Feriae Latinae*. But this is not simply a manifestation of some 'cult of personality'. Rather it is designed to show that Octavius was close to Caesar's heart as early as 47, when Sextus Gaius Caesar was still alive and active. And it is symptomatic that the elements that seem attributable to this 'rivalry' towards the other relative who was close to Caesar (and tragically eliminated in 46) all figure in Nicolaus: the dating of Caesar's first 'favours' to Octavius in 47; the proclamation against all the evidence that Octavius was the young relative 'closest' to Caesar; and the emphasis on experience of government (settlement of local conflicts) in Spain, placing Octavius by Caesar's side (summer 45), just as Sextus had gained experience at Caesar's side two years earlier in Syria (summer 47). For this reason it seems logical to suppose that Appian's dark portrait of Sextus Caesar as a 'corrupt youth' comes from Augustus (his *Memoirs*):[34] a 'replica' of the tale of *stuprum* (lewdness) that Antony had circulated about Octavius. It was never Augustus' habit to leave anything 'unfinished', or any accounts unsettled. That he realised how important it was to position himself firmly in the centre and ahead of other relatives with regard to Caesar, and that this served as the basis for his adoption by the dictator, is demonstrated by the falsifications of Nicolaus of Damascus. From the way this 'court historian' worked we can see how an unfortunate circumstance at the beginning of Octavius' career (the fact that he took second place in the dictator's graces) received the closest attention in his *Memoirs*.[35]

Notes

1 *FGrHist* 90 F 127, 17. The polemical value of these falsifications is indicated by Jacoby in his commentary (p. 268, 14–18).
2 See Chapter 26.
3 One might ask where Antony was at the time.
4 Suetonius, *Augustus* 68: 'adoptionem avunculi stupro meritum'.
5 Suetonius, *Augustus* 6.
6 Dio Cassius 43.41.
7 A reference to Caesar's incautious celebration of the triumph over the sons of Pompey.
8 Suetonius, *Augustus* 94.11.
9 Ibid.: 'conservari ut omen victoriae iussit'.
10 Ibid.: 'ne quem alium sibi succedere quam sororis nepotem vellet'.
11 Dio Cassius 43.41.2–3.
12 Suetonius' 'sibi succedere' allows both possibilities.
13 The father of Octavian. The polar opposite of the ἐκδιαιτώμενον Sextus: the whole family stood under the sign of *sanctitas*!
14 Velleius 2.59.3.
15 'Adsecutum se'.
16 So the 'miracle' of the palm tree occurred before Octavius had arrived!
17 This is the basis of Antony's insinuations.
18 This becomes clear from the connection drawn by Dio Cassius between Octavian and the 'miracle' of the palm tree on the battlefield of Munda.
19 Velleius 2.59.3.
20 Dio Cassius 43.41.
21 Velleius 2.59.4.
22 The use of the Latin imperfect is significant, indicating *habitual action* and therefore *normality*.
23 Dio Cassius 43.41.3.
24 Nicolaus was writing in c.20 BC, when almost all the eye-witnesses to the events were still alive, so there was little scope for invention.
25 Julius Obsequens (§ 66) took from Livy another miracle in connection with the Spanish campaign: the ten eagles holding bolts of lightning in their talons (*quae fulmina tenebant*), which dropped their *fulmina* and flew high into the sky and disappeared. Pompey the Younger was defeated and killed.

26 R. Syme, 'Livy and Augustus', *Harvard Studies in Classical Philology* 64 (1959), pp. 27–87. Syme may insist rather too strongly on Livy's dependence on the 'truth' of the *princeps*.

27 See J. M. Roddaz, *Marcus Agrippa* (Rome 1984), p. 34, n. 18.

28 And he himself overstated the importance of the planned Parthian campaign. (See Suetonius, *Augustus* 44.)

29 The *princeps* was given to intervening in matters close to his heart, such as the *spolia opima* of Cornelius Cossus (see Livy 4.20.5–11).

30 T. Mommsen, *Römisches Staatsrecht*, vol. I, 3rd edn (Leipzig 1887), p. 673.

31 Nicolaus of Damascus, *Life of Augustus* 5.13 (*FGrHist* 90 F 127).

32 Suetonius, *Augustus* 8.1.

33 Besides Appian, *Civil Wars* 3.9.30, and Dio Cassio 43.51.7, see *Fasti Capitolini* (ed. Degrassi) for the Roman year 710 (= 44 BC).

34 Appian, *Civil Wars* 3.77 (= 4.58).

35 Probably used by Appian at the beginning of book 3, when Octavius appears.

CHAPTER 28

'Anticato'

With Cato dead at Utica in the manner we know, *laudationes* of the republican martyr and model Stoic followed one upon another. It was Cicero, with his innate imprudence, who inaugurated the series of posthumous commemorations whose political significance as 'opposition' is plain. At the request of Marcus Junius Brutus, Caesar's favourite, but Cato's nephew and admirer,[1] Cicero began writing a *Laus Catonis* as early as April 46 BC, as soon as the news reached Rome of Cato's suicide in Africa. In the *Orator* (which followed shortly after), he stresses that the impulse for this came from Brutus: 'I would never have written it through fear of this age so unfriendly to *virtus*, had I not considered it base not to yield when you urged so strongly and kindled the memory of one so dear to me.'[2] And he goes on:

> I call you to witness (*testificor*) that it was because you asked me that I dared, albeit reluctantly, to write this book. For I wish that you should share the reproach with me, so that if I cannot defend myself against so weighty a charge, you may take the blame for imposing an excessive task on me, as I take the blame for accepting it. However, any error in my judgement will be counterbalanced by the glory of dedicating the work to you.[3]

The phrasing is all too emphatic and points to disagreeable consequences, and *testificor*, with what follows, is strongly suggestive of court action. The meaning of 'this age so unfriendly to *virtus*' is also plain. The *virtus* is clearly the political *virtus* of the hero to be celebrated, who 'commits suicide for freedom'. At first sight, it is a disconcerting expression, which might seem to go too far: an extremely harsh description of Caesar's government.[4] However, it is possible that 'this age so unfriendly to *virtus*' is the time when Brutus had suggested to Cicero the *laudatio* for Cato who had just died, that is, in the middle of a war.[5] What Cicero means to suggest (though without himself believing it) is that the climate has now changed: now the war is behind them (moreover, a war against a man whose *virtus* is debated in the controversial *laudatio*). Cicero's (fully justifiable) intention is to distinguish the climate while the civil war campaigns are taking place from periods of 'normality'. It is a legitimate perspective in a contemporary, but less understandable for us. At the same time it is a wish and a subtly flattering *captatio benevolentiae*, intended to attract a little benevolence from Caesar.

Those words were a form of insurance. Aulus Caecina, a former client of Cicero who had fought beside Pompey, writes to Cicero at the end of December 46: 'You add to my apprehension, when I see you in your *Orator* making Brutus your shield and casting about apologetically for a partner.' Caecina and Cicero are on such familiar terms that they can be quite frank with each other.[6] It is clear that those words, in the *Orator*, are not exactly pleasing: apart from anything else, Caesar's obstinate liking for Brutus was well known, so to 'make Brutus his shield' was a politically shrewd move (not to say 'opportunistic').

Caesar returned from Africa on 25 July 46: the copying of the *laudatio* had occurred in June.[7] As was usual in 'publishing' practice at the time, parts of this pamphlet were probably beginning to circulate while it was still being copied, and so Cicero hastened to formulate that clumsy 'excuse' in the *Orator*, but actual 'publication' did not occur until some months later. Whatever the case, we know from Suetonius that Caesar replied 'about the time of the battle of Munda'[8] (which was fought on 17 March 45). Since Caesar left Rome for Spain in October 46, it is likely that he had Cicero's manuscript with him, and that he intended to answer.[9] It is significant that he took it with him when he set out on that campaign; understandably, he wanted to have the terrible trials of the campaign behind him before entering the 'literary' battle.

In the meantime he had persuaded the faithful Hirtius to write another reply to the Ciceronian panegyric. The composition was quickly prepared and came to Cicero's notice by 9 May 45, while Caesar was still in Spain (he would return only in September). Caesar's reaction worried Cicero, who wrote to Atticus, 'What sort of thing Caesar's invective against my panegyric will be, I have seen from the book, which Hirtius has sent me.'[10] But Cicero needed to find a graceful way out of the situation. He noted that Hirtius' satirical pamphlet did not spare Cato, but was full of praise for him, Cicero; and that seemed to him good reason to promote the distribution of Hirtius' piece: 'I want it to be published. To facilitate that, please give your men orders.'

Two days later, on 11 May, Cicero held in his hands a letter from Hirtius which dealt (Cicero says) with what Caesar himself was planning to write. He wrote to Atticus: 'Hirtius' letter seems to me a sort of first sketch of the tirade Caesar has written against Cato, let me know what you think of it, if you can.'[11]

In the meantime, Brutus intervened with a composition of his own in praise of Cato. This too was read and annotated by Caesar, who was still in Gallia Narbonensis, on his way back from Spain. In fact Caesar made sure that Cicero saw his opinion on both pieces, Cicero's and Brutus'. And Cicero informed Atticus on 12 August 45. As usual Balbus was involved, acting as an intermediary. In his letter Caesar established an exclusively stylistic hierarchy: reading Cicero's *Cato* had enriched his range of expression,[12] while having read Brutus he felt himself the more eloquent for it. It is clear, of course, that he is joking. Without broaching the substance, Caesar makes fun of both writers, and, as usual, lavishes praise upon Cicero (in a way which does nothing, however, to calm the orator, who is aware that the content of his writing cannot have pleased Caesar).[13] As the drama moved towards its conclusion, and the preparations for that conclusion were very probably well in hand, this kind of verbal duel seems curious.

Apart from everything else, it is a duel involving more than two parties (for or against the suicidal hero). We do not know why Brutus also decided to write. Because he was disappointed by Cicero's writing? Because he felt a need to show his independence of Caesar? It is difficult to say.

What we do know, however, thanks to Cicero's correspondence with Atticus, is that Cicero did not at all like what Brutus wrote. He had Atticus convey to Brutus, in writing, a series of criticisms aimed at persuading the author to make some modifications. Atticus wrote, and he sent a copy of the reply he received from Brutus to Cicero, who reacted in a piqued and far from friendly tone.[14] It is not simply a question of vanity. Cicero was undoubtedly provoked by the fact that Brutus, in his *laudatio*, made Cato, not Cicero, the prime mover in the suppression of the Catilinarians.[15] What galled him once again was the non-recognition of his merits by one whose side he had taken, fearfully, tortuously, and at the cost of some embarrassment. So the *factiosi* could do without him! Then, while the threat remained of more adverse reaction from the dictator, and the *factio* raised its head again in Cato's name, old divisions reopened. This made it easier for Cicero to digest Caesar's reply fully and try to get a conciliatory message to him, again through Atticus. In short, the dispute over Cato, complex and long drawn out (discussion of the rights and wrongs of his suicide went on for months),[16] became a 'dress rehearsal' for the drama to come. It may even be viewed as a trial balloon, launched to test Caesar's reactions on the propaganda level. This would help explain the convergent efforts of Brutus, Fadius and Munatius Rufus.

Embarrassed at finding himself 'trapped' in the debate with Caesar on the figure of Cato, Cicero tried to extricate himself by turning, as usual, to Balbus, through whom he let Caesar know that he held his *Anticato* in high regard.[17] The initiative for this, however, came from Atticus, who had cunningly suggested to Cicero that he should write 'a more comprehensive letter' to Caesar! A neat way of suggesting that Caesar needed to be placated after the pamphlet clash. Cicero gives a detailed account of the story from the beginning, pointing out that Balbus suggested and then approved, together with Oppius, the 'sweetening' letter that Cicero contrived to send Caesar through Dolabella.

Notes

1 There was great confusion in the mind of this man. Caesar was right when he said of him, with affectionate humour, 'I know not what this young man wants, but all that he wants he wants very much' (Plutarch, *Brutus* 6.4).

2 Cicero, *Orator* 35.

3 'Tantam quaestionem': the image is maintained of a 'trial' which might be initiated against this work.

4 We may, however, rule out the possibility that words were added later by the speaker, since the letter from Aulus Caecina (see below) assumes knowledge of them.

5 The African campaign, which would end with Caesar's return to Rome at the end of July.

6 Cicero, *Letters to his friends* 6.7.4 (Caecina to Cicero). The client did not choose these words to criticise his former *patronus*. He too found himself in an awkward situation, required to compose a recantation after circulating a ferocious attack on Caesar.

7 Or so we may conclude if Cicero's letter to Tiro, his secretary (*Letters to his friends* 16.22.1), expressing his concern that the copyists cannot read his writing in the pages he has just finished, dates from the same month. See H. J. Tschiedel, *Caesar's Anticato* (Darmstadt 1981), p. 8.

8   Suetonius, *Caesar* 56.5.

9   Tschiedel (*Caesar's Anticato*, p. 9) believes that Cicero's book went into circulation in November and that it reached Caesar's headquarters in Spain at the end of the year.

10 Cicero, *Letters to Atticus* 12.40.1 (9 May).

11 Cicero, *Letters to Atticus* 12.41.4 (11 May).

12 'Legendo se dicit copiosiorem factum.'

13 Cicero, *Letters to Atticus* 13.46.2.

14 Cicero, *Letters to Atticus* 12.21 (17 March 45). So the manuscript was conceived as early as March 45.

15 This emphasis is in accord with Sallust's *Catilinarian Conspiracy*. A noteworthy coincidence of views.

16 In August 45 there appeared another laudatory *Cato*, by the Epicurean Marcus Fadius Gallus (see Cicero, *Letters to his friends* 7.24.1). Yet another was written by Munatius Rufus (see Plutarch, *Cato the Younger* 37.1). The polemics surrounding the memory of Cato were never-ending. Octavian continued the tradition into his old age. At an advanced age he gave readings of his *Reply to Brutus on Cato* [*Rescripta Bruto de Catone*] (Suetonius, *Augustus* 85.1), and required Tiberius to continue when he grew tired.

17 Cicero, *Letters to Atticus* 13.59.1 (23 August 45).

Part IV

From the Conspiracy to the Triumph of Caesarism

CHAPTER 29

Inklings of Conspiracy

In his *Defence of Marcellus* (late summer of 46 BC) Cicero had urged the senators he was addressing to be on the alert and protect Caesar from possible conspiracies. And he talked at length about the 'madness' of those who would conceive or plan an attempt on Caesar's life, even – he specifies, turning directly to Caesar – 'among the ranks of your own'. It is strange that he felt the need to point out this possibility to the Senate and, above all, to Caesar himself. 'Still, since there are in the human mind corners so dark and recesses so unexplored, let us by all means intensify your suspicions; for by so doing we shall intensify your watchfulness.'[1] These are not idle words: it is a plea that could not have come out of nothing. This may also be inferred from Cicero's indication that the attempt could be hatched 'de tuis' or 'ex eo numero qui una tecum fuerunt', as well as 'ex inimicis'.

One is tempted to observe that the insistence with which Cicero stresses that there are no more enemies suggests a wish – surprising though this may be – to signal that some such wild scheme could arise only among the Caesarians. That he has something definite in mind may be deduced from the fact that, after a brilliant demonstration that there could *not* be any potential conspirators (unless they were completely insane), he nevertheless arrives at the conclusion that the minds of men are such that vigilance must be stepped up!

When we remember that Cicero's speeches were always improvised (including the speech thanking Caesar for pardoning Marcellus), and the written versions, the ones we read, are later works, we conclude that the words that we are reading are not really from late summer 46, but *later* (how long after is unknown). It is known that Cicero was aware that while Caesar was still in Spain (spring 45) Trebonius, a Caesarian from the beginning, was preparing a plot against Caesar and attempting to involve Antony.[2] Antony did not agree, but certainly did not denounce anyone. At this point Cicero's words, written perhaps when he already knew all the facts, should be read with closer attention to their literal meaning, and not dismissed as the virtuoso hyperbole of a particularly fawning and fanciful panegyrist.

Cicero continues:

> For what man on earth is there so ignorant of life, so unversed in politics, so utterly careless of his own well-being and that of the community, as not to realize that his own well-being is bound up in yours, and that on your sole life hang the lives of all?[3]

He goes on speaking of the necessity that Caesar *remain alive*, of the foolishness, political first of all, of those who do not realise that to safeguard his life means to protect everyone. Then he again speaks explicitly of a possible coup. He says,

> For my part, as I ponder day and night upon you, as I cannot but do, it is but human chances, the doubtful issues of bodily disorder and the frailness of our common nature, at which I shudder; and I mourn that, while the commonwealth must be immortal, its existence should turn upon the mortal breath of a single man. But if to human chances and the uncertain instability of bodily health there is also added conspiracy for criminal and treacherous ends, what god are we to suppose could succour the state, should he so desire?[4]

Here the word *conspiracy* (*insidiarum consensio*) is openly uttered. It is difficult to imagine that it is a word thrown in carelessly. The threat of a plot, of Caesar's violent end at the hands of conspirators, continues to be canvassed, to Caesar and the Senate, as a real and alarming possibility.

He takes up the theme no less dramatically in the conclusion. Woe betide him who 'still keeps his soul armed'.[5] Much more honourable was he who fought fiercely and died on the battlefield (even for a losing cause). Cicero seeks a spiritual demobilisation. Every conflict, every division, so far has been either overcome by force of arms or annulled by the victor's justice. All men of sound sense must unanimously express a single wish: 'Only through your safety, Gaius Caesar, . . . can there be any safety for ourselves.' 'For this reason all of us, who have the safety of the existing frame of things at heart, urge and implore you to look to your own life and welfare.'[6] A promise, then, that anticipates the senators' oath to watch over the physical safety of Caesar, which Antony, not long after this, will throw in the teeth of Caesar's murderers, all of them members of the Senate:

> And, if I may say on behalf of others what I personally feel, since you think that some danger lurks which should be guarded against, we all

promise you not merely sentinels and bodyguards (*excubias et custo-dias*), but the shelter that our own breasts and bodies can afford.[7]

Perhaps indeed the central importance of the *Defence of Marcellus* (of its written version, of course, not the words improvised in the Senate) lies precisely here: in this insistent warning addressed not only to the chosen victim, soon to be targeted and murdered, but also, even primarily, to those anonymous scheming opponents, probably known to Cicero, never suppressed and now implacably – if unwittingly – taking Rome towards a new civil war.

In the summer of 45 BC, in Gallia Narbonensis, Trebonius tried to draw Antony too into a conspiracy to eliminate Caesar. At that time Antony was cool towards Caesar because Caesar had chosen Lepidus as *magister equitum*. Cicero's statement is very clear (and would lead to Antony's polemical rejoinder, making Cicero the true mastermind of the conspiracy):

> It is well known that you, Antony, entered into this scheme at Narbo with Caius Trebonius and, because of partnership in that design, were, we have seen, drawn aside by Trebonius at the time when Caesar was being slain.[8]

This conspiracy of Trebonius and Antony is entirely within the Caesarian camp. Later on, Trebonius would be considered 'a Caesarian who can be counted on' by Cassius and Brutus, when they decided to act.

Cicero's statement, often called into question, is valuable above all for its indications of *time and place*. While Caesar, having barely got out of Munda, where he risked losing everything and even contemplated suicide, is still grappling with the Spanish revolt, the plot against him takes shape. The military course having been unsuccessful, the terrorist one looms as the next choice, and it has its beginnings in the army's rear (in Gallia Narbonensis), among the commanders who observe events from there and inform friends in Rome.

From Narbonne Hirtius wrote to Cicero, in Rome, to inform him of the outcome at Munda.[9] Trebonius was in Gallia Narbonensis, as was Antony, who had been excluded by Caesar from both the African and Spanish campaigns, and harboured a certain grudge at being marginalised for so long. It was at Narbonne, in the late summer of 45, that a plot began to form to remove Caesar, who – contrary to expectations – had returned from Munda alive. At that time the conspirators decided to involve Antony, apparently on the basis of his behaviour and what the others thought they knew of him. How did Cicero know all this? Probably from people like Hirtius, *or from Trebonius himself* after March 44. It is difficult to dismiss this information as unreliable.

Plutarch's account[10] is much more detailed than Cicero's in the *Second Philippic* and derives directly from Trebonius. The scene is placed in a different location. The two were 'going out to meet Caesar on his return from Spain',[11] their conversations took place while they were alone for long periods together, sharing a tent and travelling in the same vehicle; Trebonius had chosen his words 'quietly and cautiously'[12] and was certain that Antony had understood, without, however, rising to the bait; nevertheless, Antony had loyally, πιστῶς, revealed nothing to Caesar. Later, when the conspiracy came to fruition, the plotters considered including Antony.

During the interminable Spanish campaign, then, a conspiracy formed within Caesar's entourage. Cicero's information about this is fairly detailed and the names he cites – Trebonius first, then Antony, at least as being aware, and, by his silence, complicit – became a source of great embarrassment. It is difficult to comprehend the complex follower psychology revolving around a leader who galvanises about his own person devotion, admiration, envy and resentment. These factors carry weight, together with many others: Caesar's authoritarian tendency, the unending civil war, the appeal of still-active power groups, as well as rivalry within the entourage of the dictator, who could speed up or hold back the careers of members of the swollen elite around him. And the dictator himself, with his disarming openness towards men of great prominence and social and family status like Marcus Junius Brutus,[13] for example, did not even realise that he irked or exasperated those who had been most loyal to him, from the very beginning, including – certainly – Antony.

In this confused situation, among mature, titled men with a record of political achievement, long engaged in concealed rivalry for the succession (whenever it might be), the unexpected arrival of an ambitious and only seemingly frail youth like Octavius at Caesar's headquarters during the Spanish campaign would at first have given rise to irritation, or to jokes and lewd guffaws, like Antony's insinuation about the young man's loss of innocence. In the late summer and autumn months of 45 BC, when there was serious anxiety at the very heart of the Caesarian camp, the appearance of that *puer* would have been cause for nothing more than some ribald soldierly humour. The serious problems of politics lay elsewhere. Antony, though informed by Trebonius of his disturbing plans (perhaps not his alone: in these months Hirtius was also in Narbonne), did not betray his party comrade, but was able to effect a reconciliation with the dictator. He was consul with Caesar for 44, obviously with Caesar's consent, a sign of harmony regained. This harmony was adversely affected, however, by the disturbing events of the feast of the Lupercalia,[14] and the irresponsible (or treacherous) performance then staged, which cost the dictator much sympathy. It is noteworthy that the very men who, in the summer of 45, were at Narbonne, while Caesar was in Spain, all received 'rewards' from the dictator: Trebonius, *consul suffectus* in 45,[15] was appointed proconsul of Asia for 43; Antony would join Caesar in the consulate of 44; and Hirtius would be named consul for 43.

The case of Trebonius is typical and helps one towards a better understanding of the conduct, the reactions and the decisions of these men. Trebonius was a convinced 'republican', whose long association with Cicero had clearly left its mark. In his time – perhaps in 60 BC when he was *quaestor* – he had opposed Clodius' attempted *transitio ad plebem* (his change of status from patrician to plebeian), which was a threat to Cicero, but in 55 it was he who, as tribune of the plebs, had proposed the extension of Caesar's term in Gaul for a further five years, as well as Crassus' and Pompey's appointments to the governorship of Syria and Spain respectively. And from 54 to 49 he had fought beside Caesar in Gaul as legate and had followed him in the civil war, taking part in the difficult siege of Marseilles (the account of which in Caesar's *Commentaries* owes a very great deal to him).[16] The crossing of the Rubicon had not created particular difficulties for this republican – further evidence that Caesar's propaganda was believed above all by his men. The praetorship in 48 had crowned this career, and the government of Spain in 47 had meant an important recognition. But there things had not gone well: Pompey the Younger had driven him from Baetica (Further Spain), and it was precisely due to Trebonius' urgent insistence that Caesar decided to intervene in person in Spain (November 46), embarking (after Alexandria) on yet another very risky enterprise. How did the experience of that campaign bring Trebonius to the point of breaking with Caesar and plotting his assassination, and trying to draw the dissatisfied Antony (replaced by Lepidus as *magister equitum*) into the venture? This is a difficult problem to solve on the basis of the documents, but an important one. The signs of a serious rupture, pregnant with consequences, may be seen here, in the new power structure which Caesar was seeking to build as he moved – uncertainly and with many 'provisional' solutions (which is what dictatorship means) – beyond the old 'republican legality'. It is at this point that some of his allies drew back and began to contemplate extreme solutions.

Notes

1 'Tantae latebrae tanti recessus [in anima sunt]': Cicero, *In defence of Marcellus* 22

2 Cicero, *Philippics* 2.14.34.

3 According to Cicero, one of the dangers facing Caesar was assassination in a coup! However, we know only of some of those coups which were planned, but failed, like that of his secretary Philemon, 'who had promised Caesar's enemies that he would poison him'. *Suetonius*, Caesar 74.1.

4 Cicero, *In defence of Marcellus* 23: 'si accedit [. . .] sceleris etiam insidiarumque consensio'.

5 Cicero, *In defence of Marcellus* 31.

6 Cicero, *In defence of Marcellus* 32: 'ut vitae, ut saluti tuae consulas'.

7 Cicero, *In defence of Marcellus* 32: 'subesse aliquid putas quod cavendum sit'.

8 Cicero, *Philippics* 2.14.34.

9 He writes to Cicero on 18 April 45; we know this from Cicero, *Letters to Atticus* 12.37A.

10 Plutarch, *Antony* 13.1–3.

11 Ibid. This is inexact: see F. Münzer, *RE*, s.v. *Trebonius*, no. 6.

12 These details can only come from Trebonius himself, who also wrote some works which are known from Cicero. See *Letters to his friends* 12.16.3: a poem about Antony composed in 44; *Letters to his friends* 15.21.2–3: a collection of Cicero's *bons mots* (see also H. Bardon, *La Littérature latine inconnue*, vol. I [Paris 1952], p. 272; p. 364 n. 1).

13 Brutus may also have been the son of Caesar, who for a long time was the devoted lover of Servilia, Brutus' mother.

14 See Chapter 31.

15 At the beginning of October: Broughton, *MRR*, vol. II, p. 304.

16 Caesar, *Civil War* 2.1–16.

CHAPTER 30

'Iure caesus'

After the hard-fought battle of Munda, the subjugation of Hispania Baetica (Further Spain) kept Caesar busy for several months. He admitted that this time he had fought not for victory but for his life,[1] and then had to confront determined resistance with no prospect of real pacification. The survivors from the defeated army had barricaded themselves in Corduba (Cordoba) and in the city of Munda; 'cleansing' those cities of these stubborn fighters, who were ready for anything, entailed considerable losses of men[2] and months of military and political effort.[3] In managing the victory Caesar abstained from his usual *clementia*, and the victors and their allies vented all their bitterness on the two cities. Land and money were needed. Not even the temple of Heracles at Gades (Cadiz) was spared.[4] Until August, that is, for another five months after the victory at Munda, Caesar had much to do in Spain. Late in September he was at the gates of Rome, but did not enter: he was preparing the triumph, which was celebrated, to widespread bewilderment, at the beginning of October.[5]

To celebrate a triumph over Roman citizens was an unheard-of act.[6]

> This was the last war that Caesar waged; and the triumph that was celebrated for it vexed the Romans as nothing else had done. For it commemorated no victory over foreigners or barbarian kings, but the utter annihilation of the sons and the family of the mightiest of the Romans, who had fallen upon misfortune; and it was not meet for Caesar to celebrate a triumph for the calamities of his country.[7]

From Caesar's point of view, the triumph was warranted because the war that had only just ended was presented as having been fought against local rebels supported by treacherous Romans. This is the fundamental propagandist premise assumed in the *Spanish War*. And in a certain sense this approach was confirmed by the evolving situation. Very soon the Spanish bandits began to show themselves again, and Sextus Pompey, Pompey's surviving son, joined them and began to achieve successes, partly because the harsh treatment inflicted on Spain turned out to be counter-productive. Naturally the magistrates charged with governing the unruly province were the ones to pay the price for this resumption of war: first Gaius Carrinas, then Asinius Pollio, who entered the province at the beginning of 44 BC and there suffered a defeat[8] that Velleius described as 'clarissimum bellum'.[9]

The victory over Spain, that is, over Pompey's sons, was the first signal of a change in style which characterised the last months of the life and government of Caesar. In comparison with the few months spent in Rome after his return from Africa (August–October 46), this autumn and winter season of 45–44, between the triumph celebrated in October and the Ides of March, presents a completely different situation, from both the human and the political point of view. It is no accident that in the summer of 46 Marcellus and Ligarius were granted clemency, while at the end of 45 the trial of Deiotarus concluded without any sentence. To Caesar it was more important to get to the bottom of the conduct of the Galatian tetrarch, who was suspected of backing the Syrian rebellion, which was still in progress.

The summer of 46 had been a time of great building initiatives (the *Forum Caesaris*, the temple of Venus Genetrix), of grand plans (the drainage of the Pontine marshes; the commencement of a new road across the Apennines to the Adriatic; the construction of a great Greek and Latin library, whose design was entrusted to the ex-Pompeian and universal scholar, Marcus Terentius Varro). It was a time of reform of the calendar, of legislation in defence of provincials (the law *de repetundis* which for two centuries, with minor alterations, regulated relations between Rome and its empire), of laws that completed the Romanisation of Gallia Transpadana, and of legal provisions on debt and the rent of houses, aimed at alleviating the effects of the long civil war on the life of the citizens – a war that had profoundly affected individual lives and left deep scars.[10]

The autumn-winter period between the Spanish triumph and the Ides of March was different: it was characterised by Caesar's determined efforts to place his personal power finally within the framework of a new order, and by mounting reactions to this openly authoritarian development. Examining these last months of Caesar's life, Napoleon observed that, beside the push to dictatorial power, Caesar decided to pay even more attention to the noble classes and to distance himself still further from the growing demands of the common people.[11] Support for this analysis by the French emperor (who again sees his own life mirrored in that of the Roman dictator) may be found in Suetonius:

> At last, in his later years, he went so far as to allow all those whom he had not yet pardoned to return to Italy, and to hold magistracies and the command of armies: and he actually set up the statues of Lucius Sulla and Pompey, which had been broken to pieces by the populace.[12]

We have already seen the importance of such symbols when Caesar restored Marius' trophies and statues. Cicero, it seems, was speaking ironically when he observed that Caesar was restoring Pompey's statues in order to safeguard his own.[13]

Another sign of this atmosphere was, according to Suetonius, Caesar's choice not to investigate the conspiracies against him that he was uncovering, but to issue an edict in which he made it known that he was aware of 'the conspiracies which were detected, and of meetings by night'.[14]

Napoleon has his own firm belief regarding Caesar's openness towards the old ruling groups: 'After Munda and the elimination of Pompey's party, the *populares* and the veterans stepped up their demands. Caesar took note of this and resorted to the old families to keep them in check.'[15] Good or bad as this analysis may be (and one would like the sources to provide confirmation of such increased 'popular' radicalism following Munda), it offers Bonaparte the opportunity to frame a sort of general theory, valid for any context, on the reconstituting of an 'aristocracy': even in the framework of a revolution that has toppled the nobility as a class, even when one tries to avoid the forming of an aristocracy in the 'Third Estate', and even of an aristocracy of workers ('elle surnage et se réfugie dans les chefs d'ateliers et du peuple').[16] So, he concludes, a leader has nothing to gain from any such 'slippage' of the aristocracy: it is preferable to keep the old aristocracy alive and make use of it in the new order, 're-establishing the old families under new leaders'.[17] This, in his opinion, was the way Caesar was turning in his last phase. It is a legitimate reading of Caesarism; however, it leaves out of account the mounting disaffection aroused in the aristocracy – that same aristocracy which Caesar was under the illusion that he had attracted – by the swing towards enduring personal power. After indicating these signals of a new openness, Suetonius notes that 'yet after all, his other actions and words so turn the scale, that it is thought that he abused his power (*abusus dominatione*) and was justly slain (*iure caesus*)'.[18] A puzzling formulation by the secretary who managed the correspondence of the emperor Hadrian,[19] but one which clearly conveys the traumatic effect on the republican aristocracy of the dictator's last decisions.

On Caesar's actions and behaviour which in some sense 'justified' the assassination, in Suetonius' view, there is an established tradition of providing a fairly stable 'list' of abuses and misdeeds, starting with the constitutional innovations – all tending towards a monocracy – introduced by Caesar after Munda, some at the beginning of 44 BC.

Suetonius summarises these innovations thus: 'He accepted excessive honours, such as an uninterrupted consulship, the dictatorship for life, and the censorship of public morals, as well as the forename Imperator, the surname of Father of his Country.'[20] Added to this are further honours (like the statue set among those of the kings and an elevated seat in the orchestra, etc.). The record of a series of 'slights' to constitutional practice follows; for example, the appointment of no fewer than eight *praefecti urbi* or the systematic debasement of the consulate, held by him 'in name only' (*titulo tenus*) and in which he had himself replaced, if only for a few months, resigning in anticipation.

> When on the eve of the Calends of January [31 December 45], one of the two consuls suddenly died [Quintus Fabius Maximus, consul since 1 October], although there were only a few hours left in the term of office, he conferred it upon one of those who had sought it [Gaius Caninius Rebilus, who thus came to be consul for a single day].[21]

But it was the following action in particular – Suetonius observes – that roused deadly hatred against him. When the Senate approached him in a body with many highly honorary decrees, he received them before the temple of Venus Genetrix without rising. Some thought that when he attempted to get up, he was held back by Cornelius Balbus.[22]

Then there were those memorable incidents which above all reveal Caesar's touchiness and ill humour, in particular the disagreement with Pontius Aquila, the tribune of the plebs, the only one who did not rise to his feet 'when Caesar himself in one of his triumphal processions rode past the benches of the tribunes'.[23] This can only have been the contentious Spanish triumph, seeing that Pontius Aquila, later also implicated in the plot, was a tribune in 45. Caesar was out of sorts and for days kept adding 'That is, if Pontius Aquila will allow me' every time he had occasion to promise something publicly.[24] Then there was the incident with the tribunes who detained an unknown man for crowning a statue of Caesar with a band of laurels. And his awkward response to the crowd who were hailing him *rex*: 'I am Caesar and no king!'[25]

The scene performed in the Senate when Caesar was given powers that the constitutional system had never foreseen was supremely ambiguous. Plutarch well captures the moment, and the danger: bowing to fate and regarding the power of one individual as a way of catching breath from the uninterrupted anguish of the civil war, 'the Romans . . . appointed him dictator for life'. But this – he explains – in reality was tantamount to undisguised tyranny, 'since the monarchy, besides the element of irresponsibility, now took on that of permanence'.[26] 'Tyranny' is not a term of abuse, but rather the result of Plutarch's effort to find a Greek equivalent, and he is very conscious of the popular-authoritarian nature of the Greek 'tyranny' of the classical age. A notable example was Pisistratus, who, according to Aristotle, had progressed, almost in logical order, from 'leader of the people and general' to 'tyrant'[27] – a fundamentally correct equivalent, despite an increasingly pejorative connotation in *tyrannos* in the Athenian democracy of the fifth and fourth centuries BC. And we know that this equivalent was prominent in the mind of Cicero, according to whom the dictator was fond of quoting those 'terrible' lines from the *Phoenicians* that we have recalled at various times.[28] Like the Greek tyranny in its early forms, the dictatorship was also intended to resolve, within a set time frame, problems and situations that could not be resolved by more traditional means. Only with Sulla did it become an instrument of political and constitutional reform that was useful to the *optimates*. With Caesar it reverted to its original function as an instrument of mediation for resolving conflicts.[29] Cicero was not making an unrehearsed or controversial statement when in his *On the state*, just before the civil war, he found a way to revive this notion, citing the dream of Scipio Aemilianus, in which Scipio was invested with the dictatorship in order to make constitutional reforms.[30] However, the idea of raising the matter by means of a dream indicated caution regarding the public reaction to this term. In order to cultivate views favourable to a form of government based on more marked personal power, Oppius, Caesar's most loyal agent, devoted himself to writing a life of Scipio Africanus Major.[31]

In the Senate sitting that launched the Caesarian dictatorship, according to the reconstruction passed on by Plutarch, it was Cicero who

proposed the first honours for him in the Senate, and their magnitude
was, after all, not too great for a man; but others added excessive
honours and vied with one another in proposing them, thus rendering Caesar odious and obnoxious even to the mildest citizens because
of the pretension and extravagance of what was decreed for him.[32]

Into the competition of the adulators slipped adversaries:

It is thought, too, that the enemies of Caesar no less than his flatter-
ers helped to force these measures through, in order that they might
have as many pretexts as possible against him and might be thought
to have the best reasons for attempting his life.[33]

This judgement on the complicity of the future assassins (as agents
provocateurs) in the authoritarian shift effected at the turn of the year
45–44 must stem from a good source. Florus was also aware of the
inner workings of the future conspirators' minds, which Cicero must
have known when he set down his *Defence of Marcellus* in written
form. They laid these honours on him – writes the historian, a distant
descendant of the Annaei – as they put the *infula* on the head of the
sacrificial animal when it is about to be slaughtered.

Certainly 'iure caesus' (justly killed) is a very harsh expression. I do
not believe this was the accepted view in Hadrian's entourage of
Caesar and his violent end, or that this judgement accorded with the
true feelings of men who showed off their old-fashioned education,
like Pliny the Younger (who claimed to be a kind of new Cicero).
Rather it seems to be the judgement of a contemporary for whom it is
not only predictable but understandable that abuse of *dominatio* must
lead to such a violent end – a contemporary who zealously catalogued
all the blunders and 'violations' committed by Caesar in his last
months, producing a list almost identical to the one we find in
Suetonius, Plutarch and Appian.[34] But what is striking about these
authors is that in their accounts this resentful cataloguing of 'violations' sits side by side with the conviction, expressed elsewhere in the
same work, that the murder of Caesar was a crime and that the assassins in the end received the punishment they deserved. As an example,
Suetonius concludes his biography of Caesar with the 'penalty' suffered by the assassins who had stabbed Caesar in the Senate: 'some
took their own lives with the self-same dagger with which they had
impiously slain Caesar'.[35] Even in Appian, with the transition from the
second book (in which Caesar falls in a crescendo of 'republican'
outrage at his excesses) to the third book (in which Caesar is the 'most

worthy' man, whose assassins one after the other paid for their crime), one sees a change of position which can only reflect a change of source.[36] In Dio Cassius, who is unforgiving in his pungent observations on Caesar's actions in life, the judgement on his murder is negative and categorical: 'For justice and the Divine Will seem to have led to suffer death themselves men who had killed their benefactor, one who had attained such eminence in both virtue and good fortune.'[37]

The sources that express the views of the Julian family stand yet further apart and are all the more clearly defined: Velleius, first and foremost, but we can imagine that Nicolaus of Damascus expressed himself in similar terms. Velleius not only adopts a position opposed to the assassination, which is an attitude common to several sources, variously inspired, but also opposes the definition of Caesar's power as *tyranny*. While Plutarch, when he describes the last measures that still further expanded the dictator's powers, stands by his view – what else was all this if not absolute monarchic power? – Velleius unequivocally rejects that definition. Where he reconstructs the conflicting views within the conspiracy – Cassius wanted to do away with Antony as well, while Brutus argued that 'citizens ought not to seek the blood of any but the "tyrant" '[38] – he adds polemically, 'for to call Caesar "tyrant" placed his [Brutus'] deed in a better light'. Velleius at this point decisively disputes the justice of the foundations, including the emotional foundations, of the conspiracy. It is self-evident that Velleius has in mind the totally negative use of the word 'tyrant' in the Roman political lexicon. In the days prior to Brutus' agreement to support the conspiracy, 'tyrant' and 'tyranny' are words which recur in his conversations with Cassius and Cassius' friends.[39]

There remains the question of whether that surprising 'iure caesus' that we read of in Suetonius is not due to the source that already, from other indications, has appeared to underlie the accounts of Suetonius, Plutarch and Appian: Asinius Pollio. Although his historical work has not survived, we do have an important letter of his to Cicero, written a year after Caesar's death.[40] In this letter we find, in strange equilibrium, an explanation of Asinius' decision to side with Caesar on the outbreak of civil war, and a shunning of Caesar's drift towards total *dominatio*, the negation of *libertas*. And it is precisely Suetonius' astonishing 'abusus dominatione iure caesus' (justly slain on account of abuse of power) that provides the nexus between them.[41]

> Furthermore, my nature and pursuits leave me to crave for peace and freedom. The outbreak of the civil war cost me many a tear.[42] But

since I could not remain neutral because I had powerful enemies on both sides, I avoided the camp where I well knew I should not be safe from my enemy's plots. Finding myself forced whither I would not, and having no wish to trail in the rear, I certainly did not hang back from dangerous work. As for Caesar, I loved him in all duty and loyalty, because in his greatness he treated me, a recent acquaintance, as though I had been one of his oldest intimates. Where I was allowed to manage as I thought best, my actions were calculated to win cordial approval in the most respected quarters. Where I obeyed orders, it was at a time and in a manner which made it clear that I had received them with reluctance. The ill will thereby incurred, highly unjust as it was, was enough to teach me how pleasant a thing is freedom and how miserable life under despotic rule.[43]

Pollio was a Caesarian; like many he was a Caesarian in the light of, and on the basis of, a calculation of the decisive factor for the conduct of a Roman politician: how many friends and how many enemies he had in the two conflicting parties. He showed loyalty to the leader, but he was not unaware of that leader's limitations or his defects. The *dominatio* he exercised ended by causing harm, directly and personally, to him, Pollio, too. Therefore, now that Caesar has been murdered, he is ready to fight to the end *pro libertate*: to make sure that some other Caesar does not emerge on the scene.[44] Pollio describes to his influential addressee an exemplary political career, which we will encounter soon when we look more closely at the composition of the conspiracy. It is fair to suppose that this way of seeing things was also reflected in the historical account that, years later, Pollio gave of the murder of Caesar. The sources that depend on him are there to testify to it.

But what were Caesar's plans for the future when he had himself invested with the 'dictatorship for life'? Could he really have believed that he could transform something which, by definition, in the popular consciousness, was an office of limited term into a lifelong appointment? It is possible that his decision was connected to some grand but ill-defined military exploits in the East that he was thought to have in mind, but the very scale of these projects meant that they were doomed to remain nebulous.[45] Perhaps too the dictatorship for life might provide a (provisional) basis on which to build, at leisure, a new constitutional structure.[46] After Thapsus he had secured the ten-year dictatorship, an office that could be renewed for ten consecutive years: what did the dictatorship 'for life' really add to a ten-year dictatorship, beyond the avoidance of the mere formality of annual renewal?[47] Since Caesar did not succeed in institutionalising his charismatic power, he did not succeed in imposing constitutional modifications either, which meant imposing them upon a body politic made up of a very select elite capable of tenacious self-defence and self-preservation. It was a process he knew very well from having practised and exploited it many times over. The difficulty of the undertaking is in a way confirmed by the fact that after a further ten years of bitter experience, of further thought and experiment (a renewable triumvirate for the restoration of the state) and of new conflicts, Octavius would choose to turn back to the past, by the 'restoration' of the 'res publica'.

On Caesar's more or less fantastic plans we have vague and vast information which is at once extensive and imprecise. The improbable route traced by Plutarch, in particular, seems to have been conceived to compete with Alexander's assault on the 'ends of the earth'[48] (so may be a product of the Alexander-Caesar comparison that has been consolidated in the historical and rhetorical tradition).[49] There is, however, a contemporary voice that deserves attention, that of Cicero, who leaves only the merest hint in a letter to Atticus, written scarcely two months after Caesar's death. It is the famous letter in which Cicero considers what to him seems the disastrous outcome of the Ides of March, and sets down his view of the 'liberators': 'though our courage was that of men, believe me we had no more sense than children'.[50] But then, continuing his survey of events, he adds a quite different comment, though a fleeting one, on the 'pointlessness' of the Ides of March: 'Caesar would never have come back.'[51] In Cicero's opinion, at least (and Cicero knew him well), Caesar would have plunged deeper and deeper into a remote and dangerous venture (such as the Parthian campaign?), perhaps ending it on a battlefield. The all-absorbing reality of war had ceased to be the instrument with which to control Rome (this had originally been the true aim of the campaign in Gaul); now that he, the victor in the civil war, was discovering the elusiveness of power, war came to seem an increasingly attractive and fulfilling alternative to domestic politics. We do not know whether Cicero's appraisal sprang from a flash of intuition or merely from a moment of disillusionment. Months later, Cicero himself, having returned to the fray, would extol before the Senate the necessity and grandeur of the deed accomplished by the 'liberators' and would revoke, so to speak, the reflections mentioned in this letter. There remains the question whether, in that brief reference in a private letter to his old friend, he nevertheless offered a glimpse of a truth that is valuable for an understanding of the desperate mentality of his beloved and hated lifelong rival.[52]

Notes

1 Plutarch, *Caesar* 56.4.
2 *Spanish War* 32–41.
3 Dio Cassius 43.39.
4 Dio Cassius 43.39.4–5.
5 Suetonius, *Caesar* 37.1; Plutarch, *Caesar* 56.7; Dio Cassius 43.42.
6 *Précis des guerres de César* par Napoléon, écrit par M. Marchand sous la dictée de l'Empereur [1819] (Paris 1836), p. 207. Napoleon notes that neither Marius nor Sulla had dared go so far.
7 Plutarch, *Caesar* 56.8–9. The participation of the two legates Fabius and Pedius, great-nephews of the dictator, in the triumph was seen as being particularly offensive, as well as being ridiculous. Dio Cassius 43.42.2.
8 Dio Cassius 45.10.
9 Velleius 2.73.2.
10 The law which reduced the number of those who received grain at the expense of the state (Suetonius, *Caesar* 41.5; misunderstood by Plutarch, *Caesar* 55.5, as evidence of a decline in the population) was intended to counter arbitrary acts (such as those introduced by Clodius' legislative amendments in 58). It was also evidence of profound disruptions in the social composition of the capital.
11 Napoleon, *Précis*, pp. 208–9.
12 Suetonius, *Caesar* 75.4. They had been destroyed when word came of the defeat of Pompey at Pharsalus (Dio Cassius 43.18.2).
13 Plutarch, *Caesar* 57.6.
14 Suetonius, *Caesar* 75.5.
15 Napoleon, *Précis*, p. 209.
16 A remarkable premonition of the phenomenon of the 'worker aristocracy'.
17 Napoleon, *Précis*, p. 210.
18 Suetonius, *Caesar* 76.1.
19 On the political ideology of Suetonius, see the balanced treatment by E. Cizek, *Structures et idéologies dans les 'Vies des douze Césars' de Suétone* (Bucharest and Paris 1977), p. 179. The reference to Pliny as a 'model' is particularly important.
20 Suetonius, *Caesar* 76.1.
21 *CIL* I², pp. 28, 158. Cicero comments ironically, 'ita Caninio consule scito neminem prandisse!' (*Letters to his friends* 7.30.1).
22 Suetonius, *Caesar* 78; cf. Livy, *Periocha* 116.
23 Suetonius, *Caesar* 78.2.

24 Ibid. On Aquila's role in the conspiracy see Appian, *Civil Wars* 2.113; Dio Cassius 44.38.3.

25 Suetonius, *Caesar* 79.

26 Plutarch, *Caesar* 57.1.

27 Aristotle, *Athenian Constitution* 22.3.

28 Cicero, *On duties* 3.82; Euripides, *Phoenicians* 524; Suetonius, *Caesar* 30.5.

29 We may note in passing that in modern political parlance right up to the late nineteenth century the word 'dictator' was the property of the 'left' (from Garibaldi's dictatorship to the 'dictatorship of the proletariat'). See C. Vetter, 'Dittatore e dittatura nel Risorgimento', *Studi storici* 39 (1998), pp. 767–807, and its bibliography.

30 Cicero, *On the state* 6.12: 'dictator rem publicam constituas oportebit, si impias propinquorum manus effugeris' ('it will be your duty as dictator to restore order in the commonwealth, if only you escape the wicked hands of your kinsmen').

31 Gellius 6.1.1; Carisius, in H. Keil, *Grammatici latini* (Leipzig 1855, 1859), vol. I, p. 147. Hyginus, Augustus' librarian, also wrote a biography of this 'princeps in re publica'.

32 Plutarch, *Caesar* 57.2.

33 Plutarch, *Caesar* 57.3.

34 Suetonius, *Caesar* 76–9; Plutarch, *Caesar* 60–6; Appian, *Civil Wars* 2.107–10. For partial lists see Livy, *Periocha 116*, and Dio Cassius 44.1–12.

35 Suetonius, *Caesar* 89. These are the exact last words of the book.

36 In the third book, in which Octavian first appears, Appian must have paid much attention to Augustus' *Memoirs*; in the second he relied primarily on Asinius Pollio's *Civil Wars*. In this context it is not important whether he used 'intermediate' sources, or which they might have been.

37 Dio Cassius 48.1.

38 Velleius 2.58.2.

39 Plutarch, *Brutus* 7.7; 10.6.

40 Cicero, *Letters to his friends* 10.31 (16 March 43).

41 Suetonius, *Caesar* 76.1.

42 With some justification, he speaks as if a civil war had broken out in 50–49 and was still in progress.

43 Cicero, *Letters to his friends* 10.31.2–3 (Asinius to Cicero).

44 But his letter contains a cautious limitation, which points to numerous possible developments: 'omnes enim cives plane studeo esse salvos' (Cicero, *Letters to his friends* 10.31.5).

45 Plutarch, *Caesar* 58.6–7: an expedition with a route including Parthia, Pontus, Hyrcania, the Caspian, the Caucasus, Scythia, and back to Italy by way of Germany and Gaul resembles the product of some Jules Verne fantasy. Suetonius (*Augustus* 8), less extravagantly, speaks only of a campaign against the Parthians and another against the Dacians.

46 There are some grounds, and a documentary basis, which point to a dictatorship *rei publicae constituendae*. See the discussion on this in Broughton, *MRR*, vol. III (Suppl.), pp. 107–8.

47 The move towards a dictatorship of indefinite duration occurred before the expiry of the fourth dictatorship (in January 44). The document cited by Josephus (*Antiquities of the Jews* 14.211) is evidence of this.

48 The expression is from Seneca, *Suasoria* 1.1.

49 Notable evidence of it is provided by Plutarch's paired 'lives', in addition to the comparison between the two compiled by Appian at the end of book 2 of his *Civil Wars*.

50 Cicero, *Letters to Atticus* 15.4.2 (24 May 44).

51 Cicero, *Letters to Atticus* 15.4.3: 'ille enim numquam revertisset'.

52 On the vexed question of Caesar's kingly ambitions, the most pertinent objection is that formulated by Napoleon (*Précis*, p. 214): the term *rex*, he notes, was impractical; the Romans were accustomed to seeing kings in the ante-rooms of their pro-magistrates! See F. Cassola and G. Labruna, *Linee di una storia delle istituzioni repubblicane*, 3rd edn (Naples 1991), pp. 382–3. Much has also been written on the deification to which Caesar aspired in his lifetime: the most radical advocacy of this thesis will be found in G. Dobesch, 'Wurde Caesar zu Lebzeiten in Rom als Staatsgott anerkannt?', Suppl. XLIX of *Jahreshefte. Österreichisches Archäologisches Institut, Wien*, vol. II (Vienna 1971), pp. 20–49. But it is unlikely that Caesar went further than a generalised 'cult of personality'.

CHAPTER 31

The Lupercalia Drama

The most striking and theatrical incident was provoked by Antony, at the very moment when rumours of an imminent, openly monarchical shift in Caesar's aspirations were being nourished from several sides. Once again suspicion turned to the possible role of Cleopatra as the moving force behind the scenes, especially since she had borne Caesar a son. This led to a persistent rumour that the dictator was about to move his seat permanently to Alexandria.[1] Suppositions concerning these alleged 'Oriental' plans were finally shown to be false only when Caesar's will was read after his death. Then not only was the preeminent position of Octavius seen, but also the complete absence of Cleopatra's son from Caesar's testamentary arrangements.[2] Also exploited was the alleged Sibylline prophecy according to which only a king would be able to defeat the Parthians. And soon the name was put about of the man who would place before the Senate the proposal which logically flowed from that prophecy.[3]

As for Antony, he was no longer openly out of favour with Caesar: on the contrary, he was his colleague in the consulate for the year 44 BC. But he was not reappointed *magister equitum*, and had to resign himself to being appointed *consul suffectus* (deputy consul) by Dolabella.[4] On 15 February 44, during the festival of the Lupercalia, he became the central figure in a spectacular event: an attempt to crown Caesar king. Here is the fullest account there is of the incident, taken from the *Life of Augustus* by Nicolaus of Damascus, the loyal biographer of Caesar's 'son':

> The events which happened as follows especially urged on those united against him. There was a golden statue of him on the rostra, as had been voted. This appeared with a diadem around its head – the Romans are very suspicious of a diadem and consider it a symbol of slavery. When the tribunes, Lucius and Gaius, came upon it, they ordered one of their attendants to climb up, take it down and throw it away. When Caesar learned that this had been done, he called the Senate to the temple of Concord and brought charges against the

tribunes. He said that these men secretly set in place the diadem so that they might openly insult him and seem to have done a brave deed by dishonouring his statue, because they had no respect for the Senate or for him. He further charged that their action was an indicator of some deeper motive and of their conspiracy. He asseverated that if somehow they could bring him into disrepute with the people, suggesting that he desired power in an illegal form, they themselves would begin the revolution and kill him. When he had made his allegations, since the Senate agreed with him, he banished them. The exiles left the country and other tribunes took their place.

The people began to shout that he be a king and that there no longer be any delay in proclaiming him king, since Fortune had already done so. However, Caesar said that he would indulge the people in every way because of their kindness towards him, but he would never give them this, and he asked their forgiveness for thwarting them by preserving their ancestral forms of office. He said that he preferred to hold the consulship legally than a kingship illegally.

Such was the discussion at that time, and afterwards a festival took place at Rome during the winter – a festival called the Lupercalia – in which old men and young men, naked, anointed and wearing a belt, hold a procession, abusing and striking with goat-skin straps those who happen upon them. Marcus Antonius was chosen overseer of the festival at that time. He advanced through the Forum, as was the custom, and the rest of the crowd followed with him. First of all, Antony held out the laurelled crown – a diadem had been conspicuously threaded through it – to Caesar, who was sitting upon a golden throne, on the so-called rostra, wearing a purple cloak, and since the place from which Caesar used to speak to the people was high, Antony was hoisted up by his fellow office-holders and placed the diadem at Caesar's feet. The crowd began to shout that the crown be placed upon Caesar's head and were urging Lepidus, the master-of-the-horse, to do this; but he hesitated. Meanwhile, Cassius Longinus, one of the conspirators, so that he might more easily escape detection by acting as if he were well-disposed towards Caesar, got in first, picked up the diadem and placed it upon Caesar's knee. Publius Casca was also in on the plan. While Caesar was refusing the honour and the people were cheering, Antony, who was naked and covered in oil, just as he was in the procession, quickly ran forward and placed the diadem on Caesar's head. Caesar, however, took it off and threw it into the crowd. Those at the back of the crowd clapped at this, but those close in began to shout that he accept it and not reject the gift of the people. Opinions were divided over the happenings.

Some were annoyed because the attempted crowning manifested Caesar's power, which was greater than was consistent with a democracy. Others thought that they would win his favour by co-operating, while others spread the report that Antony had done this not without Caesar's consent. Many were willing that he be an undisputed monarch. Diverse rumours spread through the crowd. Therefore, when Antony crowned him again, the people shouted spontaneously, 'Long live the King.' Caesar, however, would not accept it and ordered it to go to the temple of Jupiter Capitolinus, because it was an honour more suited to a god. The same people clapped him again as had before. (There is also another version current that Antony acted as he did, so it was thought, because he wished to win Caesar's favour and because he nursed the ambition of being made his son.)

Finally, having saluted Caesar, Antony gave the diadem to some of his attendants to place on the head of the statue of Caesar nearby. They did as ordered. Therefore, in the occurrences of that time, this event more than any other spurred on the conspirators, because it had provided outstanding visible evidence for the ambitions of Caesar, which they had suspected existed.[5]

Plutarch adds an important detail: Caesar, annoyed by the performance and also by its disastrous outcome, stands up and bares his neck, declaring that 'anyone who pleased might smite him there'.[6] By this bitter, dramatic gesture Caesar can only have been making plain in public the risk attached to any such initiative. At the same time he was saying that anyone who attempted to push him towards monarchic rule wanted his death.

Antony's gesture at the Lupercalia is prima facie ambiguous, puzzling and impolitic. All clues must be considered, because the behaviour of these men is never consistent: after the event they all strive – Cicero no less than Antony – to reconstruct for themselves a consequent and *consistent* pattern of behaviour. Hence also the reciprocal gibes which Cicero and Antony exchanged. Cicero accused Antony of laying the ground for Caesar's murder with his Lupercalia comedy,[7] and this should not be seen as merely a polemical retort, provoked by Antony's serious charge that Cicero was the true inspiration behind the conspiracy. We should not overlook Plutarch's report, according to which Caesar was informed at precisely that time of plots against his person being hatched by Antony, in addition to Dolabella.[8] Perhaps Cicero is hinting at something of the sort. Everything is elusive when one tries to understand the behaviour of political figures and supporting actors in a time of dictatorship. Account should also be taken of the independent actions of supporters and followers who 'no longer understand' their leader,[9] and begin to act secretly *on their own*. Antony is certainly uneasy, and so is Dolabella. Antony is fighting with Dolabella, and it hurts that Caesar favours him. In the meantime some are urging 'extreme' measures to provoke a popular reaction.[10] Perhaps Antony too is among those who no longer understand what Caesar is planning after the dictatorship for life, which, combined with the consulship renewable for ten years, is already an outrage. It is possible that *the farce of the Lupercalia has its origins here*. It would be wrong to try to understand the actions of these men before the Ides of March in the light of what they did afterwards.[11] The episode of Trebonius and of his 'contact' with Antony in the summer of 45 BC must not be forgotten.[12]

Cicero maintained then that, by his actions at the Lupercalia of 15 February 44, Antony 'had sealed the fate' of Caesar. This no doubt means that his actions brought the conspiracy forward, and clearly he does not exclude the possibility that Antony acted *deliberately*. However, this statement also contains an *item of information* (we do not know how truthful): that the conspiracy entered its operative phase *as from 15 February*. By these words Cicero reveals his familiarity with the hidden background to the plot.[13]

But Cicero's words (if they are not merely a defensive reply to Antony's accusations) also contain the suggestion that, had it not been for that scene at the Lupercalia, Caesar would still be alive. And this can only mean that the conspirators at that point were not of one mind. Until that moment, writes Nicolaus of Damascus,

> Those in the plot never came together openly but in secret and in small numbers at the houses of one another, and, as usually happens, the men contemplating so momentous a deed suggested and put into motion many ideas as to how and where the murder should be committed. Some men proposed that they attack him while he was walking along the so-called Sacred Way (he often used this road), while others suggested that they assail him during the elections, since he was compelled to cross a certain bridge in the field in front of the city to appoint the magistrates. In this case, they would be assigned different tasks so that some of them would push him off the bridge and the others would make the assault upon him and kill him. However, another group wanted to kill him when gladiatorial games were being held (this was soon), when no one would entertain suspicions seeing arms being prepared for the assassination, because of the nature of the competition. The majority of the assassins insisted that they kill him while he was attending a meeting of the Senate.[14]

To consolidate they needed a provocation. And they had it on the day of the Lupercalia. Was it by chance that while Antony acted out his role in the performance Gaius Cassius was beside him, ready to take an active part in the proceedings?[15]

From this point of view it can truthfully be said that, to the very end, the Caesar affair was open to opposing results. But another question also remains open: was Antony's Lupercalia role *a miscalculation*, a gesture of senseless servility, a mise-en-scène *arranged with Caesar*, or simply a provocation?

In a passage in his *Second Philippic*, Cicero says that by then Antony was afraid of Caesar the dictator.[16] This may be a further pointer to consider in trying to understand the scene at the Lupercalia. In spite of the extreme uncertainty over the meaning of that mysterious episode, there is much to suggest that it was a provocative gesture by a man filled with a deep fear of the dictator (*metus dictatoris*), rather than an expression of monarchical enthusiasm by a follower anticipating the wishes of his master. Apart from everything else, as Cicero observes, dictatorship 'had already usurped the might of regal authority'.[17]

Notes

1 Nicolaus of Damascus, *Life of Augustus* 20.68; Suetonius, *Caesar* 79. But it was Cleopatra who, despite some difficulty, took up residence in Rome.

2 This, I believe, is what Nicolaus of Damascus means in *Life of Augustus* 20.68.

3 Suetonius, *Caesar* 79.4. This refers to Caesar's uncle on his mother's side, Lucius Aurelius Cotta, a member of the council of fifteen, who was entrusted with the Sibylline Books.

4 As deputy consul, he would assume the office when Caesar departed for the East.

5 Nicolaus of Damascus, *Life of Augustus* 20ff. (§§ 69–75).

6 Plutarch, *Antony* 12.6.

7 Cicero, *Philippics* 1.84–7; 3.12; 13.17; 31; 42.

8 Plutarch, *Caesar* 62.10.

9 After the dictatorship for life, what were his plans? What weight would the other magistrates have in the constitutional picture?

10 Plutarch, *Caesar* 57.2–3.

11 Soon after the Ides of March, Antony found himself faced with the problem posed by Octavius, who assumed the role of Caesar's 'political heir'.

12 See Chapter 29. Plutarch had other information concerning such plots against Caesar: *Brutus* 8.2; *Antony* 11.6; *Moralia* 206ff. It suited

Octavian to keep alive such knowledge: a further reason for Plutarch to find more evidence.

13 The extent of Cicero's awareness remains uncertain, however.

14 Nicolaus of Damascus, *Life of Augustus* 23.81.

15 His presence at the place where Caesar and the *magister equitum* usually performed the ritual, as well as his active role in the performance, cannot be explained by his position of *praetor peregrinus*.

16 Cicero, *Second Philippic* 91: 'ob metum proximi dictatoris'.

17 Cicero, *First Philippic* 3: 'vim regiae potestatis obsederat'.

CHAPTER 32

The Dictatorship

> Caesarism [. . .] is entrusted with the task of 'arbitration' over a historico-political situation characterised by an equilibrium of forces heading towards catastrophe.
>
> Gramsci

It was the 'expansion' of the dictatorship that led to the crisis. Caesar's decision to identify his own real power (unprecedented in its extent) indefinitely with the traditional, constitutional dictatorship was not in reality a matter of choice. The dictatorship was the only instrument that allowed him freedom of action with respect to his followers. Here we shall review the stages through which the 'revitalisation' of the dictatorship had been achieved by the beginning of the civil war.

In an aside in the second book of his *Commentaries* on the civil war, in admirably modest and impersonal style, Caesar reports his own nomination as dictator. Returning home from Spain (August–September 49 BC) he passes through Tarragona, then Narbonne, and finally Marseilles. 'There he learns that a law had been passed about a dictator, and that *he himself* had been nominated dictator by the *praetor* M. Lepidus.'[1] Apart from the pleasant 'surprise' with which Caesar learns that *he himself* has been nominated to the dictatorship,[2] we should note the constitutional difficulty. According to the current regulations, the dictator had to be nominated by a consul: but in 49 both the consuls, Gaius Claudius Marcellus and Cornelius Lentulus Crus, had fled from Italy with Pompey. Hence the need for a new law permitting the magistrate highest in rank after the consuls, that is the *praetor*, to appoint a dictator. Lepidus, who had been duly elected to the praetorship in the previous year, put an end to a critical situation by nominating Caesar. He gave Caesar a veneer of legality, a highly controversial one, it is true, but this only served to make his position more favourable: the appearance of legality was essential.

Obviously the procedure that was followed was extremely questionable. Did a *praetor* have the right, in the *absence* of more senior
bearers of state office, to initiate legislation, especially on a matter as
delicate as the appointment of a dictator?

By the end of March, Cicero was expressing all his doubts about possible procedures of this kind in his letters to Atticus.[3] It was not difficult to guess that Caesar would be tempted to assume the dictatorship.
Besides, Caesar had been continually sending out signals that could
easily be interpreted (and this is how Cicero interpreted them) as
advances to eminent 'non-aligned' personages – Cicero was one – who
might support a legitimisation of his position. Now that the rift was
final he was, formally speaking, from a constitutional standpoint, an
'armed bandit' roving around Italy, unexpectedly deprived of legitimate
powers, and he had no intention of remaining in that unfavourable and
vulnerable position. Therefore – among other things – he wrote to
Cicero, each time calling him, with punctilious deference, *imperator*,[4]
not only to show his magnanimity, but also to seek advice and political
support. 'First I beg you, since I trust I shall quickly reach Rome, to let
me see you there, and employ your advice, favour, position and help of
all kinds' (5 March), and a few days later: 'I could wish you to meet me
at Rome that I may avail myself of your advice and resources, as usual,
in everything.' Cicero sent Atticus copies of both letters.[5] These insistent but ill-defined requests alarmed the already anxious and uncertain
Cicero. Shortly after receiving the first, he wrote to Atticus to forewarn
him of a very awkward request to *appear* to support Caesar in exploiting the *auctoritas* of a *praetor* (Lepidus!) in order to end his delicate
'illegal' position. He laments the fact that Caesar sends him expressions
of his respect, along with requests for 'counsel' and support. He well
understands where these requests will lead: to the problem of how
Caesar might secure his own investiture as dictator, since this, Cicero
foresaw, was the path by which Caesar would choose to legalise his own
authority, which he was still exercising only de facto. But, he adds,
quoting Homer, 'then let the wide earth swallow me!' And in clarification of his position he reasserts: 'But in our state books it is set down
that it is illegal not only for consuls to be created by the *praetors*, but
for the very *praetors* themselves, and that it has never been done.'[6] Some
days later Cicero writes again to Atticus, going into more detail and
showing increasing perplexity:

> he will want, I am sure, a decree of the Senate and a decree of the
> augurs (we shall be hurried off to Rome or harassed, if we are absent),

so that the *praetor* may hold an election of consuls or name a dictator, both acts unconstitutional. Though, if Sulla could arrange to be
named dictator by an interrex, why should not Caesar?[7]

Plutarch writes, incorrectly, that Caesar was appointed dictator by the
Senate (*Caesar* 37.2). In reality the Senate had been convened by
Caesar at the beginning of April 49 BC outside the city of Rome
(because 'a proconsul could not convoke the Senate and could not participate in the sitting in the city without deposing the *imperium*'),[8] but
after three days of sitting they had made no progress on any of the
items on the agenda. An end to the deadlock was achieved by Lepidus
– clearly on Caesar's suggestion – with the initiative which is acknowledged by Caesar in the *Commentaries*. A generally reliable source like
Dio Cassius says that Lepidus 'advised the people in his capacity as
praetor to elect Caesar dictator',[9] while Appian gives the more simplistic statement that the people elected Caesar dictator.[10] It has been
pointed out that the word employed by Dio ('advised' the people)
refers to a *contio* (an informal gathering of the people) rather than to
a comitial assembly.[11] This would also explain the expression used by
Appian and would resolve the problem surrounding the judicial form
to which Lepidus resorted in order to secure Caesar's nomination as
dictator. A crucial contribution was the popular support for the law
that authorised the *praetor* – in exceptional circumstances – to nominate the dictator. This was an 'exception' which not even Cicero, fully
mindful of the Sullan precedent, totally opposed. There is no substantial conflict between the sources here. It is entirely possible that
Lepidus sought popular support, or at least a semblance of it, for a
decision so fraught with disturbing consequences (and which would
ultimately result in Caesar's assumption of the dictatorship for life).
There is, however, by Dio – or his source – a very clear underscoring:
Lepidus in this operation acted 'against the traditional laws' (παρὰ τὰ
πάτρια). This signifies that the tradition to which Dio referred in these
books, presumably that of Livy, was distancing itself from Caesar's
'dictatorship': Augustus' constitutional political line would also turn
radically and demonstratively away from it.[12]

Caesar assumed the dictatorship *rei gerendae causa*, a magistracy
of limited duration always provided for in the Roman constitutional
system, with his customary self-assurance (he did not even appoint a
magister equitum) and with the intention of giving a firmer 'constitutional' guise to his own authority. He had barely taken office when he
convened the electoral meetings and had himself elected consul for the

following year (48 BC) with the *praetor* of the year 54 Publius Servilius Isauricus, an ex-supporter of Cato who had gone over to Caesar on the eve of the civil war and then remained his very loyal follower, and afterwards a very loyal follower of Octavius. In this way, at the start of the new year, Caesar found himself holding the dual role of dictator and consul. Nor did he hesitate to force the current regulations on delicate questions like the *praetors'* duties (distributed by him, and not by drawing lots) and the division of the provinces. In spite of these distortions, which were intended as signals of the freedom of action that Caesar reserved for himself in wartime and perhaps later, this was clearly no *dictatura rei publicae constituendae* (dictatorship for the restoration of the state), but precisely *dictatura rei gerendae causa*.[13] He used it, however, not only as a simple quasi-legal expedient to consolidate his position and advance from *rebel* to *consul in office*, but also to *implement a programme of government*.

His first acts as dictator, on his return to Rome, were clearly based on the traditional requests of the *populares*, but they were carried out with shrewd caution and the intention of not frightening the property-owners. Debts were not cancelled – a dominant and, in the eyes of the property-owners, typically 'Catilinarian' request. Instead, what might be termed a principle of 'equidistance' was established: debts had to be honoured, but the amounts would be set by reference to the pre-war value of the property, and to this end 'arbiters' were created to guarantee and supervise the course of the operation. The fact that Caesar gives much prominence to this measure at the start of the second commentary is highly significant.[14] The *Commentaries* are the vehicle of his propaganda on all levels, not only for questions concerning responsibility for the outbreak of the conflict, but also for other issues: the legitimacy of his power, his acts of government, the behaviour of his friends and enemies at war, his magnanimity in dealing with them, and so on. Here it is important for him to explain that he has refrained from falling in with the politically subversive tendencies characteristic of times of civil war. He established those rules – he specifies – 'to remove fear of *tabulae novae*': wording which in the Roman political struggle classically expressed the *populares'* request to cancel debts, and which, not long ago and in circumstances all too familiar to Caesar, had been the most persuasive and effective of Catiline's slogans.[15] While the worst suspicions were circulating about Caesar's true intentions, Cicero also wondered if he was about to move against the well-to-do by proclaiming *tabulae novae* against them.[16] In presenting the fairness to all classes of his decision on the burning problem of debt, Caesar deliberately dwells at unusual length on a political consideration designed to please all right-thinking people. Demands of this kind, he observes, are 'apt to follow war and civil strife'. But with the measure he had adopted, he concludes, the fear of subversive measures is dispelled, while at the same time an *existimatio aequa*, a *'fair estimate' to the advantage of the debtors*, was guaranteed.[17] And to reaffirm the fair and non-revolutionary character of his measure, a few chapters further on he provides a detailed description of the turmoil caused by the *praetor* Marcus Caelius Rufus, who espoused 'the cause of the debtors'.[18]

Since Caesar clearly does not mean, in the *Commentaries* on the civil war, to tell the domestic story of Rome during the conflict, it is evident that this 'digression' into internal politics in the course of the military account has a purpose: to demonstrate that the new government not only knew how to govern, but, if necessary, how to use a firm hand against intriguers and fomenters of social chaos. The description of the disorders provoked by Caelius Rufus is masterly from the propagandist viewpoint. The thread running through the account is that Caelius continually brandishes the threat of 'turning to Caesar' to obtain support for his radical programme, and instead he is liquidated by Caesar's men. Caesar 'unmasks' the suspicious extremism of Caelius: he *says* he wants to 'take refuge with Caesar', but in fact he secretly he makes contact with Milo, Clodius' assassin, who had disappeared in 52 BC and retired to Marseilles after the sentence from which Cicero had not been able to save him.[19] In his turn, Milo comes out of the shadows and he, the murderer of Clodius, confidently takes up the cause of the disgruntled debtors, and does so proclaiming himself 'Pompey's emissary'![20] There could be no more striking example of the 'unprincipled' nature of the agitation. Milo, in league with Caelius (who refers to Caesar), does not hesitate to press for the same 'extreme' programme but in Pompey's name, and to resort to the slaves confined in their *ergastula* (slave compounds) in the Hirpine countryside.[21] The genuine Caesarians, Quintus Pedius and Gaius Trebonius, do their duty and oppose the two intriguers, who are both liquidated.[22] Caelius does not hesitate *in extremis* to play one last card, bribing Caesar's reserve troops (Gauls and Spaniards) stationed in Thurii, but he is killed by them. 'Thus', comments Caesar, concluding this effective 'didactic' digression, 'the first outbreak of a serious movement, which kept Italy harassed by the burden of work imposed on the magistrates by the crisis, came promptly and easily to an end.'[23]

Another measure that Caesar points out, with due emphasis, at the beginning of the second commentary is the one regarding the reinstatement into civil life of those convicted of bribery under the *Lex Pompeia de ambitu*. It is well known that corruption was the normal and pervasive practice in the electoral struggles of the 'free republic'. Ever since the triumvirate had fixed in advance the electoral results in the vote for the chief magistracies, nobody – perhaps not even the upright Cato – could maintain he had nothing to do with the practice of electoral 'dealing'. Therefore the trials for 'fraud' were only an extension of the struggle between the parties, and had nothing to do with morality. Everyone knew this and the trials ended variously, depending on the balance of forces. Hence the law which Caesar presents in his *Commentaries* in a spirit of unalloyed party solidarity: it sprang from the trials initiated and directed by the opposing party. Far-reaching amendments were needed to rectify their effects and ensure the political reintegration of those who had suffered. Here too Caesar weighs his words very precisely: first of all the initiative for the operation is attributed, as is correct on the procedural level, to the *praetors* and tribunes; then he adds vaguely that some (*nonnullos*, so not a great number) will benefit by the measure. However, from the context it appears that it cannot have been quite as he says, seeing that the victims of those unjust trials were not exactly few 'in those critical times when Pompey had kept in Rome a detachment of his troops as a bodyguard (*praesidia legionum*)' and 'the trials had been carried through, *each in a single day*, with one set of judges hearing the evidence and another voting on the issue'.[24] And here he adds a clarification: that at the beginning of the conflict some of these 'political prisoners' had offered to collaborate with him, but he had preferred that their rehabilitation should not occur through his personal clemency, but by '*iudicio populi*'. He did not want to appear either ungrateful in repaying the assistance he had received, or arrogant in usurping a right which belonged to the people.[25] And to complete the group of politically symbolic measures, he also wanted to annul a shameful measure that still remained as part of Sulla's legacy: he returned in full the civil rights of the children of the exiles.[26]

This move sent a very clear propaganda 'signal' of compensation that was almost 'owed' to the *popularis* party. There was, then, in this first, very short dictatorship of Caesar – which ended immediately after the passing of those measures, coinciding with the *Feriae latinae* of the year 48 BC, when Caesar travelled to Brindisi to confront Pompey directly[27] – a skilful blend of moderation and political clarity. At a time when Caesar was re-enacting Sulla's decision to use the institution of the dictatorship (having obtained it, like Sulla, by the most brazen of means), an anti-Sulla signal was more necessary than ever. Necessary because the watchword of his programme had been anti-Sullan from the start. His 'manifesto', the open letter to Oppius and Balbus (written at the end of February 49 BC), a copy of which also reached Cicero, contained the firm statement: 'I do not intend to imitate Sulla.'[28] And in the rousing speeches with which he had stirred up his troops after crossing the Rubicon, when he had produced before them the tribunes of the plebs who had been driven from Rome, victims of the faction which controlled the Senate, his dominant theme had been that his personal enemies were about to eliminate those last guarantees of the tribunes' freedom that Sulla had left untouched.

However, as we well know, the policy 'manifesto' was clear on one other point: Caesar did not intend to present himself as being beholden *to any particular party*. 'Let us see', he had written in his 'open letter' to Oppius and Balbus at the critical moment of the conflict, when he found himself simply in the position of a rebel against the legally constituted authority,

> if by moderation we can win all hearts (*omnium voluntates*) and secure a lasting victory [he speaks of victory when he has only a few legions on his side and the war has yet to be fought!], since by cruelty others have been unable to escape from hatred and to maintain their victory for any length of time except L. Sulla, whose example I do not intend to follow.

In these lines it is usual – and quite correct – to give emphasis to the reference to Sulla. But, to those able to read between the lines, Caesar may also be seen distancing himself from the model of Marius, the man who continued to be a 'myth' of the Roman plebs, and whose statues he himself, as a *popularis*, had had restored.[29] To whom else could he be referring when he speaks of those who clung to the illusion that *crudelitas* could bolster their power, and lost it because of the *odium* they incurred? Clearly to Marius and Cinna, whom he knew well. He had followed in their wake; as a young man he had suffered Sulla's persecution for his loyalty to that faction, but he knew very well where they had gone wrong, where that faction had revealed its weaknesses and the narrowness of its horizons. When his time came, he would also re-erect Pompey's statues and those of Sulla, torn down by the crowd in the enthusiasm over Caesar's victory.[30]

It can certainly be claimed that the words written to Oppius and Balbus were merely propaganda, and this is no doubt true from a 'technical' point of view. A letter of that kind, written to people who were his closest 'comrades-in-arms', makes no sense if it was intended *only for those two addressees*. It was intended for all the others. It was written so that those two could make its contents known. And it has come down to us because Balbus passed it at the right time to Cicero (a man Caesar fully intended to have on his side, or at least in a neutral position), and Cicero sent a copy of it to Atticus (who put it away and then published it with the other letters sent to him by Cicero). But propaganda does not mean falseness, although it is commonly understood in a pejorative sense. The politician's skill lies precisely in putting about propaganda which is demonstrably fairly consistent with the facts. And this is one of Caesar's major advantage points over his opponents. *Omnium voluntates reciperare*: these are not simply seductive words designed to sway senators who are wavering and confused by the civil war. This is a programme to be implemented immediately: from the moment when, for the first time, between the surrender of Marseilles and the departure for Pharsalus, Caesar is able to exploit the instrument of the dictatorship.

Notes

1 Caesar, *Civil War* 2.21.5.
2 'Seseque dictatorem dictum'.
3 Cicero, *Letters to Atticus* 9.9.3; 9.15.3.
4 Cicero's title after the military successes in Cilicia, a title he certainly did not hold at this time.
5 Cicero, *Letters to Atticus* 9.6A; 9.16.
6 Cicero, *Letters to Atticus* 9.9.3 (17 March 49 BC).
7 Cicero, *Letters to Atticus* 9.15.2 (25 March).
8 F. De Martino, *Storia della costituzione romana*, 2nd edn, vol. III (Naples 1973), p. 228.
9 Dio Cassius 41.36.1.
10 Appian, *Civil Wars* 2.48.196.
11 On the discussion of the constitutional problems connected with Caesar's dictatorship, see De Martino, *Storia della costituzione romana*, pp. 228–31 (and in particular n. 37).

12 The fact that an 'Augustan' historian like Dionysius of Halicarnassus stresses that the brutal murder of Romulus by the senators in the Senate was a consequence of his turn towards tyrannical rule is a clear indication of his condemnation of Caesar's 'errors'.

13 Compare this hypothesis of Mommsen with De Martino, *Storia della costituzione romana* p. 232.

14 Caesar, *Civil War* 3.1. It is fair to describe this so-called third book as the 'second' commentary. See the edition of *Bellum civile* edited by A. Klotz, 2nd edn (Leipzig 1952), p. vi, and the one edited by P. Fabre (Collection Budé), vol. I (Paris 1936), pp. xvi–xvii.

15 See Sallust, *Catilinarian Conspiracy* 20.13 and 21.2; Cicero, *Catilinarian* 2.8 and 18, and more generally Suetonius, *Caesar* 42.3.

16 Cicero, *Letters to Atticus* 5.21.13.

17 Caesar, *Civil War* 3.1.2–3.

18 Caesar, *Civil War* 3.20.1. On Caelius, see Chapter 22.

19 Caesar, *Civil War* 3.21.4.

20 Caesar, *Civil War* 3.22.1: 'sent dispatches to the effect that in what he was doing he was acting by the order and authority of Pompey'.

21 Caesar, *Civil War* 3.21.2.

22 Both died painfully. Trebonius plotted against Caesar and was assassinated by Dolabella in Asia in 43 BC. Pedius became a colleague in Octavius' consulate after the coup in August 43, but died suddenly at the beginning of the proscriptions, which he opposed.

23 Caesar, *Civil War* 3.22.4. On all of this see Chapter 22.

24 Caesar, *Civil War* 3.1.4.

25 Caesar, *Civil War* 3.1.5.

26 Plutarch, *Caesar* 37.2. Dio Cassius (41.18.2) puts this at the beginning of the conflict, when Caesar had just invaded Italy and had not yet embarked upon his Spanish campaign against Afranius and Petreius. However, it is much more likely that it occurred as a result of the initiatives taken after formalisation of his powers.

27 Caesar, *Civil War* 3.2.1.

28 Compare Cicero, *Letters to Atticus* 9.7C: 'quem imitaturus non sum'. On this see Chapter 19.

29 Suetonius, *Caesar* 11; Plutarch, *Caesar* 6.1. This episode has been variously dated, but is from the beginning of his career.

30 Suetonius, *Caesar* 75.4.

CHAPTER 33

Epicureans in Revolt?

The historian who claimed that persons of Epicurean belief dominated the conspiracy against Caesar, and that Epicureanism, creatively reformulated in the fifth book of Lucretius, underpinned the anti-monarchic rebellion of these 'Epicureans in revolt', was Arnaldo Momigliano.[1] His belligerent essay is compelling but largely unfounded, especially in its central tenets: that the conspirators and later republican fighters were mostly 'unconventional' (that is, politically committed) Epicureans, and that Lucretius was their formative reading. It remains a good article on the aesthetic level, extolling the 'heroic' nexus between Epicureanism in philosophy and militant libertarian republicanism in politics. For Momigliano, writing that daring essay was a kind of catharsis, after years of prose calibrated according to its compatibility with the 'controlled tolerance' of fascism and that of the *Enciclopedia Italiana*.[2] For the sake of his thesis he expands the circle of the Epicureans,[3] and, if by chance any are hostile to the conspiracy or want nothing to do with it, they are enlisted all the same. This is the case with Statilius, an 'Epicurean' who, Plutarch clearly affirms, immediately rejected the advances of the person who wanted to bring him into the conspiracy – no less a figure than Marcus Junius Brutus in person. That man might not be the same Statilius who had been in Africa with Cato and then died at Philippi: at least, there is no reliable confirmation of it. But, even if he were, it should be pointed out that, despite a glorious 'republican' career, he flatly refused to join the conspiracy. His example, then, would serve if anything to demonstrate the Epicureans' *lack of enthusiasm* for that way of fighting, not their support. Equally incredible are the deductions concerning Philodemus' book *On the good king according to Homer*, which, apart from everything else, was written in the house of Caesar's father-in-law. For Momigliano, that book was definitely 'an appeal for moderation' written 'in the years of Caesar's dictatorship'.[4] How this can be deduced from the title of the work, and from the fact that Piso, Caesar's father-in-law and host of the good Philodemus, was 'a moderate', Zeus alone knows. Almost anything can be asserted, except that Caesar – after the victory – needed appeals 'for moderation'. It was his *clementia* that was his downfall, as the audience that boldly applauded the line of verse from Pacuvius' *Armorum iudicium*, which was recited at the funeral games in Caesar's honour, well knew: 'Saved I these men that they might murder me?'[5] If one wished to indulge a taste for the hypothetical, one could just as well argue a diametrically opposite case: that the good Philodemus' treatise on the monarchy – if it really was intended to be topical – was a declaration *in favour of* the monarchy, which was in the air during Caesar's last months.

Republican enthusiasm, then, imposes blinkers from the very start: even the date of Cassius' 'conversion' to Epicureanism is incorrect. For Momigliano it is 46 BC, and the source to support this date is Cicero's letter to Cassius (*Letters to his friends* 15.16),[6] in which he jokes about the unsatisfactory translation of the Epicurean εἴδωλον as *spectrum*. That letter, however, which for unclear reasons has been dated in the year 45 BC, shows that Cassius' 'conversion' must have come about some time earlier. Cicero writes, 'it is now two or three years since you were seduced by the wiles of Miss Pleasure (Epicureanism) into serving notice of divorce on Lady Virtue (Stoicism)'.[7] He is speaking of a 'conversion' that occurred much earlier: if 'biennium aut triennium' (period of two or three years) means anything, it seems that Cassius had loudly proclaimed himself an Epicurean and behaved accordingly soon after the defeat at Pharsalus, when he went over to Caesar's side. It was, then, a gesture of submission, even one of conformist support for a philosophy whose adherents were said to include Caesar, rather than its opposite, a decision to take up the struggle against tyranny and against Caesar.[8]

As Momigliano's argument progresses, these ardent republican Epicureans are reduced to Cassius alone. To see M. Valerius Messalla Corvinus as one of them is a fantasy, since Horace says of him that he is 'steeped in Socratic lore'.[9] In the end Momigliano gives up: 'nothing can explain his [Cassius'] switch from orthodox Epicureanism to heroic Epicureanism'.[10] In fact, further studies have shown how confused and inauthentic was the Epicureanism that Cassius began to profess at a certain point.[11] The truest portrait of Cassius is probably by Appian, who depicts him with all his physical and intellectual energies single-mindedly intent on war, on the struggle, just as gladiators in the arena focus all their energy on their opponents.[12] This portrait has nothing in common with the public behaviour inspired by the philosophy of the Garden.

Perhaps Cassius' 'conversion' to Epicureanism is not a purely private event. Even Caesar's polemical relentlessness in *Anticato* against the hero of Stoicism who was continuing to win over so many, especially among the young, is not the product of a purely philosophical opposition. Cicero – as we have seen – informs us about Cassius' 'conversion'. His correspondence with Cassius, a very small part of which is preserved in book 15 of the *Letters to his friends*,[13] is the most important source on this subject, not only because it provides a chronology ('two or better three years ago'), but also because it jokingly yet clearly suggests an unfortunate external factor behind this conversion. Of particular importance is the point where he says that Cassius had been dislodged from his original Stoic belief *vi hominibus armatis* (by the force of armed men),[14] that is, following Caesar's victory at Pharsalus and the surrender of Cassius, who became *ipso facto* the victor's lieutenant. Although put humorously, it gives a clear indication of chronology: in going over to Caesar after Pharsalus (August 48), Cassius also discarded his Stoic convictions and embraced Epicureanism, the philosophy of his new master. Cicero expresses himself in allusions, indirectly suggesting that Cassius had been under compulsion, and pretending in jest that he wishes to ask the *praetor* to intercede and restore Cassius in his former estate (the Stoic philosophy).[15]

Cassius' behaviour throughout the civil war was rather puzzling, at least judging from what Cicero says, be it only through hints. The most important letter for the reconstruction of Cassius' behaviour is the one from Cicero in Brindisi to Cassius in August 47.[16] Cicero recalls their long conversation ('sermo familiaris meus tecum', etc.) before the outbreak of the conflict and during its early stages. It seems clear that both were in a state of some consternation ('hoping for peace and hating civil bloodshed'), and resolved to place their hopes in the outcome of a single battle which they thought imminent. It was a hope dashed by the unforeseen duration of military operations and the time lost in the Alexandrian war, thanks to which Cicero was still stranded at Brindisi, alarmed by Pompey's rearmament in Africa, and waiting in vain for Caesar to return. At the end of this important letter Cicero provides a piece of valuable and surprising information. He says that Cassius had written to him from Luceria (Lucera) – in the spring of 49, therefore, before Pompey and the republican 'general staff' left Italy – and urged him *not* to embrace Pompey's cause, but to remain in Italy.[17] It is an obvious sign of Cassius' lack of confidence in the army he had joined.

Shortly after Pharsalus, Cassius had chosen not just to surrender, but to join Caesar. Cicero enviously reminded him: 'You made for a quarter where you would be present at the making of decisions and able to foresee events to come', receiving 'the best comfort for an anxious mind'.[18] It seems almost to describe the tasks and benefits of an 'infiltrator', of one who has positioned himself close to the figure whose decisions and actions he wants to know in advance. Moreover, Cicero also knows that as early as 47 BC, when Caesar visited Cilicia after leaving Syria, Cassius had organised an attack on the dictator that came within a hair's breadth of success.[19] A speedy transfer, then, to the side of the victor, followed immediately by an attempt to get rid of him: this may be the earliest existing report of an attempt on Caesar's life. And already it reveals the ambivalence of Cassius' behaviour: he reluctantly follows Pompey, immediately goes over to Caesar after Pharsalus, straight away gains his trust, becomes his adviser, and embraces his philosophical beliefs, then attempts to murder him, even before the idea of a conspiracy has taken shape in the minds of others.[20] Once again this seems to be the shrewd, calculating and decisive behaviour of an infiltrator.

The rest of the correspondence (there is very little) between Cicero and Cassius before the Ides of March of 44 BC is evasive and raises suspicions. It is not clear, for example, to what extent the discussion of Catius' *spectra* and the uncouth Roman Epicureans can be read for what it first seems to be, a purely philological disquisition with little purpose, since it deals with things that are well known to both of them. Or is it a private joke concealing some deeper meaning? We recall what Cicero and Atticus wrote about the advisability of resorting to a coded language.[21] Then there is the clear expression of hostility, by Cassius in the same letter, towards Pompey the Younger, and his significant statement that he prefers 'the old easy-going master' (Caesar, it seems) to a cruel new one (Pompey the Younger). Is this a re-emergence of the hostility towards Pompey that prompted Cassius to write his letter from Luceria with advice to Cicero, which Cicero regretted not having followed? Does it point to a now irreparable rift between the unyielding Pompeians and the 'young ones' who surrendered after Pharsalus? Perhaps too there is the underlying fear that, if Pompey the Younger were victorious, his first victims would be those erstwhile comrades-in-arms who had deserted him at the first setback.

All of Cassius' behaviour, then, appears to be marked by ambivalence. His 'conversion' has convinced neither ancient nor modern scholars. When Seneca (*Letters to Lucilius* 83.12), for example, observes that 'all his life Cassius drank only water', he means above all to point out a mode of life far from relaxed Epicurean ease and much more in keeping with the ascetic harshness of an exemplary Stoic. But it is mainly the prolix argument that Cassius inflicts on Brutus, reported in Plutarch's *Life of Brutus*,[22] that arouses suspicions. The theory there set forth, which denies the value of feelings and calls them 'notoriously deceptive', stands wholly within the Platonic-Aristotelian tradition and in complete opposition to Epicurean doctrine. Cassius' thesis that visions (such as the ghost seen by Brutus before Philippi) have no substance but are figments of our imagination is at odds with the Epicurean idea according to which those visions are real and so prove the existence of the gods.[23] Plutarch tells us that Cassius, before joining in the attack on Caesar in the Senate, 'turning his eyes toward the statue of Pompey before the attack began, invoked it silently', and comments that such a gesture by Cassius was very strange, seeing that he was close to the doctrines of Epicurus. Plutarch expresses himself cautiously here: he does not say that Cassius professed Epicureanism as his philosophy (or his 'faith'); he says that 'he was not averse, ἀλλότριος, to the Epicurean doctrines'.[24]

It is also very strange that Brutus, a well-known authority on Greek philosophy, should need Cassius' banal and inconsistent explanations. Strange too that Cassius, as an 'Epicurean', should always be invoked in relation to a single subject: the theory of the *imagines*/εἴδωλα. This is what he discusses with Brutus, according to Plutarch,[25] and Cicero teases him about it,[26] taking as his starting point Catius' poor translation (*spectra*) of the term that is usual in Epicurus' texts. The impression is given that Cassius does not know much else.

Plutarch's account is important in another respect. Perhaps it was Messalla, his source, who enhanced his hero's philosophical consistency by making him speak as an Epicurean even *in articulo mortis* (at the moment of death), on the eve of Philippi, thus responding indirectly to the doubts of those who saw Cassius' 'conversion' as closely linked with his surrender to Caesar. Cassius' correspondence with Cicero, on the other hand, offers first-hand documents in which the hero speaks directly. And yet they are tortuous documents, not only because of their ironical, almost paradoxical tone, but especially because of the strange 'complicity' between the two correspondents, who should have been 'crossing swords', so great is their philosophical disagreement.[27]

And yet, most of all the impression remains that Cassius and Cicero were speaking of something else under the veil of their philosophical debate. The suspicion takes shape if one considers Cassius' letter in reply to Cicero's 'provocation'. Apart from the jokes about the painful translation of εἴδωλον as *spectrum*, Cicero had rebuked Cassius, three years late,[28] for having 'divorced himself from virtue' two or three years previously. And Cassius replies, again explaining to Cicero what Cicero knows full well and has taught to others (for example, when he has Torquatus speak in *De finibus*), that Epicurus is not against virtue: Epicurus deems that pleasure requires 'a life conducted with nobility and justice'.[29] But he does not stop there; he gives examples from contemporary politics and the behaviour of particular individuals. 'Thus it is that Pansa,' he continues, 'whose goal is *Pleasure*,[30] retains Virtue [*virtutem retinet*].' And immediately afterwards he expands on this: 'And those whom you and your friends call *Pleasure-lovers*[31] are *Good-lovers and Justice-lovers*, practising and retaining all the virtues [*virtutes et colunt et retinent*].'[32]

Here Cassius, prudently and under the guise of philosophy, is providing a piece of new information: the behaviour and actions of Pansa (the consul), and certain people whom he does not name but identifies by reference to their Epicurean beliefs, *are guided by virtue*. It is known that the security of private correspondence is generally short-lived, and especially so in the letter-writing of the ancients. Cicero writes to Atticus (July 59, during Caesar's first consulate):

> Some time I will give you a clear account if I find a very trusty messenger; or if I veil my meaning you will manage to understand it. In these letters I will call myself Laelius and you Furius: and convey the rest *in riddles*.[33]

It is likely that the message contained in these lines is that the conduct of certain people, known to both of them, is *guided by virtue*. No doubt he means political 'virtue', but his more precise meaning is obscure.

Cassius continues with hints that are even less transparent, if his words are to be taken literally: 'And so Sulla,' he writes, '*whose judgement we must respect* [*cuius iudicium probare debemus*], saw that the philosophers were at loggerheads: instead of trying to discover what was good, he went and bought up all the goods he could find!' (A reference to the acquisition en masse of goods belonging to those who had been exiled.) These appear to be casual words, but of course they are not. For one thing, they reveal a detached scepticism with regard to philosophical disputes over 'what is Good', making fun of them by playing on *bonum* (in the philosophical sense) and *bona* (in the material sense). This kind of mockery ill befits a defender of the 'Epicurean idea of Good' in dispute with adherents of other philosophies, which is the way Cassius wishes to present himself in the first part of his letter. The word-play is possible only because of the somewhat surprising reference to Sulla.[34] The statement 'we must respect Sulla's *iudicium*' is also puzzling. Tyrrell and Purser get round it by saying that the expression is ironic: but that would only make sense if it made sense to involve Sulla in this discussion, which began as a defence of the Epicurean ἡδονή against its detractors! The dialectical somersault by which one proceeds from a discussion of the primacy of Pleasure/Virtue to a gratuitous play on the words *bonum/bona* (Good/goods) seems essentially to be based on the phrase 'we must respect Sulla's judgement'. But what is the purpose of such a declaration? In Roman politics it would have sounded decidedly odd: especially in a dialogue between people who – like Cicero at that period – have repeatedly declared their *abhorrence* for the Sullan model. We should bear in mind, however, that it was Sulla who desired the physical elimination of the young Caesar, and that he had replied harshly to those who had intervened to save him: 'Have your way and take him; only bear in mind that the man you are so eager to save will one day deal the death blow to the cause of the aristocracy [*optimates*].'[35] Is this perhaps the 'judgement of Sulla' which 'we must respect'? The skilful interweaving of this question with the philosophical theme of Good, a theme into which Sulla is unexpectedly introduced, serves to make clear that the discussion is not about philosophy, but rather a *iudicium* of Sulla, which must be approved: in short, a clear *reminder* of the necessity of at least doing now what Sulla had been unable to do.

Even more cryptic are the words that follow: 'I have borne his death with fortitude.' Why would Cassius, who at the time was still a child, have been distressed by Sulla's death (78 BC)? But here too a hint will be concealed, since immediately afterwards a connection between Sulla and Caesar is established: 'Caesar will not let us miss him [Sulla] long.'[36] The unusual expression might mean that Caesar is to be eliminated, so we shall no longer have to 'miss' Sulla, that is, it invokes the figure who wanted to eliminate Caesar once and for all.

With the end of this part, which has some meaning only if it is seen as a coded message,[37] Cassius emphasises that *now, at this point in his letter*, he is returning to political matters (and therefore what has gone before is not political). He writes: 'Now *to get back to public affairs*, let me know in your reply how things are going in Spain.' It is the end of January in the year 45 BC and Caesar is grappling with the most difficult campaign of the long civil war, against Pompey's sons, in Further Spain.[38] Cassius continues, showing his preference for a victory by Caesar over one by Pompey the Younger, of whom he paints a harsh and alarming portrait. A portrait in which he counts on Cicero's approval: '*You know* what a fool Gnaeus is, how he takes cruelty for virtue,[39] how he thinks we always made fun of him.' (After the defeat at Pharsalus, Cicero himself had almost fallen victim to the cruelty of Pompey the Younger.) Behind these words are, certainly, hatred and reciprocal intolerance, and above all the different paths that, after Pharsalus, were taken on the one hand by Cicero and Cassius (and Brutus), and on the other by the sons of Pompey and Cato: another war is involved, fought in Africa and lost at Thapsus, one that caused a rift between these 'ex-Pompeians'. So (writing, moreover, 'in clear') while the military prospects are extremely uncertain, Cassius can say here that he 'would rather have the old easygoing master than try a cruel new one'.[40]

This letter, written a year before the attempt on Caesar's life, in which Cassius was the prime mover, is a document that we can only partially decipher. It comes at the end of book 15 of Cicero's *Letters to his friends*, in a batch of letters which testify to the close ties between Cicero and two figures from different groups who stood out most clearly in the plots against Caesar: Cassius and Trebonius. This letter should not be read in isolation; it assumes significance in its documentary context: from it emerges vividly a Cicero who is the confidant of those most determined to destroy the dictator.

Notes

1 See his review of B. Farrington's *Science and Politics in the Ancient World* (1939), *JRS*, 31 (1941), pp. 149–57 (also in A. Momigliano, *Secondo contributo alla storia degli studi classici* [Rome 1960]). I refer particularly to the second part of this review, entitled 'Epicureans in Revolt'.

2 His article 'Roma. Impero' in the *Enciclopedia Italiana di scienze, lettere ed arti* (Rome 1936), vol. XXIX, is a typical example. In it he wrote that Caesar 'had created an image of himself which drew on the deepest

currents of all of ancient history' (p. 628); of the conspirators he writes that they confused their own freedom with 'freedom itself' (p. 629; a remark with much truth in it).

3 Thanks to C. Castner, *Prosopography of Roman Epicureans* (Frankfurt 1988), we now have a clearer picture. Castner too (p. 31) finds the thesis developed in 'Epicureans in Revolt' untenable.

4 Momigliano, *Secondo contributo*, p. 380.

5 Suetonius, *Caesar* 84.

6 Momigliano, *Secondo contributo*, p. 379.

7 Cicero, *Letters to his friends* 15.16.3.

8 This objection against Momigliano was raised by J. Carcopino, *Les Secrets de la correspondance de Cicéron* (Paris 1947), vol. II, p. 247, n. 6.

9 Horace, *Odes* 3.21.9.

10 Momigliano, *Secondo contributo*, p. 387.

11 See Castner, *Prosopography*, p. 31.

12 Appian, *Civil Wars* 4.133, 561.

13 Most of their correspondence is at the beginning of book 12.

14 Cicero, *Letters to his friends* 14.16.3.

15 On this see the very valuable commentary by R. Y. Tyrrell and L. C. Purser, *Correspondence of M. T. Cicero*, vol. IV, 2nd edn (Dublin and London 1918), p. 523.

16 Cicero, *Letters to his friends* 15.15.

17 Cicero, *Letters to his friends* 15.15.4.

18 '[ut] futura animo prospicere posses': Cicero, *Letters to his friends* 15.15.3.

19 Cicero, *Philippics* 2.26. There is no reason to assume any confusion on the part of Cicero with the Lucius Cassius mentioned by Suetonius, *Caesar* 63.

20 It would soon occur to the Caesarians themselves, as we know from *Philippics* 2.34.

21 Cicero, *Letters to Atticus* 2.19 and 20.

22 Plutarch, *Life of Brutus* 37.

23 See Castner, *Prosopography*, p. 31, and above all F. E. Brenk, 'In Mist Apparelled: Religious Themes in Plutarch's *Moralia* and *Lives*', *Mnemosyne*, Suppl. 48 (1977), p. 124, n. 14.

24 Plutarch, *Caesar* 66.

25 Plutarch is apparently relying on the evidence of the book by Messalla Corvinus.

26 Cicero, *Letters to his friends* 15.16 (February 45).

27 Cassius speaks of 'omnes Catii et Amalfinii mali verborum interpretes' (15.19) just as contemptuously as Cicero in his *Tusculanae*. In *Civil Wars* 2.112, Appian wonders whether the 'clash' between Brutus and Cassius over the praetorship was staged to give the appearance of dissension between them and dispel the impression of excessive closeness. The

theory which Appian formulates (with his source) reinforces the view of Cassius's 'conversion' to Epicureanism as cold-blooded and calculating.

28 'Iam biennium aut triennium est . . .'

29 This precept is found in his *Letter to Menoeceus* (= Diogenes Laertius 10.132).

30 He uses the Greek word, meaning to indicate a follower of Epicurus.

31 In Greek again, as a technical term from philosophical polemics.

32 Cicero, *Letters to his friends* 15.19.2–3 (Cassius to Cicero).

33 Cicero, *Letters to Atticus* 2.19. Tyrrell and Purser confuse this letter 'in riddles', which may not have survived, with *Letters to his friends* 5.7, in which Cicero says that he would like to play the same role vis-à-vis Pompey that Laelius played vis-à-vis Scipio. Cicero himself says here (*Letters to Atticus* 2.20) that there is no need to resort to the code of changing Atticus' name.

34 Sulla, however, was not personally involved in the acquisition of the exiles' property.

35 See Chapter 1.

36 This is followed by, 'He has other victims of justice to offer us in his place' (*Letters to his friends* 15.19). This is utterly obscure, and Tyrrell and Purser are prudently silent about it.

37 'If I have to write in fuller detail to you I shall hide my meaning under covert language', wrote Cicero to Atticus in another letter in 59 BC (*Letters to Atticus* 2.20).

38 Cicero, *Letters to his friends* 15.19.4.

39 The term 'virtue', so central to this letter, is used again.

40 'Malo veterem et clementem dominum habere quam novum et crudelem experiri.' The portrait of Pompey the Younger is a 'Sullan' one. This is made clearer by the preceding sentence, in which Sulla is invoked not in order to praise him, but for the sake of obscure allusions.

CHAPTER 34

The Hetairia of Cassius and the Recruitment of Brutus

There is a tradition that pays particular attention to the role of Cassius in the events leading to Caesar's murder. It emerges here and there in the sources and may well provide a valuable element of information. The clearest text is also the most interesting: Plutarch's account of the coup at the beginning of his *Life of Brutus*, which uses sources very close to the events and the protagonist. He relies on *Brutus* by Emphylos, the Rhodian rhetorician who remained Brutus' friend and confidant to the very end, as well as the biography written by Brutus' stepson, Marcus Calpurnius Bibulus, the son of the first marriage of Porcia (Brutus' wife and Cato's daughter) to Bibulus, Caesar's colleague in the consulate of 59 BC.[1] These are primary sources of the first rank, and the whole of Plutarch's account bespeaks a view favourable to Brutus, which derives from Plutarch's own intellectual sympathies as well as from those sources.

Describing the beginning of the conspiracy, Plutarch tells how Brutus was gradually won over by Cassius to the idea of eliminating the 'tyrant' by assassination, despite the very high favour he enjoyed with Caesar. Here Plutarch uses a particularly significant expression: 'Indeed, had he wished it, he might have been first among Caesar's friends and exercised the greatest power; but the party (*hetairia*)[2] of Cassius drew him away from such a course.'[3] In the rest of his account Plutarch clearly describes the further efforts of 'Cassius' *hetairia*' to draw Brutus in. Since Brutus was still ill-disposed towards Cassius, who had done his best to obstruct his appointment as urban *praetor* for the year 44,[4] Cassius did not approach him directly but sent 'his friends' (the *hetairia*, to use Plutarch's term). These friends made unremitting efforts to persuade Brutus, continually pointing out that Caesar meant to 'tempt' and 'soften' him; and exhorted him not to accept 'the tyrant's kindnesses and favours'.[5]

All these events, be it noted in passing, deserve attention because they reveal the determination and long-term vision behind Cassius' actions. Cassius sensed the vulnerable points in Brutus' psychology, and, notwithstanding the friction caused by their rivalry for the urban praetorship, he decided to focus on him. Brutus, as a nephew of Cato, was an excellent 'ornament' and living monument to Caesar's reconciliation policy. Cassius prudently chose arguments that could pierce the psyche of a man of whom Caesar, his fatherly protector, said, 'I know not what this young man wants, but all that he wants he wants very much.'[6] And he orchestrated a campaign to win over the man who would be the 'heart and soul' of the conspiracy.

The expression 'the *hetairia* of Cassius' has its analogue in Appian's *Civil Wars*, a particularly valuable account. At the end of book 2, in the story of the attempt on Caesar, the phrases 'the party of Cassius' and 'Cassius and his friends'[7] recur several times. This probably means that the group headed by Cassius kept its identity even after the conspiracy widened to include other followers (beginning with Brutus) and became operational. There is, then, in the sources closest to the events and protagonists,[8] and therefore the most important, an awareness of the existence of a politically active circle, sufficiently organised to merit the term *hetairia*, led by Cassius; and for some time Cassius had been working with determination to prepare his spectacular coup.

Plutarch had no doubt that the real author of the conspiracy was Cassius. It was he who, with his *hetairia*, urged Brutus to join the conspiracy,[9] and he who, after due preparation by the 'friends', went to Brutus to overcome his last hesitations.[10] There is one further striking detail: Cassius shows that he knows *who* is covering the city with inscriptions urging Brutus to act. According to Plutarch, Cassius asked him the awkward question:

> Dost thou think that thy tribunal was covered with inscriptions by weavers and hucksters, *and not by the foremost and most influential citizens*? From their other *praetors* they demand gifts and spectacles and gladiatorial combats; but from thee, as a debt thou owest to thy lineage, the abolition of the tyranny.[11]

Just before this, Plutarch informs us of the powerful effect of that 'mural' campaign on Brutus' thinking: 'Brutus was exhorted and incited to the undertaking by many arguments from his comrades, and by many utterances and writings from his fellow citizens.'[12] 'Besides, the praetorial tribunal of Brutus himself was daily found covered with such writings as these: "Brutus, art thou asleep?" and "Thou art not really Brutus".'[13] Brutus is *praetor* in 44 BC: this strong and decisive pressure on him occurs precisely in the weeks prior to the assassination.

Why Brutus? His presence was crucial to the conspiracy. This becomes clear from a review of his career. At the start of the civil war, the choice Brutus made had seemed baffling: he had sided with Pompey even though Pompey had treacherously plotted the assassination of his father. (It was certainly Cato's influence that led to this choice, which no one foresaw as possible.) But he was a favourite of Caesar, who ordered his officers to spare him at Pharsalus.[14] And Caesar preferred him to Cassius in the clash over the praetorship.

Brutus obviously cannot be termed a 'Caesarian'. Until the eve of the assassination he was a figure outside all parties. The conspirators, incited, of course, by Cassius, finally agreed to act *only on condition that Brutus took the lead*.[15] Only thus could the two 'streams' of the conspiracy, the 'Pompeian' current and the Caesarian, which had grown more and more hostile to the dictator (Decimus Brutus, Trebonius, etc.), join forces, despite their different backgrounds. Brutus was seen as the figure who guaranteed both sides, but above all he reassured those who were preparing to betray Caesar. Here Plutarch provides valuable information when he observes that Brutus was predestined to be 'first in the city with none to dispute him, could he have endured for a little while to be second to Caesar'.[16] In his turn Brutus invoked the name of Cicero in his public speeches immediately following the assassination (or even in the Senate), because he wanted to appeal to those who had been reconciled to Caesar (and who had made compromising statements of their position in public, like Cicero in *In defence of Marcellus*). The reference to Cicero sounded like a call to those who were not of the ultra-Pompeian faction. And it is no accident that Decimus Brutus, a Caesarian and a conspirator, also refers to Cicero: otherwise it would not be at all clear why a copy of Decimus Brutus' dramatic and highly confidential note to Brutus and Cassius of 16 March, when it seemed to him that everything was turning for the worse, reached Cicero as well, among whose letters it may be found,[17] together with Cicero's subsequent correspondence with Decimus Brutus. Again, Decimus Junius Brutus Albinus, consul designate for 42, enters into the conspiracy because he is told that Brutus is directing the enterprise.[18] Decimus Brutus, says Plutarch, 'had Caesar's confidence',[19] but he acquiesces, it is certain, precisely because of the presence of Brutus.

Brutus' ability as a man who could unite opponents of such diverse, even opposite, political backgrounds is confirmed by the episode of Ligarius' recruitment into the conspiracy. Ligarius considered himself still a 'Pompeian', and for his continuing friendship towards the dead

Pompey he had been denounced to Caesar and pardoned, thanks in part to the intervention of Cicero. The scene described by Plutarch has an eloquent pathos: Ligarius, who is ill, is affectionately scolded by Brutus ('what a time this is to be sick!'). Guessing Brutus' meaning, he immediately raises himself in bed, grasps Brutus' right hand and says: 'Nay, Brutus, if thou hast a purpose *worthy of thyself*, I am well.'[20] (This 'worthy of thyself' is the recurrent leitmotif of the anonymous inscriptions rampant in the city during these months.)

The picture that emerges clearly from the first part of Plutarch's *Brutus*, in which chapters 8–17 are all about the conspiracy and its preparation, is of Cassius leading a group whose orientation may be called 'Pompeian'. It is an aggressive group, and for this reason slow to develop a following. It is with the overture to Brutus that the conspiracy gains substance and joins with the 'Caesarian conspiracy'.

At the time of the final deliberations there were some who suggested that Antony should be involved. Trebonius opposed this, recalling that in Spain Antony had not agreed, even if he had *loyally* not denounced anyone. Others concluded from the Spanish events that Antony should be killed as well (and from the *Life of Brutus* we know that Cassius pressed for this), but Brutus objected.

If these pieces are put together, we understand better how the different 'streams' of the conspiracy came together. It can easily be inferred that the suggestion of involving Antony came from the Caesarian conspirators, perhaps in view of the *loyalty* with which he had kept silent about Trebonius' advances the previous summer. Antony's loyalty, it was seen then, was not to Caesar, but to the conspirators (or better to the Caesarians, who were by now impatient with the dictatorship). But Cassius' *hetairia* countered that, precisely because he had held aloof at the first attempt, Antony was dangerous and should also be eliminated. This proposal was turned down. Brutus opposed it, and once again Brutus played the key role. It was agreed that Antony should not be assassinated (and this at any rate is a success for the Caesarian conspirators, and perhaps above all for Trebonius, who owed a great deal to Antony's loyalty); but Trebonius had to take care to keep him away from the Curia when the conspirators made their move.

Notes

1 Bibulus the Younger fought at Philippi (October 42) under Brutus. He was therefore already grown up in 44, and it is clear that he had collected the confidential communications of Brutus and especially his mother

Porcia, who died shortly before her husband (see Cicero, *Letters to Brutus* 1.9.2). Porcia was fully informed about the conspiracy (see Plutarch, *Brutus* 13).

2 The Greek term ἑταιρεία must have been deliberately chosen. It is a technical term from Athenian political discourse, of which Plutarch had expert knowledge.

3 Plutarch, *Brutus* 7.4.

4 According to Appian (*Civil Wars* 2.112, 466), it cannot be ruled out that the contest between the two for the urban praetorship was an act, staged 'so that they might not seem to have a common understanding with each other'. This theory seems somewhat improbable in view of the detailed account given by Plutarch of the steady rapprochement between Cassius and Brutus after their contest for the praetorship. The suspicions of Appian (or, presumably, of his source) are nevertheless interesting in themselves. They show that in this sort of political situation such camouflages may be suspected and could be taken seriously by those who undertook to set down the events. Dio Cassius (44.14), recounting the scene known to Plutarch in which Porcia is let into her husband's secret (the preparation of the conspiracy), makes Brutus the prime mover and the one who 'drew in Cassius'. But Plutarch's account of the competition for the praetorship, as well as his accurate description of the '*hetairia* of Cassius', incline one to the belief that Dio Cassius, by simplifying things (see 44.14.3), confused the picture.

5 Plutarch, *Brutus* 7.4.

6 Plutarch, *Brutus* 6.4.

7 Appian, *Civil Wars* 2.121, 508; 122, 511; 123, 515; 142, 593, etc.

8 Certainly Appian's source as well.

9 Plutarch, *Brutus* 7.

10 Plutarch, *Brutus* 10.

11 Plutarch, *Brutus* 10.3.

12 Plutarch, *Brutus* 9.3.

13 Plutarch, *Brutus* 9.4.

14 Plutarch, *Brutus* 5.1.

15 Plutarch, *Brutus* 10.1.

16 Plutarch, *Brutus* 8.2, and earlier (7.4): 'Had he wished it, he might have been first among Caesar's friends and exercised the greatest power.'

17 Cicero, *Letters to his friends* 11.1.

18 Plutarch, *Brutus* 12.5.

19 Plutarch, *Brutus* 12.5. Among other things he held control of an important 'military' instrument, the gladiators' school.

20 Plutarch, *Brutus* 11.

CHAPTER 35

A Conspirator's Realism: Cassius Settles for the Second Rank

In his *Life of Brutus* Plutarch presents the reconciliation of Brutus and Cassius. Cassius is driven to make peace by one politically decisive consideration: everyone he approaches with the proposal of a violent attempt to eliminate Caesar replies that he would be party to it only if Brutus were to take the lead. Should Brutus refuse, then any such enterprise must be considered a failure, precisely because Brutus had rejected it![1] This is why Cassius decided to restore the contact with Brutus that had been broken off when he found himself competing with him for the praetorship.[2] The first question he asked him – during their first meeting after the rupture – was whether he intended to take part in the Senate meeting on 1 March, the sitting at which, it was said, Caesar's friends would propose the elevation of Caesar to *king*. Brutus replied that he would stay away. 'What if we are summoned there as *praetors*, what shall we do then, my good Brutus?' 'I will defend my country to the death', he replied. At this point Cassius, seeing Brutus well disposed, deployed what he considered the very effective argument of the 'anonymous' propaganda that for some time had been inciting Brutus to action. The rest is well known: Brutus joined and began seeking support, and, apart from the occasional refusal, he was personally successful.

   This account stems from sources close to Brutus and his family – Bibulus and Emphylos – or from Messalla Corvinus, if the source of the account is in Cassius' circle instead. If it is to be believed, it not only supports the view that the rift between Brutus and Cassius was staged, but also provides a definite chronological point of reference. When the conversation between the two occurs, the Senate sitting of 1 March is close, so one might also wonder whether this scene occurred before or after Antony's failed attempt to place the diadem on Caesar's head at the feast of the Lupercalia on 15 February. It seems most likely that that disastrous and counter-productive move had not yet happened, and that, precisely because of this, a Senate sitting dedicated to the 'coronation' of Caesar was feared. There exists the less likely possibility that, after the Lupercalia fiasco, some still wanted to take the 'monarchic' initiative to the Senate. This second conjecture seems less probable because the public setback (whatever Antony's motives might have been) could only have served to discourage a repeat performance within a few days and, moreover, in an assembly utterly inappropriate for an anti-constitutional proposal of such significance. We do not know if the scheduled sitting of the Senate on 1 March actually took place. Certainly the one that Cassius said he feared did not occur: no source mentions a meeting of the Senate to consider a proposal to proclaim Caesar king.

The most probable scenario, then, is the one based on the evidence provided in Plutarch's *Life of Brutus*. Before the Lupercalia, but certainly in February, Cassius decides to approach Brutus. By this time he has been able to establish that, without the involvement of Brutus, very few will follow him, apart from his own *hetairia*.[3] He has had no contact with Brutus since Caesar gave preference to his rival in the contest for the praetorship. From this we may deduce that for a time Cassius had thought of acting alone, solely with his own men. When he realised that it would be impossible without the contribution of a key figure with a large following like Brutus, he attempted an approach. He used two arguments to obtain Brutus' assent: (a) if Caesar really were crowned by the highest constitutional organ of the republic, the coming Senate sitting of 1 March could put an end to any hope of deliverance; (b) the anonymous inscriptions that daily urged Brutus to tyrannicide were the work of prominent citizens, Cassius claimed, so all the more worthy of Brutus' attention.

It is plain, then, that Brutus was drawn in because he was crucial to the success of the conspiracy, and *only in the final phase* of an intrigue begun by Cassius well before. That intrigue had stalled because of the limitations imposed by the figure of Cassius himself in the eyes of possible converts.

Cassius' genius lay in knowing at what point to step back and settle for a subordinate position to a leader who was more widely accepted,[4] while keeping a 'nucleus' of his own loyal followers, whom Appian, for example, still calls 'Cassius' men' even after the conspiracy has achieved its end and events are rapidly unfolding. Cicero, who was kept out of the operational phase, but who probably knew what was going to happen and therefore did not go to the Senate on 15 March, was closer to Cassius than to Brutus before and after the assassination.[5] Cassius hardly ever got his way in the most important matters (the elimination of Antony in addition to Caesar, a proposal supported by Cicero as well; or Antony's request for a grand funeral for Caesar). Each time Brutus adopted a decision favourable to Antony, and each time that decision was shown by subsequent events to be harmful. At least, the historical accounts at our disposal would suggest this conclusion.

Notes

1 Plutarch, *Brutus* 10.
2 Appian, *Civil Wars* 2.113. On this episode and the testimony of Appian, see Chapter 34, n. 4.
3 Plutarch, *Brutus* 10.1.
4 Plutarch must have had his reasons for dedicating a *Life* to Brutus but not to Cassius, although he possessed biographical material about both of them. (There was nothing to prevent him writing a 'double' life, as he did in the case of the Gracchi brothers.) A *Life of Cassius* was written by Oppius, a loyal follower of Caesar with a penchant for biography. (See Carisius, in H. Keil, *Grammatici Latini*, vol. I, p. 147.) This was most probably a polemical work inspired by Caesar.
5 This may be why the tradition which is closest to Brutus, used by Plutarch in his *Life of Brutus*, maintains that Cicero was 'kept in the dark' (Plutarch, *Brutus* 12.2). It is legitimate to wonder if Cicero was one of Cassius' conspiratorial 'contact men'.

CHAPTER 36

Some Unexpected Refusals

Having related the reconciliation of Brutus and Cassius, Plutarch informs us that both began to get in touch with their friends. But he really only relates the steps taken by Brutus.[1] This is not surprising, seeing that he is writing Brutus' biography, and in any case he has already said that Cassius has been busy for some time.

According to Plutarch, Brutus received only two noes: both from persons who had had very close ties to Cato and would later die at Philippi in the republican ranks – Statilius[2] and Favonius. The latter was described in this context by Plutarch as 'the devoted follower of Cato',[3] with the explanation that he was 'more impetuous and frenzied than reasonable in his pursuit of philosophy'.[4]

We can infer from this that Cassius had not yet approached them. The task fell to Brutus, Cato's nephew. According to the sources Plutarch uses here, Brutus – on meeting them – approached the subject indirectly,[5] and within the framework of a philosophical debate, at which the jurist Labeo was also present. The topic of conversation must have been the best form of government, or perhaps whether monarchy was legitimate or tolerable, and the means, legitimate or otherwise, of opposing it. This much may be deduced from the answers Brutus received. Favonius, the fanatical Catonian, said that 'civil war is worse than illegal monarchy'. Statilius was scornful, and said that 'it did not become a wise and sensible man to be thrown into turmoil and peril for the sake of feeble and foolish folk'. It was Labeo, not Brutus, who replied to both, and from this Brutus deduced that Labeo would support the conspiracy.

The response of the two Catonians might have been simply due to the (awkward?) way that Brutus had guided the not too cryptic discussion. Apart from anything else, anyone taking part in this sort of conversation under a dictatorship may fear a provocation. Nevertheless the categorical rejection of Brutus' advances by these two Catonians is surprising. Favonius is too well known for his total political devotion to Cato, from the beginning of his career to the final outcome, for his reply ('civil war is worse than illegal monarchy') not to give rise to some questions. Ronald Syme has put forward those strong words as proof of the *weariness* of even that part of the ruling class which had enjoyed the *libertas* reserved only for oligarchs, a limited *libertas* characteristic of the Roman republic. Syme is speaking of the state of mind that made the Augustan solution possible and largely accepted. He points out: 'to a patriotic Roman of republican sentiments even submission to absolute rule was a lesser evil than war between citizens', and quotes Favonius' reply to Brutus on the subject.[6] In reality there is a chronological discrepancy in such reasoning. Syme is explaining how and why in the end Augustus was 'accepted', even by the most valiant champions of *libertas* in the ruling classes, when in fact that realistic and dispassionate comment by Favonius is from March 44, a little prior to Caesar's murder, which would be followed by another very long cycle of civil wars. Nevertheless, such a short circuit may make sense. If Favonius spoke in this way to dampen Brutus' proselytising zeal, that is probably due to the fact that by now the Caesarian dictatorship was felt as an evil to which one should resign oneself, even if one was 'a devotee of Cato', as Plutarch calls Favonius, who later did not hesitate to fight and die at Philippi. At that moment, then, in spite of all that was written after the event (the famous list of Caesar's abuses of power as a cause of widespread outrage against him), it was only a very small circle that considered the elimination of Caesar to be possible. And that circle probably made its decision amidst the excitement aroused among these opponents by the dramatic Spanish campaign, and perhaps also because of rumours of plots being hatched within the Caesarian camp itself.

It is possible, however, that in the case of Favonius his Stoic faith played a role. (Statilius, on the other hand, is described by Plutarch as 'an Epicurean'.)[7] On one page of *De beneficiis* Seneca dwells on Brutus' action. His judgement is very clear: 'Although in other respects Brutus was a great man, in this particular he seems to me to have acted very wrongly, and to have *failed to conduct himself in accordance with Stoic teaching*.'[8] And he sets forth a tightly argued case against the murder of Caesar:

> Either he was frightened by the name of king, though a state reaches
> its best condition [*civitatis status*; the best guarantee of stability]
> under the rule of a just king, or he still hoped that liberty could exist

where the rewards both of supreme power and of servitude were so great, or that the earlier constitution of the state could be restored after the ancient manners had all been lost, that equality of civil rights might still exist and laws maintain their rightful place there where he had seen so many thousands of men fighting to decide, not whether, but to which of the two masters, they would be slaves!

The last point is an obvious reference to Pharsalus: not, of course, to Thapsus, because that would involve a condemnation (impossible from Seneca) of the figure and political convictions of Cato. And in any case Brutus had fought at Pharsalus, not at Thapsus, or anywhere else. Those who saw Pharsalus, claims Seneca, could not have faith in a revival of *libertas*: meaning, liberty would not be established in the absence of a large enough number of citizens able to value it, want it and defend it; the complete opposite of the spectacle seen at Pharsalus. These lines contain a compressed theoretical formulation of the pointlessness of Caesar's murder, in keeping with the *principle* according to which the most balanced constitutional form is the government of a 'just king'. Favonius, in his reply to Brutus, had been even more categorical (but fully in accord with this view), when he had affirmed that even an *un*just king would be preferable to civil war. Naturally, once Caesar had been eliminated, Favonius, like Statilius, returned to the renewed conflict in which right – or 'virtue', as Horace put it – was obviously, in his eyes, on the side of the liberators. He did not consider Brutus' way of doing things – the regicide – acceptable; but for Seneca, too, that had been a choice 'out of keeping with Stoic teaching'.

Notes

1 Plutarch, *Brutus* 10.4.
2 Perhaps the same Statilius as is mentioned by Plutarch in his *Life of Cato* (see F. Münzer, *RE*, s.v. *Statilius*, no. 2 [1929]).
3 Plutarch, *Brutus* 12.3.
4 Plutarch, *Brutus* 34.4.
5 Plutarch, *Brutus* 12.3: πόρρωθεν.
6 R. Syme, *The Roman Revolution* (Oxford 1939), p. 2 and n. 1.
7 This did not, however, prevent him from trying to commit suicide with Cato (assuming that this is the same Statilius).
8 Seneca, *De beneficiis* 2.20.2.

CHAPTER 37

Cicero – an Organiser of the Conspiracy?

Speaking in the Senate on 19 September 44 BC, in the absence of Cicero, Antony made a serious accusation: 'When Caesar had been slain, Brutus, whom I name with respect, at once lifting high his bloody dagger, shouted for Cicero by name, and congratulated him on the recovery of freedom'.[1] From Brutus' remark (which Cicero does not deny) Antony concluded, perhaps rightly, that Cicero was not unaware of the conspiracy. In the *Second Philippic*, a savagely Demosthenian reply that was never delivered, Cicero accurately quotes Antony's words and hits back with a detailed and deadly polemical retaliation: he recalls the blackest stain on Antony's 'Caesarian' career – his complicity in the plan to assassinate Caesar the previous year, shortly after Munda. Cicero's reminder was also a gift to Octavian, since at the time he actually published this damaging pamphlet he was already in touch with Octavian.[2]

In his answer Cicero establishes, rightly, a connection between Antony's compromise the previous summer and the strange moment during the assassination when Trebonius, who had informed Antony about the conspiracy a year earlier, kept him out of Pompey's Curia while the others carried out the stabbing. Here Cicero expresses himself in a way that at first sight might lead one to think that Cicero himself was a witness: '[you] who were, *we have seen* [*vidimus*], drawn aside by Trebonius at the time when Caesar was being slain' (*Philippics* 2.34). But strictly speaking *vidimus* (we saw) must refer to what happened *outside* Pompey's Curia, which would force one to conclude that Cicero was outside, not within. In reality *vidimus* should probably be understood in a more general sense: 'Trebonius could be seen keeping you far from the scene'. A reference, then, to a not insignificant detail which was at that point common knowledge, a detail that *some had seen* and everyone knew.

Not even the words written a month later (27 April 44) to Atticus, when Cicero speaks of 'the joy of feasting my eyes on the just death of a tyrant',[3] necessarily mean that Cicero was present at the moment of the attack. Those words could apply in the more likely event that Cicero, like many others, arrived on the scene a little later, or else they may refer to any other moment between the assassination and the dictator's dramatic funeral.

What matters here is not the detail in itself. Rather, both the matter of Cicero's presence or absence at the moment of the attack and the vexed question of his responsibility as a 'prompter' can shed light on the dramatic events, as well as on the intentions and positions of the conspirators. It is not only a question of his note to Basilus (*Letters to his friends* 6.15), generally dated 15 March, the very day of the bloody deed. Every so often some scholar declares that this note, exulting at some unnamed venture in which Basilus is involved, is too 'savage', too 'brutal' to be Cicero's response to the news that immediately spread of Caesar's murder.[4] In recent years as skilful an interpreter of Cicero as Shackleton-Bailey has considered it necessary to erase the bad impression provoked by that note, maintaining that Cicero was present at the assassination, so did not need to get the details from Basilus. This wish to eliminate 'blemishes' stems from a prim sense of propriety, which overlooks the ferocity of the political struggle and of political odium in the Roman republic. There are no private matters that would justify such an exultant and unbridled outburst from Cicero. Moreover, Cicero's bloodthirsty insistence when he says to Cassius that, had he been invited to supper on the eve of the Ides, he would have supported the killing of Antony too, as well as the cold sarcasm with which he imagines – in the *Second Philippic* – telling Antony to his face, 'if that stylus had been mine, as is said, believe me, I would have made an end, not of one act only, but of the whole story',[5] are eloquent in themselves.

In his speech of 19 September Antony had skilfully stressed Cicero's moral responsibility (and not only moral) in the assassination. And he had recalled a scene whose accuracy Cicero does not deny: the one in which, just after Caesar had been stabbed, Brutus, his dagger still bloody, had invoked Cicero's name, 'congratulating him on the recovery of freedom'.[6]

Now, not only is it difficult to imagine that this compromising declaration of moral authorship of the murder occurred with Cicero *present*, but one might also wonder what exactly Brutus meant by it, assuming that he really uttered these words. Antony was not present, so he also relates from hearsay. And Cicero in the *Second Philippic* can be pleased with the anecdote (by then flattering from his point of view) without giving too much thought to the accuracy of his rival's assertion. He even ventures a somewhat extravagant interpretation. Brutus, he claims, sang his praises, rejoicing with him at liberty regained: 'because he had done a deed exactly like those deeds I myself had done, he called me especially to witness that he had appeared as a rival of my fame [*mearum laudium*]' (*Philippics* 2.28). So the elimination of Caesar was like the elimination of Catiline and the leaders of that earlier conspiracy. This interpretation of Brutus' invocation is certainly mistaken and sophistic. We know from Cicero that Brutus, in his piece in praise of Cato, published exactly a year before the Ides of March, thoroughly belittled Cicero's role in the suppression of the Catilinarians and gave Cato the greatest credit. And Cicero showed himself very annoyed by this when writing to Atticus on 17 March 45 (*Letters to Atticus* 12.21.1)

It does not seem then that Brutus had the same high regard for Cicero's consular services as Cicero himself. Cicero's best-intentioned friends knew how much he had exaggerated his own contribution to the Catilinarian affair (although he had chosen to spare Caesar, who was also under fire). Certainly, Brutus had urged Cicero to defend the memory of Cato,[7] drawing a very piqued reply from the dictator as a result. That he even would have accepted Cicero as the very symbol of the republican restoration seems at least problematic, however much Cicero liked the idea.

But this is not enough to provide an *organising* accomplice in the conspiracy. Cicero's public declarations matter less than the fact that, in a private letter to Cassius, he says: 'the madman [Antony] declares that I was a leader [*princeps*] in your noble enterprise. If only I had been! He would not be giving us any trouble.'[8] The historian Carcopino, on the other hand, finds a more interesting and ingenious solution to this complex problem than Antony's schematic denunciation. Carcopino had personal experience of a difficult period in French political life (Vichy), and of the devious paths that are taken in resisting authoritarian rule. He supposed that Cicero must have exerted upon Brutus a subtle moral pressure, a subtle 'blackmail in the name of the ancestors', pushing him towards the terrorist option. Difficult though it is to go deeply into the psychology of historical figures (who, besides, are known to us primarily from Cicero's letters), Brutus certainly did not remain insensitive to the anonymous campaign of slogans on walls and monuments in the streets of Rome, of which Suetonius and Plutarch provide details, shortly before the assassination. Certain phrases used by Cicero indicate that he is alluding to that campaign, without naming it.[9] It is no less certain that a politically 'suffering' intellectual, like Cicero under Caesar's dictatorship, uses words with a violence that is purely in the mind: when the time comes to move on from words to action he is gripped by paralysis. Intellectuals are extremists and radicals only within their own imagination: they do not always understand the material implications, the practical consequences of their words; they do not always foresee that others will take them literally, and turn their words into *actions*, into *facts*. When Cicero recalls the Brutus of old who 'toppled Tarquin', he does not say that he really imagines Brutus, overcome by this great vision, reaching for his dagger. His war with the dictator, whether in his *Praise of Cato* or his *Defence of Marcellus*, remained always a war of words.

Cicero's attitude to Caesar, his contemporary and fellow student of Greek in adolescence, whose career had started a little later than his own (he was merely a *praetor*-designate in the year when Cicero was already an illustrious consul), differed greatly from his attitude to Sulla, to take the most obvious example. To Cicero, Sulla was a great man of the generation before his own, in power when he was scarcely starting out. His dictatorship, despite the shameful matter of the proscriptions, had been a painful necessity. This was the view that Cicero had formed, although his judgement varied with changing times and circumstances. Caesar, on the other hand, appeared to him in a completely different light: as a contemporary who, at various critical moments, could have been restrained or even stopped, if only things had gone as they should have gone, and if Cicero had not been betrayed, first by one, then by another, and if he had not been let down by Pompey, who had cynically held fast to the 'triumviral' pact. Here Cicero has a much closer perspective, and is far less inclined to accept whatever happens as preordained or inevitable. His close familiarity and direct involvement also gave rise to the idea which he had nurtured within himself during the years 47–44: that nothing that had happened was final or conclusive. Notwithstanding the strained protestations in his 'Caesarian Orations', notwithstanding the temptation to make himself the Aristotle of this new Alexander,[10] Caesar was to Cicero a *provisional* victor, one who could yet fall. He would not have plunged headlong into the political fray, to a suicidal end, against Antony, if he had not profoundly believed that republican normality *could begin again*, despite the spectacular series of unforeseeable successes of that snobbish and opportunist contemporary of his. He did not realise that times had changed, or perhaps rather, he could not accept that Caesar was the protagonist and beneficiary of a new era. Because of this, the murderous initiative of the 'liberators' did not appear foolish to him, but legitimate and above all politically feasible. He was 'ready' for it.

Notes

1 See Cicero, *Philippics* 2.28 and 30 (= *ORF* no. 159, VII Malcovati).
2 Cicero states in a letter that Octavian has begun to visit him (*Letters to Atticus* 14.11.2, 20 April 44).
3 Cicero, *Letters to Atticus* 14.14.4: 'laetitiam quam oculis cepi iusto interitu tyranni'.
4 E. T. Merrill (*Classical Philology*, 8 [1913], pp. 48–56) sees this note as referring to private matters going back to 47 BC; J. Carcopino, *Les Secrets de la correspondance de Cicéron*, 9th edn (Paris 1957), vol. II, p. 41, uses words like 'savage joy', 'inhuman', 'more ruthless than a dagger-blow'.
5 Cicero, *Philippics* 2.28. A *graphium* (stylus) is a pointed implement for writing on wax tablets.
6 Cicero, *Philippics* 2.28.
7 Cicero, *Orator* 10.35.
8 Cicero, *Letters to his friends* 12.3. Or see another letter, which begins with the words, 'A pity you did not invite me to dinner on the Ides of March!' (*Letters to his friends* 12.4.1).
9 See Cicero, *Letters to Atticus* 13.40.1.
10 Cicero, *Letters to Atticus* 12.40.2 (9 May 45). It is no accident that this was written two months after Munda, when the last chance was lost.

CHAPTER 38

The Serious Mistake of Dismissing the Escort

Suetonius, who is well informed about reports of warnings reaching Caesar before the conspiracy,[1] wonders whether Caesar actually *wanted* to die, given that exhaustion had led to physical decline – a question which, he says, has already been explored by others. He paid no attention, it is said, to omens or 'the reports of his friends'.[2] Suetonius also records the view that Caesar felt safer after the senators had sworn to protect him,[3] and therefore made the mistake – which made possible his murder – of dismissing his bodyguard. A third opinion, which Suetonius duly records, is actually very close to the theory of those who said 'he *wanted* to die': this view held that he preferred to confront those perils, once and for all, rather than live constantly in fear of them. It is probable that *each one of these suggestions* captures part of the truth and helps to understand Caesar's baffling decision to dismiss his armed escort.

But the most important evidence comes from Caesar himself, reported again by Suetonius in the same chapter. Caesar used to say, and Suetonius records his words verbatim, that:

> it was not so much in his own interest as in that of his country that he remained alive; he had long since had his fill of power and glory; but if aught befell him, the commonwealth would have no peace, but would be plunged in civil strife under much worse conditions.[4]

In a condensed biography of the 'tyrannicide' Marcus Junius Brutus, Matthias Gelzer compares this theory, which he terms 'more profound', with the view expounded several times by Cicero, when confronted with the disappointing political outcome of Caesar's murder.[5] Cicero labelled the assassins as having 'the courage of men, but the blind policy of a child',[6] meaning that the slaughter of the Ides of March ought to have included Antony as well. Left alive and dangerous, as the inheritor of Caesar's policies, Antony was in a position to undo everything that the 'liberators' had achieved. For Cicero, it was a matter of better defining the target: with Antony eliminated too, the game would have been over and the old order would have returned. For Caesar, his possible violent physical elimination meant, on the contrary, resumption of the civil conflict on a grand scale and with greater virulence. Cicero's view places responsibility for the conflict, endemic in the last century of the republic, upon ambitious individuals: as soon as they are removed, order will return. Caesar clearly recognises *that there are greater forces* involved in the conflict, which would end (so he imagined) with his victory. These forces would not remain inactive after the violent removal of their leader. This analysis of Caesar's is, incidentally, much more 'profound' (to use Gelzer's expression) than the inflexible and irrelevant explanations with which, in the *Commentaries*, he accounts for his decision to reopen the civil wars.[7] In those chapters we hear the leader speaking in propaganda terms to explain that he took action to safeguard the trampled rights of the tribunes of the plebs. But in the reflection written when the conflict was behind him, and recorded by Suetonius, Caesar's words are not mere propaganda – they have substance. They show that he was aware not only of the nature of the conflict from which he had only just emerged victorious; he was also fully aware of the nature of the conflict to come, unleashed by his violent death, whether he feared that death or hoped for it.

Obviously, in Caesar's reflection reported by Suetonius there is no concession to historical determinism. It is not a matter of asserting the 'pointlessness' of a conspiracy (even if it achieved its aim) in the face of the 'fated march' of history. On the contrary, Caesar meant to outline the unprecedented and alarming scenario that his violent death would produce (and did produce).

It is clear that in its way the conspiracy was *successful*. And it can hardly be claimed that such acts are 'politically useless'. They are never politically useless when they succeed, but the consequences may go beyond all the calculations and expectations of the conspirators. Not even the victory of the Caesarians at Philippi could be taken for granted. Instead of conflict among the triumvirs, there could have been further conflict between Caesarians and 'liberators' (or, even within the broad ranks of the 'liberators'). The forces involved were far too substantial and socially significant simply to vanish into thin air merely as a result of the tyrant's death. Caesar had needed years to wear down and disperse a group like Pompey's (49–45 BC). The assassination set everything in turmoil again. Because the forces in the field were deep rooted, a vast, new 'Pompeian' camp arose, which held the Caesarians in check until October 42 at least: not to speak of the vigorous revival of Sextus Pompey, who dominated the sea until 35, and could deal with the triumvirs as an equal, thanks to the balance of forces. Caesar's observation that a conspiracy against him would be, at the least, inadvisable was not determinism but foresight.

Notes

1 Suetonius, *Caesar* 81. Plutarch is even better informed. See Plutarch, *Caesar* 63–5 and *Brutus* 14–16.
2 Suetonius, *Caesar* 86.1.
3 An oath warmly supported by Cicero in *In defence of Marcellus*.
4 Suetonius, *Caesar* 86.2.
5 In *RE*, s.v. *Iunius*, no. 53, col. 991, 1–13.
6 Cicero, *Letters to Atticus* 14.21.3. Cf. also 15.4.2 and elsewhere in his correspondence (e.g. his letter to Cassius in *Letters to his friends* 12.4.1; see Chapter 37, n. 8).
7 See the beginning of the first *Commentary* of his *Civil War*.

CHAPTER 39

The Dynamics of the 'Tyrannicide'

> . . . let even
> the Senate itself wait – and find out at once
> what important message Artemidorus has for you.
>
> Cavafy

The evening before the assassination, Caesar was among the guests at supper at the house of Marcus Lepidus, his *magister equitum*, and the discussion turned to the question: what kind of death would be best? While the rather strange conversation lingered on this question – a cryptic warning? – Caesar, when his turn came to speak, said that he would by far prefer a sudden and unexpected death.[1] He had expressed the same preference ('*subitam et celerem*') before, in the context of another philosophical dialogue, in the margin of a passage on the death of Cyrus in Xenophon's *Cyropaedia*.[2] In Cicero's *Cato the Elder*, written shortly before the murder of Caesar, that passage is translated into Latin with a commentary. It is not at all improbable that, during a reading of *Cato the Elder* in which Caesar was taking part, the dictator had made that note about his preference for a 'sudden and unexpected' death. Obviously this cannot be proven. But the conversation on the eve of the assassination is somewhat enigmatic. There is nothing unusual, given the situation, about conversations consisting of allusive questions or innuendo, designed to pass a veiled message. We should recall the procedure followed by Brutus when he was recruiting followers for the conspiracy. He visited Favonius and Statilius, when Labeo was present, and, in Plutarch's words, 'put them to a very similar test [that is, to see if they might join him] by the round-about method of a philosophical discussion'.[3] But he received negative responses from both of them. This is a procedure similar to the one used at Lepidus' table, the evening before the attempt on Caesar, when somebody steered the conversation to the topic of the most desirable manner of death.

Incidents like this make one think of a Caesar hounded by those who want to kill him, and, therefore, also 'pestered' by those bent on the opposite, who try, with more or less cryptic warnings, to save him. One should not forget, as proof of the 'pressure' from all those around the dictator, that the morning after Lepidus' rather gloomy supper, the morning of the assassination, Decimus Brutus, one of the conspirators who will soon stab him, steals up to Caesar (in Caesar's own house!) and, as Caesar ponders whether to go out or stay at home and 'put off what he had planned to do in the Senate', exhorts him to come to the Senate and not disappoint 'the full meeting which had for some time been waiting for him'.[4] Caesar is controlled by the conspirators, and perhaps the person who introduced that strange topic of conversation the previous evening could find no other way to make himself understood and warn the victim.

The night before the Ides of March was one of nightmares. Calpurnia, Caesar's wife, dreamt that the roof of their house was falling in and her husband was assassinated on her lap. She believed that at that moment the bedroom door sprang open by itself.[5] Some said that it was not the roof, but a gable end that had been added to Caesar's house on a Senate decision 'for decoration and honour'.[6] Caesar also had a nocturnal vision before the dawn: he dreamt he was floating in the air, flying above the clouds, and clasping the hand of Jupiter.[7] A megalomaniac dream, perhaps, but eloquent in its way.

Caesar had never taken too seriously the cumbrous apparatus of superstition that so obtrusively governed Roman public life. His totally secular cast of mind allowed him to take a detached view of those beliefs, which were of primary importance in daily affairs. But there was a public aspect to it all, which he was able to keep in mind. He did not put off his departure for Africa when it meant confronting Scipio, Juba and Cato: certainly he was not dissuaded by the fact that during the sacrifice one of the animals had escaped.[8] But when, on disembarking, he stumbled and fell, he turned the bad omen to good, exclaiming: 'Teneo te, Africa!' almost as if he had thrown himself down to kiss the ground. A very well-known prophecy ordained that the name of the Scipios should remain forever undefeated in Africa: hence his decision, which was reassuring especially for his troops, since a Cornelius Scipio led the opposing army, to have a Scipio in camp also, a little-known and disgraced member of the *gens Cornelia*.

And yet, at dawn on that 15 March, Calpurnia's unusual anxiety alarmed him. Added to this, the soothsayers reported to him that the sacrifices were giving inauspicious signs,[9] so he thought of cancelling the Senate meeting and sending Antony to dismiss the senators.

Just at this moment a man intervened who enjoyed the complete confidence of the dictator to the extent that he was listed in his will among the minor heirs, Decimus Junius Brutus Albinus. The familiarity of the relationship between Caesar and Decimus was such that Caesar was not surprised to see him in the house so early in the morning. The task assigned to Decimus Brutus by the conspirators was a very delicate one: he was to keep an eye on Caesar to see that he did not change his mind and actually went to the Senate. Decimus Brutus adopted a jokingly non-religious tone and began to mock the soothsayers,[10] while urging Caesar not to postpone the sitting because this would seem like an insult to the Senate: it was Caesar who had convened it, and many senators had already been waiting for a long time in Pompey's Curia.[11] Plutarch reports in full the pressing arguments employed by the zealous conspirator: was there perhaps a need to send someone to inform the senators, who were already sitting and waiting, that they should go home and return when Calpurnia had had better dreams? And would this not vex them? Would this not provoke the murmurings of the envious ones? And what reply should we make when they denounce this behaviour as tyrannical? If it really seemed necessary to postpone the sitting, he concluded, at least Caesar should appear in person in the Senate to inform the senators of the postponement! After which Decimus Brutus took him by the hand and led him, one could almost say pushed him, out of the house.[12] It was the fifth hour when Caesar, urged on by Decimus Brutus, set out. Just then something unexpected occurred: a slave from another house, who had been trying his hardest to get close to Caesar, pushed his way through the crowd, entered Caesar's house, and presented himself to Calpurnia, asking to be held in her care until Caesar's return. He was the first of the messengers that morning who sought to reveal something to Caesar without success.

In the meantime the conspirators were on their way to the Senate. Brutus armed himself and made haste from home, alone. He had told his wife Porcia everything, since she had won his trust, even in political matters, by demonstrating a resistance to pain worthy of a daughter of Cato. The others gathered at Cassius' house; from there they hurried, all together, taking with them Cassius' son, who that day was assuming the *toga virilis*.[13] First they stopped in the Forum; then they set off, still as a group, towards Pompey's Portico, where the sitting was to be held.

Some of the conspirators, Brutus among them, were *praetors*. Their duties included giving hearings, listening to petitioners, and settling disputes. In one unforeseen incident, an obstinate petitioner rejected Brutus' judgement, lost his self-control and began to shout that he would appeal to Caesar. Unperturbed, Brutus replied with something approaching defiance: 'Caesar does not prevent me from acting according to the laws, nor will he prevent me.'[14]

In the meantime another person had come out of Brutus' house unobserved. He was a Greek, Artemidorus of Cnidus, a teacher of Greek rhetoric and son of the Theopompus of Cnidus to whom Caesar, shortly after Pharsalus, had granted the freedom of the city. In Rome, Artemidorus was on familiar terms with Brutus' circle and he suspected, or knew, enough to hurry to warn Caesar. According to Appian, he reached the Curia too late.[15] According to Plutarch, however, Artemidorus, who had written down his message about the imminent assassination attempt, managed to get close to Caesar and tell him to read the scroll at once (instead of passing it, as he usually did, without even reading it, to one of his secretaries). But, astonishing though it seems, Caesar was unable to read it, although he tried repeatedly, distracted each time by the crowd and the petitioners' insistent and bothersome demands.[16]

He still had it in his hand when at last he entered the Senate. Spurinna, too, the *haruspex* who some time before had forewarned Caesar of danger 'no later than the Ides of March', came up to him among the crowd while he was slowly approaching the meeting place. Caesar did not fail to tease him: 'The Ides of March have come,' he said, 'and brought me no harm!' And Spurinna retorted that they had indeed come, but they had not yet gone.[17]

Meanwhile the conspirators' impassivity and sangfroid were exposed to unexpected tests. A man approached Casca, took him by the right hand, and said to him: 'You hid the secret from us, Casca, but Brutus has told me everything.' However, it immediately became clear (or the stranger wished to make it clear) that he was referring to something quite different.[18] A little while later a senator, Popilius Laenas, went up to Brutus and Cassius and said in a low voice: 'I join you in praying for the accomplishment of what you have in mind, and exhort you not to delay, for the matter is on men's tongues.'[19] The two were alarmed because this alluded without doubt to the conspiracy: it was plain that someone had talked.

At that moment, just after Popilius' unforeseen remark had chilled them, a servant from Brutus' house came running in, announcing that Porcia was dying. At home Porcia could not stop worrying.

> Porcia, being distressed about what was impending and unable to bear the weight of her anxiety, could with difficulty keep herself at home, and at every noise or cry, like women in the Bacchic frenzy, she would rush forth and ask every messenger who came in from the Forum how Brutus was faring, and kept sending out others continually.[20]

At one point she fainted as she sat, surrounded by her servants. The colour drained from her face, her voice failed completely and she collapsed. Fearing that she had died, the servants began to lament and neighbours crowded in. Hence the report that reached Brutus in the difficult moment produced by the seemingly provocative words of Popilius Laenas.

Brutus stayed where he was: given the sensitivity of the moment, he could not abandon his accomplices. He did not dare to hurry home, in spite of his grief.[21]

At length Caesar arrived, in a litter, rather dispirited by the unfavourable omens, and still determined to defer any important decisions to another sitting.[22] Scarcely had he stepped down from the litter when Popilius rushed up to him – the senator who shortly before had unexpectedly gone up to Brutus to exhort him 'not to delay'. The conspirators thought all was lost. They feared the worst and exchanged glances to indicate that they were ready to kill one another rather than be captured.[23] Cassius had already put his hand on his dagger, and so had others, and they were already preparing to unsheathe their weapons when Brutus noticed, from Popilius' bearing, that he was not denouncing them but was asking a favour of Caesar. Brutus did not utter a word (he could not, because others were there who were not in the conspiracy) but his beaming face signalled to Cassius and the others that there was nothing to fear. A moment later, Popilius kissed Caesar's hand and moved away: and it was clear that their conversation had been about his business, nothing else.[24]

While this was happening the senators had entered the atrium and the conspirators had taken their places round the chair on which Caesar was seated. Trebonius alone remained outside, because he had the task of preventing Antony from going in, of detaining him outside the Curia.[25] Antony's compliance on that occasion, and in spite of such a tense day full of warning signs, was and remains surprising. Cassius, on entering the atrium, glanced up at the statue of Pompey, invoking his help.[26] It was Tillius Cimber who set things in motion by throwing himself at Caesar's feet with a petition: he was interceding for his brother in exile. All of them joined the request, kissing the dictator's hands and breast.[27] In Plutarch's *Life of Brutus*, as also in Suetonius' *Caesar*, the dictator is already seated when Tillius Cimber begins his plea and the other conspirators gather round. In his *Life of Caesar*, on the other hand, Plutarch divides the scene into two parts. First: Caesar enters the atrium and the group of conspirators divides, some taking up their positions around the chair in which Caesar will sit, while the others walk towards him with Cimber, who is throwing himself at his feet and accompanying him towards the chair, all the while continuing his entreaties. Second: Caesar takes his seat and Tillius with both hands grasps Caesar's toga and pulls it down, exposing his neck (this was the agreed signal). Casca and his brother, the first to stab, throw themselves on Caesar and wound him. Caesar shouts: 'Why, this is violence!' (according to Suetonius), or 'Impious Casca, what doest thou?' (according to Plutarch). In Suetonius' account and in the *Life of Brutus* the assault takes place while Caesar is 'trying to get up', but the sequence of events is the same. Suetonius adds one detail: Caesar, after the first blow inflicted by Casca, seizes the arm of his assailant and wounds him with his stylus,[28] but he is immediately struck by other blows and overwhelmed.

In his *Life of Caesar*, Plutarch indulges in some pathos when he describes Caesar's last moments.

> But those who had prepared themselves for the murder bared each of them his dagger, and Caesar, hemmed in on all sides, whichever way he turned confronting blows of weapons aimed at his face and eyes, driven hither and thither like a wild beast, was entangled in the hands of all; for all had to take part in the sacrifice and taste of the slaughter. Therefore Brutus also gave him one blow in the groin.[29]

Plutarch adds that Caesar did his best to defend himself:

> He darted this way and that and cried aloud, but when he saw that Brutus had drawn his dagger, he pulled his toga down over his head and sank, either by chance or because pushed there by his murderers, against the pedestal on which the statue of Pompey stood.

Suetonius gives different information. Caesar attempts to leap to his feet (in Suetonius the assault occurs when Caesar is already seated in the middle of the atrium):

> When he saw that he was beset on every side by drawn daggers, he muffled his head in his robe, and at the same time drew down its lap to his feet with his left hand, in order to fall more decently, with the lower part of his body also covered.[30]

He utters a single groan and does not say a single word. Suetonius adds that, 'some have written that when Marcus Brutus rushed at him, he said in Greek, "You too, my child?" '[31] A dramatic detail. In this story the word 'child' is intended literally and refers to the widespread view that Brutus was the product of Caesar's relationship with Servilia, Brutus' mother, who nurtured a deep and abiding passion for Caesar, which was at odds with the political orientation of all her menfolk (beginning with her brother Cato). This story, reported by Suetonius for the sake of completeness, conflicts with his own account, in which Caesar dies without uttering a word – only a single groan. In Plutarch's *Life of Caesar* this detail is present, but still as the opinion of 'some people'; however, in his *Life of Brutus*, it is stated as a fact, for the obvious reason that here Brutus is the hero of the account, and this story accentuates his central position in the event, including its final stage.

The doctor Antistius, a surgeon whose name is known from Roman medical literature,[32] examined the corpse and pointed out that, of twenty-three stab wounds, only one had been mortal, the second of those that Caesar received full in the chest.[33]

The detail of the corpse rolling to the feet of Pompey's statue also serves the purpose that Plutarch set himself in his *Caesar* (it is absent from his *Brutus*). In the *Life of Caesar* the account of the assassination begins with the observation that it cannot be a matter of chance that the entire scene occurs in a place that had been designed by Pompey, and it closes with the statue of Pompey drenched with Caesar's blood: 'one might have thought that Pompey himself was presiding over this vengeance upon his enemy, who now lay prostrate at his feet, quivering from a multitude of wounds'.[34]

The conspirators did not even have the courage to throw Caesar's body into the Tiber, as they had intended to do.[35] Instead they launched into ineffective public statements about their political motivation, while the other senators gave way to hysteria and panic around them. The corpse remained in the now deserted atrium for some time, until three slaves laid it on a stretcher and carried Caesar home, with one arm hanging down.

Notes

1 Suetonius, *Caesar* 87.1.
2 Suetonius, *Caesar* 87.1.
3 Plutarch, *Brutus* 12.
4 Suetonius, *Caesar* 81.4.
5 Suetonius, *Caesar* 81.3. According to Plutarch, *Caesar* 63.8, the windows as well.
6 Plutarch, *Caesar* 63.9. Plutarch relies on Livy, who relates this episode in book 16 of his *History of Rome*.
7 Suetonius, *Caesar* 81.3
8 Suetonius, *Caesar* 59.
9 Plutarch, *Caesar* 63.11.
10 Plutarch, *Caesar* 64.2.
11 Suetonius, *Caesar* 81.4.
12 Plutarch, *Caesar* 64.3–6.
13 Plutarch, *Brutus* 14.4.
14 Plutarch, *Brutus* 14.7.
15 Appian, *Civil Wars* 2.116.486.
16 Plutarch, *Caesar* 65.2–3.
17 Suetonius, *Caesar* 81.4.
18 Plutarch, *Brutus* 15.2.
19 Plutarch, *Brutus* 14.4; Appian, *Civil Wars* 2.115. At this point Appian's account accords fully with Plutarch's. Popilius Laenas figures in three letters from Cicero to Atticus in March 45 as a person to whom Cicero entrusts delicate tasks. His name always appears with that of Statilius, who may be the same Statilius whom Brutus tried without success to draw into the conspiracy. (See Plutarch, *Brutus* 12.3.)
20 Plutarch, *Brutus* 15.5.
21 Plutarch, *Brutus* 15.9.
22 Plutarch, *Brutus* 16.1.
23 To Plutarch this detail is certain, *Brutus* 16.3. It is confirmed by Appian, *Civil Wars* 2.116.487.
24 Plutarch, *Brutus* 16.4–5; Appian, *Civil Wars* 2.116.487.
25 Plutarch, *Brutus* 17.1. In his *Life of Caesar* (66.4) Plutarch says that Decimus Brutus was the one who detained Antony outside the Curia, but Cicero (*Philippics* 2.34) affirms that it was Trebonius.
26 In *Caesar* 66.2, Plutarch observes that this gesture ill accords with Cassius' Epicurean sympathies, but he adds that in the excitement of the moment departures from behavioural norms are understandable.
27 Plutarch, *Brutus* 17.3.

28 Suetonius, *Caesar* 82.2: 'Cascae brachium arreptum graphio traiecit.'
29 Plutarch, *Caesar* 66.9–10.
30 Suetonius, *Caesar* 82.2.
31 καὶ σὺ τέκνον
32 Scribonius Largus, p. 209 Helmreich.
33 Suetonius, *Caesar* 82.3.
34 Plutarch, *Caesar* 66.13.
35 Suetonius, *Caesar* 82.4.

CHAPTER 40

'Where's Antony?'

> 'Where's Antony?'
> – Fled to his house amazed.
>
> Shakespeare, *Julius Caesar*

This exchange between Caesar and Trebonius, in Act III, Scene 1, of *Julius Caesar*, follows immediately after the fatal dagger-blows which end the dictator's life. Shakespeare was a diligent reader of the ancient sources, and had culled from them and exploited a crucial and awkward point: the panic to which Antony gave way, having been detained by Trebonius outside Pompey's Curia while the assassination was taking place inside; and a little later Antony's attempt to reach an understanding with the assassins, with particular attention to the inner feelings of Brutus, the more moderate of the leading conspirators, who brandished their 'red weapons' while crying 'Peace! freedom! and liberty!' rather than 'freedom and liberty' (Act III, Scene 1, line 110). As we know from Cicero, some months earlier, while Caesar was in difficulty in Spain, Trebonius had been in contact with Antony – a fact which was potentially embarrassing to both parties, and for this reason Trebonius now had the task of keeping Antony away from the scene. To enter upon the minefield of conjecture would be futile, but it is very difficult to imagine a politician and man of action as experienced and circumspect as Antony suspecting nothing at all: it was far from normal for him to be stopped on some pretext on his way into the Senate, least of all on a day of great tension when Caesar himself, usually so contemptuous of superstition, had seemed reluctant to enter the Senate.

Shortly after the murder, with the conspirators still in the Curia, Antony sends a message of conciliation and political understanding:

> Mark Antony shall not love Caesar dead
> So well as Brutus living; but will follow
> The fortunes and affairs of noble Brutus

Through the hazards of this untrod state
With all true faith.

(Act III, Scene 1, lines 133–7).

Shakespeare plays skilfully on two possible readings of the lines he gives to Antony in this scene: on the one hand Antony is truly 'amazed', as Trebonius puts it after seeing him slip away as soon as word comes that the plotters have achieved success, and prepared to make common cause with the new conquerors; on the other, by his strategy of accommodation with Brutus and the others he is already planning his own coup. In a sense the words which best reveal the ambiguity of his position are those he utters at the end of this long scene to the servant of young Octavius:

Yet stay awhile;
Thou shalt not back till I have borne this corse
Into the market-place: there shall I try,
In my oration, how the people take
The cruel issue of these bloody men.

Yet the words with which he approaches the assassins and achieves his wish – to have a public commemoration for the dead man – are conciliatory: 'Friends am I with you all, and love you all' (Act III, Scene 1, line 220), the same words with which Cicero expresses to Minucius Basilus his joy at the success of the conspiracy: 'Tibi gratulor, mihi gaudeo. Te amo, tua tueor' ('Congratulations. I am delighted on my own account. Be sure of my affection and active concern for your interests') (*Letters to his friends* 6.15). Shakespeare's Antony is not feigning willingness to co-operate; he really is prepared for genuine co-operation if public reaction to the coup is favourable.

The scene in which Antony speaks to the assassins while Caesar's body lies beside them on the floor is an invention, of course. Shakespeare, who relied mainly on Appian,[1] knew full well that after the murder the assassins took refuge on the Capitol and that only some time later could Antony reach agreement with them not to launch criminal proceedings, in the name of public order (*Civil Wars* 2.124.520). This scene is of pivotal importance in the play: it sets the scene for Antony's speech to the people, a speech which resolves a situation of extreme uncertainty and prepares the downfall of the liberators. It is a key moment, but a totally invented one, or rather, one which goes beyond what the sources say, making subjective use of the evidence. Here the playwright hits the mark by placing his focus on the ambivalence of Antony's position, imagining his words and actions in the hours following the assassination. 'For your part, / To you our swords have leaden points', says Brutus to him amiably. And Brutus cannot be called naïve.

Shakespeare presents Antony immediately after the Ides of March as one who is almost sympathetic – whether sincere or not – to the conspirators. The playwright thus displays the same historical intuition as may be seen in Antony.

The sources provide no shortage of indications of Antony's careful tactics. These lead one to surmise that, after the Ides of March or the hours immediately after the coup, Antony feared that the plotters were fully in control, and therefore gave them to understand that he was on their side and grateful that they had spared him. But in the hours that followed he realised that the situation was still fluid and did not seem to favour the 'liberators'.[2] At that point he decided to put himself forward as leader of the party of Caesar.

Notes

1 Plutarch in his *Caesar* says nothing about what Antony said or did immediately after the assassination.
2 On this see M. A. Levi, *Ottaviano capoparte*, vol. 1 (Florence 1933), pp. 1–17.

CHAPTER 41

Caesar's Body: How to Turn Victory into Defeat

In the moment in which the conspirators leave the body of the dictator unattended and abandon the idea of getting rid of it by throwing it into the Tiber, they lose everything. The Caesarians begin to regain ground when they are able to make political and emotional capital out of the corpse, whose cumbrous presence weighs increasingly heavily, and in the end decisively, on Roman politics. Shakespeare recognised the 'potential' of this corpse when in Antony's (partly imagined) speech before the bloodstained body he captured the mood of the urban plebs.

In the very first moments after the murder, Brutus and the others make every possible effort to get the situation under control. Their efforts are mostly doomed to failure. The fact that for a brief moment they seemed to have succeeded is demonstrated by Antony's panic: he dresses as a plebeian and flees.[1] Brutus tries to talk to the senators, but they are bent on fleeing with all speed from the scene of the attack they have witnessed. Neglecting to dispose of the body and proceeding to a renunciation of all Caesar's works, they can think of nothing better than to go to the Capitol, waving their daggers and calling on imaginary citizens – the streets are deserted and the shops shut – to 'make the most of their freedom'. At the Capitol they wait a short while. Eventually some senators appear, and a small crowd, urging the conspirators to leave the Capitol.[2] Taking fresh heart, the group moves down to the Forum, where Brutus is hoisted onto the rostra and begins to speak. The crowd listens in silence. Then Cinna comes forward and begins to denounce Caesar. At this the crowd erupts in violent anger and the conspirators beat a hasty retreat back to the Capitol.[3] Brutus fears the crowd will storm the hill and that all will be lost.

Thus in the space of a few hours the conspirators lose all the advantages of surprise and the confusion of their opponents, by trying to present to the people some abstract 'freedom'.

Antony quickly realised that the plotters had no plan for the hours immediately following the coup and that they (or Brutus, at least) were counting on the purifying effects of 'tyrannicide' and the word 'freedom'. He promptly shed his disguise and resorted to two ploys which proved successful. He sent his son to the 'liberators' as a 'hostage', thus persuading them to come down from the Capitol, and let it be widely known that Cassius was dining at the house of Antony and Brutus at the house of Lepidus.[4] The next morning he was greeted in the Senate as the man who had saved the city from a new civil war.[5] And despite the opposition of Cassius, but with the consent of Brutus, he succeeded in having Caesar's will read out in the Senate, and in ensuring that the dictator was not buried secretly and without honour.[6] In his *Life of Brutus*, as we know, Plutarch in his account of the conspiracy relies above all on two sources very close to the man who epitomises the assassination. For this reason his view of Brutus' decisions in those first hours is highly significant: 'In allowing Caesar's funeral rites to be conducted as Antony demanded, he committed a fatal error.'[7] This was the opinion which formed among Brutus' colleagues. It can also be seen in the barely concealed criticisms set down by Cicero in his letters, especially in his famous letter to Cassius,[8] in which he regrets not having had his say while the plot was being prepared, and thus failing to name Antony as the next target of the assassins. (Cassius and his *hetairia* had sought in vain to have Antony murdered too.) In the months following the Ides of March, while the situation in Rome shifted in favour of the Caesarians,[9] a kind of complicity emerged between Cicero and Cassius, which, to judge from the surviving correspondence, had already shown itself in the months before the assassination. There was no such understanding between Cicero and Brutus. Brutus was restrained in his feelings for Cicero, in spite of the deference with which Cicero continued to dedicate his books to him, one after another. Brutus may have privately thought that he might be able to come to an agreement with Antony – a good compromise between true *nobiles*.

Antony was well aware of what Caesar had written in his will, which was made on 13 September 45 and entrusted to the care of the Vestals. It was opened at the request of Lucius Calpernus Piso, Caesar's father-in-law, at Antony's house.[10] Thus he also knew, for example, that Caesar had nominated as his heir, more precisely 'among his heirs in the second degree',[11] the formerly devoted Decimus Brutus, who on the morning of the Ides had delivered Caesar into the hands of his murderers almost by force. And several of the plotters were named as possible guardians for his (adopted) son Octavius, now Gaius Julius Caesar Octavian, should the need arise for a guardian. There was therefore an abundance of material which would show the 'liberators' in a bad light if the provisions of the will were read out in public, even without his bequests and donations to the people.[12]

On 20 March the body was carried to the Forum. The lying in state was skilfully managed for maximum effect. The choice of venue, above all, was felicitous: the Field of Mars, and a site beside the tomb of Julia, Caesar's beloved daughter, who for as long as she lived had been the guarantee of a stable relationship between Pompey, her husband, and Caesar, her father.[13] As a setting, a gilded shrine was constructed before the rostra, in shape reminiscent of the temple of Venus Genetrix, Caesar's ancestress and a deity supremely dear to the Romans. The bier was made entirely of ivory, with coverlets of purple and gold (the colours representing power), showing up clearly the toga Caesar had been wearing at the time of the murder.[14] With more than twenty knife-rents, it did much to enhance the drama of the scene, even without the display of the body itself. When Antony began his speech and sensed the rising mood of the crowd, like a good actor he seized the dead man's toga and held it aloft so that all could see the cuts,[15] and deliberately stirred up the emotion, provoking a riot which resolved itself in a scene of deification of the body. Cremation took place amidst a popular outburst by a crowd bent on vengeance, filled equally with rage and mysticism.

Plutarch paints the following picture:[16]

> Some cried out to kill the murderers, and others, as formerly in the case of Clodius the demagogue, dragged from the shops the benches and tables, piled them upon one another, and thus erected a huge pyre; on this they placed Caesar's body, and in the midst of many sanctuaries, asylums, and holy places, burned it.[17] Moreover, when the fire blazed up, people rushed from all sides, snatched up half-burnt brands, and ran round to the houses of Caesar's slayers to set them on fire.[18]

This is a somewhat perfunctory account, leaving certain facts without illumination, as can be seen from Suetonius' account. The shrine in which Caesar's dagger-pierced toga was displayed, among other items, was left on the Field of Mars for several days for the benefit of those who wished to place gifts by the bier. Funeral games were held, and musicians and actors dressed up, using garments of Caesar's 'from the equipment of his triumphs'. Suggestive verses were sung, such as those from 'The Contest for the Arms' of Pacuvius, containing the line, 'Saved I these men that they might murder me?'[19] At this the crowd erupted.[20] The event was skilfully managed. Antony had a herald recite the *senatus consultum* in which all members of the Senate pledged to protect the person of Caesar.[21]

When the bier was brought down to the Forum with the body of the dictator, carried by magistrates and ex-magistrates, emotions reached fever pitch. They were further excited by an additional piece of theatre, a scene which clearly required stage-management, reported by Appian: in order to work the crowd to a frenzy it was necessary to display the wounded body, but this was not possible. Instead,

> somebody raised above the bier an image of Caesar himself made of wax. The body itself, as it lay back on its couch, could not be seen. The image was turned round and round by a mechanical device [*mechané*; a truly theatrical contraption], showing the twenty-three wounds in all parts of the body and on the face, that had been dealt to him so brutally. The people could no longer bear the pitiful sight presented to them.[22]

Then came the release of pent-up feeling, and the fire was lit. In a fevered atmosphere of apotheosis, amid calls for revenge, differing proposals were heard as to where to cremate the body. With heated debate raging (some urging cremation in the temple of Jupiter on the Capitol, others in the Hall of Pompey – to continue a kind of play of symbols), two heavily armed men, with swords at their sides and javelins, set fire to the bier.[23] Thus it was that there arose the gigantic funeral pyre of which Plutarch speaks, onto which everything was thrown, including the clothes that the actors and musicians tore off their own backs. It remains unclear who orchestrated the surprise of the wax effigy of Caesar, and who arranged the armed men to resolve the matter of the venue.[24]

At this point, in all three of his *Lives* dealing with the funeral of Caesar,[25] Plutarch places the murderers at the centre of attention. He relates the assault on their homes, and its tragic 'coda': the brutal murder of Gaius Helvius Cinna, mistaken by the enraged mob for the *praetor* Lucius Cornelius Cinna (who the day before had delivered a violent speech against Caesar, when Brutus came down from the Capitol and tried to make a speech).

Suetonius, on the other hand, takes a different tack, with an apparent narrative inversion. He concentrates primarily on the impressive spectacle of the homage paid to Caesar's ashes by foreigners: 'At the height of the public grief a throng of foreigners went about lamenting each after the fashion of his country, above all the Jews, who even flocked to the place for several successive nights.'[26] This point is important as it helps us to see the true dimensions of Caesar: a victim of the traditional Roman political caste, lionised by peoples who were distant but still constituted a significant presence in the multi-ethnic kaleidoscope of the capital of the empire.

Not that Suetonius overlooks the other side of the event: the crowd's lust for revenge, the assault on the homes of the 'liberators'; the murder by mistake of Gaius Helvius Cinna, a grimly significant episode of rampant brutality, which emerges with full clarity only in Suetonius' account:

> They slew Helvius Cinna [. . .] supposing him to be Cornelius Cinna, who had the day before made a bitter indictment of Caesar and for whom they were looking; and they set his head on a spear and paraded it about the streets.[27]

The mutilation of the body (of Cinna, but the same fate awaited the conspirators if only the crowd could break through the cordon of troops with which they had surrounded themselves) was the instinctive response to the collective violation which the conspirators had wrought upon the body of Caesar.

The spontaneity of the acts witnessed at the funeral is striking. Antony by his speech and his orchestration had awakened forces that he himself was uncertain what to do with: should they be encouraged or suppressed? It is clear that the days of the funeral rites tilted the scales towards the Caesarians, above all towards Antony, the incumbent consul, who, after a moment of panic, returned to the scene as a consummate stage-manager. The martyred body of Caesar did him great service in allowing him to turn the situation around.

But some spontaneous displays of opposition, continuing and even spreading, must have been alarming for him. The most persistent was the phenomenon of the so-called 'false Marius'. This individual gave himself out to be the son of Marius the Younger and grandson of Marius the Great, and therefore a close relative of Caesar himself, whose aunt Julia was married to Gaius Marius. If he was really the son of Marius the Younger, this would make Amatius ('false Marius') a second cousin of Caesar, in the same relation to Caesar as Sextus Caesar (also the son of Caesar's cousin), to whom the dictator had entrusted the province of Syria in 47 BC. This man, by trade an eye-doctor,[28] probably a former slave, displayed ability and determination. During Caesar's long absence in Spain in 45, numerous colonies of veterans, towns and important *collegia* had adopted him as their *patronus*, accepting his claim of a blood-relationship.[29] In addition, several women of the family had recognised him, except for Atia, the mother of Octavius, who for obvious reasons was anxious to protect her son against possible rivals. Amatius, however, managed to gain the trust of the young Octavius, who held him in high regard but as usual left the last word to Caesar as 'head of the family'.[30] But when Caesar returned from Spain he sent Amatius out of Italy.[31] After Caesar's death Amatius reappeared, having established relations with Cicero as well,[32] and used the site of Caesar's cremation as his platform for agitation.

Amatius had an altar constructed and initiated a cult of Caesar as a deity, thus becoming, with the broad approval of the urban plebs, the true founder of the cult of *Divus Julius*. 'He collected a band of reckless men and made himself a perpetual terror to the murderers.'[33] Antony had him suddenly arrested and executed without trial, on the pretext of the threats he had made against Brutus and Cassius. The Senate pretended to be scandalised by this illegal procedure, writes Appian, while remaining basically content because at last Brutus and Cassius could breathe easily.[34] The elimination of Amatius led to insurrection among his followers, who enjoyed broad support among the townsfolk and were openly hostile to Antony. They attempted to put forward demands for the consecration of the altar which Amatius had built to Caesar in the place where the body had been cremated, along with regular sacrifices, but they were dispersed by force. It is symptomatic of the changes then in train that some busts of Caesar were removed from their pedestals and secretly destroyed in various workshops. Amatius' supporters tried to set fire to these workshops, but the reaction by Antony's troops was brutal. Some were killed, the others captured, 'and of these the slaves were crucified and the freemen thrown over the Tarpeian rock'.[35] The Alexandrian historian comments that in this way, 'the extreme fondness of the plebeians for Antony was turned into extreme hatred. The Senate was delighted, because it believed that it could not rest secure otherwise about Brutus and his associates.'[36]

Notes

1 Plutarch, *Brutus* 18.3. In Plutarch's *Life of Antony* (14.1) Antony puts on 'slave's clothing'. He is said to have done the same the year before, on hearing that Caesar had died at Munda (*Antony* 10.8).
2 Plutarch, *Brutus* 18.4–5.
3 Plutarch, *Brutus* 18.6–7.
4 Plutarch, *Brutus* 19.2–3.
5 Plutarch, *Antony* 14.4, ἀνῃρηκέναι δοκῶν ἐμφύλιον πόλεμον.

6 Plutarch, *Brutus* 20.1.

7 Plutarch, *Brutus* 20.2, τοῦ παντὸς σφαλῆναι.

8 Cicero, *Letters to his friends* 12.4.1. (See Chapter 37, n. 8, and Chapter 38, n. 6.)

9 Leaving aside the unknown factor of the first disconcerting moves by the very young Octavius, who all at once reappeared as 'Caesar's son'.

10 Suetonius, *Caesar* 83.1.

11 Suetonius, *Caesar* 83.2.

12 Ibid.: 'to the people he left his gardens near the Tiber for their common use and 300 sesterces to each man'.

13 It was no accident that Lucius Domitius Ahenobarbus had opposed the solemn burial for Julia. At the time (like Cato and others) he had been at war with both.

14 Suetonius, *Caesar* 84.1.

15 Plutarch, *Brutus* 20.4.

16 Plutarch, *Brutus* 20.4.

17 This implies that the holy places were thus profaned.

18 A similar but briefer account is given in Plutarch's *Life of Antony* 14.7–8.

19 This may be from the lament of Aiax before his suicide.

20 Appian, *Civil Wars* 2.146.611.

21 Suetonius, *Caesar* 84.2.

22 Appian, *Civil Wars* 2.147.612–13.

23 Suetonius, *Caesar* 84.3.

24 In Appian's account the sequence of events is slightly different: the attempt to set fire to the murderers' houses and the murder of Cinna take place immediately after the showing of the wax effigy. Only after the attack on the murderers has failed is the funeral pyre raised and ignited. There is also an attempt by the crowd, foiled 'by the priests', to bury Caesar 'with the gods' on the Capitol (Appian, *Civil Wars* 2.148.615). If this is correct it shows how far the situation had slipped out of Antony's control.

25 Plutarch, *Caesar* 68.2–3; *Brutus* 20.3–6; *Antony* 14.8.

26 Suetonius, *Caesar* 84.5. See also Chapter 24.

27 Suetonius, *Caesar* 84.5.

28 Valerius Maximus 9.15.1: 'ocularius medicus'.

29 Ibid.

30 Nicolaus of Damascus, *Life of Augustus* 32–3.

31 According to Valerius Maximus 9.15.1.

32 Cicero, *Letters to Atticus* 12.49.1.

33 Appian, *Civil Wars* 3.2.3. Appian speaks of Amatius in most respectful tones.

34 The other assassins had by one means or another disappeared from Rome.

35 Appian, *Civil Wars* 3.3.9.

36 Appian, *Civil Wars* 3.4.10.

CHAPTER 42

The Wind

A fragment of Livy, most probably from book 116 (a 'definitive' portrait of Caesar following the account of his death),[1] raised a question mark over Caesar's entire career. By citing it Seneca introduced a new angle, which has its own profound poetry – an analogy with the wind: 'As things are, however, it could be said of winds what was commonly said of Julius Caesar, as reported by Titus Livy; it is uncertain whether it was better for the state that Caesar had been born or not.' It would be wrong to read this as a hostile judgement on Caesar. Rather it stems from a state of profound perplexity: because nobody would categorically 'condemn' the wind, although everybody knows what destruction it can wreak. And in fact Seneca continues:

> Indeed, whatever is useful and necessary from the winds cannot be balanced by the things which the madness of mankind devises for its own destruction. Even if they do cause harm by the wrongdoing of men who use them evilly, not on this account are the winds evil by nature. Actually, Providence and that god who is the organiser of the universe did not arrange to move the atmosphere by winds and to distribute winds from all directions (lest anything become barren because of inactivity) only so that we might fill up our fleets with armed soldiers to seize part of the deep waters and only so that we might seek out an enemy on the sea or even beyond the sea!

The profundity of this analogy is breath-taking. Seneca teeters on the brink of a decision which he fails to take. Through the metaphor of the wind, he helps us see Caesar as a whirlwind. Almost all the expressions he applies to the wind might also refer to the political and above all military career of the dictator. When he refers, for example, to 'misuse' of the wind, by going to seek out enemies on the sea or beyond the sea, this can only be an allusion to his expedition to Britain, which many judged to be pointless, a classic 'futile slaughter', motivated, some thought (admittedly those ill-disposed to Caesar's military adventures), by his greed for pearls.[2] And when he refers in the same note, apparently in a purely meteorological sense, to the usefulness of the winds, as an antidote to the 'decay' resulting from immobility, we are reminded of a famous 'wartime speech' by the great German philologist Wilamowitz in 1914:[3] Wilamowitz blamed a 'dead calm' and the resultant spiritual decay following the *pax Augusta* for the decline of the Roman empire.

The uncertainty over the provenance of the manuscript notwithstanding, it goes without saying that Seneca's suggestive analogy (making use of Livy) points to Caesar and not to Gaius Marius.[4] It should also be underlined that this comparison between Caesar and the wind leads us into the heart of the spiritual and moral tension which gave birth to Seneca's *Natural Questions*: the contrast between the world of political history and the world of nature – the former often irrational and incomprehensible, the latter reassuring and deserving of diligent study.

Livy, then, concludes his portrait of Caesar with this memorable judgement, reflecting deep ambivalence. If Augustus called Livy 'the Pompeian',[5] one of Livy's pages which must have supported this opinion would have been this one, perhaps the most important and the most thoughtful in Livy's eight books on the civil war. The mind of the *princeps* was such that we cannot say with certainty, at this distance from the events, that Livy's view would have displeased Augustus, even if it was equivocal on the historical role of his adoptive father. And 'Pompeian' was most probably no insult from Augustus, since his own form of government appeared closer to the role of *princeps* and protector, which Pompey would have favoured, than to the dictatorship which his adoptive father had created, and which eventually destroyed him. Octavian had begun life as a dutiful son, justly eager for vengeance, who built his fortunes as a party leader on the greatness and the legacy of Gaius Julius Caesar, but he ended his long career as a statesman with the restoration of the republic, becoming *princeps* on the basis of the constitution, and restored the old tradition. Livy the historian might well pronounce an equivocal judgement on the man who had inflicted upon the republic five terrible years of almost unbroken civil war and left no workable model for the reordering of the state. Augustus could not have shared this view, but he could well have condoned it. In private, at least, he would have acknowledged that without Caesar he would have remained the son of Gaius Octavius from Velletri (Velitrae). And as for Livy, if he was harsh in his judgement of Caesar, this was due not only to the detached and critical eye with which the Paduan provincial looked upon all the men of the civil war – one needs only to think of his severe judgement of Cicero as a would-be proscriber![6] – but also to his narrow-mindedness: until he had personal evidence to the contrary,[7] Livy really believed that Augustus had restored the republic. And from this perspective all of Caesar's works could seem a prolonged and costly crisis leading inevitably to failure.

But from Seneca we also learn something else, which the philosopher probably drew from Livy: namely, that the judgement to which Seneca, through his analogy with the wind, gave immense ethical and historical depth was current ('vulgo dictatum') before Livy adopted it. In spite of the popularity so ably won and so long enduring, Caesar left much puzzlement in the mind of later generations: like those citizens who, according to Plutarch, when they saw the 'liberator-murderers' holding forth, were respectful towards Brutus while at the same time thinking of Caesar. These are the people, who, in Shakespeare's critical and contemptuous presentation, first admire Brutus' bloodstained dagger, and are then swayed by Antony's oratory to sympathise with Caesar.

Where do the roots of this ambivalence lie? Not in nostalgia for the values which Brutus, the usurer, Stoic and fundamentalist republican, propounded in tedious speeches. 'The many', the recipients of the benefits of his able demagogy, his slogans, gifts and the direct advantages flowing from his conquests, wondered whether – assuming the question is meaningful – it might have been better if Caesar had never been born. This question may have had more profoundly humane origins: the human cost of eight years of foreign wars and five of civil war.

The 'black book', the calculations by Pliny and Plutarch, of millions upon millions of dead weighed heavy. It also weighed heavy upon the minds of those who judged Caesar favourably. It was the human cost which lay at the root of that doubt. But that cost was not sufficient to cancel out the greatness of his deeds and the transformations he wrought. After the Caesarian storm, the republic could no longer remain the same, and it did not, in spite of the 'republican alchemy' of his adopted son. Perhaps in Caesar's harsh but realistic judgement the transformations were worth the cost: the resistance of the old order, so dear to the usurer-heroes, had forced him to apply the same brutal measures which Sulla had used to guarantee the dominance of the *nobilitas* in the old city-state only a few years earlier.

A French *libertin* and essayist of the seventeenth century once wrote that Caesar's weakness lay in the vagueness of his plans. This essayist, who had reflected at length, some time before Montesquieu, on the history of Rome, was Charles de Saint-Denis, seigneur de

Saint-Évremond, called Saint-Évremond for short. He framed his critique of the long-term effects of the works of Caesar in an elegant dissertation on the meaning of the word 'vaste' for the Académie française. He took as his point of departure Caesar's 'fantasy' – to use his words – of 'making war on the Parthians when it would have been better to secure the support of the Romans'. And in an apparent contradiction he traces all the actions of that great 'man of action' back to his *uncertainty*:

> In this state of uncertainty, in which the Romans were neither citizens nor subjects and Caesar was neither magistrate nor tyrant, in which he broke all the laws of the republic without being able to establish his own, confused, lost in vast ideas of his own grandeur, incapable of ordering his thoughts any more than his affairs, Caesar offended the Senate and put his trust in the senators. He trusted disloyal and ungrateful people, who, preferring freedom to his virtues, chose to murder a friend and benefactor rather than have a master over them. Praise his vast spirit: it cost Caesar his empire and his life.[8]

At the end of his *Second Philippic*, one of his harshest speeches, Cicero sketches the following picture of Caesar:

> In him there was genius, calculation, memory, letters, industry, thought, diligence; he had done in war things, however calamitous to the State, yet at least great; having for many years aimed at a throne, he had by great labour, great dangers, achieved his object; by shows, buildings, largesses, banquets he had conciliated the ignorant crowd; his own followers he had bound to him by rewards, his adversaries by a show of clemency: in brief, he had already brought to a free community – partly by fear, partly by endurance – a habit of servitude.[9]

Untroubled by the fact that his *In defence of Marcellus* had been circulating for more than a year, Cicero concludes his *Second Philippic* by contrasting Caesar and Antony, favouring the former, of course, but still with the clear intention of restoring proper proportions to the figure of the dictator recently cut down. His portrait of Caesar ranks with the many acute portraits which recur throughout Roman historiography. It was not intended to be a one-sided denigration (and it is not). It seeks to be balanced, eschewing anything that smacks of the clichés of the encomium (which mark even *In defence of Marcellus*). Even the widely acknowledged *clementia Caesaris* here becomes *clementiae species*, a mask or show; the military conquests are 'great' but 'calamitous to the State'; his personal gifts are undeniable, but the true passion of this disquieting life so prematurely terminated was the *regnum* (that is, the flagitious antithesis of the aristocratic ideal of the *libera res publica*); he has appeased the people, seducing them in demagogic fashion with material temptations; even his adversaries (or some of them, at least) have been unable to resist his persuasive skill. What is missing from this portrait is an accusation against the dead man, one usually levelled against the Caesar of the early period: the charge of having passed into law or imposed, or of having tried to impose, the traditional 'revolutionary' programme of an assault on wealth. This was the programme that Caesar had spent the early part of his career cultivating. Cicero's silence is certainly not intended to conceal anything. Rather it signals recognition of the novelty, the unprecedented nature of Caesar's dictatorship, standing far apart from all familiar models. It was this novelty which led Plutarch (or his source) to imagine the scene of Caesar's painful 'confession' in the Senate during his turbulent first consulship: 'crying with loud adjurations that he was driven forth into the popular assembly against his wishes, and was compelled to court its favour by the insolence and obstinacy of the Senate'.[10] When they killed him his assassins did not realise that they had eliminated the best and most far-sighted mind of their class.

Notes

1 It has been preserved thanks to Seneca, *Natural Questions* 5.18.4.
2 Suetonius, *Caesar* 47. (Gibbon believed this.)
3 U. von Wilamowitz-Möllendorff, 'Weltreich des Augustus', in *Reden aus der Kriegszeit* (Berlin 1915).
4 The Geneva manuscript (Z) has *de C. marior*, not *de Caesare maiori* (*maiore*). It is unlikely that Seneca regarded Marius as responsible for the great watershed in Roman history, or that Marius' place in history was a regular subject of debate for those who came later (*vulgo dictatum*). The comparison with Livy's *Periocha* 80 is tenuous.
5 Tacitus, *Annals* 4.34.
6 Fr. 61 Weissenborn-Müller.
7 See L. Canfora, *Studi di storiografia romana* (Bari 1993), pp. 183–4.
8 Saint-Évremond, *Dissertation sur le mot de vaste* (1665–70), now available ed. D. Bensoussan (Paris 1998), p. 130.
9 Cicero, *Philippics* 2.116. See Chapter 15.
10 Plutarch, *Caesar* 14.3.

Chronology

For the events in Caesar's life up to the end of the Gallic wars the dates we have are mostly approximate. For the years of the civil war, on the other hand, the sources, above all Caesar's *Commentaries*, give exact dates. In these cases the dates usually refer to the pre-Julian calendar and the Julian calendar (following the systems of Le Verrier and Groebe).

The pre-Julian calendar, based on the lunar year (355 days), made provision for the addition of an intercalary month of 22 or 23 days every two years, so that in a four-year cycle an average year-length of 366 days could be achieved, matching the solar year. The arbitrariness of the extra months, controlled by the *pontifex maximus*, had led to an increasing disjuncture between the civil and the astronomical calendars. It was only Caesar's reform of 46 BC which achieved the complete and final harmonisation of the two calendars, from 1 January 45 BC. To stabilise the chronological equivalence between pre-Julian calendar and Julian dates, two systems are applied: one devised by U. Le Verrier (adopted by Napoleon III, *Histoire de Jules César*, vol. II [Paris 1866], pp. 456–84), and one by P. Groebe (in W. Drumann and P. Groebe, *Geschichte Roms in seinem Übergange von der republikanischen zur monarchischen Verfassung* [Leipzig 1906], 2nd edn, vol. III, pp. 753–827). The abbreviations used for the historical sources are given at the end of the Chronology.

All dates in the Chronology are BC.

1 Events up to the Gallic campaigns

12 or 13 July 100	Birth of Caesar. (Vell. Pat. 2.41.2; Plut., *Caes.* 69.1; Suet., *Caes.* 88; App., *Civil Wars* 2.106.149; Dio Cass. 47.18.6; Macr., *Sat.* 1.12.34; *Fast. Amit.*, p. 189; *Fast. Ant.*, p. 208)
87	Caesar is *flamen Dialis*. (Plut., *Caes.* 7.1.3; Suet., *Caes.* 1.1; Vell. Pat. 2.43.1)

85	Death of Gaius Julius Caesar the father. (Pliny 7.181; Suet., *Caes.* 1.1)
83	Caesar is divorced from Cossutia and marries Cornelia, daughter of Cinna. (Plut., *Caes.* 1.1; Suet., *Caes.* 1.1)
82	Caesar refuses to repudiate his wife and leaves Rome to evade Sulla. (Vell. Pat. 2.41.2; Plut., *Caes.* 1.1; Suet., *Caes.* 1.1–2; 74.1; Dio Cass. 43.43.4)
81	Takes part in the siege of Mytilene on the orders of *propraetor* Thermus. (Suet., *Caes.* 2.1; [Aurelius Victor], *On famous men* 78.1)
80	As Thermus' legate, goes to the court of Nicomedes IV of Bithynia. (Plut., *Caes.* 1.7; Suet., *Caes.* 2.1; 49.3; Gell. 5.13.6; Dio Cass. 43.20.2; [Aurelius Victor], *On famous men* 78.1)
78	Death of Sulla. Caesar returns to Rome. (Plut., *Caes.* 4.1; Suet., *Caes.* 3)
77–76	Prosecutes Dolabella and Gaius Antonius Hybrida. (Vell. Pat. 2.43.3; Asc., pp. 26, 74; Plut., *Caes.* 4.1–2; Suet., *Caes.* 4.1; Gell. 4.16.8; [Aurelius Victor], *On famous men* 78.2)
75–74	During a voyage to Rhodes, is captured by pirates and held on Pharmacussa. Assembles a small force and takes part in the third war against Mithridates. (Vell. Pat. 2.41.3; Plut., *Caes.* 1.8–2; Val. Max. 6.9.15; Suet., *Caes.* 4.1–2; [Aurelius Victor], *On famous men* 78.3)
73	Returns to Rome. Is elected to the college of *pontifices*. (Vell. Pat. 2.43.1)
72 or 71	Military tribune. (Plut., *Caes.* 5.1; Suet., *Caes.* 5)
70	First consulate of Pompey and Crassus. (Cic., *Verr.* 2.3.123; Sall., *Cat.* 38.1; *Fast. Cons.*, pp. 486–7)
69	Quaestor in Further Spain under *praetor* Gaius Antistius Vetus. Delivers the eulogies for his aunt Julia and his wife Cornelia. (*Spanish War* 42.1; Vell. Pat. 2.43.4; Plut., *Caes.* 5.2–4; 5.6; Suet., *Caes.* 6–8; Dio Cass. 37.52.2; 41.24.2)
68	Marries Pompeia. (Plut., *Caes.* 5.7; Suet., *Caes.* 6.2)

67	Supports the *Lex Gabinia*. (Plut., *Pomp.* 25.8)
66	With Cicero supports the *Lex Manilia de imperio Pompeii*. (Dio Cass. 36.43.2–4)
65	Curule *aedile*. (Caes., *Civil War* 3.16.3; Vell. Pat. 2.43.4; Plut., *Caes.* 5.9–6.3; Suet., *Caes.* 10; Dio Cass. 37.8.2)
63	Elected *pontifex maximus*. Speaks in Senate against death penalty for Catilinarians. (Sall., *Cat.* 49.2–51; Cic., *Letters to Atticus* 12.21.1; Vell. Pat. 2.43.3; Plut., *Caes.* 7–8; Suet., *Caes.* 14; Gell. 5.13.6; Dio Cass. 37.36.1–2; 44.1)
62	*Praetor*. (Cic., *Letters to Atticus* 2.24.3; Vell. Pat. 2.43.4; Dio Cass. 37.44) After the scandal provoked by Clodius during the feast of Bona Dea, rejects Pompeia. (Cic., *Letters to Atticus* 1.12.3; 13.3; Plut., *Caes.* 10; Suet., *Caes.* 6.2)
61	Sent to Further Spain as *propraetor*. Operations against the Lusitanians. (Cic., *Balb.* 43; Liv., *Per.* 103; Vell. Pat. 2.43.4; Plut., *Caes.* 12; Suet., *Caes.* 18.1; App., *Iber.* 102; App., *Civil Wars.* 2.8; Dio Cass. 37.52–3)
60	Triumvirate with Pompey and Crassus. (Cic., *Letters to Atticus* 2.3.3; Liv., *Per.* 103; Vell. Pat., 2.44.1–3; Plut., *Caes.* 14.1–2; Suet., *Caes.* 19.2; App., *Civil Wars* 2.9; Dio Cass. 37.55–7)
59	Consul for the first time. Marries Calpurnia. (Liv., *Per.* 103; Plut., *Caes.* 14.1–2.8; Suet., *Caes.* 19.2; 21; Dio Cass. 44.41.3–4; *Fast. Capit.*, p. 57)
March 58	Leaves for Gaul. (Caes., *Gallic War* 1.7.1; Plut., *Caes.* 17.5)
April–June 58	Campaign against the Helvetii. Defeat of the Helvetii at Bibracte. (Caes., *Gallic War* 1.2–29; Liv., *Per.* 103; Strab. 4.3.3; Plut., *Caes.* 18; App., *Gallic history* fr. 1.3.15; Dio Cass. 38.31–3)
July–September 58	Campaign against the Germanic tribes. Occupation of Vesontio (Besançon). Defeat of Ariovistus. (Caes., *Gallic War* 1.30–54; Liv., *Per.* 104; Plut., *Caes.* 19; App., *Gallic history* fr. 1.3; Dio Cass. 38.34–50)
Autumn 58– winter 58–57	Spends the winter in Gallia Cisalpina. (Caes., *Gallic War* 1.54.2–3; Plut., *Caes.* 20.1–3)

Spring–summer 57	Campaign against the Belgae. Defeat of the Belgae coalition on the Axona (Aisne). Publius Crassus subjugates the peoples of Armorica. (Caes., *Gallic War* 2; Plut., *Caes.* 20.4–10; App., *Gallic history* fr. 1.4; Dio Cass. 39.1–5)
4 September 57 (16 August 57; 17 August 57)	Cicero returns from exile to Rome. (Cic., *Letters to Atticus* 4.1.4–5; Liv., *Per.* 104; App., *Civil Wars* 2.16; Dio Cass. 39.9.1)
Late/early September 57	Senate decrees a fifteen-day *supplicatio* for Caesar's achievements. (Caes., *Gallic War* 2.35.4; Cic., *Balb.* 61; Cic., *Prov. cons.* 25–7; Cic., *Letters to his friends* 1.9.14; Plut., *Caes.* 21.1; Suet., *Caes.* 24.3; Dio Cass. 39.5.1.)
Late summer 57	Publius Crassus carries out the first reconnaissance of the coast of Britain. (Strab. 3.5.11)
Autumn 57– winter 57–56	Caesar spends the winter in Gallia Cisalpina. (Caes., *Gallic War* 2.35.4; Plut., *Caes.* 21.3–5; App., *Civil Wars* 2.17; Dio Cass. 39.5.1)
April 56	Meeting in Luca with Pompey and Crassus: renewal of the triumviral pact. (Plut., *Caes.* 21.6; Plut., *Pomp.* 51.4–8; App., *Civil Wars* 2.17–18)
Summer– autumn 56	Military operations against the Alpine peoples. Naval warfare against the Veneti (battle of Quiburn). Crassus' expedition to Aquitania. Operations against the Morini and the Menapii. (Caes., *Gallic War* 3; Liv., *Per.* 104; Dio Cass. 39.40–6)
Autumn 56– winter 56–55	Caesar spends the winter in Gallia Cisalpina. (Caes., *Gallic War* 3.29.3)
55	Second consulate of Pompey and Crassus. *Lex Pompeia Licinia* extends Caesar's proconsulate in Gaul for five years. (Caes., *Gallic War* 4.1.1; Vell. Pat. 2.46.1; Plut., *Pomp.* 52.1–4; App., *Civil Wars* 2.17–18; Dio Cass. 39.27–31; *Fast. Cons.*, pp. 494–5)
Spring–summer 55	Campaign against the Usipetes and the Tencteri. First crossing of the Rhine. (Caes., *Gallic War* 4.1–19; Liv., *Per.* 105; Luc. 2.570; Plut., *Caes.* 22–3.1; Suet., *Caes.* 25.2; App., *Gallic history* fr. 1.5.18; Dio Cass. 39.47–9)

Late September–early November 55 (early August–late September 55)	First expedition to Britain. (Caes., *Gallic War* 4.20–36; Liv., *Per.* 105; Vell. Pat. 2.46.1; Luc. 2.571–2; Plut., *Caes.* 23.2–4; Suet., *Caes.* 25.2; App., *Gallic history* fr. 1.5; Dio Cass. 39.50–2)
Autumn 55–winter 55–54	Senate decrees a twenty-day *supplicatio*. Caesar moves to Gallia Cisalpina and visits Illyricum. (Caes., *Gallic War* 4.38.4–5.1; Plut., *Caes.* 24.1; Suet., *Caes.* 24.3; Dio Cass., 39.53.2)
Summer 54	Second expedition to Britain. Caesar defeats Cassivellaunus. (Caes., *Gallic War* 5.5–23; Cic., *Letters to Atticus* 4.15.10; 4.18.5; Cic., *Letters to Quintus* 3.1.25; Dio Cass. 40.1–3)
September 54	Death of daughter Julia, wife of Pompey. (Liv., *Per.* 106; Vell. Pat. 2.47.2; Plut., *Caes.* 23.5–7; Suet., *Caes.* 26.1; App., *Civil Wars* 2.19)
Autumn 54	Insurrection of the Eburones, led by Ambiorix. (Caes., *Gallic War* 5.26–52; Liv., *Per.* 106; Plut., *Caes.* 24; Dio Cass. 40.4–11)
Autumn 54–winter 54–53	Revolt of the Senones and the Treveri. Caesar spends the winter in Gaul. (Caes., *Gallic War* 5.53–8; Dio Cass. 40.11.2)
Winter–summer 53	Expeditions against the Nervii, Carnutes, Senones, Treveri and Menapii. Second crossing of the Rhine. Caesar crushes the Eburones. (Caes., *Gallic War* 6; Plut., *Caes.* 25.3–5; Dio Cass. 40.32)
12 June 53	(31 May 53; 9 May 53) Death of Crassus at Carrhae in the expedition against the Parthians. (Caes., *Gallic War* 3.31.3; Liv., *Per.* 106; Vell. Pat. 2.46.4; Plut., *Crass.* 31.1–6; App., *Civil Wars* 2.18; Dio Cass. 40.27)
Autumn 53–winter 53–52	Caesar spends the winter in Gallia Cisalpina. (Caes., *Gallic War* 6.44.3–7.1.1; Dio Cass. 40.32.5)
18 January 52 (1 January 52; 8 December 53)	Murder of Clodius at Bovillae. (Caes., *Gallic War* 7.1.1; Cic., *Mil.* 27; 45; Liv., *Per.* 107; Vell. Pat., 2.47.4; Asc. p. 31; Suet., *Caes.* 26.1; App., *Civil Wars* 2.21; Dio Cass., 40.48.2–3)
February 52	General rising in Gaul, led by Vercingetorix. (Caes., *Gallic War* 7.2–5; Liv., *Per.* 107; Plut., *Caes.* 26–7; Dio Cass. 40.33–41)

End of intercalary month 52 (end of February 52; early February 52)	Pompey nominated as sole consul. (Cic., *Letters to Atticus* 7.1.4; 8.3.3; Liv., *Per.* 107; Vell. Pat. 2.47.3; Plut., *Caes.* 28.7; Plut., *Pomp.* 54.6–9; App., *Civil Wars* 2.23; Dio Cass. 40.50.4; *Fast. Cons.*, pp. 496–7)
Spring 52	Capture of Vellaunodunum, Cenabum, Noviodunum and Avaricum. (Caes., *Gallic War* 7.15–28; Liv., *Per.* 107; Flor. 1.45.23; Dio Cass. 40.34)
May–June 52	Caesar defeated at Gergovia. (Caes., *Gallic War* 7.39–53; Liv., *Per.* 107; Suet., *Caes.* 25.2; Flor. 1.45.24–5; Dio Cass. 40.35.4–36.5)
August– September 52	Siege and capture of Alesia. (Caes., *Gallic War* 7.68–89; Liv., *Per.* 108; Vell. Pat. 2.47.1; Plut., *Caes.* 27.1–8; Flor. 1.45.23; Dio Cass. 40.40)
27 September 52 (25 September 52; 3 September 52)	Surrender of Vercingetorix. (Caes., *Gallic War* 7.89.3; Plut., *Caes.* 27.9–10; Flor. 1.45.26; Dio Cass. 40.41)
Autumn 52– winter 52–1	Caesar spends the winter at Bibracte. Senate decrees a twenty-day *supplicatio*. (Caes., *Gallic War* 7.90.7–8; Suet., *Caes.* 24.3; Dio Cass. 40.50.4)
Winter–summer 51	Campaigns against the Biturigi and Carnutes. War with the Bellovaci. Siege of Uxellodunum. Last operations in Gaul. ([Caes.], *Gallic War* 8.1–44; Liv., *Per.* 108; Dio Cass. 40.42–3)
1 May 51 (22 April 51; 31 March 51)	Cicero leaves to take up proconsulate in Cilicia. (Cic., *Letters to his friends* 2.8; 3.2; Plut., *Cic.* 36.1)
Autumn 51– winter 51–50	Caesar spends the winter in Gaul. ([Caes.], *Gallic War* 8.46.6)
Spring 50	After a foray into Italy, Caesar returns to his army in Gaul. ([Caes.], *Gallic War* 8.50–2.3)
April 50 (February–March 50)	First proposal of Curio in the Senate. ([Caes.], *Gallic War* 8.52.4–5; Liv., *Per.* 109; App., *Civil Wars* 2.27; Dio Cass. 40.62)
1 December 50 (7 November 50; 16 October 50)	Curio's proposal, presented again, is adopted. (Liv., *Per.* 109; App., *Civil Wars* 2.30)
December 50 (November 50)	Caesar returns to Italy. ([Caes.], *Gallic War* 54.5; Liv., *Per.* 109)

2 FROM THE RUBICON TO THE IDES OF MARCH

1 January 49 (6 December 50; 14 November 50)	Curio reads Caesar's letter in the Senate. (Caes., *Gallic War* 1.1.1; Plut., *Caes.* 30.3; Plut., *Ant.* 5.5; Suet., *Caes.* 29.2; App., *Civil Wars* 2.32; Dio Cass. 41.1)
4 January 49 (9 December 50; 17 November 50)	Cicero returns from Cilicia. (Cic., *Letters to Atticus* 7.3; 8.2; Cic., *Letters to his friends* 16.11.2; Plut., *Caes.* 31.1.)
7 January 49 (12 December 50; 20 November 50)	*Senatus consultum ultimum.* In the night the tribunes Mark Antony and Quintus Cassius flee to Ravenna. (Caes., *Civil War* 1.5.3–5; Cic., *Letters to his friends* 16.11.2; Dionysius of Halicarnassus, *Roman Antiquities* 8.87.7–8; Liv., *Per.* 109; Plut., *Caesar* 31.2; Plut., *Ant.* 5.8–10; Vell. Pat. 2.49.3; Suet., *Caesar* 31.1; 33.1; App., *Civil Wars* 2.33; Dio Cass. 45.27.2; 46.11.2–4.)
Night of 11 January 49 (16 December 50; 24 November 50)	Caesar crosses the Rubicon. (Plut., *Caes.* 32.4–8; Plut., *Pomp.* 60, 3–4; Vell. Pat. 2.49.4; Suet., *Caes.* 32; App., *Civil Wars* 2.35; Dio Cass. 41.4.1.)
12–15 January 49 (17–20 December 50; 25–8 November 50)	Occupation of Ariminum (Rimini), Pisarum (Pesaro), Fanum, Ancona and Arretium (Arezzo). (Caes., *Civil War* 1.8.1; 11.4; App., *Civil Wars* 2.35; Dio Cass. 41.4.1.)
17 January 49 (22 December 50; 30 November 50)	Pompey censured in Senate sitting. Flight of Pompey. (Caes., *Gallic War* 1.14.1–3; Plut., *Caes.* 33.4–6; 56.5; Plut., *Cato the Younger* 52.1–3; Plut., *Pomp.* 60.6–8; App., *Civil Wars* 2.37; Dio Cass. 41.6.1)
18 January 49 (23 December 50; 1 December 50)	Flight of the consuls and the Senate. (Caes., *Civil War* 1.14.1–3; Plut., *Caes.* 34.1; App., *Civil Wars* 2.37; Dio Cass. 41.7)
22 January 49 (27 December 50; 5 December 50)	Labienus defects to Pompey at Teanum. (Cic., *Letters to Atticus* 7.11.1; 12.5; 13A.3; Plut., *Caes.* 34.5; Plut., *Pomp.* 64.5; Dio Cass. 41.4.2–4)
23 January 49 (28 December 50; 6 December 50)	Pompey leaves Teanum. (Cic., *Letters to Atticus* 7.13A.3; 8.11B.2)

1–4 February 49 (4–7 January 49; 13–16 December 50)	Occupation of Iguvium (Gubbio) and Auxium (Osimo). (Caes., *Civil War* 1.12–13; Luc., 2.466–8)
5 February 49 (8 January 49; 17 December 50)	Arrival of the Twelfth Legion. Occupation of Firmum Picenum and Ascolum. Flight of Lentulus. (Caes., *Civil War* 1.15.3; 16.1; Luc., 2.466–8)
15–21 February 49; (18–24 January 49; 27 December 50 to 2 January 49)	Arrival of the Eighth Legion. Siege and capture of Corfinium. Caesar frees Lucius Domitius Ahenobarbus. (Caes., *Civil War* 1.18–23; Liv., *Per.* 109; Plut., *Caes.* 34.7–8; Vell. Pat. 2.50.1; Suet., *Caes.* 34.1; App., *Civil Wars* 2.38; Dio Cass. 41.10.2)
16 February 49 (19 January 49; 28 December 50)	Mark Antony takes Sulmo (Sulmona). (Caes., *Civil War* 1.18.2)
19 February 49; (22 January 49; 31 December 50)	Pompey leaves Lucera. (Caes., *Civil War* 1.24.1; Cic., *Letters to Atticus* 8.9.4)
21 February 49 (24 January 49; 2 January 49)	Pompey leaves Canusium (Canossa). (Caes., *Civil War* 1.24.1; Cic., *Letters to Atticus* 8.14.1; 9.1.1)
25 February 49 (28 January 49; 6 January 49)	Pompey reaches Brindisi. (Caes., *Civil War* 1.24.1; Cic., *Letters to Atticus* 9.10.8; Plut., *Caes.* 35.2)
1 March 49 (1 February 49; 10 January 49)	Caesar arrives in Arpi. (Caes., *Civil War* 1.23.5; Cic., *Letters to Atticus* 9.3.2)
4 March 49 (4 February 49; 13 January 49)	The consuls sail with thirty cohorts for Dyrrhachium (Durazzo). (Caes., *Civil War* 1.25.2; Plut., *Caes.*, 35.2; Plut., *Pomp.* 62.3; App., *Civil Wars* 2.39; Dio Cass. 41.12.1)
9 March 49 (9 February 49; 18 January 49)	Caesar reaches Brindisi with six legions. (Caes., *Civil War* 1.25.1; Cic., *Letters to Atticus* 9.3.2; 13A.1; 18.2; Plut., *Caes.* 35.2)
11 March 49 (11 February 49; 20 January 49)	*Lex Roscia* on the extension of citizenship to the Transpadanians. (Plut., *Caes.* 37.2; Dio Cass. 41.36.3)
17 March 49 (17 February 49;	Pompey flees from Brindisi to Durazzo. (Caes., *Civil War* 1.28.3; Cic., *Letters to Atticus* 9.15A;

26 January 49)	Plut., *Caes.* 35.2; Plut., *Pomp.* 62.5; App., *Civil Wars* 2.40)
18 March 49 (18 February 49; 27 January 49)	Caesar occupies Brindisi. (Caes., *Civil War* 1.28; Plut., *Pomp.* 62.6; Dio Cass. 41.12.3)
31 March 49 (2 March 49; 9 February 49)	Caesar returns to Rome. (Plut., *Caes.* 35.3; App., *Civil Wars* 2.41; Dio Cass. 41.15.1)
1 April 49 (3 March 49; 10 February 49)	*Conventus senatorum* held outside the city. (Caes., *Civil War* 1.32.2; Cic., *Letters to Atticus* 9.17.1; 10.1.2; Cic., *Letters to his friends* 4.1.1; Plut., *Caes.* 35.4; Dio Cass. 41.15.2)
6 April 49 (8 March 49; 15 February 49)	Caesar sets out for Massilia (Marseilles). (Caes., *Civil War* 1.33.4)
19 April 49 (21 March 49; 28 February 49)	Caesar outside Marseilles. (Caes., *Civil War* 1.34.1)
22 April 49 (24 March 49; 2 March 49)	Curio leaves for Sicily. (Caes., *Civil War* 1.30.2)
23 April 49 (25 March 49; 3 March 49)	Cato flees from Sicily. (Caes., *Civil War* 1.30.5; Cic., *Letters to Atticus* 10.16.3)
4 May 49 (4 April 49; 13 March 49)	Siege of Marseilles begins. (Caes., *Civil War* 1.36; Liv., *Per.* 110; Vitr. 10.16.11–12; Luc. 3.375ff.; Dio Cass. 41.19.3–4)
5 June 49 (6 May 49; 14 April 49)	Caesar leaves Marseilles for Spain. (Caes., *Civil War* 1.36.5)
7 June 49 (8 May 49; 16 April 49)	Cicero leaves Formiae to join Pompey. (Cic., *Letters to his friends* 14.7)
22 June 49 (23 May 49; 1 May 49)	Caesar arrives in Ilerda (Lérida). (Caes., *Civil War* 1.41.1)
26 June 49 (27 May 49; 5 May 49)	Battle of Ilerda (Lérida). (Caes., *Civil War* 1.43–7)
27 June 49 (28 May 49; 6 May 49)	First sea battle off Marseilles. (Caes., *Civil War* 1.56–8; Luc. 3.509–762)
25–6 July 49 (24–5	Afranius and Petreius withdraw to Otogesa.

June 49; 2–3 June 49)	(Caes., *Civil War* 1.63.3)
28 July 49 (27 June 49; 5 June 49)	Caesar blocks the advance of Pompey's forces towards the Ebro. (Caes., *Civil War* 1.68–72)
29 July 49 (28 June 49; 6 June 49)	Pompey's forces withdraw to Lérida. (Caes., *Civil War* 1.73)
31 July 49 (30 June 49; 8 June 49)	Second sea battle off Marseilles. (Caes., *Civil War* 2.4–7)
2 August 49 (2 July 49; 10 June 49)	Capitulation of Afranius and Petreius at Lérida. (Caes., *Civil War* 1.84; Liv., *Per.* 110; Plut., *Caes.* 36.2; Luc., 4.337–40; *Fast. Amit.*, p. 191; *Fast. Ant.*, p. 208; *Fast. Maff.*, p. 79; *Fast. Vall.*, p. 149)
8 August 49 (8 July 49; 16 June 49)	Curio sails for Africa. (Caes., *Civil War* 2.23.1; Luc. 4.583–4)
11 August 49 (11 July 49; 19 June 49)	Curio lands in Africa. (Caes., *Civil War* 2.23.1; Luc. 4.584–5)
16 August 49 (16 July 49; 24 June 49)	Battle of Utica. (Caes., *Civil War* 2.33–4)
20 August 49 (20 July 49; 28 June 49)	Defeat and death of Curio in battle on the Bagrada river. (Caes., *Civil War* 2.39–42; Liv., *Per.* 110; Vell. Pat. 2.55.1; Luc. 4.734–98; App., *Civil Wars* 2.45)
7 September 49 (5 August 49; 14 July 49)	Caesar in Cordoba. (Caes., *Civil War* 2.21.1)
17 September 49 (15 August 49; 24 July 49)	Caesar in Cadiz. (Caes., *Civil War* 2.21.3; Liv., *Per.* 110.2; Dio Cass. 41.24.1–2)
25 September– 1 October 49 (23–8 August 49; 1–6 August 49)	Caesar in Tarragona. (Caes., *Civil War* 2.21.5; Dio Cass. 41.24.3)
Mid-October 49 (first half of September 49; second half of August 49)	Caesar is appointed dictator. (Caes., *Civil War* 2.21.5; Plut., *Caes.* 37.2; App., *Civil Wars* 2.48; Dio Cass. 41.36.1–2)
Late October 49 (late September	Caesar back in Marseilles; the city capitulates. (Caes., *Civil War* 2.21.5–22; Liv., *Per.* 110; Dio

49; late August– early September 49)	Cass. 41.25.3)
November 49 (October 49; September 49)	Ninth Legion mutinies in Placentia (Piacenza). (Luc., 5.237–373; Suet., *Caes.* 69; App., *Civil* *Wars* 2.47; Dio Cass. 41.26–35)
2–12 December 49 (28 October–7 November 49; 6–16 October 49)	Caesar in Rome; assumes the dictatorship and is elected consul for the year 48. (Caes., *Civil* *War* 3.2.1; Plut., *Caes.* 37.1–2; App., *Civil* *Wars* 2.48)
13 December 49 (8 November 49; 17 October 49)	Caesar leaves for Brindisi. (Caes., *Civil War* 3.2.1)
22 December 49 (17 November 49; 26 October 49)	Caesar reaches Brindisi. (Caes., *Civil War* 3.2.1–3)
4–5 January 48 (28–9 November 49; 6–7 November 49)	Caesar sails from Brindisi and lands in Palaeste (Paleste). (Caes., *Civil War* 3.6.3; Plut., *Caes.* 37.4; Luc. 5.460; App., *Civil Wars* 2.54; Dio Cass. 41.44.3)
6–7 January 48 (30 November–1 December 49; 8–9 November 49)	Occupation of Oricum and Apollonia. (Caes., *Civil War* 3.11.3–12; Plut., *Caes.* 37.4)
11 January 48 (5 December 49; 13 November 49)	Caesar camps on the left bank of the Apsos. (Caes., *Civil War* 3.13.5; Plut., *Caes.* 38.1; App., *Civil Wars* 2.56)
27 March 48 (16 February 48; 25 January 48)	Mark Antony lands at Nymphaeum. (Caes., *Civil War* 3.26.4; Plut., *Caes.* 39.1; Luc. 5.720; App., *Civil Wars* 2.59)
3 April 48 (23 February 48; 1 February 48)	Caesar and Mark Antony join forces. (Caes., *Civil War* 3.30.6)
8 April 48 (28 February 48; 6 February 48)	Pompey the Younger attacks Caesar's fleet at Orikon. (Caes., *Civil War* 3.40)
9 April 48 (1 March 48; 7 February 48)	Pompey camps at Asparagium. (Caes., *Civil* *War* 3.41.1; Plut., *Caes.* 39.1)
12 April 48 (4 March 48; 10 February 48)	Pompey makes camp at Petra and Caesar at Durazzo. (Caes., *Civil War* 3.42.1)

c.15 April 48 (*c*.17 March 48; *c*.13 February 48)	Caesar tries to encircle Pompey. (Caes., *Civil War* 3.43)
25 June 48 (16 May 48; 24 April 48)	Combat near Durazzo. Pompey's first attempt to breach the blockade. (Caes., *Civil War* 3.51–3; Plut., *Caes.* 39.4; Suet., *Caes.* 68.3; Flor. 2.13.40; Dio Cass. 41.50.3–4)
6 July 48 (26 May 48; 4 May 48)	Pompey breaks out. (Caes., *Civil War* 3.62–71)
17 July 48 (6 June 48; 15 May 48)	Defeat at Durazzo. (Caes., *Civil War* 3.69; Plut.,*Caes.* 39.4–8; Plut., *Cato the Younger* 54.8–10; App., *Civil Wars* 2.62)
18 July 48 (7 June 48; 16 May 48)	Caesar sets out from Durazzo for Thessaly. (Caes., *Civil War* 3.75.1–2; Plut., *Caes.* 39.10)
20 July 48 (9 June 48; 18 May 48)	Caesar reaches Apollonia. (Caes., *Civil War* 3.78)
29 July 48 (18 June 48; 27 May 48)	Caesar and Domitius Calvinus join forces at Aiginion. (Caes., *Civil War* 3.79.7)
31 July 48 (20 June 48; 29 May 48)	Gomphoi is taken. (Caes., *Civil War* 3.80.7; Plut., *Caes.* 41.7; App., *Civil Wars* 2.64; Dio Cass. 41.51.4)
2 August 48 (22 June 48; 31 May 48)	Pompey arrives at Larissa. (Caes., *Civil War* 3.82.1)
3 August 48 (23 June 48; 1 June 48)	Caesar reaches the plain of Pharsalus. Pompey and Scipio join forces. (Caes., *Civil War* 3.81.3–82; Plut., *Caes.* 42.1)
9 August 48 (29 June 48; 7 June 48)	Battle of Pharsalus. (Caes., *Civil War* 3.88–9; Liv., *Per.* 111; Plut., *Caes.* 44–5; Plut., *Pomp.* 69–72; Plut., *Brut.* 4.6–7; App., *Civil Wars* 2.76–81; Dio Cass. 41.58–60)
10 August 48 (30 June 48; 8 June 48)	Caesar leaves Pharsalus and reaches Larissa. (Caes., *Civil War* 3.98.3; Plut., *Caes.* 48.1)
11 August 48 (1 July 48; 9 June 48)	Caesar leaves Larissa. (Plut., *Caes.* 48.1)
13 August 48 (3 July 48; 11 June 48)	Pompey sails from Amphipolis; Caesar arrives shortly afterwards. (Caes., *Civil War* 3.102; Plut., *Caes.* 48.1)

16 August 48 (6 July 48; 14 June 48)	Pompey reaches Mytilene. (Caes., *Civil War* 3.102.4; Plut., *Pomp.* 74.1)
19 September 48 (7 August 48; 16 July 48)	Caesar in Asia. (Caes., *Civil War* 3.105.1)
23 September 48 (11 August 48; 20 July 48)	Pompey reaches Cyprus. (Caes., *Civil War* 3.102.5; Plut., *Pomp.* 77.1)
28 September 48 (16 August 48; 25 July 48)	Pompey assassinated. (Caes., *Civil War* 3.104.3; Liv., *Per.* 112; Plut., *Pomp.* 79; App., *Civil Wars* 2.85; Dio Cass. 42.4)
2 October 48 (19 August 48; 28 July 48)	Caesar lands at Alexandria. (Caes., *Civil War* 3.106.1; Liv., *Per.* 112; Plut., *Caes.* 48.2; Suet., *Caes.* 35.1; Dio Cass. 42.7.3)
7 October 48 (24 August 48; 2 August 48)	Caesar summons Ptolemy XIII and Cleopatra to Alexandria. (Caes., *Civil War* 3.107.2–109; Plut., *Caes.* 48.9; Dio Cass. 42.9.1)
2 November 48 (19 September 48; 28 August 48)	Achillas has Ptolemy's ambassadors murdered. (Caes., *Civil War* 3.109.5)
Early November 48 (second half November 48; late August 48)	Marcellus besieges Cassius Longinus at Ulia. (*Alexandrian War* 61)
6 November 48 (23 September 48; 1 September 48)	Caesar decides to keep Ptolemy with him. (Caes., *Civil War* 3.109.6)
9 November 48 (26 September 48; 4 September 48)	Achillas lays siege to Caesar in Alexandria. (Caes., *Civil War* 3.111; Plut., *Caes.* 39.5)
11 November 48 (28 September 48; 6 September 48)	Caesar has the ships in harbour set alight and seeks help from the Asiatic states. (Caes., *Civil War* 3.112.6; *Alexandrian War* 1; Plut., *Caes.* 49.6; Dio Cass. 42.38.2)
17 November 48 (4 October 48; 12 September 48)	Execution of Potheinus. (Caes., *Civil War* 3.112.12; Plut., *Caes.* 49.5; Plut., *Pomp.* 80.7)
2 December 48 (18 October 48; 26 September 48)	Arsinoe has Achillas murdered by Ganymede. Ganymede receives command of the army. (*Alexandrian War* 4; Dio Cass. 42.40.2)

10 December 48 (26 October 48; 4 October 48)	Thirty-Seventh Legion disembarks west of Alexandria. (*Alexandrian War* 9.3)
11 December 48 (27 October 48; 5 October 48)	Caesar wins back the Thirty-Seventh Legion. Sea battle. (*Alexandrian War* 10–11)
19 December 48 (4 November 48; 13 October 48)	Domitius Calvinus marches with four legions from Comana in Pontus towards Nicopolis. (*Alexandrian War* 35.3)
28 December 48 (13 November 48; 22 October 48)	Battle of Nicopolis; Pharnakes defeats Domitius Calvinus. (*Alexandrian War* 39–40; App., *Civil Wars* 2.91; Dio Cass. 42.46.2–3)
29 December 48 (14 November 48; 23 October 48)	Gabinius arrives in Illyria. (*Alexandrian War* 43.1)
6 January 47 (20 November 48; 29 October 48)	Caesar takes the island of Pharos. (*Alexandrian War* 17; Plut., *Caes.* 49.7; Dio Cass., 42.40.3)
7 January 47 (21 November 48; 30 October 48)	Battle at heptastadium mole. (*Alexandrian War* 19–21)
17 January 47 (1 December 48; 9 November 48)	Caesar sets Ptolemy free. (*Alexandrian War* 24.3–4; Dio Cass. 42.42.3–4)
20 January 47 (4 December 48; 12 November 48)	Defeat of Gabinius in Illyria. (*Alexandrian War* 43)
6 February 47 (19 December 48; 27 November 48)	Naval battle of Canopus. (*Alexandrian War* 25.5–6)
23 February 47 (5 January 47; 14 December 48)	Vatinius sails for Illyria with his ships. (*Alexandrian War* 44)
Late February 47 (mid-January 47; December 48)	Death of Cassius Longinus. (*Alexandrian War* 64.3)
6 March 47 (16 January 47; 25 December 48)	Battle of Pelusium; Antipater's troops seize the city. (*Alexandrian War* 26.2; Josephus Flavius, *Antiquities of the Jews* 14.130; Dio Cass. 41.41.1–2)
15 March 47	Battle of the Jewish Camp. (*Alexandrian War*

(25 January 47; 3 January 47)   27.4–5; Josephus Flavius, *Jewish War* 1.191–2; Josephus Flavius, *Antiquities of the Jews* 14.131–2)

16 March 47 (26 January 47; 4 January 47)   Sea battle off the island of Tauris between Vatinius and Marcus Octavius. (*Alexandrian War* 46)

19 March 47 (29 January 47; 7 January 47)   Caesar goes out to meet Mithridates; at the same time Ptolemy begins his march. (*Alexandrian War* 28.1)

27 March 47 (6 February 47; 15 January 47)   Battle of the Nile and capitulation of Alexandria. (*Alexandrian War* 32; Plut., *Caes.* 49.9; Dio Cass. 42.43; *Fast. Caeret.*, p. 66; *Fast. Maff.*, p. 74)

28 June 47 (9 May 47; 17 April 47)   Caesar sails from Alexandria for Syria. (*Alexandrian War* 33.5)

17 July 47 (27 May 47; 5 May 47)   Caesar reaches Tarsus. (*Alexandrian War* 66.2)

22 July 47 (1 June 47; 10 May 47)   Caesar reaches Mazaca. (*Alexandrian War* 66.3)

28 July 47 (7 June 47; 16 May 47)   Deiotarus comes as a supplicant to Caesar. (*Alexandrian War* 67)

2 August 47 (12 June 47; 21 May 47)   Battle of Zela; defeat of Pharnakes. (*Alexandrian War* 74–6; Liv., *Per.* 113; Plut., *Caes.* 50.2; App., *Civil Wars* 2.91; Dio Cass. 42.47)

29 August 47 (9 July 47; 17 June 47)   Birth of Caesarion. (Plut., *Caes.* 49.10)

September 47 (July 47; June 47)   Mutiny of Tenth and Eleventh Legions in Campania. (Plut., *Caes.* 51.2; App., *Civil Wars* 2.92–4; Dio Cass. 42.30.1; 52–3)

26 September 47 (2 August 47; 11 July 47)   Caesar lands at Tarentum. (Plut., *Caes.* 51.1; Plut., *Cic.* 39.4)

4 October 47 (11 August 47; 20 July 47)   Caesar reaches Rome. (Plut., *Caes.* 51.1)

Early December 47 (early October 47; mid-September 47)   Caesar leaves Rome for Lilybaeum. (Plut., *Caes.* 52.2)

17 December 47 (23 October 47; 1 October 47)   Caesar reaches Lilybaeum. (*African War* 1.1; Plut., *Caes.* 52.2)

25 December 47 (31 October 47 9 October 47)	Caesar departs for Africa. (*African War* 2.4; Plut., *Caes.* 52.2; App., *Civil Wars* 2.95)
28 December 47 (3 November 47; 12 October 47)	Caesar lands at Hadrumetum. (*African War* 2.5–3; Plut., *Caes.* 52.3)
29 December 47 (4 November 47; 13 October 47)	Caesar camps at Ruspina. (*African War* 6.7)
1 January 46 (5 November 47; 14 October 47)	Occupation of Leptis. (*African War* 7.1)
3 January 46 (7 November 47; 16 October 47)	The dispersed fleet arrives. (*African War* 11.1–3)
4 January 46 (8 November 47; 17 October 47)	Battle of Ruspina. (*African War* 12.19; Plut., *Caes.* 52.3.6)
6 January 46 (10 November 47; 19 October 47)	Scipio leaves Utica. (*African War* 24.1)
12 January 46 (16 November 47; 25 October 47)	Scipio joins forces with Labienus and Petreius. (*African War* 20.2)
22 January 46 (26 November 47; 4 November 47)	Thirteenth and Fourteenth Legions arrive. (*African War* 37.1; Plut., *Caes.* 52.6)
Night of 25–6 January 46 (night of 29–30 November 47; 7–8 November 47)	Caesar leaves his camp and advances to the plain of Uzitta. (*African War* 37.1–2; Plut., *Caes.* 52.6)
27 January 46 (1 December 47; 9 November 47)	Caesar tries in vain to provoke combat. (*African War* 41–2)
17 February 46 (20 December 47; 29 November 47)	Juba and Scipio join forces. (*African War* 48.2)
28 February 46 (31 December 47; 5 December 47)	Ninth and Tenth Legions arrive. (*African War* 53; Plut., *Caes.* 52.6)

14 March 46 (14 January 46; 15 January 46)	Caesar marches from Uzitta to Aggar. (*African War* 67.1)
17 March 46 (17 January 46; 18 January 46)	Zeta occupied. (*African War* 68.2)
22 March 46 (22 January 46; 23 January 46)	Attempts to provoke combat. (*African War* 75.1)
23 March 46 (23 January 46; 24 January 46)	Caesar marches on Sarsura. (*African War* 75.2)
24 March 46 (24 January 46; 25 January 46)	Caesar reaches Tisdra. (*African War* 76.1)
26 March 46 (26 January 46; 27 January 46)	Caesar returns to Aggar. (*African War* 76.2)
4 April 46 (4 February 46; 5 February 46)	Caesar marches from Aggar to Thapsus. Scipio follows. (*African War* 79.1–2; Plut., *Caes.* 53.1)
5 April 46 (5 February 46; 6 February 46)	Scipio tries to block the northern isthmus at Moknine, near Thapsus. (*African War* 80.3; Plut., *Caes.* 53.1; Dio Cass. 43.7.3)
6 April 46 (6 February 46; 7 February 46)	Battle of Thapsus. (*African War* 83; Liv., *Per.* 114; Plut., *Caes.* 53.4; App., *Civil Wars* 2.96–7; Dio Cass. 43.7–8)
Early April 46 (early February 46; early February 46)	Pompey the Younger arrives in Spain. (*African War* 23.3; Dio Cass. 43.29.2–30.1)
Evening of 8 April 46 (8 February 46; 9 February 46)	News of the battle of Thapsus reaches Utica. (Plut., *Cato the Younger* 58.13; App., *Civil Wars* 2.98)
9 April 46 (9 February 46; 10 February 46)	Caesar sends Messalla to Utica. Cato convenes the Council of the Three Hundred. (*African War* 86.3; 88.1; Plut., *Cato the Younger* 59.3)
10–11 April 46 (10–11 February 46; 11–12 February 46)	Uzitta and Hadrumetum captured. (*African War* 89.1–2)
Night of 12–13	Cato commits suicide. (*African War* 88.3–5; Liv.,

April 46 (12–13 February 46; 13–14 February 46)	*Per.* 114; Plut., *Caes.* 54.2; Plut., *Cato the Younger* 70; App., *Civil Wars* 2.98–9; Dio Cass. 43.11)
14 April 46 (14 February 46; 15 February 46)	Messalla reaches the gates of Utica. (*African War* 88.7)
16–17 April 46 (16–17 February 46; 17–18 February 46)	Caesar reaches Utica in the evening and enters the town the next day. (*African War* 89.5–90.1)
29 April 46 (1 March 46; 2 March 46)	An embassy comes from Zama. (*African War* 92.1)
5 May 46 (6 March 46; 7 March 46)	Caesar reaches Zama. (*African War* 92.4)
17 May 46 (18 March 46; 19 March 46)	Caesar returns to Utica. (*African War* 97.1)
13 June 46 (14 April 46; 15 April 46)	Caesar sails from Utica. (*African War* 98.1; Plut., *Caes.* 55.1)
15 June 46 (16 April 46; 17 April 46)	Caesar reaches Caralis (Cagliari). (*African War* 98.1; Plut., *Caes.* 55.1; Dio Cass. 43.14.2)
27 June 46 (28 April 46; 29 April 46)	Caesar leaves Cagliari. (*African War* 98.2)
25 July 46 (25 May 46; 26 May 46)	Caesar reaches Rome. (*African War* 98.2; Plut., *Caes.* 55.1; Dio Cass. 43.14.2)
August 46 (June 46; June 46)	Celebrations of the four triumphs: *ex Gallia, ex Aegypto, ex Ponto, ex Africa de rege Iuba.* (*Spanish War* 1.1; Liv., *Per.* 115; Plut., *Caes.* 55.2; Suet., *Caes.* 37.1; App., *Civil Wars* 2.101; Dio Cass. 43.19.22)
25–6 September 46 (24–5 July 46; 25–6 July 46)	Consecration of the *Forum Iulium* and the temple of *Venus Genetrix.* (Plut., *Caes.* 55.4; App., *Civil Wars* 2.102; Dio Cass. 43.22.2; *Fast. Pinc.*, p. 48; *Fast. Vall.*, p. 151)
Second intercalary	Caesar sets out for Spain. (Plut., *Caes.* 56.1;

month 46 (early November 46; early November 46)	Suet. *Caes.* 56.5; App., *Civil Wars* 2.103)
Early December 46 (early December 46; early December 46)	Caesar reaches Obulco. (*Spanish War* 2.1; Strab. 3.4.9; Dio Cass. 43.32.1)
19 February 45	Capitulation of Ategua. (*Spanish War* 19.6; Dio Cass. 43.33.2–34.5)
17 March 45	Battle of Munda. (*Spanish War* 31.8; Liv., *Per.* 115; Plut., *Caes.* 56.2–6; App., *Civil Wars* 2.104; Dio Cass. 43.35.4–38.4)
12 April 45	Caesar in Cadiz. In Hispalis the head of Pompey the Younger is displayed to the people. (*Spanish War* 39.3; Vell. Pat. 2.55.4; Plut., *Caes.* 56.6; App., *Civil Wars* 2.105)
30 April 45	Caesar in Hispalis. (Cic., *Letters to Atticus* 13.20.1)
June–August 45	Octavius joins Caesar in Spain. (Nic. Dam., *Aug.* 21–2; Vell. Pat. 2.59.3; Suet., *Aug.* 8.1; Dio Cass. 43.41.3)
13 September 45	Caesar writes his will in his villa in Lavicum. He adopts Octavius. (Liv., *Per.* 116; Suet., *Caes.* 83.1)
Early October 45	Caesar reaches Rome. Celebration of the triumph over the sons of Pompey. (Liv., *Per.* 116; Vell. Pat. 2.56.3; Plut., *Caes.* 56.7; Suet., *Caes.* 37.1; Dio Cass. 43.42)
14 January 44	Caesar is *imperator*, consul, and for the fifth time dictator. (Plut., *Caes.* 56.1)
26 January 44	Following the conclusion of the *Feriae Latinae* in Alba, Caesar returns to Rome. (Plut., *Caes.* 60.3; Suet., *Caes.* 79.1; App., *Civil Wars* 2.108; Dio Cass. 44.10.1)
14 February 44	Caesar is officially declared dictator for life. (Liv., *Per.* 116; Plut., *Caes.* 57.1; Suet., *Caes.* 76.1)
15 February 44	Feast of the Lupercalia: Caesar refuses the royal crown. (Nic. Dam., *Aug.* 71–5; Liv., *Per.* 116; Plut., *Caes.* 61.1–6; Dio Cass. 44.11.2–3)
15 March 44	Assassination of Caesar. (Nic. Dam., *Aug.*

88–90; Liv., *Per.* 116; Plut., *Caes.* 66.4–14; Plut., *Brut.* 17.3–5; Suet., *Caes.* 82.1–2; App., *Civil Wars* 2.117; Dio Cass. 44.19.3–5)

ABBREVIATIONS AND PRINCIPAL CLASSICAL SOURCES

Corpus Caesarianum:
African War [*de Bello Africo*]
Alexandrian War [*de Bello Alexandrino*]
Caes., *Civil War* [*de Bello Civili*]
Caes., *Gallic War* [*de Bello Gallico*]
Spanish War [*de Bello Hispaniensi*]

App., *Civil Wars* = Appian, *The Civil Wars*
App., *Gallic history* fr. = Appian, *Gallic history* fragments
App., *Iber.* = Appian, *Wars in Spain* [*Iberia*]
Asc. = Asconius, *Commentary on five Orations of Cicero* [*Commentarii in orationes Ciceronis*]
[Aurelius Victor], *On famous men* [*de Viris Illustribus*]
Cic., *Balb.* = Cicero, *In defence of Balbus* [*pro Balbo*]
Cic., *Letters to Atticus* = Cicero, *Letters to Atticus* [*Epistulae ad Atticum*]
Cic., *Letters to his friends* = Cicero, *Letters to his friends* [*Epistulae ad Familiares*]
Cic., *Letters to Quintus* = Cicero, *Letters to brother Quintus* [*Epistulae ad Quintum Fratrem*]
Cic., *Mil.* = Cicero, *In Defence of Milo* [*pro Milone*]
Cic., *Prov. cons.* = Cicero, *On the consular provinces* [*de Provinciis Consularibus*]
Cic., *Verr.* = Cicero, *Against Verres* (*Verrine Orations*) [*in C. Verrem*]
Dio Cass. = Dio Cassius, *Roman History*
Dionysius of Halicarnassus, *Roman Antiquities* [*Antiquitates Romanae*]
Flor. = Annaeus Florus, *Epitome* [*Epitome bellorum omnium annorum*]
Gell. = Aulus Gellius, *The Attic Nights* [*Noctae Atticae*]
Josephus Flavius, *Antiquities of the Jews* [*Antiquitates Judaicae*]
Josephus Flavius, *Jewish War* [*de Bello Judaico*]
Liv., *Per.* = Livy, *Summaries* [*Periochae*]
Luc. = Lucan, *Pharsalia*
Macr. = Macrobius, *Saturnalia*

Nic. Dam., *Aug.* = Nicolaus of Damascus, *Life of Augustus*

Pliny = Pliny the Elder, *Natural History* [*Naturalis Historia*]

Plut., *Ant.* = Plutarch, *Life of Antony*

Plut., *Brut.* = Plutarch, *Life of Brutus*

Plut., *Caes.* = Plutarch, *Life of Caesar*

Plut., *Cato the Younger* = Plutarch, *Life of Cato the Younger*

Plut., *Cic.* = Plutarch, *Life of Cicero*

Plut., *Crass.* = Plutarch, *Life of Crassus*

Plut., *Pomp.* = Plutarch, *Life of Pompey*

Sall., *Cat.* = Sallust, *The Catilinarian Conspiracy* [*de Catilinae Coniuratione*]

Strab. = Strabo, *Geography*

Suet., *Aug.* = Suetonius, *Augustus*

Suet., *Caes.* = Suetonius, *Caesar* [*Divus Iulius*]

Suet., *de Vita Caesarum* = Suetonius, *The Lives of the Caesars*

Val. Max. = Valerius Maximus, *Memorable Deeds and Sayings* [*Facta et Dicta Memorabilia*]

Vell. Pat. = Velleius Paterculus, *History of Rome* [*Historiae Romanae*]

Vitr. = Vitruvius, *On Architecture* [*de Architectura*]

Fast. Amit. = *Fasti Amiternini*, in *Inscriptiones Italiae*, XIII.2, ed. A. Degrassi (Rome 1963), pp. 185–200

Fast. Ant. = *Fasti Antiates Ministorum Domus Augustae*, ibid., pp. 201–12

Fast. Caeret. = *Fasti Caeretani*, ibid., pp. 64–8

Fast. Capit. = *Fasti Capitolini* [*Fasti Consulares et Triumphales Capitolini*] in *Inscriptiones Italiae*, XIII.1, ed. A. Degrassi (Rome 1947), pp. 1–142

Fast. Cons. = *Fasti Consulares*, ibid., pp. 346–533

Fast. Maff. = *Fasti Maffeiani*, in *Inscriptiones Italiae*, XIII.2, ed. A. Degrassi (Rome 1963), pp. 70–84

Fast. Pinc. = *Fasti Pinciani*, ibid., pp. 47–9

Fast. Vall. = *Fasti Vallenses*, ibid., pp. 146–52

Bibliography

ABBREVIATIONS

ASNP   *Annali della Scuola Normale di Pisa*
CIL   *Corpus Inscriptionum Latinarum*
FGrHist F. Jacoby, *Die Fragmente der griechischen Historiker*, vols I–II, Berlin 1923–30; vol. III, Leiden 1943–58
HRR   H. Peter, *Historicorum Romanorum reliquiae*, vol. I, Lipsiae, 1914; vol. II, Lipsiae 1906 [Stutgardiae 1967 ed. stereotypa]
ILS   H. Dessau, *Inscriptiones Latinae selectae*, vols I–IV, Berlin 1892–1916
JRS   *Journal of Roman Studies*
MRR   T. R. S. Broughton, *The Magistrates of the Roman Republic*, vols I–II, Cleveland OH 1951–2; vol. III (Suppl.), New York 1986
ORF   E. Malcovati, *Oratorum Romanorum Fragmenta*, Augustae Taurinorum, 1955
RE   A. Pauly and G. Wissowa, *Realencyclopädie der klassischen Altertumswissenschaft*, Stuttgart 1893–1980
Syll.³ W. Dittenberger, *Sylloge Inscriptionum Graecarum*, vols I–IV, Leipzig 1915

THE *CORPUS CAESARIANUM*

The Collection Lemaire (vols 1–4, Paris 1819–22) includes the Byzantine translation of books 1–7 of the *Gallic War*. Note also the 'classic' commentary by F. Kraner, W. Dittenberger and H. Meusel on the *Commentaries* (Weidmann: Berlin; latest edn rev H. Oppermann: 18th edn 1960 for the Gallic War, 16th edn 1959 for the Civil War).

A valuable collection of the *Commentaries* and the three *Wars* was produced by A. Pennacini et al. and published in 1993 by Einaudi and Gallimard, with the somewhat inappropriate title 'Opera omnia'.

(It does not contain the letters from Cicero's correspondence with Atticus, or the fragments.) Note in particular the commentary by Albino Garzetti on the *Gallic War* and the translation by Antonio La Penna of the *Civil War*.

For the *Gallic War* and the *Civil War*, the following editions remain essential:

C. Julii Caesaris *Bellum Gallicum*, ed. Otto Seel (Leipzig: Teubner 1961, 3rd edn 1977) is of value above all for the collected documents on Caesar and his works. For the text, however, the critical apparatus of W. Hering (Leipzig: Teubner 1987) is more cautious and reliable.

L.-A. Constans' slim volume, *Guide illustré des campagnes de César* (Paris: 1929) is a vital addition to the study of the Gallic War.

On the civil war the editions by Alfred Klotz and Pierre Fabre are valuable and complement each other: C. Iulii Caesaris, *Commentarii*, vol. 2, *Commentarii belli civilis*, ed. Alfred Klotz (Leipzig: Teubner 1957); César, *La guerre civile*, vols 1–2, ed. Pierre Fabre (Paris: Les Belles Lettres 1936).

The remainder of the *Corpus Caesarianum*, including fragments of lost works and letters, is in vol. 3 of Alfred Klotz's edition of 1927 (Leipzig: Teubner 1957).

However, for each of the wars it is necessary to have recourse to the specialised editions, with both textual and interpretative improvements: César, *Guerre d'Alexandrie*, ed. J. Andrieu (Les Belles Lettres: Paris 1954); Pseudo-César, *Guerre d'Afrique*, ed. A. Bouvet, new edn J.-C. Richard (Les Belles Lettres: Paris 1997); [C. Iulii Caesaris], *Bellum Hispaniense*, ed. Giovanni Pascucci (Le Monier: Florence 1965).

For the few surviving letters, documents and fragments of lost correspondence, the primary collection is by Paolo Cugusi, in vol. 2 of *Epistolographi Latini minores* (Paravia: Turin 1976), pp. 72–112 (with commentary in the second part of the volume). It should be pointed out that this collection also contains information on letters which Caesar wrote (but which have not necessarily been included in collections) as well as on the *collections* of Caesar's letters which were compiled and circulated *as such* at one time or another (probably not immediately, to judge from Suetonius' comments). The primary source of information here is Suetonius' *Life of Caesar* 56.6. A corpus of 'autographs' of letters from Caesar to Cleopatra was passed on to Octavian by Cleopatra herself (Dio Cassius 51.12.3) shortly after Actium. It is characteristic that Suetonius makes no mention of these among the collections of Caesar's letters in existence in his day, yet it is hardly likely that Octavian would have destroyed them.

An example of the very useful work that can be done on the fragments is Hans Jürgen Tschiedel's edition of the fragments of the *Anticato* (Wissenschaftliche Buchgesellschaft: Darmstadt 1981).

ANCIENT SOURCES

Of the contemporary sources the most important is clearly Cicero: his letters, his Catilinarian and 'Caesarian' speeches, and his so-called 'Philippics'. Cicero's testimony on Caesar is broad and at times contradictory. The annotated editions using a single chronological order regardless of the collection are to be preferred: R. Y. Tyrrell and L. C. Purser, *Correspondence of M. T. Cicero* (Hodges Figgis and Longmans Green: Dublin and London, vol. 1, 1904 [3rd edn], vol. 2, 1906 [2nd edn], vol. 3, 1914 [2nd edn], vol. 4, 1918 [2nd edn], vol. 5, 1915 [2nd edn], vol. 6, 1933 [2nd edn], vol. 7, 1901 [index]); and L.-A. Constans, J. Bayet and J. Beaujeu (Collection Budé: Paris, vol. 1, 1940–vol. 11, 1996). D. R. Shackleton-Bailey's attempt to impose chronological order within each collection is less successful. Nevertheless, Shackleton-Bailey's commentary on the *Letters to Atticus* (Cambridge University Press: Cambridge 1965), preceded by an important introduction on the history of the text (vol. 1, pp. 59–76), is extremely valuable. Fragments of Cicero's correspondence (in vol. 3 of Watt's *Bibliotheca Oxoniensis* [Oxford 1958, 2nd edn 1965]) display traces of the practice of the ancient grammarians, who collected both Caesar's letters to Cicero and vice versa (pp. 153–6); but the tradition was marred by confusion between Caesar and Octavian (both referred to as Caesar).

As for Asconius and his valuable commentary, written in the time of Nero, on Cicero's speeches, the edition generally used is by A. C. Clark (*Q. Asconii Pediani, Orationum Ciceronis quinque enarratio* [Bibliotheca Oxoniensis: Oxford 1907]). Attention is sometimes given also to the text offered by A. Kiessling and R. Schoell in the Berlin edition (Weidmann: Berlin 1875). The commentary by Bruce A. Marshall, *A Historical Commentary on Asconius* (University of Missouri Press: Columbia 1995), is also worth noting.

The life of Caesar was treated in ancient sources both in monographic form (the *Lives* of Plutarch and Suetonius) and within the framework of historical narrative.

For Plutarch's *Life of Caesar* the historical commentary by Albino Garzetti, with a good Italian translation, is essential (La Nuova Italia: Florence 1954). The text is that established by Konrat Ziegler in *Plutarchi Vitae* 2.2 (Teubner: Leipzig 1968). For Suetonius the text by Maximilianus Ihm remains irreplaceable (Suetonii, *De vita Caesarum libri VIII* [Teubner: Leipzig 1907]). Unfortunately there is no modern historical commentary on Suetonius' *Life of Caesar*: the work by H. Doergens (Leipzig 1864) is disappointing and verbose; the somewhat pedantic work by H. E. Butler and M. Cary is fairly serviceable (*Svetonii Tranquilli Divus Iulius* [Clarendon Press: Oxford 1927]), though marred by some surprising errors (e.g. p. 70, where it is repeatedly stated that Gaius Memmius was a consul, although the ruin of his career is well known). Isaac Casaubon's commentary on Suetonius' *Twelve Lives* (1595, 2nd edn Geneva 1596) still renders useful service. Among the Italian translations, that by Felice Dessì, with a good introduction by Settimio Lanciotti, stands out (BUR: Milan, 3rd edn 1989).

Of the historical narratives, those of Sallust, Velleius Paterculus, Annaeus Florus, Appian and Dio Cassius have survived. Some histories which gave ample treatment to Caesar – those of Seneca the Elder, beginning in 133 BC, and Asinius Pollio, beginning in 60 BC – did not survive until the Middle Ages, but it is possible that Lucan's *Pharsalia* (*Bellum Civile*) partly relies on them. Of Livy's work relevant to the period only the summaries (*Periochae*) have survived. No account is taken here of minor or minimal treatments such as *de Viris Illustribus* by Aurelius Victor.

Sallust, a follower of Caesar, gives much space to him in *The Catilinarian Conspiracy*: it contains the only surviving version, quite possibly a reliable one, of one of Caesar's speeches, delivered in the Senate in December 63 BC. The edition of Sallust by Alfred Kurfeß, reprinted many times (Teubner: 3rd edn Leipzig 1957, latest reprint 1991) is the most reliable, and Alfred Ernout's translation is as usual admirable (*Salluste* [Collection Budé: Paris 1941, 3rd edn 1960]). In Italian one should read the translation by Lidia Storoni (BUR: Milan 1976). The so-called letters of Sallust *ad Caesarem senem* are a later fabrication.

On Velleius, the historian who wrote in the time of Tiberius, the recent text with commentary by Maria Elefante (Olms-Weidmann: Hildesheim, Zurich and New York 1997) does not supersede that by C. Stegmann von Pritzwald (Teubner: Leipzig, 2nd edn 1933). In Italian the translation by Leopoldo Agnes (UTET: Turin 1969) is more reliable than that by Rusconi.

Annaeus Florus wrote during the time of the emperor Hadrian (AD 118–37). The edition referred to is that by Enrica Malcovati: L. Annei Flori, *Quae exstant* (Istituto Poligrafico dello Stato: Rome, 2nd edn 1972).

For the second book (entirely devoted to Caesar) of Appian's *Civil Wars*, unlike the other books of the same work, there is no historical commentary. (Appian was the Alexandrian historian at the time of Fronto and Antoninus Pius.) The critical text for reference remains that of Ludwig Mendelssohn, revised by Paul Viereck (Teubner: Leipzig 1905). The good English translation in the Loeb Library, by Horace White, has the drawback of departing from the paragraph division of the Teubner text.

For Dio Cassius (who in the time of the Severi wrote his *History of Rome* in Greek, in no fewer than 80 books), the edition by U. Ph. Boissevain (Weidmann: Berlin 1905, repr. 1955 vols 1–4; vol. 5, *Index Graecitatis*, ed. W. Nawijn) is unsurpassed. Books 37–44.20 deal mainly with the story of Caesar. Dio Cassius takes much from Livy and perhaps also from Caesar's *Commentaries*.

For the fragments of Livy's lost books, see the edition by W. Weissenborn and H. J. Müller (vol. 10 of the annotated Livy), (Weidmann: Berlin [1880], 3rd edn 1962, pp. 167–80).

MODERN SOURCES

The most reliable reconstruction of the various stages of Caesar's public career is to be found in vol. 2 of *Magistrates of the Roman Republic* [= MRR] by T. R. S. Broughton (American Philological Association: Cleveland OH 1952), under the years 81–44 BC. Note also the corrections in vol. 3 (Supplement, Scholars Press: New York 1986), pp. 105–8. T. P. Wiseman's *New Men in the Roman Senate (139 BC–AD 14)*, University Press, Oxford 1971, is very useful. On Caesar's life up to the time of the triumvirate, H. Strasburger, *Caesars Eintritt in die Geschichte* (Neue Filser, Munich 1938), is irreplaceable. In matters of chronology and referencing, Broughton's dry but exhaustive treatment, with that of Strasburger (in particular the tables on pp. 7–23), replaces two valuable works by Paul Groebe: one which occupies a large part of the volume devoted to the *gens Iulia* in W. Drumann's rewritten *Geschichte Roms* (Borntraeger, vol. 3, 1906, pp. 125–684 and 695–827); and the later (1918), more schematic and compact, in the entry 'Iulius' (No. 131) of Pauly-Wissowa (= *RE*). The concluding part of this entry (*Caesar als Schriftsteller*, cols

259–75) is by Alfred Klotz. Political interpretations of Caesar's work will be found in the following groundbreaking studies (not overlooking the *Précis des guerres de César* [1819] by Napoleon I, published by Marchand in 1836): *Römische Geschichte*, by Theodor Mommsen (1854–6); *L'Histoire de Jules César* (1865–6), completed by Stoffel for the civil war period; Eduard Meyer, *Caesars Monarchie und das Prinzipat des Pompejus* (Cotta: Stuttgart and Berlin, 3rd edn 1918); *Caesar*, by Matthias Gelzer (Deutsche Verlags-Anstalt: Stuttgart and Berlin 1921, 1940, 1960); *César*, by Jérôme Carcopino (Presses Universitaires de France: Paris [1935] 1968). Ronald Syme's *Roman Revolution* (Clarendon Press: Oxford 1939) remains essential, as does his collection of essays on Roman history (*Roman Papers*, ed. E. Badian [vol. 7 by A. R. Birley], vols 1–7 [Clarendon Press: Oxford 1979–91]). *The Last Generation of the Roman Republic* (University of California Press: Berkeley, Los Angeles and London 1974) is a thorough study by E. S. Gruen. All these works are rather more enjoyable than the somewhat overwhelming biography by Christian Meier (Severin und Siedler: Berlin 1982).

For all judicial and constitutional matters connected with Caesar's political actions, the essential work is still Francesco De Martino's *Storia della costituzione romana*, vol. 3 (Jovene: Naples 1973).

On the granting of citizenship to the Transpadanians, see the following, at least: E. Gabba, *Italia romana* (Ed. New Press: Como 1994), ch. 21, esp. pp. 242–3; G. Bandelli, 'Colonie e municipi delle regioni transpadane in età repubblicana', in *Le città nell'Italia settentrionale romana (Atti, Trieste 1987)* (Ed. École française de Rome: Rome 1990), pp. 251–77, esp. 260–3; also, more generally, W. Eck and H. Galsterer (eds), *Die Stadt in Oberitalien und in den nordwestlichen Provinzen des Römischen Reiches* (Verlag Philipp von Zabern: Mainz 1991), esp. the contribution by F. Cassola.

For the broad field constituted by the 'reception' of the figure of Caesar through the ages, see the contributions to the collection in honour of M. Rambaud, *Présence de César* (Les Belles Lettres: Paris 1985); also the painstakingly precise entry 'Caesar im Mittelalter' in *Lexikon des Mittelalters*, 2 (Artemis: Munich and Zurich 1983), cols 1351–60, not to mention the entry for Caesar in the Dutch dictionary *Van Alexandros tot Zenobia* (SUN: Nijmegen 1987–9), largely devoted to Caesar's 'reception'. Above all, see Zwi Yavetz, *Julius Caesar and his Public Image* [1979] (Thames and Hudson: London 1983), esp. ch. 1. and also Maria Wyke (ed.), *Julius Caesar in Western Culture* (Blackwell: 2006).

On the difficulty the sources of the time of Augustus and Tiberius found themselves in with regard to the republican 'hero', see Lily Ross Taylor, 'Catonism and Caesarism', in *Party Politics in the Age of Caesar* (University of California Press: Berkeley and Los Angeles 1949), pp. 162–82, and the essay by Arturo De Vivo, 'La morte negata: Caton Uticense nella "Storia" di Velleio', in *Costruire la memoria: Ricerche sugli storici latini* (Loffredo: Naples 1998), pp. 49–62.

The delicate position of Mark Antony during the last months of Caesar's life is described by R. F. Rossi, 'Antonia fra Cesare ed i con-giurati', in *Marco Antonio nella lotta politica della tarda repubblica romana* (Università di Trieste 1959), pp. 33–63.

On Caesar's death see J. P. V. D. Balston, 'The Ides of March', *Historia*, 7 (1958), pp. 80–94 (with the judgement, 'without the immense prestige of Brutus' personality [. . .] the conspiracy could never have taken place'); also some chapters of U. Gotter, 'Der Diktator ist tot!', *Historia Einzelschriften*, 10 (Steiner Verlag: Stuttgart 1996), and the first chapter of Jochen Bleicken, *Augustus: Eine Biographie* (Alexander Fest Verlag: Berlin 1998). On the religious and political aspects of Caesar's funeral, see A. Fraschetti, *Roma e il principe* (Laterza: Rome and Bari 1990), pp. 46–59.

For bibliographical guidance see the materials in vol. 1.3 (1973) of *Aufstieg und Niedergang der Römischen Welt* (de Gruyter: Berlin and New York), pp. 457–87, and the bibliography by M. De Nonno, P. de Paolis and C. Di Giovine in *Lo spazio letterario di Roma antica*, vol. 4 (Salerno: Rome 1991), pp. 302–8.

Index

Achillas, 190–1, 194, 195, 199,
    200–1
Actium, battle of, 76, 204
Actorius Naso, Marcus, 45
Adcock, F. E., 174, 183n
Aedui, 100, 101–2, 110–11
Aemilius Lepidus Paullus, Lucius,
    131
Afranius, 167, 174, 233, 235
African War, 234
agrarian legislation, 78–9
Agrippa, Marcus, 250–1
Albinus, Aulus, 175
Alchaudonios the Arab, 238
Alesia, siege of, xii, 111
Alexander the Great, 17–18, 114,
    118, 277
Alexandria
    capitulation of, 203
    fire in, 200–1
    Hellenism, xv
    Lucan, 198–9
    Mommsen, 195, 199–200
    pars oppidi, 198
    Pompey's head, 188
    as trap, 179, 188, 194–5
Alexandrian War, 204
    Caesar, 201–2
    Caesar, Sextus Julius, 221,
        239
    Cleopatra, 196
    Deiotarus, 223–4
    Delta, battle of, 209
    Jews, 211, 214
    Mithridates, 210, 213–14
Allobroges, 54

Amatius (false Marius), 341–2,
    343n
Ambiorix, 101, 108, 112–13
ambitus see corruption
amicitia, 159–61, 204
Ampius, Titus, 25
Antigonus, 220
Antioch, 218, 220–1
Antipater
    Alexandria, 211
    Caesar, Sextus Julius, 222
    changing sides, 220
    Jewish soldiers, 202–3
    Josephus, 209, 213
    Mithridates, 213
    rebels, 237
    Strabo, 210
Antistius, doctor, 331
Antistius Vetus, Gaius, 16, 17, 90
Antistius Vetus, Gaius, governor of
    Syria, 238
Antonius, Gaius, 85
Antony, Mark, ix
    Amatius, 342
    assassination of Caesar, 317,
        334–6
    attempted crowning of Caesar,
        281–3
    Brindisi, 176
    Brutus, 334–5
    Caesar, 133, 186, 266
    Cassius, 275, 285
    Cicero, 283–4, 322–3
    Commius, 112
    consul suffectus, 281
    consulship, 54

Antony, Mark (*cont.*)
  Dolabella, 185–6, 281, 284
  Durazzo, 176
  factio, 142
  fleeing Rome, 145
  harshness, 232
  liberators, 336, 337–8
  life threatened, 309, 322–3, 338
  Lupercalia, 311–12
  magister equitum, 175, 231
  Octavius, 204, 246, 266–7
  to Senate, 264–5
  Trebonius, 263–4, 265, 266, 267, 284, 317, 329–30, 334
Apollodorus, carpet merchant, 197
Apollonia, 176, 246, 251
Appian of Alexandria
  Amatius, 343n
  Caesar, 274–5, 340
  Caesar, Julius Sextus, 253
  Cassius, 297–8
  Cinna, 343n
  Civil Wars, 18, 75, 307, 310n
  deaths in Gaul, 121
  Pollio, 134
  Shakespeare's source, 335–6
Appius Claudius Pulcher, 6, 29, 35
Aquitani, 103
Aremorican tribes, 103
Ariovistus, 102, 232
Aristobulus, 220
aristocracy, 33, 63–4, 100, 271, 302, 346
Aristophanes, 140n
Aristotle, 273
Arsinoe, 199, 201, 203
Artemidorus of Cnidus, 328
Arverni, 102, 107–8, 110
Asconius Pedianus, Quintus, 7, 57
Asia Minor, 219 (map)
Asinius Pollio, Gaius
  Alexandrian War, 214–15
  amicitia, 159
  Cicero, 159–60
  civil war, 65, 72–6, 134, 135
  Delta battle, 210

Dolabella, 231
Further Spain, 113
Histories, 131
killing of Caesar, 275
letter to Cicero, 76, 275–6
Pharsalus, 26, 70
Rubicon, 144, 146–7
Spanish defeat, 270
Timagenes, 215
triumvirate, 89
Assandrus, 225, 236
Ategua, 240
Atticus *see* Cicero, Marcus Tullius, letters to Atticus
Augustus, Emperor (formerly Octavius), x
  Apollonia, 246
  censorship, 73–4
  on Livy, 345
  Memoirs, 246, 250, 251
  principate, xiv–xv
  Senate's proceedings, 78
  Velleius, 67
Auletes *see* Ptolemy XII Neos Dionysos
Autronius, Lucius, 45
Autronius, Publius, 12
Avaricum, 110

Bacon, Francis, 203
Balbus, Cornelius, 272
  Caesar's letter to, 150, 151, 153, 155–6, 293–4
  as intermediary, 65, 94, 133–4, 171, 258
Balbus, Marcus Atius, 245
Balbus, Titus Ampius, 138
Balkan campaign, 176
Basilus, Minucius, 318, 335
Bayle, Pierre, 77n
Belgae, 98–9, 121
Bellum Hispaniense, 16
Bibracte, battle of, 102, 122
Bibulus, Marcus Calpurnius
  aedile, 18, 19
  break with, 78–9

consulship, 27–8, 42, 66
Durazzo, 176
edicts, 43–4
Bibulus the Younger, 306, 309–10n, 311
Bithynia, 10–11
Bobbio, Norberto, 37
Bochus II, 235
Bona Dea festival, 83–4, 85
Borges, Jorge Luis, ix–x
Bosphorus, 225
Brambach, J., 206n, 207n
Brecht, Bertolt, ix, x, xiv, 27
bribery, 28, 291, 292; *see also* corruption
Brindisi, 170–1, 175, 176, 230
British expedition, 30, 92, 100, 106–7
Brutus, Decimus, 19, 174–6, 243n, 308, 326–7, 338
Brutus, Marcus Junius
  allegiances, 160
  Antony, 334–5
  Caesar, 257, 266, 268n
  Cassius, 275, 306–7, 311, 312–13, 314
  on Cato, 47, 256, 258
  Cicero, 28–9, 46–7, 258–9
  killing of Caesar, 325, 327–8, 330–1
  Plutarch, 42
  Pompey, 7n
  praetorship, 307–8
  Seneca on, 315–16
  Stoicism, 24
  unifying influence, 308–9
  usury, 28
Butler, H. E., 137, 149n

Caecilius Bassus, Quintus, 236–7, 243n
Caecina, Aulus, 257
Caelius Rufus, Marcus, 99–100, 175, 184–5, 291
  tribune, 133, 145
  uprising, 42, 50

Caepio, Servilius, 69
Caesar, Julius, x–xi, xiii
  aedileship, 18–19, 20, 44
  To the Bithynians speech, 11
  Cato, 163
  Civil War, 133
  consulship, 44, 64, 68, 78–82, 175
  corpse, 331–2, 337, 339–42
  death, x, 42, 308–9, 317, 322, 334–6, 342
  dictatorship, 152, 175, 212, 230, 231, 285, 292–3
  divorce, 84
  early life, 3–7
  Gallic War, xi–xii
  magister equitum, 50
  Pompey, 65–6, 120–1, 191–2, 193–4
  pontifex maximus, 23–5, 78–9, 83, 161, 211
  populace, 87, 89, 167, 348
  praetor, 25, 39, 43
  relationship with soldiers, 91–4, 174, 182n
  sexuality, 89, 246
  threats against, 47–8, 263–4
  wills of, 238–9, 338–9
  see also Commentaries
Caesar, Sextus Julius
  Appian, 253
  death of, 245
  Josephus, 243n
Caesar, Sextus Julius (*cont.*)
  murdered, 237, 238–9, 245
  Syria, 221–2, 236
  Varro, 175
Caesarion, 203–4, 235, 281
Caesarism concept, xi, 42, 174, 229, 271, 287
calendar changes, 241n
Calpurnia, 69, 326–7
Calvinus, Gnaeus Domitius, 35
Cambridge Ancient History, 105
Campanian Territory, 94, 231–2
Caninius Rebilus, Gaius, 272

Carbo, Gnaeus Papirius, 49
Carcopino, J., 104, 180n, 319
Carnutes, 108, 109
Carrinas, Gaius, 270
Cary, M., 88–9, 137, 149n
Casca, Publius, 282, 328, 330
Cassius, Gaius, 298–9
    Alexandria, 222
    Antony, 275, 285
    Appian, 297–8
    Brutus, 275, 306–7, 311,
        312–13, 314
    Cicero, 222–3, 313n, 338
    civil war, 298–9
    Epicureanism, 297–8
    hetairia, 306–7, 312, 338
    letter to Cicero, 230, 241n,
        298–9, 300–3
    Lupercalia, 282
    Pharsalus, battle of, 298
    Pompey's statue, 330
    Stoicism, 297–8, 300
    on Sulla, 301–2
    Syria, 237
Cassius, Lucius, 222
Cassius Longinus, Lucius, 49
Cassius Longinus, Quintus, 133,
    142, 145, 235
Cassivellaunus, 107
Catilinarian conspiracy, 18
    Caesar, 25, 39, 41–2
    Cicero, 46, 317, 318–19
    death sentence, 86
    Plutarch, 55
    rumour, 43–4
    Sallust, 34
Catiline
    attacked, 48
    Catulus, 58
    electoral defeat, 54
    extortion, 34
    Gelzer, 50
    promises to electorate, 49
    propraetorship, 34
Cato, Marcus Porcius
    Brutus, 47, 160

on Caesar, 119
Calpurnia, 69
Cicero, 256, 325
Corfu, 233
Defence of the Rhodeans, 58
ejected from Senate, 88
elections, 28, 292
imprisonment, 80
laudationes, 256
Plutarch, 74
Pompeians, 230
republican war, 230, 241n
Scipio, 233
senate speech, 54, 55–6
suicide, 41, 46, 162–3, 164n,
    235, 256
Catullus, Gaius Valerius, 35, 98, 107
Catulus, Quintus Lutatius, 5, 24,
    57, 58
Cavafy, K. P., 325
Celtic tribes, 98–9, 99–101, 122
censorship, 73–4, 77n
Cethegus, Gaius Cornelius, 49, 54
Cévennes, 109–10
Charles V, xi–xii
Charles VIII, xi
Christina, Queen, xii
Cicero, Marcus Tullius, 23, 33
    Ad Axium, 44
    Antony, 283–4, 322–3
    Asinius Pollio, 159–60
    Basilus, 335
    Brindisi, 230
    and Brutus, 28–9, 46–7, 258–9
    Caesar, 39–40, 48, 206n, 320–1
    Cassius, 222–3, 313n, 338
    Cassius's letters, 230, 241n,
        298–9, 300–3
    Catilinarian conspiracy, 34, 46,
        317, 318–19
    Cato, 256, 325
    Cilicia, 28, 132–3
    On the consular provinces, 90
    consulship, 46, 54
    De amicitia, 159, 160
    De consiliis suis, 43

Defence of Marcellus, 120,
263–5, 274, 347
Defence of Murena, 37
Deiotarus, 221, 239
On duties, 40, 44, 138–9
election of, 24
exiled, 86
First Catilinarian, 58
Fourth Catilinarian, 43, 56–7,
59
Gallic war, 98
Laus Catonis, 46–7, 256
letter to brother, 35–6, 37
letter to Caelius, 99–100
letter to Cassius, 297, 338
letters to Atticus, 64–5, 68, 79,
150–1, 170, 171–2, 257–8,
288–9, 317–18
Letters to his friends, 298, 318
on liberators, 277–8
Lex Manilia, 19
Marius, 90
Matius, 159–60
Miloniana, 57
Octavius, 317
Orator, 256–7
Philippics, 123n
Pompey, 153–4, 171–2
returned from exile, 90
Second Catilinarian, 49
Second Philippic, 119–20, 285,
317, 318–19, 347
On the state, 273
Sulla, 320
Tiro, 160
triumvirate, 67
Lex Tullia de ambitu, 20
Verrine Orations, 36
Cicero, Quintus Tullius, 37, 98,
108, 222
Cilicia, 4, 9–10, 18, 28, 132–3, 237
Cimber, Tillius, 330
Cinna, Gaius Helvius, 340, 341,
343n
Cinna, Lucius Cornelius, 14, 49,
337, 340

citizenship, 81, 130, 174
civil war, 30–1
Asinius Pollio, 65, 72–6
deadlock, 165
Livy, 75, 244n
Marius, 63
Plutarch, 65–6
political exit, 152
Pompey, 141
Rubicon, 151
Senate, 141
Spain, Further, 303
stages, 230
tribunes, 133–4
Claudius Marcellus, Gaius, 287
clementia, 229, 269, 270, 297,
347–8
Cleon, 58
Cleopatra, 205, 207n
Caesarion, 203–4, 235, 281
Commentaries, 196–7
Dio Cassius, 197–8
Plutarch, 194–5, 197
Pompey, 190
power, 188
succeeding to throne, 190
clientship, 34
Caesar, 16–17
Josephus, 212–13
Pompey, 63, 173
provinces, 90–1
Ptolemy, 192
Lex Clodia, 85–6
Clodius Pulcher, Publius, 91
becoming pleb, 83, 85
Clodius Pulcher, Publius (*cont.*)
Bona Dea festival, 83–4
Caesar, 27
death of, 70, 127, 185
praetorship, 86–7
sacrilege, 84, 147n
Trebonius, 267
comitia, 78, 79
Commentaries, xi, xii, xiii, xv,
49–50
Alexandrian War, 196

Commentaries (cont.)
  Caelius Rufus, 184–5
  Cato, 163
  Cleopatra, 196–7
  ethnography, 98, 112
  extremists, 186n
  Labienus, 108
  nomination as dictator, 287,
    288–9
  Numerius, 156
  plundering treasury, 31
  as propaganda, 99, 290
  recruiting in province, 128
  relations with soldiers, 92
  reliability, 215
  Rubicon, 146
  sources, 133
  supplicatio, 122
Commius, 101, 112
Condé, Louis II de Bourbon, xii
coniuratio Italiae, 136n
constitutional innovations, 272
consulship
  Caesar, 44, 64, 68, 78–82, 175
  Cicero, 46
  Crassus, 35
  election campaign, 27–8
  Memmius, 35
  Metellus, 72
  nobility, 33
  Pompey, 35
Corduba, 240, 269
Corfinium, 152, 154–5, 156n,
    160–1, 165, 167–9, 176
Corfu, 233
Cornelia, 3, 5, 15, 16
Lex Cornelia de maiestate, 37
Cornificius, Quintus, 238
corruption, 33–4, 35, 36; *see also*
    bribery
Cotta, commander, 108
Cotta, Gaius Aurelius, 3, 12, 14
Cotta, Lucius, 6
Crassus, Marcus Licinius
  Caesar, 15, 18–19, 24, 27, 40,
    46, 71n

consulship, 35, 95
  death of, 127
  dictatorship, 44–5, 50
  Pompey and Caesar, 65–6
  tribunes of the plebs, 14
Crassus, Publius Licinius, 103, 106
Crastinius, 178, 183n
Cremutius Cordus, xv, 72, 73
Creticus, Antonius, 12
Crixus, 19
Curio, Gaius Scribonius, 133, 141
  Africa, 173, 175, 232
  debts paid off, 131–2, 147
  fleeing, 145
Curio the Elder, 45
Curius, Quintus, 40, 54
Curtius, Ludwig, 250
Cyprus, 189, 199
Cyrenaica, 233
Cyrus, 325

death, preferred manner, 325
death penalty, 57
debts, 24
  cancellation, 185, 231
  election campaigns, 26–7
  political, 34
  populares, 290–1
  relief, 80, 132, 185–6
Deiotarus, 221, 223–4, 237, 239,
    270
Delta, battle of, 209–10
Demosthenes, 58
dictatorship, 279n
  Caesar, 152, 175, 212, 230, 231,
    285, 292–3
  consul sine collega, 127
  Crassus, 49, 50
  expanded, 275–6, 287
  nomination, 287–8
  populares, 290–1
  rei gerendae causa, 289–90
  Senate, 273–4, 289
  Sulla, 137, 320
Dio Cassius, 215
  Caesar's return to Rome, 186

Cleopatra, 197–8
  killing of Caesar, 275
  Lepidus, 289
  Octavius, 245, 247, 251–2
  Pompey, 114n, 206n
  Porcia, 310n
  Ptolemy's death, 193–4
  Spain, 249–50
Dio Chrysostom, 100
Diodorus Siculus, 60n, 198
Diodotos, 58
Dioscorides, 200
Diphilus, actor, 80
Disraeli, Benjamin, 63
Divus Julius, 342
Dolabella, Gnaeus Cornelius
  Antony, 281, 284
  Macedonia, 6
  remission of debts, 185–6
  uprising, 42, 50
Dolabella, Publius Cornelius, 231,
  232
Domitius Ahenobarbus, Lucius
  against Caesar, 182n
  consulship, 35, 94–5
  Corfinium, 152, 156n, 165,
    167–9, 175–6
  eve of Pharsalus, 49
  Marseilles, 173–4, 176
  Napoleon's plan, 167
  pontificate, 161
Domitius Calvinus, 201, 220, 221,
  224
Druids, 100
Durazzo, 165, 170, 176–7

Eburones, 100, 108, 109
Egypt, 188, 189, 195–6, 203–4
elections
  in absentia, 130, 135
  consulate, 27–8
  corruption, 33–4, 35, 36, 292
  costs of campaigns, 26
  debts, 26–7
  gladiatorial spectacles, 19–20
embezzlement, 36

emergency powers, 127
Emphylos, 306, 311
Engels, Friedrich, 105
Ennius, Quintus, 79
Ephesus, 220
Epicureanism, 23–5, 57, 211, 296,
  297–8
ethnography, 98, 112
Eunoë, African queen, 45
Euripides, 138, 140n, 273
Euryptolemos, 59
exiles, 292
extortion, 30, 34, 36, 80–1, 90
Ezechias rebellion, 210–11

Fabius, Quintus, 240
Fabius Maximus, Quintus, 272
Fadius Gallus, Marcus, 259
farmers, 80
Farrington, Benjamin, 23–5
fasces, 191, 196
Favonius, 165–7, 169, 314–15,
  316, 325
Fenestella, 11
Feriae Latinae, 252–3, 293
flamen Dialis, 3, 12, 161
Florus, Lucius Annaeus, 67, 75,
  239, 274
Forum Caesaris, 270
Forum Iulium, 128
Fronto, Marcus Cornelius, 75
funeral games for Caesar, 297,
  339–40

Lex Gabinia, 19
Gabinius, Aulus, 189, 200
Gaetulia, 234
Gaguin, Robert, xi
Gallia Cisalpina, 88, 90–1, 95, 98,
  128–9, 132
Gallia Comata, 88
Gallia Narbonensis, 265
Gallia Transalpina, 132, 175
Gallia Transpadana, 18, 81, 90
Gallic tribes, 100, 107–8
Ganymede, 201

Gaul, 88, 99 (map)
  civilisation destroyed, 118
  ethnography, 98, 112
  insurrection, 109
  legions, 95, 102–3, 109, 132
  Marius, 89
  massacres, 110
  monarchy, 100
  pacification, 112
  punishments by Caesar, 109
  revolt, 107
  Roman victories, 89–90
  Romanisation of, 113–14, 118,
    121–2
  see also Gallia entries
Gellius, 6, 11
Gelzer, Matthias, xiv, 48–9, 50, 322
genocide, 118
gens Julia, 3, 68, 71n
Gergovia, 110
Germanic peoples, 101
Germany, 92–3
Giannelli, Giulio, 105–6
Gibbon, Edward, xiv, 30, 106
Giglio, 173
gladiator teams, 19–20
Goethe, W. von, 118, 123
Gracchus, Gaius, 36, 48
Gracchus, Tiberius, 48, 75
grain ration, 28
Gramsci, Antonio, 287
Greece, 23, 165–7, 170
Greek language, 24, 74, 191
guerrilla warfare, 104, 107

Hadrian, Emperor, 272, 274
Hadrumetum, 233–4
Helvetii, 101, 102
Henri IV, xii
Herod, 213, 222
Hirtius, 257–8, 265–6, 267
Hispania Baetica, 269
historiography, 58, 192
Homer, quoted, 288
homines novi, 33
Horace, 72, 73, 74, 77n, 297

Hortensius, Quintus, 6
Hybrida, Gaius Antonius, 6–7
Hypsicrates, 214, 215
Hyrcanus, 203, 209, 210, 212–13,
  220

Idumaeans, 202–3, 222
Illyricum, 88
Lex de imperio magistratuum,
  130
Indutiomarus, 108
inimicitia, 162, 163
intelligence service, 20, 94
Isauricus, Publius Servilius, 4, 10,
  24, 175, 290
iure caesus verdict, 274, 275

Jerusalem, 211
Jewish Camp, battle of, 213–14
Jewish community, 210–11, 213,
  340–1
Jewish soldiers, 202–3, 209
Josephus Flavius, 226n
  Antipater, 209
  Caesar, Sextus Julius, 221–2,
    243n
  clientship, 212–13
  Jews, 210
  in Rome, 210–11
  Strabo, 213, 215
Juba, king of Numidia, 175,
  229–30, 233, 235
Jugurtha, 33–4, 234
Lex Julia, 80
Julia, aunt of Caesar, xiii, 15–16
Julia, city, 240
Julia, daughter of Caesar, 69, 339
Julia, sister of Caesar, 245
Jullian, Camille, 102, 105, 121
Juncus, Marcus, 10–11, 16–17

kingship, 273, 280n, 281–3, 311;
  see also monarchy

Labeo, 314–15, 325
Labienus, Titus

Alesia, 111
allegiances, 162
    Caesar, 174, 182n
    death of, 241
    funeral, 162
    Gallic revolt, 107, 108
    legatus pro praetore, 162
    and legionary, 234
    Pharsalus, 177
    Pompey, 25, 177
    Scipio, 233
    Spain, 236, 240
    Treveri, 109
    tribune of the plebs, 162
land distribution, 80
Las Cases, Emmanuel, Conte de,
    xii
laudationes, 256, 257
legationes liberae, 81
legions
    Alaudae, 129
    Campania, 231–2
    Gaul, 102–3, 109, 132
    Lilybaeum, 232
    Spain, 167
Lentulus, consul, 31
Lentulus Crus, Lucius Cornelius,
    132, 142, 287
Lentulus Spinther, Publius
    Cornelius, 154–5, 160–1,
    168–9
Lentulus Sura, Publius Cornelius,
    49
Lepidus, Marcus, 175
    magister equitum, 5–6, 8n, 186,
    282, 325
    nominating Caesar, 287, 289
Lepidus, Marcus Emilius, 4–5, 8n,
    14, 43, 49
Lérida, siege of, 174–5
liberators, 230, 243n, 277–8, 321,
    336, 337–8, 341
Licinius Macer, Calvus, 14
lictors, 78
Ligarius, 270, 308–9
Lilybaeum, 229, 232

Lingones, 110
Livy, Titus, 58, 66, 67
    Caesar's influence, 344, 345–6
    civil war, 75, 244n
    miracles, 254n
    Octavius, 251–2
    Periochae, 215
    Rubicon, 146
    Spain, 249–50
    triumvirate, 68, 75
Louis XIII, xii
Louis XIV, xii
Luca meeting, 94, 104, 118, 127
Lucan, 32n, 192–3, 198–9, 207n
Lucceius, Lucius, 27–8
Lucretius, 34–5
Lucullus, Lucius, 64
Lupercalia, feast of, 267, 281–3,
    285, 311–12
Lycomedes of Bithynia, 223

Mandubracius, 107
Lex Manilia, 19
Marat, Jean Paul, xiii
Marcellus, Gaius Claudius, 131,
    132, 270
Marcellus, Marcus Claudius,
    129–30, 131
Marchand, M., xii
Marchesi, Concetto, 93, 121
Marcius Rex, Quintus, 18
Marcus Aurelius, 11
Marinone, N., 36
Marius, false *see* Amatius
Marius, Gaius, xiii, 3, 15, 20, 89,
    161, 234, 271
Marius the Younger, 15
marriage alliances, 35, 69
Marseilles, 172, 173–4, 176
Marxist-Leninist view, xiv
Mashkin, N. A., 43
massacres, 104–5, 109, 110, 121
Matinius, P., 29
Matius, Gaius, 159–60
Mazarin, Jules, xii
Memmius, Gaius, 34–5, 36

Memphis, 203
Menapii, 104, 109
Messalla Corvinus, Marcus
    Valerius, 297, 300, 311
Metellus, consul, 16, 73
Meyer, Eduard, 48, 149n
Miletopolis, 63
milites Gabiniani, 195, 199
Milo, Titus Annius, 57, 86–7, 185,
    291
miracles *see* supernatural
    phenomena
Mithridates of Pergamon, 12, 201,
    202–3, 209
    Alexandrian War, 210, 213–14
    allies, 222
    Antipater, 213
    Bosphorus, 225
    historical accounts of, 215
    murdered, 236
Mithridates VI, 224–5
Momigliano, Arnaldo, xiv, 296–8
Mommsen, Theodor
    Alexander the Great, 118, 119
    Alexandria, 195, 199–200
    Caesar, xv
    Catiline, 48
    History of Rome, 167
    massacre, 105
    monarchy, 140n
    Rome, 240
monarchy, 48–9, 100, 139, 140n,
    204, 273; *see also* kingship
Montesquieu, C.-L. de S., 141
monuments restored, 20
Morini, 104
Mosca, Gaetano, 37
Munatius Plancus, 57
Munatius Rufus, 259
Munda, battle of
    Caesar's difficulties, 238–9
    Cato, 46
    Hirtius, 265–6
    palm shoot, 247–8, 252
    Pompey's sons, 174, 229,
        236

mutiny, 181n, 231–2
Mytilene, 4, 58

Nabataeans, 210
Napoleon I, 229
    Caesar, xii–xiv, 93, 270–1
    Cleopatra, 195
    Durazzo, 177
    Pharsalus, 179
    on Pompey, 165–7
    Précis des guerres de César, 105
    suicide, 239
Napoleon III, xi, 121
Narbonne, 109, 265–6, 267
Nervii, 93, 108, 109
Nicias, 170
Nicolaus of Damascus
    Augustus, 252
    killing of Caesar, 275, 284–5
    Life of Augustus, 281–3
    Octavius, 245, 246, 248–9, 251,
        254
Nicomedes, 4
Nicomedes III, 10
nobiles see aristocracy
nobilitas see aristocracy
Novius Niger, 39
Numerius Magius, 155, 156, 158n
Numidia, 234

Obulco, 240
Octavia, 69
Octavian war, 230
Octavius, Gaius, 248–9
Octavius (later Augustus), 41
    adoption, 245, 248, 252–3
    Amatius, 342
    Antony, 204
    Cicero, 317
    coniuratio Italiae, 136n
    as consul, 59–60
    Dio Cassius, 245, 247
    family background, 245
    guardians nominated, 338–9
    as heir, 238–9
    personality cult, 253

pontificate, 161
reconstructing Caesar's image,
    x
res publica, 277
Spain, 245–6, 251, 266–7
triumvirate, 67
Velleius, 248–9
oligarchy, 33
Oppius
    as agent, 94, 133–4, 273
    Caesar's letter to, 150, 151, 153,
        155–6, 293–4
    Life of Cassius, 313n
optimates
    aristocracy, 302
    Bibulus, 27–8
    Plutarch, 24–5
    Pompey, 63, 171
    populares, 20, 42
    Sulla, 152, 273
Orgetorix, 100
Oricum, 176
Orosius, 146

Pacorus, king of Parthians, 238
Pacuvius, Marcus, 297, 339
palm shoot sign, 247–8, 252
Pansa, 175, 301
Parthians, 218, 222, 237, 281
Pascal, Blaise, 207n
Pauly-Wissowa, xiv
pearl fishery, 30, 344
Pedius, Quintus, 156, 175, 237–8,
    240, 291
Peducaeus, Sextus, 175
Pelusium, battle of, 209
Petra, 176
Petrarch, Francesco, 188
Petreius, 167, 174, 233, 235
Petronius, 32n
Pharmacussa, 9
Pharnakes, 120, 220, 223
Pharnakes II, 224–5
Pharos, 201–2
Pharsalus, battle of
    Cassius, 298

casualties, 26, 70, 131, 178–9
Domitius, 176
Labienus, 177
Pompey, 49, 134, 174, 178–9
psychology of war, 178
Seneca, 316
Syria, 218, 220
Philippe of Orléans, xii
Philippi, battle of, 72
Philodemus, 296, 297
Picenum, battle of, 167–8
Pinarius, Lucius, 238
pirates, 9–10, 11, 14, 19
Pisistratus, 144–5, 273
Piso, Gaius, 24, 90
Piso, Gnaeus Calpurnius, 45–6
Piso, Lucius Calpernius, 296–7,
    338
Pistoia, battle of, 39
Pius, Antoninus, 75
Placentia, 181n
plebs, 14, 43; *see also* populace
Pliny the Elder, 32n, 118, 120, 121
Pliny the Younger, 274
Lex Plotia, 14
Plutarch
    Alexander the Great, 17–18
    Asinius Pollio, 134
    Brutus, 42
    Caesar, 4, 48, 92, 339, 340
    on Cassius, 300, 307–8
    Catiline conspiracy, 55
    Cato, 74, 88
    Cato the Younger, 121
    Cicero, 139
    civil war, 65–6
    Cleopatra, 194–5, 197
    Gaul, 118, 121
    Juncus, 10–11
    killing of Caesar, 274, 275, 327
    Life of Antony, 197
    Life of Brutus, 300, 306, 309,
        310n, 313n, 330, 331, 338
    Life of Caesar, 42, 83, 91–2,
        330, 331
    Life of Cicero, 57

Plutarch (*cont.*)
  Life of Crassus, 14–15
  Pharsalus, 131
  pirates, 9, 11
  Pompey, 69, 182–3n, 190–1
  pontifex maximus, 24–5
  praetorship, 17
  prosecutions, 6–7
  Rubicon, 144
  Statilius, 296
  Sulla, 3
  Trebonius, 266
  triumvirate, 68, 74
  tyranny, 273
Pollio *see* Asinius Pollio, Gaius
Polyaenus, 11
Polybius, 23–4, 25n
Pommereul, Baron de, xii–xiv
Pompeia, 84
Lex Pompeia de ambitu, 292
Lex Pompeia Licinia, 130
Pompeian war, 230
Pompeians, 230, 231, 323–4
Pompeius, Quintus, 57
Pompeius Strabo, Gnaeus, 49
Pompey, Sextus, 230, 235–6, 240,
  269–70, 324
Pompey the Great, 80, 107, 114, 133
  Balkan campaign, 176
  and Caesar, xiii, 5, 19, 65–6, 99,
    120–1
  on Caesar, 137
  Caesar's will, 238–9
  Cicero, 171–2
  Cicero on, 153–4
  civil war, 141
  Cleopatra, 190
  clientship, 17, 63, 173
  consulship, 35, 95, 127–8, 130
  Crassus, 65–6
  death of, 179, 183n, 188, 191–2,
    244n
  divorce, 64
  Durazzo, 165
  expelled from Syria, 218
  extortion, 30

father, 49
Greece, 165–7
Julia, 69
legions, 70n, 172–3
Lepidus, 5
Marseilles, 173
Octavia, 69
offices held, 17
optimates, 63, 171
Pharsalus, 134, 178–9
Plutarch, 69, 182–3n
as proconsul, 135n1
Scipio, 142
statue of, 331
Tacitus, 76
tribunes of the plebs, 14, 153
Pompey the Younger, 235–6
  Cassius on, 299
  cruelty, 303
  as *imperator*, 240
  killed, 254n
  Scipio, 233
  Trebonius, 267
pontifex maximus, 23–5, 49, 78–9,
  83, 161, 211
Pontius Aquila, 272
Popilius Laenas, 328–9, 332n
populace, 80, 83, 167, 346, 348
populares
  Caesar, 3, 14, 43, 47, 50, 68, 87,
    89, 271
  dictatorship, 290–1
  optimates, 20, 42
  Senate, 86
Porcia, 306, 310n, 327, 329
Potheinus, 190, 194, 195
power
  abuses, 315
  duality, 175
  legitimacy, xiii
  pontifex maximus, 78–9, 83,
    161, 211
  republican, xv
praetorship
  Caesar, 25, 39, 43
  Clodius, 86–7

grain ration, 28
  Memmius, 35
  Pompey, 17
  provinces, 84
pro-magistrates, 175
propraetorship, 34, 46, 81, 113, 233
provinces
  clientship, 90–1
  extortion, 36, 81, 90
  granted to Caesar, 88
  praetorship, 84
  recruitment, 128–9
  slaves, 108, 118
Ptolemy XI, 189
Ptolemy XII Neos Dionysos, 189
  clientship, 192
  death of, 190, 193–4
  extortion, 30
  Pompey, 179, 183n, 188
Ptolemy XIII, 190, 196, 199, 202, 203, 209–10
Ptolemy XIV, 199, 203
Publius Clodius Pulcher *see* Clodius Pulcher, Publius
Purser, L. C., 302
quaestorship, 15, 16, 17, 81, 90
Quiberon, Bay of, 103–4
Quintius, Lucius, 14

Rabirius Postumus, Gaius, 189
Ravenna, 143, 145
rebellion, 235–6, 269–70
recruitment, 128–9, 135n
rei publicae constituendae, 45
religious office, 23–5
res publica, xi, 277
Rhine bridge, 109
Rhodes, 7, 12, 58
Roddaz, 250–1
Roman Empire, 166 (map)
Roman fleet, 103–4
Rosenberg, Arthur, 48
Rubicon river, 17, 69, 121, 139, 143–7, 149n, 151
Ruspina, 233, 234

Sabinus, commander, 108
Sabis, river, 93
sacrilege, 36, 84, 147n
Saint-Évremond, 346–7
Salamis, people of, 29
Sallust
  Caesar and Crassus, 46
  Caesar's Senate speech, 54–60
  Catilinaria, 45
  The Catilinarian Conspiracy, 40–1
  Cato's Senate speech, 55–6
  civil war, 231–2, 235
  corruption, 33–4
  Epistulae ad Caesarem senem, 56
  Gelzer, 49
  Histories, 75
  Invectiva in Ciceronem, 57
  as tribune of plebs, 57
Sambre, battle of, 93, 102–3
Sardinia, 175
Saturninus, 162
Scaptius, M., 29
Scipio, Publius Cornelius, 273, 326
Scipio, Quintus Metellus, 49, 232–3, 235
Scipio Aemilianus, 273
Scipio Nasica, Quintus Caecilius Metellus Pius, 128, 142
scorched earth tactics, 110
Seeck, Otto, 77n
Lex Sempronia iudicaria, 36
Senate
  Caesar, 139, 272–3
  Cato ejected, 88
  civil war, 141
  dictatorship, 273–4, 289
  emergency powers, 127
  populares, 86
  purged, 147n
  record of proceedings, 78
  Sallust, 54–60
Seneca the Elder, 75, 192
Seneca the Philosopher, 344–5
  De beneficiis, 315
  Letters to Lucilius, 300

Seneca the Philosopher (*cont.*)
  Marius, 348n
  Natural Questions, 345
Senones, 109
Septimius, 191
Sequani, 100, 102
Serapion, 200
Sertorius, 5, 10, 14, 63
Servilia, 160, 268n, 331
Severus, Septimus, 247
Shackleton-Bailey, D. R., 318
Shakespeare, William
  Julius Caesar, ix–x, 206n, 334–6
Shaw, George Bernard, 201
Sibylline prophecy, 281
Sicily, 170, 175
Sidon inscription, 212
Silanus, Decimus Julius, 54, 57
Sittius, 235
slaves, 26–7, 108, 118, 122
Social War, 33
soldiers
  Caesar's relationship with, 91–4,
    174, 182n
  mass desertion, 234
  mutiny, 181n, 231–2
  rewards, 167–8
  war booty, 128
soothsayers, 326–7
Spain
  campaign, 174–5
  Dio Cassius, 249–50
  legions, 167
  Livy, 249–50
  Octavius, 251
  Pompey's troops, 172–3
  propraetorship, 113
  quaestorship, 90
  rebellion, 235–6, 269–70
  return to, 229
  Velleius, 249–50
Spain, Further, 16, 175, 269, 303
Spanish War, 241, 269
Spartacus, 14, 19
Spurinna, 328
state treasury, 30–1, 169

Statilius, 296, 314–15, 325, 332n
statues, restored, 271, 293, 294
Stoicism, 297–8, 315–16
Strabo, 198, 210, 213, 214–15
Strada, Giacomo, xii
street riots, 127
Suetonius, xv
  Alexander the Great, 17–18
  Alexandria trap, 188
  Augustus, 246, 252
  Caesar, xiii, 7, 41, 330
  Caesar/Pompey, 30, 47–8, 79, 92,
    131, 137, 225, 340–1
  Catilinarian conspiracy, 39
  Cato ejected from Senate, 88
  Clodius, 85
  debts, 24, 26–7
  edicts, 44
  Egypt, 203–4
  gladitorial games, 20
  intelligence service, 20
  killing of Caesar, 271–2, 274,
    275, 322, 323
  Lepidus, 5
  Mithridates' general, 12
  Munda, 247–8
  Pharsalus, 131, 134
  pirates, 9, 11
  plebs, 14
  plunder, 30
  Pollio, 134
  restoring statues, 271
  royalty, 16
  Rubicon, 144, 145–6, 147,
    149n
  Senate, 82n, 88, 139
  Sulla, 3
  three-cornered pact, 66
  tyranny, 137–8
suicide, 239
Suleiman the Magnificent, xii
Sulla, Faustus, 235
Sulla, Lucius Cornelius, 152–3, 154
  on Caesar, 3–4, 137
  Cassius, 301–2
  Cicero on, 320

death of, 4
dictatorship, 137, 320
freedom of tribunes, 293
legacy of, 14
and Lepidus, 5
optimates, 152
outlawing enemies, 151
tribunes of the plebs, 14, 153
tyranny, 273
Sulla, Publius, 45, 161
Sulpicius Rufus, Servius, 131,
175
supernatural phenomena, 220,
247–8, 252, 254n
superstition, 23–4, 25n, 326–7
supplicatio, 99, 104, 122
Syme, Ronald, xi, xv, 59, 69–70
killing of Caesar, 315
Pollio, 75–6
The Roman Revolution, xiv,
75–6, 123, 140n
Syria
Caesar, 220, 226n
Caesar, Sextus, 236
Cassius, 237
Cleopatra, 190
Pharsalus, 218, 220
Pompey, 231
revolt, 231, 237–8, 239

tabulae novae, 290–1
Tacitus, 6, 58, 75, 76, 100, 138
Tanusius Geminus, 44, 45, 46,
123n
Tarentum, 225
Tarsus, 223
Tasgetius, 108
Teanum, 169
Tencteri, 104, 105, 109, 119, 121,
122
Tenth Legion, 232, 241
Thapsus, battle of, 120, 163, 231,
235, 276–7, 303, 316
Themistocles, 169–70
Theodotus, 190, 192, 194
Theophrastus, 25n

Thermus, Marcus Minutius, 4
Thrasea, xv
Thucydides, 56–7, 57–8
Thurii, 185
Tiberius, 73
Timagenes of Alexandria, 73–4,
215
Tiro, Tullius, 160
Tolstoy, Leo, 93–4
Toynbee, Arnold, 28
treason, 36
Trebellus, 231
Trebonius, Gaius, 175, 291
Antony, 265, 266, 267, 284, 317,
329–30, 334
conspiracy, 309
Marseilles, 174
republican, 267–8
in Spain, 235
threats against Caesar, 263–4
Treveri, 109
tribunes, 131, 133–4, 153
tribunes of the plebs, 14, 57, 145,
153
tribunes of the soldiers, 14, 15
triumphal celebrations, 229–30,
269
triumvirate, 65–7, 73
Asinius Pollio, 89
Livy, 68, 75
Luca meeting, 94, 104, 118, 127
Plutarch, 74
Velleius, 75
Tubero, Quintus Aelius, 243n
Lex Tullia de ambitu, 20
tyrannicide, 312, 317–18, 322, 338
tyranny, 13n, 137–8, 149n, 172,
273–8, 275
Tyre, 236–7
Tyrrell, R. Y., 302

Umbrenus, 54
uprisings, 42, 127, 291–2, 342; *see
also* mutiny
Usipetes, 104, 105, 109, 119, 121,
122

usury, 28
Utica, 233–4

Valerius Maximus, 132
Varro, Marcus Terentius, 67, 167,
    175, 182n, 270
Varro Atacinus, 98
Varus, Attius, 232, 233, 236
Vatinius, 88, 176
Velleius Paterculus
    Asinius Pollio, 270
    Cato, 55
    Lex Clodia, 85
    Curio's debts, 132
    death of Pompey, 194
    deaths in Gaul, 121
    Dolabella, 66
    flumen Dialis, 12
    killing of Caesar, 275
    Octavius, 248–9
    pirates, 9–10, 14
    quaestorship, 17
    Spain, 249–50
    triumvirate, 66, 67, 75
Veneti, 103–4
Ventidius, 57
Vercingetorix, 101
    Alesia, 111
    Arsinoe, 203
    death of, 112
    massacre avoidance, 111–12
    monument, 121
    revolt, 109, 110, 127
    unifying role, 107–8
Verres, trial of, 36
Verus, Lucius, 57
Vestal Virgins, 3
Vettius, Lucius, 39
Vibullius Rufus, 173, 176
virtus, political, 256–7, 301
votes, trade in, 33, 37

war booty, 128
war chariots, 107
warfare, 180n, 346
wealth/power, 33
Weil, Simone, 123
Wilamowitz, U. von, 345
writing, public records, 78

Xanten massacre, 104–5
Xenophon, 59, 60n, 325

Zela, 225, 241